THE SELF EXPLAINED

Also from Roy F. Baumeister

Breaking Hearts:
The Two Sides of Unrequited Love
Roy F. Baumeister and Sara R. Wotman

Handbook of Self-Regulation:
Research, Theory, and Applications, Third Edition
Kathleen Vohs and Roy F. Baumester, Editors

Meanings of Life
Roy F. Baumeister

The SELF EXPLAINED

Why and How We Become Who We Are

Roy F. Baumeister

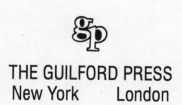

THE GUILFORD PRESS
New York   London

Library of Congress Cataloging-in-Publication Data

Names: Baumeister, Roy F., author.
Title: The self explained : why and how we become who we are / Roy F.
   Baumeister.
Description: New York, NY : The Guilford Press, [2022] | Includes
   bibliographical references and index.
Identifiers: LCCN 2021042450 | ISBN 9781462549283 (cloth)
Subjects: LCSH: Self-realization. | Self—Social aspects.
Classification: LCC BF637.S4 B393 2022 | DDC 158.1—dc23/eng/20211109
LC record available at *https://lccn.loc.gov/2021042450*

About the Author

Roy F. Baumeister, PhD, is Professor Emeritus of Psychology at Florida State University and at the University of Queensland in Australia. One of social psychology's most highly cited researchers, Dr. Baumeister has been conducting research, teaching, and thinking about the human self since the 1970s. His work spans multiple topics, including self and identity, self-control, interpersonal rejection and the need to belong, sexuality and gender, violence and evil, self-esteem, self-presentation, emotion, decision making, consciousness and free will, and finding meaning in life. He has written approximately 700 professional publications as well as numerous books for professionals and the general public. Dr. Baumeister is a recipient of awards including the Distinguished Lifetime Achievement Award from the International Society for Self and Identity and the William James Fellow Award, the highest honor of the Association for Psychological Science.

Acknowledgments

Many people have read all or part of the manuscript for this book and provided helpful comments. All errors and problems are my fault and responsibility, not theirs, of course. But I am very grateful for their suggestions.

In particular, I am grateful to Bill von Hippel, Eli Finkel, and Nathalie André, who offered extensive comments on the full manuscript. I also was greatly helped by comments from JongHee Kim, Evan Anderson, and Jenn Veilleux. John Tierney read several chapters and offered great help for how to organize the book and write it better.

A particular thanks to the students in my Psychology 4881 seminar, who read the book in draft form and provided plenty of valuable suggestions and support. In alphabetical order, they were: Debbie Chow, Nicole Delmo, Tallara Drew-Hazou, Chloe-Emily Eather, Rhiarna Harris, Morgan Hodgson, Cassandra James, Bryan Lee, Tao Li, Weiwei Liang, Nigel Lim, Kevin Lin, Caitlin McClure-Thomas, Shane McKenzie, Madison Neve, Hannah Newsome, Yu Wen Ong, Ayu Namira Paramecwari, Megan Puckering, Yingying Tang, Manh Quan Tran, Karen Nicole Urivna Castellanos, Harriet Wilson, and Joanna Wilson. Special thanks to Yingying Tang, who reread the entire book after the semester was over and offered additional comments.

Kayne Lim, who has worked with me for several years, was a terrific help. Among other things, he was invaluable in helping run the seminar, which had to switch to online class meetings after the first week.

Another quasi-seminar on the book was also quite helpful as I finalized the manuscript. Amber Price, Rebecca Clarke, and Meg Jankowski met biweekly with Dianne Tice and me to offer their impressions and reactions.

Jayson Brady, my superb research assistant, found valuable sources for key points. Lingjie Mei, an earlier research assistant, also was quite helpful, especially when I was trying to get serious about moving this along toward the first complete draft.

This final version of the book is the brainchild of Barbara Watkins, a distinguished developmental editor at The Guilford Press. She is to be thanked for transforming the conceptual structure, organization, and train of thought for the book, as well as deleting large amounts of material. She also fixed some mistakes. Any mistakes or stupidities that remain are my responsibility because I wrote the early version of the manuscript, but if the book is any good, it is largely because of her.

Last, I am very grateful to my wife and research partner, Dianne Tice, who not only read the entire manuscript and offered helpful comments but also provided invaluable support.

A Note on Sources

Let me begin by apologizing to all the many fine researchers who have contributed to our understanding of human selfhood, but whose work is not specifically cited in this book. The research literature is unmanageably vast and always increasing. I've done my best to pull together a great deal, but no one knows more than I do that plenty of good stuff was missed. Moreover, the editing process deleted about 20% of the total manuscript, including both text and references, and my decision was to trust the process and accept almost all the cuts. So there are many of you whom I wished to cite but was overruled.

There is also a stylistic choice. Modern writing in professional psychology journals has gotten to the point where authors frequently cite a source in almost every sentence. I often write like that myself. But to most readers, researcher names are nonsense syllables, and I did not want the book to read that way. Hence, I have struggled to balance the scholarly duty of citing specific sources with making this an easily readable book. In particular, I have relied heavily on review articles in many places, rather than citing specific original studies. I hope this enables scholars who wish to learn more or to dispute some conclusion to find the evidence they want, while freeing up the text to be more user-friendly.

Another issue is that research has become ever more collaborative, and so many articles have half a dozen authors, sometimes far more. To keep reference citations from cluttering up the text, I mostly just cite first author names, though the others are duly acknowledged in the References. The main exception has to do with citing papers by myself with multiple coauthors, when I was the first author. I am grateful to and deeply appreciative of my coauthors, and as a small sign of appreciation, I have sought to include their names.

Contents

ONE **THE REMARKABLE HUMAN SELF**

1. What Is the Self?   3
2. The Self in Social Context   10
3. How the Modern Western Self Took Shape   22
4. Different Societies Make Different Kinds of Selves   36
5. Four Pitfalls of Self Theories: 42
   No Self, Multiple Selves, Authentic True Selves,
   and Self-Actualization

TWO **WHY DO WE HAVE SELVES?**

6. Some Beginnings of Self   65
7. How Baby Grows Up to Have a Working Self   74
8. Human Groups Need (and Shape) Selves   94
9. Moral Reputation as a Foundation of Self   104
10. The Unity Project: The Unfinished Business   114
    of Stitching the Self Together

THREE **KNOW THYSELF**

11. Self-Awareness   129

12. What Sort of Knowledge Is Self-Knowledge?   139

13. Why Know Thyself?   152

14. Building Self-Knowledge: 165
    How People Learn about Themselves

15. Self-Esteem   175

16. Accuracy and Illusion in Self-Beliefs   192

FOUR **THE SELF AS ACTIVE AGENT**

17. The Self in Action   217

18. Self-Regulation and Self-Control   231

19. Decision Making, Autonomy, and Free Will   251

FIVE **THE SELF IN RELATION TO OTHERS**

20. The Interpersonal Self   271

21. The Self as Group Member   280

22. Self-Presentation   289

23. Self as Close Relationship Partner   304

SIX **PROBLEMS OF SELF**

24. Problems of the Modern Self   317

25. The Stress of Self, and Some Escape Routes   326

26. Selves and Mental Illness   335

27. The Deep Puzzle of Self-Defeating Behavior   348

28. Ways the Mind Can Organize Self-Beliefs   360

Epilogue The Self: A Summary   369

References   377

Index   407

PART ONE

THE REMARKABLE HUMAN SELF

CHAPTER 1

What Is the Self?

There is nothing like a human self anywhere else in nature. It's a key to what it means to be a human being. Consider some of the features of the human self. It is aware of itself, not just slightly but extremely, and is capable of extremes of self-criticism and self-love. Yet, it often registers disapproval, even disgust, when other people display how much they love themselves. It directs action and acknowledges moral responsibility for its acts. It can perform roles yet transitions easily out of them, often shifting smoothly among multiple roles. It alertly champions its own needs: If there's one thing the self knows how to do, it's to be selfish! It's no accident that much antisocial, disruptive, obnoxious behavior is described as *self*-ish. But the human self is also capable of extraordinary self-sacrifice. It is aware of itself extending far into the past and future, and it can in fact tell stories about itself that link its actions across time. And like a self-programming computer, it regulates and adjusts itself extensively, responding to inner needs and external circumstances, including complex sets of rules.

The self includes a psychological structure, based in the brain but operating in a society full of symbols and information. Modern societies assign you a specific name at birth, and you have a lifetime record of career, legal problems, family, education, earned licenses and credentials, commitments, medical records, and credit rating. Thus, you have an identity within society.

Meanwhile, inside your own mind, you have a concept of self, or if not a single concept, a collection of information about yourself (some of which is probably wrong). But the self-concept is not the same thing as the self, any more than a map of France is the same thing as France. There is an entity, a something, that the self-concept refers to and represents.

3

That's what I seek to explain. It's not (just) your body, nor your personality, though both of those are relevant. Nor is it just the self-concept.

The self is your social identity and your inner processes that enable you to operate your body successfully in society, securing your livelihood. The self exists at the interface between the human animal body and the complicated social structures that we call society and culture. That's what this book seeks to explain.

SYSTEM, PROCESS, PERFORMANCE

Being a thing is one way to exist. There are other ways. Processes and systems are also real. Performances are real. The self is not a thing. It is better to think of the self as a system, a process, or a performance. A system connects multiple pieces or parts into coordinated functioning. A process is a set of changes that are causally linked across time, one leading to the next. In a performance, one entity acts in meaningful ways as part of a group. In contrast, a thing is generally the same across time. Human selves are always in flux, dealing with new situations, learning, adapting, and they operate as organized systems. The body is a thing. It is a specific physical entity. Self starts with body but becomes more than the body. Moreover, even the body is not just a thing. It includes ongoing processes. The body dies but usually continues to exist (hence burial). Death means the cessation of the system that sustained life.

Likewise, the self-concept can be deemed an entity, though not a physical item. Perhaps it would be more precise to say, the collection of self-beliefs is an entity. Self is more than the collection of self-beliefs, though those are important.

Neither the body nor the collection of self-beliefs is merely a thing. The body is an organized system, in which all the parts are interconnected.

Consider the parable of the ship of Theseus. The ship was made of boards, and gradually, over time, every one of the boards was replaced— yet everyone treated it as the same ship. The lesson to draw from this parable is that the ship's identity resides not in the boards themselves but in the organizing system. The set of boards that made up the original ship would not have been called a ship when they were merely stacked lumber in the shipyard. Only when they were put together into a functioning unity did the boards become a ship. And when this organized, functioning unity set sail, it retained its identity even as the boards were replaced. The ship's identity lay in the functioning system. The system organized the boards in a useful way, so as to float on the water and move across it. The boards could be replaced as long as the system remained intact (i.e., the ship still floated and sailed).

The reality of the self clearly does not reside in molecules. The self resides more in the organizing system imposed on the physical body. It keeps changing despite having unity over time, so the organizing system is also a process. And the process is based substantially on performing a role in the social system.

The self exists at the interface between the body, which is a physical thing composed of molecules (though animated by biochemical processes that all living things need), and the society, which includes other people as well as plenty of information, shared symbols, and other nonphysical things. Participating in society is how human creatures solve the problems of survival and reproduction.

WHAT THE SELF ISN'T AND MORE OF WHAT IT IS

The self begins with body, but it is far more than body. Children use the terms *self* and *body* almost interchangeably, suggesting that body awareness is a crucial early step. But self-awareness goes far beyond feeling your body. The self that purchases real estate, promises sexual fidelity, or grapples with a moral dilemma, cannot easily be explained as a purely physical item.

The self is not the body, or not just the body, indeed by far.

The self is not part of the brain. This may be a bit difficult to accept at first, as many experts assume that there must be some crucial center tucked away in some part of the brain that really is your self. But despite a couple decades of searching the far corners of the brain, no such self center has been found. A number of brain researchers have been so dismayed by this that they have concluded the self is an illusion (e.g., Hood, 2012).

Let's be clear. There are no human selves without brains. Moreover, everything the self does is matched and supported by some event in the brain. Perhaps a computer analogy will help. If the brain is like a computer, then the self is like one of the programs it is running. There is no particular piece of the computer that corresponds to the program. Rather, the program exists in the organized system that coordinates what many little pieces in the computer are doing. In similar fashion, the self is not a piece of the brain so much as it is the program, the organizing system that coordinates what the neurons are doing so as to produce a civilized human being, a responsible member of society. Of course, without a computer (a purely physical thing), a program would not accomplish anything. The self is the animal body plus the programming. Even more precisely, the self is the process of the animal body *executing* the programming.

The self is part of the interface between the basic human animal body and the broader society. The society includes language, culture, and shared systems for getting things done.

Another common mistake about the self is to equate it with the self-concept. Mostly when you read a book about the self, it covers a great deal of research on how people think about themselves: self-esteem, self-knowledge, self-illusions, and much more. Self-knowledge will be covered in this book, too, but do not confuse the self-concept with the self. Self-knowledge, by definition, is knowledge about the self, rather than the actual self. Again: A map of France is not the same as France itself.

On the other hand, a self needs some understanding of itself in order to act effectively. In that sense, the self-concept is a useful part of the self. Still, it is not the whole thing. The self acquires a stock of information about itself as a vital way of helping it do what it has to do. The self thus uses its self-concept on a regular basis. It may even be fair to regard the self-concept as one of the working, moving parts of the self. But a concept does not belong to a group, whereas a self does. A concept does not make decisions and accept moral responsibility, whereas a self does. By confusing self-concept with self, we risk missing out on many important aspects of self.

DEFINING KEY ASPECTS OF THE SELF

There are three main aspects of self (Baumeister, 1998): self-knowledge, executive function, and the interpersonal being. Unity of self across time is another key feature of self.

> 1. *Self-knowledge.* This is based on being aware of self, including self-concepts, self-insights, and self-esteem. Human consciousness turns around to recognize its source, so we are aware of ourselves. Indeed, we develop elaborate systems of beliefs and theories about ourselves.
>
> 2. *Executive function.* This is the self that does things. It makes choices, seeks control, and regulates itself. Without this aspect, the self could not do anything.
>
> 3. *Interpersonal being.* The self exists primarily in a network of social relationships. It adjusts itself to social pressures and demands. It seeks validation from others, and in other ways it exists in relation to others rather than as a self-contained unit. This occurs at two different levels, at least. We relate to individuals, based on our relationships to them. And we relate to large groups, by identifying with them and operating as a member of the group. In both, the purposes and functions of the self involve relating to other people.
>
> 4. *Unity across time.* The self involves unity. Identity differentiates oneself from others and has continuity across time. It serves as a

point of reference for conversation, experience, and action, as well as within the social structure (e.g., these are Joe's gloves). The self has lots of little parts and pieces that are somehow integrated into an organized system, though integration and organization remain imperfect.

Additional Important Terms

● *Culture.* Culture is a kind of social system that shares information, produces resources based on interlocking sets of complementary roles, takes advantage of trade, accumulates knowledge in the group, and so on.

● *Society.* Society is the culture plus the people. It comprises the people living within and enacting that system.

● *Doxa.* This is the group's shared beliefs, ones that go without saying, the culture's common stock of knowledge.

● *Identity.* The terms *self* and *identity* are sometimes used interchangeably, but here they will have a slightly different emphasis in terms of inner versus outer. Identity emphasizes your position in society or within a smaller social system (e.g., father, salesclerk). The self emphasizes inner processes, including knowledge of self, information processing, making decisions, and guiding action. In a sense, the self inhabits and operates the identity.

● *Morality.* This is the society's set of rules and criteria that define various actions as good or bad. Morality supports cooperation by way of reputation.

EVOLUTION AND CULTURE

I don't think evolution can provide anything close to a full explanation of the self. But it is a solid starting point. Culture will be abundantly needed, though even there, culture still builds on nature—even when it goes far beyond it.

My own thinking came to a stunning change when I started seeing culture as a biological strategy (Baumeister, 2005). Every species has to solve the problems of survival and reproduction, in order to sustain life. Humankind has solved these problems in a very unusual way, which is to create culture. In purely biological terms, human culture has been extremely successful. The human population has ballooned from the original woman (or group of sisters) to nearly 8 billion in just a couple of hundred thousand years—while most other mammal populations have seen declines, many into extinction. My best guess is that all the traits that make us human, setting us apart from other animals, are rooted in biological adaptations to make culture work for us. The human self is one of these.

That's a crucial point. Evolution laid the foundations for the human self. But the self evolved in order to make culture possible. Selves enabled culture, and culture has enabled our species to thrive.

A LOOK AHEAD

Part One of the book addresses basic questions on how to think about the self. First off, how does the individual fit in to society, and indeed is the self shaped more by society or by individual choice and action? Both have been argued, and both have good points. Chapter 2 describes how the self results from active interplay of the individual animal and the symbolic society. Along with that, how does this compare to what other animals have? Next, I look at different kinds of human selves. Chapter 3 explores how the modern Western self took shape over time. Chapter 4 looks at cultural differences in self. In Chapter 5, I try to ward off four important misconceptions about the self. The first is that the self is an illusion; it is not. Nor is the self a multiplicity of separate selves, though that idea keeps resurfacing every generation. Those who speak of multiple selves do have some important phenomena to contribute, but the idea that one person is different selves is ultimately unworkable and leads to absurdities. I then consider the powerfully beckoning idea of the True Self, but it is probably more a mirage and ideal than a reality. I then turn to self-actualization. Everybody wants it though nobody's sure what it is. There is probably something to self-actualization, but so far research has not managed to fill in the vague concept with real stuff.

Part Two asks, "Why do we have selves?," especially the complicated human kind? A big part of the answer lies in making productive social systems possible. Chapters 6 and 7 look at some beginnings of self, including child development, which reveals the process of selves taking shape. Chapter 8 elaborates on why groups need selves. Chapter 9 describes why moral reputation is a foundation of self, and Chapter 10 discusses why unity over time is a key to self yet always unfinished.

Parts Three through Five consider three essential parts of the self. Part Three explores self-knowledge: Why and how people accumulate it, and why it's sometimes inaccurate. What is special about the human kind of self-awareness? What are its effects? What purpose does self-awareness serve? Part Four covers the active part of the self: how it makes decisions, exerts control, and alters itself. Part Five deals with interpersonal aspects of self.

The chapters in Part Six examine problems of self, ways that selves fail to function as one would like, including stress, self-defeating behaviors, and mental illness.

Throughout the chapters ahead, I explore a number of main themes. First, the self is interpersonal and its job is to connect the individual to the group. The human self originates as the brain learns to perform a role in the social group. Second, the self's reputation—how others see you—is crucially important. Third, the human self extends across time mainly because that is what human social systems demand. Fourth, the brain applies organizational systems to construct the unity of the self, which is not a given inevitability but rather the result of an ongoing process.

Humans are much more than animals—but we are nevertheless animals. The next chapter compares human selfhood to its animal precursors, while also considering culture and society as the environment in which the human animal operates.

KEY POINTS

- The self is not thing. Think of it as a system, a process, or a performance. Human selves are always in flux.
- The self is your social identity, and your inner processes that enable you to operate your body successfully in society, securing your livelihood.
- The self exists at the interface of human body and the social structures of society and culture.

CHAPTER 2

The Self in Social Context

$\mathbf{M}$any thinkers have pondered the self as something existing in a single mind, only distantly or secondarily immersed in interpersonal relations. But much of what the self does is tied up with interactions and relationships with other people. Let's consider what features of the self you would not need if you lived a totally solitary life.

How much of a self would you have if you never interacted with other people? You would not have any roles in social systems, such as being a police officer, assistant manager, teammate, employee. You would not own anything. If you had a cup, it would be "the cup" not "my cup." It only becomes "my cup" if other people are present, and you want them not to use your cup. A solitary self would not have language either, and so all the information about self that is captured in language would be absent. You would not even need a name or an address, let alone a Social Security number. You would not have a moral reputation to maintain, or indeed any sort of reputation, because reputations exist in the minds of others. Moreover, much self-knowledge comes from interacting with others, including seeing how they treat you and how you compare against them, so most self-knowledge would be absent.

A totally solitary self would be hardly like you at all. Indeed, it would not be you, in essential ways, because so much of who you are has come from your interactions with other people and with society at large.

This may sound like a caricature, but biologists note that most living creatures do live alone. The benefits of having other members of one's species around are limited, and the costs may outweigh them. If food is scarce, having other creatures like yourself nearby means they will eat the food that you want and need. It's probably no accident that grass-eating animals sometimes form large herds. Usually, there is plenty of grass, so nobody has to worry about not getting fed if others eat. Others might also take the mate you want. So solitude has some clear advantages.

Only a relatively few species are social. Humans are probably the only species that is not only social but extensively cultural. Small beginnings of culture can be found in several dozen species, but nothing like human-kind's (de Waal, 2001). The human self is designed not just for belonging to a social group but also for performing roles in a complex group that has shared knowledge and that cooperates based on shared understandings and communication.

If you lived by yourself, you would still have some aspects of self. Obviously, you'd still have the integrity of your body. A falling stone might hit your toe or the dirt next to it. The brain, far from the toe, will try to make sure the falling stone hits the dirt rather than the toe, so it recognizes some unity of self that includes the toe. That doesn't require a social group or cultural context. But plenty of selfhood does.

NATURE AND CULTURE

Are we born with a self, or is it learned? For decades, nature versus nurture has been the battleground on which social scientists have disputed and debated countless phenomena. In this context, however, I prefer the term *culture* over *nurture* since it is broader; nurture, after all, is a way that children learn culture. The fact that babies do not have much in the way of self is not sufficient to tilt the answer in culture's favor because nature's gifts unfold and develop slowly over time. For example, menstruation is not present at birth, but no one argues that girls only menstruate because their culture pressures them to do so. Intelligence, too, unfolds slowly over the years—but most experts think it has a strong genetic and innate aspect. Even so, it may not develop to its inborn potential because of lack of stimulation, poor nutrition, abusive parenting, and other problems. A baby's intelligence exists as potential. The genetic part is how well that baby could grow up given an optimal environment.

Advocates of nature and culture both have ample valid points regarding the self. The way forward lies not in favoring one over the other but in recognizing how they combine. Usually when disputes go on unresolved for decades, it's not because one side is right and the other is wrong. It's because they both have valid points but are framing the problem differently and therefore talking past each other.

The human self is mainly a cultural phenomenon, but its roots are firmly grounded in nature and evolution. And indeed, some fairly extraordinary things had to happen in evolution to enable human selves. *Nature made us for culture*: Most of the traits that make us human, that define the difference between us and other primates, are biological adaptations to make culture possible (Baumeister, 2005).

Culture became part of the environment that selected winners and losers. Today's human race is descended from some early humans and not others, and the factors that decided which ones became our ancestors included being able to flourish within culture. Biology measures success by survival and reproduction. The successful ones were those who lived longest and produced the most offspring who in turn lived long enough to produce children. In that sense, grandchildren are nature's measure of success.

In human history, the biologically successful individuals were the ones who worked well within the emerging culture. Traits that improved participation in cultural society had advantages for survival and reproduction. Language is a good example. Chimps and other apes do not talk. They only use limited sign language. In contrast, all humans talk. Evolutionary forebears who talked better seem to have spread their genes more widely than their tongue-tied or otherwise inarticulate peers. All over the world, when groups of people are together, they typically talk and talk, unlike all other species. Natural selection among humans favored the talkers.

To frame this in evolutionary context: A certain kind of hairless primate evolved the capacity to create a psychological self so that it could survive and reproduce better. This was part of a broader movement by which these primates (humankind) evolved the ability to create culture because culture enabled them to survive and reproduce far better than any other primates, *mainly by creating more resources* (starting with food) (Harris, 1997; Henrich, 2018), and sharing them.

Nowadays, worldwide, most mammal populations are declining, while the human population continues to rise, buoyed by improvements in both survival and reproduction. The total population count of humankind has risen sharply, especially by reductions in child mortality. Indeed, the population has gone from one woman (or a few sisters) to almost 8 billion living bodies in about 200,000 years. Likewise, survival has increased by leaps and bounds. No other species on earth has tripled its average life expectancy by virtue of its accumulated knowledge and collective practical interventions. Such rare advances indicate the power of culture to serve biology. What does that have to do with the self? Cultural systems work best insofar as each individual member has one of these biologically based selves.

So we must understand the self as a cultural phenomenon that serves nature's goals. Cultures are there to help the bodies survive and reproduce. All cultures need selves and use them to make the cultural systems function effectively. As one obvious example, it would be impossible to have a market economy without selves. Who would buy, sell, or own stuff, or even spend money, if there were no selves?

The self is thus a combination of nature and culture, indeed a very particular kind of combination. It is a tool of culture that benefits nature (survival, reproduction). The self emerges as *a cultural solution to a natural problem*. The natural problem is the basic biological challenge that all creatures must solve, namely how to sustain life, typically measured in terms of survival and reproduction. Human beings survive and reproduce extremely well. Indeed, our species is flourishing so well that we are crowding out most of the other mammals.

The implication is that humankind, alone among the mammals, is doing something very well. Indeed, the reason other mammal populations are declining is bound up with our thriving. We crowd them out of their habitats. Selves are part of the recipe by which human beings are surviving and reproducing far more successfully than other mammals. Selves enable our social systems to work their powerful magic, to our benefit and unfortunately to the detriment of many others.

So, to reiterate: *The human self is a cultural solution to a natural problem.*

How the Self Is Made

How does self come into existence? For the past couple of decades, neuroscientists seemed sure that the brain had to be a key part of explaining everything. Well, I'm convinced that the brain has to be an active participant in any answer, but still: Does the self emerge from the brain's inner processes, or is the brain merely forming the self as a way of dealing with its social environment?

Here, I pull together the three fields I have studied: psychology, sociology, and philosophy. Psychology starts inside the individual and gradually works outward. Sociology works in the opposite direction, starting with society as a whole and its major institutions, and working slowly down toward the individual. Both perspectives are useful for understanding the self. Philosophers, whose role is to be the expert thinkers, would approve of both approaches.

A classic article by sociologist Ralph Turner (1976) put a novel twist on the question of where the self comes from. Unlike some others, he did not just take one side as correct. Instead, he proposed that different cultures and different historical periods shifted the emphasis between the inner self and the outer one.

His terms are self as institution versus impulse. They have not caught on in the research community but the distinction is profound and important. *Impulse* is what you feel inside. Is the self what goes on in the daily privacy of your inner mind? Is the self in how you think and feel about yourself from moment to moment? In contrast, *institution* is how society designates you. Is the self how you act in public and participate in society? Is the self your name and job, family membership, bank account, police record, and/or educational credentials? It doesn't matter what rebellious, grumpy, or inappropriate thoughts you have in your stream of consciousness. Rather, what matters is what you do and say out in front of everybody.

Both the public self and the private self are real, and both are important. The question of which one is the real one, the stronger or more important one, has no single answer. Scientists at different times and different places have traded off the two, sometimes emphasizing one, sometimes the other.

Turner says that ceremonies matter much more when the institutional self is on top, as opposed to the impulse self. Ceremonies are emphasized in societies that think of the individual self mainly in terms of its public performances. For example, weddings and funerals are big deals and highly scripted. When the inner, impulsive self is on top, your inner feelings are what matter and what define who you are. In that case, the wedding or funeral ceremony is done at a bit of distance, with a slightly detached or even mocking attitude among some participants. The official aspect of marriage is not an identity-defining event but just a piece of paper, when the reality is what you feel for each other inside, not whatever words were recited in church that one peculiar afternoon. But to the institution-self folks, of course, what you said in church in front of everyone is what matters, and your fluctuating feelings about your spouse from day to day are at worst a minor distraction, and nobody's problem but your own.

To return to the key question: Does society or the individual make the self? I like the analogy of a buffet. Individuals are not just passive products of giant social forces. Rather, they are individual animals, with wants and needs, and able to make choices. Society lays out the buffet: It defines what kinds of self are possible and lays them out, though some people have more access to various choice ones than others. Nonetheless, the individual has some latitude to choose among society's offerings. Both individual and society have crucial roles in creating each particular self.

Celebrity impersonators offer a helpful example. They work hard on creating a version of themselves—as someone else! Some people spend considerable time, effort, and money trying to pass as a duplicate of a famous person. The famous models to copy come from the culture, typically including such film stars and musicians as Elvis Presley, Dolly Parton, and Cher, but the individual chooses and then works to approximate the original. The extent to which they go is evident from an anecdote in Dolly Parton's memoir (see Aman, 2020). The singer and film star was in Los Angeles and happened to hear of a celebrity look-alike contest nearby, in which several people were impersonating her. For a lark, Dolly decided to sneakily enter the contest dressed as herself. She lost! (And to a man.) Apparently, the judges thought that several men were better copies of her than she was of herself.

Let's try for a moment to embrace the perspective that society is the main and fundamental set of forces, and society can mold individual people any way it wants.

The Soviet Union had more power to shape individual selves than almost any other modern culture. (Rivals for that title are other major Communist and totalitarian countries, like North Korea.) Consider how much advantage society had over the individual. The society controlled the flow of information, the newspapers, the universities, the education systems. It controlled jobs and housing.

Yet, it failed. The Soviet Union couldn't produce people who would live out its principles and create the kind of society it dreamt of. At one point, the rulers decided that in the interests of fairness and abolishing class privilege, children should be raised in common, and parents should not do anything special for their own children. This practice was a spectacular failure and was soon retracted. The Israeli communes (kibbutzim) tried the same ideal but again quickly gave up. Sometimes society doesn't get its way at all.

Still, society is not helpless. The buffet analogy works. Society sets the table from which the individual makes choices. That's how the self is made. An autonomous animal with its own wants and needs makes choices—but these choices, and often even the value basis for making them, come from society. Like a person selecting his or her plateful from a lavish buffet, the end product, the meal that the particular person eats, is a product of both the inner workings of the individual and the systems and collective productions of society.

DO OTHER ANIMALS HAVE SELVES?

How and why did humankind develop a form of selfhood so different from what all other creatures have? Some coverage of what other animals lack in terms of human selfhood would be one clue to the answer.

Some years ago I read a letter by a dog owner who loved his dog but hated its name. The dog had been named before he acquired it, and he did not want to put the dog through the emotional turmoil and "anguish" of a name change. He thought the dog was like a person who is attached to having a particular name. Yet, dogs don't mind at all having their names changed. I have changed dogs' names a couple of times, and they don't seem to mind at all; they adjust readily to the new name. Whatever sound you make when giving them a treat is fine. However, a dog can tell the difference between getting a biscuit itself and another dog getting the biscuit. That's self in action. Dogs get used to having their own bowl and place to nap, and groups of dogs soon work out hierarchies and other basic relationships. So there are some beginnings or precursors to selfhood. Still, they don't seem to fully get the difference between them and you.

Consider some aspects of the human self that are mostly or indeed utterly absent in other animals.

Moral Responsibility

The human self can recognize moral obligations and principles, and people adjust their behavior accordingly—sometimes to their own considerable disadvantage. You keep your promises even when you don't want to. In fact, that's precisely the point of promising.

Reputation Concerns

People are acutely aware of how others perceive them and adjust their behavior so as to influence others' views of them. They know that reputation can differ from reality and keep track of both. They adjust their behavior based on false or unfair impressions others may have of them.

Connections across Time

People know that they are the same person today as they were years ago and will be years from now, despite various changes. They borrow money and spend it with a commitment to pay it back years in the future (e.g., when mortgaging a house), and they succeed at paying it back. They debate how much money to save for rainy days, children's college fund, retirement. They reminisce about their childhoods, make plans for events decades into the future.

Complex and Dynamic Self-Concepts

People form a complicated understanding of themselves, some of which is correct, most of which is in the plausible range. The self-concept is also linked loosely to their reputations and to a set of self-evaluations, which together form a level of self-esteem that fluctuates somewhat from one day to another. They defend their self-esteem against negative messages, but they also do revise it sometimes.

Introspection

People focus their attention on their inner thoughts and feelings, and indeed sometimes they use these inner reactions to evaluate possible courses of action and other plans.

There may be more on that list. Still, it's enough to make one thing clear. Although humans are animals, we are a very special breed. Human brains seem capable of creating a form of selfhood that is far beyond what is seen elsewhere among all the animals on our big and diverse planet. Nature has created all manner of quirky creatures: dinosaurs and viruses, bugs and elephants, platypuses and penguins. But the human being represents one of nature's most extraordinary experiments and most successful innovations.

The human self is presumably a product of evolution, but it moves far beyond what evolution has wrought elsewhere. Yes, we'll need a bit of biological perspective to understand the human self—but biology enabled human beings to become far more than other animals. When human beings reproach each other as "animals," it is an insult. People expect each other to be more than animals.

THE SELF'S MAIN FUNCTIONS

To understand what something is, you try to figure out what it was made to do: what its function or purpose is. What problem did the human self evolve to solve? This can be answered at multiple levels. Survival and reproduction are basic problems. The higher, more interesting levels are all about social integration. Let's start at the bottom.

Survival and Reproduction

In nature, survival and reproduction are the basic problems because they enable life to continue. The ultimate functions of the self are to enable the animal body to survive and reproduce. The brain is there to help the body that contains it (and maybe its genetic offspring). In complicated human societies, the self still has to take care of itself and children, within the rules of the society. It uses society's systems, like supermarkets, hospitals, governments, schools, and banks, to take care of self and offspring.

The solitary organism does not have much need for a self. All it needs is perhaps just a rudimentary sense of bodily unity. The hands should take action to protect the feet, for example, because if the feet are damaged, it will become hard to get food.

Social Integration

With social life, the importance of self increases. With culture, it increases vastly more. Socially, the most basic job for the self is to secure acceptance by the group. Life alone is not really an option. In the most famous example of equivalence, Socrates was offered the choice between exile and death, and he chose death. The self has to know society's rules and criteria of value, adjust to them, find some way to hold a position. One job of the self is to get the body integrated into a social group. Among humans, survival and reproduction come only by participating in the social group. We are not like hyenas, snakes, or other solitary animals that survive on their own.

Integration into society, by means of connecting with others, is a central task for the self, even if people do not necessarily recognize that is what they are doing. Early in life, the task is to get others to like you. As the child matures, acceptance comes to depend on respect, too.

Competence and Morality

Respect has two aspects: competence and morality. For example, to be well respected as a plumber, you essentially have to do two kinds of things consistently. First, you have to fix people's sinks and toilets so they function properly (competence). Second, you have to charge a fair price, keep promises and fulfill contracts, back up your work with guarantees (e.g., come back to fix mistakes), and in other ways demonstrate honesty and related virtues (morality).

Integration into society likewise usually involves forming and maintaining some close relationships. The self must attract other people who are amenable to forming a mutual attachment. And then it must act so as to keep the others willing to continue the relationship.

Communication and Cooperation

What psychological traits enabled human society to flourish? The consensus seems to emphasize two big things, communication and cooperation. Humans communicate and cooperate far more and far better than others. Human society succeeds based on communication and cooperation, plus their combination (e.g., discussing plans). The human self has to learn to communicate and cooperate, so as to participate in society and help producing more resources.

Groups that work together and share information can achieve much more than collections of individuals working by themselves. The self needs to participate in this cooperation, and that includes attracting others to cooperate.

Choosing How to Act

In order to get integrated into society, the self has to behave in particular ways. Choosing how to act is a vital function of the self, and thus another of its main jobs. The self makes choices. It has to integrate multiple levels of information and come up with a decision about what muscle movements to make and what sound waves to expel (what to do and say)—understanding that the social implications extend far beyond the physical facts of movement and sound. Standing up in church and reciting wedding vows, for example, will have consequences that can last for decades, including opportunities and constraints, and how other people treat you.

Indeed, choices are not only a product of the self's inner activity but also help create the self. Existentialist philosophy emphasized that self and identity are the result of choices one makes over the years, great and small. For example, people choose whom to wed, and those choices define who they are afterward ("Mr. and Mrs. Jones"). Thus, the self engages in a complex process of re-creating and re-defining itself. The inner processes of self confront sets of options and make choices among them, and as a result the self is modified.

Reputation

The self has to construct and maintain a concept of itself *in other people's minds* (Goffman, 1959; Schlenker, 1980). Reputation management is vital, both for being liked and later, in its more advanced cultural form, for being respected. Respect is not a momentary phenomenon but something that is earned by accumulated actions, as seen and judged by others.

The ongoing concern with having a good reputation can hardly be overstated. The human brain evolved in substantial part to be able to create and maintain a good reputation. Reputation management requires one to consider oneself from the perspective of other people—thus to anticipate and mentally simulate what they are thinking. And then one adjusts one's behavior based on how one assumes others will react to and evaluate it.

A White partygoer who remembers a joke and then refrains from telling it because someone might think it is racist has not done anything visible, but plenty of complex mental activity has happened: listening and understanding the conversation, having an association to the joke, wanting to tell it so as to make others laugh and perhaps to impress them with one's wit, mentally rehearsing it in preparation for telling it, comparing the joke to standards of what is offensive, evaluating whether others might be offended, and then suppressing the impulse so as to say nothing.

Alert readers may have noticed that I have emphasized the process of creating a good image of self in other people's minds—not in one's own mind. The desire for self-esteem has been much discussed in social psychology, and indeed some entire theories about self (such as social identity theory; e.g., Hornsey, 2008; Tajfel, 1978; Tajfel & Turner, 1979) start from the assumption that people wish to think well of themselves. Despite having spent decades studying self-esteem (e.g., Baumeister, 1993; Baumeister, Campbell, Krueger, & Vohs, 2003), I cannot regard the desire for self-esteem as a viable starting point for understanding the self, or as a given (innate) psychological fact. I discuss this further in Chapter 15. The human brain did not evolve for the sake of maximizing self-esteem. It is, however, fundamentally concerned with cultivating others' esteem for its reputation—starting perhaps with being regarded as the sort of person with whom others will cooperate.

FUNCTIONS OF THE SELF IN MODERN CULTURE

Thus far I have outlined basic functions of the self that may have been found in most times and places. Selves may have performed those jobs in different ways, but the need for acceptance and the striving for a good reputation to attract cooperative partners are probably found everywhere. The modern Western society we live in has certainly compiled additional jobs for the self. The freedom of the modern self, and the complexity of modern society, offer the self unprecedented options for choice and self-definition—as well as new sorts of dangers (e.g., online identity theft). An adult in modern society participates in massive exercises in cooperative interactions among strangers, whether this be standing in line for concert tickets, paying taxes, working in a large organization, donating to charity, or voting in elections.

Responsible Autonomy

A modern adult self has to exhibit *responsible autonomy*. Autonomy means that the self is competent to make choices and decide its actions in ways that can take care of itself within the society's rules. Responsibility means understanding the consequences of one's actions, including from society's perspective, and incorporating that knowledge into one's choices. Responsible autonomy is required of the functioning modern self in diverse contexts, such as renting an apartment, dating and mating, jury duty, managing one's money, and driving a car. Even a day at the beach requires responsible autonomy: You're welcome to enjoy yourself as long as you obey rules for proper parking, wear garments that reveal no more than the permitted amount of skin, avoid interfering with other bathers, and obey posted signs regulating activities to promote water safety.

KEY POINTS
- Selfhood requires a social group or cultural context.
- The human self is a cultural solution to a natural problem. It is a tool to enable the human body to survive and reproduce by virtue of participating in society with culture.

- A key function of the self is social integration, which at its most basic level is to secure acceptance by a group.
- Group acceptance is first managed by getting others to like you. Acceptance then comes to depend on respect, which includes competence and morality.
- Human societies succeed based on communication and cooperation.
- Choosing how to act is a vital function of the self.
- Reputation management is vital for being liked and respected.
- The modern self has to exhibit responsible autonomy. Autonomy means being competent to make choices that take care of one's self. Responsibility means understanding and accepting the consequences of one's choices.

CHAPTER 3

How the Modern
Western Self Took Shape

As described in Chapter 2, selfhood requires a cultural context. Yet, most research on the self is based on modern Americans. For this reason, it's good to also consider self in alternative contexts. There are two ways of doing this: looking at other times and at other places. This chapter looks at the self over time. The next chapter looks at self in other cultures.

"This above all: to thine own self be true," said Polonius to his son, Laertes, the buddy of Shakespeare's eponymous Hamlet. This classic line comes at the end of assorted other bits of advice, such as listen more than talk, think before acting, and minimize sexual mischief. Being true to self was a new sort of advice: The Ten Commandments, for example, prohibited lying to others but said nothing about being true to yourself. The value of this new advice, Polonius explains, is that if you are true to yourself, you won't be false to anyone else.

Polonius's assertion is probably wrong; it is quite possible to be true to oneself while lying to others. Narcissists and psychopaths may be quite true to themselves but blithely mislead, deceive, and exploit others. Still, Polonius's comment is important. The Shakespearean age was newly fascinated with the idea that people could pretend to be something they were not. Sincerity had emerged as an important new virtue (Trilling, 1971). Polonius thought being true to yourself would enable you to be sincere with others. That's just one of the many problems of self.

We have moved from early societies in which people had no problems with who they were, to a modern culture in which problems of self are rife and kaleidoscopic. What happened? How did something as simple as the self become such a mysterious quagmire?

The self exists as a way of connecting an animal body with a complex social system marked by rules, symbols, norms, ownership, and reputations. As the social system became more complex, the demands on the self increased. These contributed to stress. There is no single explanation for why modern individuals have struggled with certain problems of self and identity more than the ancients. There is no basic, universally true version of selfhood that would enable people of all eras and cultures to be comfortable in their skins. But we can map out how the problems have grown and changed. If the self emerged to enable the animal to belong to a culture, then as culture changes, the self probably changes too. Let's review how this happened.

I shall use the most studied versions of both culture and self, namely the self in the history of Western civilization. This will start from the early Middle Ages and come up to the present (see Baumeister, 1986, 1987, for earlier reviews). Some other forms of selfhood from quite different cultures are examined in the next chapter. Here, we focus on commonalities, major trends and widespread changes.

COLLECTIVE IDENTITY IN THE EARLY MIDDLE AGES

A dozen centuries ago, perhaps, the very idea of a person was a "functional" concept (MacIntyre, 1981). That is, there was a built-in purpose (function) for every human being. Knowing who you were mainly meant doing your job(s) in society. The goal of life was to achieve salvation, which meant going to heaven after death. Feelings and personality traits were sideshows or distractions needing to be suppressed. People were equated with their roles in society, and mostly they were born into those roles, with minimal alternative options. They dressed accordingly, so everyone would immediately know each other's place in society.

The initial separation between inner and outer self appears to have been in the selves of others, not in the elusiveness of your own inner self. Consider briefly life in medieval Europe. There was not much travel. Most people lived in small farming villages. Everybody knew everyone—indeed, often knew them from birth to death. Cities were rare, and a great many people, perhaps most, never set foot in a large city. Faking was rare and difficult. Many societies had laws requiring people to dress according to their social rank. You could tell right off who was a duchess and who was a fishwife. They knew who they were, and everybody else also knew it. Clergy wore special clothes, too. Identity was obvious on the outside, and there wasn't much thought devoted to its possible hidden realms.

A person was equated with his or her role in society, very much including social rank. Today, one speaks of social class instead of rank, but long before there was class consciousness, social rank was what mattered.

Society had a more differentiated and rigid hierarchy than it does today. Moving up or down was generally not even possible. Medieval Christians liked to think of society as a body, and so each person had his or her place in it. St. Augustine's much-quoted phrase aptly captured the medieval theory of self: A person should not aspire to change position in society, any more than a finger should wish to become an eye.

There was no broad sense that society was improperly formed and hence to blame for individual woe. A common idea was "the great chain of being," which clearly recognized that everyone was interconnected (Nisbet, 1973). You could not really live apart from the station to which you had been assigned by God and fate (in modern terms, by the circumstances of your birth). You were put on earth as a particular link in the great chain, and you belonged there. Being chained to your particular position in society also meant that social mobility was rare. Serfs did not get promoted to become dukes. Scholars today debate how much social mobility exists in various societies, but most are very open compared to the rigid medieval social structure.

Thus, the relation of an individual to society was understood as firmly based on several key factors. First, there was no conception of inner self or potential that defined the self as existing apart from the roles that defined his or her place in society. You were your job. (Notice that many surnames originated that way: Smith, Taylor, Cooper, even Baumeister [architect].) Second, there was a strong sense that life would be meaningful, and would be rewarded by fulfillment (salvation in heaven), if you just did your assigned duties. The Christian beliefs that dominated the early Middle Ages emphasized collective salvation (Aries, 1981). That's why people wanted to be buried in sanctified church graveyards.

Henrich (2020) noted that the extensive changes in Catholic Church law during early medieval times in Europe may have meant the Church gradually took over marriage and family. Weddings were held and registered in churches; babies were brought there for baptism, and so on. As part of its program of cracking down on sex (likely an appealing feature of early Christianity in the Roman Empire, where sexual license had become extensive, leading to disease and other problems), it began prohibiting marriage to cousins and other traditional practices. The cumulative effect of these reforms would be to weaken the extended family clan that had been the basis of almost all human societies in the world. The Church emphasized the nuclear family rather than the extended one.

The breakup of the extended family led gradually toward greater individualism. Traditionally, everything was decided among the clan, but now people learned to work and cooperate with non-kin. If there was a business, instead of hiring people mainly from the extended family, people hired non-kin. Crucially, this enabled hiring to be based on merit rather than family ties, so business functioning improved. In other respects as well, people could make their own decisions rather than deferring to the clan's decision makers, usually the oldest members. And people slowly became able to shape their lives based on their own talents and ambitions, instead of having their life course determined by the clan.

In the 12th century, beliefs also shifted to focus on individual judgment and salvation. That put much more focus on how the individual lived his or her life. Everything you did was measured by God in moral and religious terms, and when your life was over, the accumulated record would be judged.

Crucially, the new belief in individual judgment upped the importance of morality. Whether you acted virtuously or not came to be considered a big factor in whether you would get to heaven. Morality is ultimately a matter of individual choice and responsibility, so this was a boost to views of individualistic selfhood. This represented a big change. The culture began to assign greater importance to the individual life, rather than seeing the individual merely as part of a group. The individual self mattered in a new way.

Late medieval Europe saw the beginnings of capitalism and central government, and the new individuality may be linked to them. As one sign, the old traditional societies would punish an entire family for one person's offense, sometimes to the extent of killing the entire clan. Most modern societies punish only the wrongdoer and leave his family alone. That was a major change based on government-enforced rule of law.

It is easy to see how this change in responsibility might make a difference. If your cousin might do something that would get you and the rest of the family all killed, you would adopt a different attitude toward your cousin than would apply in an individualistic culture. If only the cousin will be punished for the cousin's misdeeds, then you can live and let live.

EARLY MODERN PERIOD: WHAT YOU SEE IS NOT WHAT YOU GET

Another big step occurred in the 16th century (Trilling, 1971). As Western civilization changed, it developed a new and greatly expanded sense that much of the self is hidden. Today, we take it for granted that many aspects of a self can be concealed, or revealed only deliberately in the social context of trust. Modern society likes to assume that every person has secrets, unconscious fears and desires, undiscovered talents, and other private things. It was not always thus. It took a long, gradual process to separate the idea of self from the surface appearance. For example, who you are is tied up with being someone's spouse and having a particular job, but if you divorced and changed jobs, you would still be you. It took society a long time to appreciate that.

Intellectuals were fascinated with the difference between appearance and reality, such as Bishop Berkeley's famous philosophical analysis starting with whether the clouds were really pink at sunset. There was also Machiavelli's advice to aspiring politicians, that how you should think is different from what you should say and how you should act. The rise in geographical and social mobility, and the ongoing increase in urban populations and city life generally, gradually undermined the old system in which a stranger could be known at 50 meters' distance (Sennett, 1974).

The 16th century—the time of Shakespeare, Queen Elizabeth I, and the Spanish Armada—was fascinated with the theater, including the idea of playing roles. Lionel Trilling's (1971) epochal book *Sincerity and Authenticity* documented this change. Plays changed and evolved. In the Middle Ages, if a character was supposed to be evil, he might be named "Evil" and might even wear a sign designating him as such. But then a new kind of character appeared, called a "villain." (The term, not incidentally, was related to the term for being a peasant: moral wickedness was associated with lower classes.) As a literary character, the villain represents a step forward in sophistication. The audience is led to understand early on that this person is evil—but the other characters in the play do not know he is evil. Often, the suspense of an early modern play revolves around whether the main characters will recognize the villain's wicked plans in time to avoid their own downfall. This provided a moral twist on a more basic theatrical innovation, which is the use of multiple perspectives. That, too, showed an increasing sensitivity to differences among selves (Weintraub, 1978).

Why did sincerity suddenly gain in importance as a virtue? Presumably, people had come to see that insincerity was a common problem. Translated into self terms, society was facing up to the fact that plenty of people were not really who they appeared to be; they were different inside from outside. The virtue of sincerity meant your inner self matched your outward appearance, including clothes and actions.

A perennial problem with understanding human selfhood is the question of what, exactly, is supposed to be known. "Know thyself" can mean a variety of different things, and it has. On this, the self has been a moving target.

The original problem of other people pretending to be someone they were not mainly took the form of pretending to be of higher social rank than they were entitled. The challenge was to know the selves of others, that is, to know what their position and rank in society were. The practical benefit was not succumbing to pretensions of grandeur.

Two key changes complicated this considerably. One was the gradual elaboration of self to include personality, including feelings and desires, alongside social rank. The second was the gradual conceptual separation of the person from rank and roles (MacIntyre, 1981). Putting these together meant that knowing someone's self became quite a different project from what it had been. Before, one wanted to know where the person stood in the hierarchy of society, and how well people performed their assigned roles. Afterward, you wanted to know all sorts of inner traits and patterns.

To be sure, knowing personality traits and moral propensities was undoubtedly important in early evolutionary history. I have said that moral reputation was one of the foundations of self. But in the small bands of hunters and gatherers, you could get to know someone very well over a long period of time. There was not the challenge of sizing up individual strangers, the way that became important as society moved out of the Middle Ages into the increasingly urban-based society of the early modern period.

One definition of *city* is as a place where a person regularly encounters strangers. Most cities are much older than the countries they are now in. Cities changed the forms of social interaction, concentrating people together so that interactions with strangers became important.

The separation of the individual from his or her roles was needed for multiple reasons. One is that people could and did seek advantage by pretending to have higher status than that to which they were entitled. Another was social mobility: it was actually possible to move up or down in social class. Families and even individuals did rise and fall in their position in society. They could change homes and even jobs. No longer were you your job or role—you were the actor who played that role. You would still be yourself on some later day even if you played a different role.

All of this meant that the self was not worn on the surface, as in previous eras. Where was it, then? The culture gradually began to think that the real self was hidden inside you somewhere. The Romantic period (late 1700s, early 1800s) showed an increased interest in artists because of their supposedly rich inner lives (Weintraub, 1978). Readers wanted to know what kind of person the artist was, deep down inside. Today, actors and athletes are many of the most famous people, and the public loves to see them on talk shows hoping to find out what they are really like inside (see Gabriel et al., 2016).

THE DIFFICULTY OF SELF-KNOWLEDGE

The medieval mind did not believe much in the inner self, nor did it think there was much of importance there that would be worth knowing. To the extent people did search inside and examine themselves—Plutarch was a famous example (Weintraub, 1978)—the purpose was to evaluate how well one resembled the religious ideals of virtue, duty, and piety. It was not "What am I really like deep down inside?" but "How well do I measure up to the way we are all supposed to be?" This is in keeping with what we have already seen: the self emerged to perform roles in the social system. Selfhood is less a matter of inner treasures coming to light and more a matter of the brain figuring out how to be accepted by performing these roles.

Historians generally agree that the Puritans were more self-conscious than their predecessors and greatly upped the stakes on self-knowledge (Greven, 1977; Weintraub, 1978). Puritanism flourished in Europe earlier and more briefly than in North America, so it had a more lasting effect on the latter. One sign is the great many soul-searching diaries and other autobiographical writings they left behind.

There was good reason for all this. Calvin highlighted a theological conundrum. If God knows everything, then he must know whether you will end up in heaven or hell. In a sense, your eternal fate is already determined. Calvin added that the signs were sufficiently clear. Although Calvin said not to waste time and energy trying to ascertain whether you were one of God's chosen few, it must have been hard to resist wondering about one's eternal fate.

As Puritans scrutinized their thoughts and feelings for revealing marks of sinfulness or virtue, they gradually realized that they might be engaging in wishful thinking. (Probably the first recognition of this was in others— "She thinks she's one of the Elect destined for heaven, but obviously she's not.") Did you perform that good deed because you are really good—or were you just trying to convince yourself you're good (thus committing the sin of pride)?

Calvin's views are no longer widely accepted, even among Protestant Christians. But the recognition of self-deception has had lingering consequences. It made self-knowledge suspect forever after. It's always possible that you could be fooling yourself.

To illustrate: The French thinker Guy de Montaigne wrote some autobiographical essays in the 1500s, when writing about oneself was still pretty unusual. At one point he offered a tongue-in-cheek justification for this. He said that although his topic, himself, was hardly as important as what other writers tackled, this lack of profundity might partly be offset by the fact that he at least knew his topic better than any other writers knew theirs. The implication was that self-knowledge was the most direct and impeccable form of knowledge. A couple of centuries later, such an assertion could not be made because people had come to realize that self-knowledge is systematically distorted by wishful thinking. The downward spiral of the prestige of self-knowledge escalated after the Puritans.

The low point in the cultural view of self-knowledge was probably Freudian psychoanalysis, in the first half of the 20th century. It assumed that by spending several hours every week for many years with an expensive and highly trained professional, a person might at best hope to make some progress toward correct self-knowledge.

COMPLICATED MODERN IDENTITY

The forming and maintaining of a self grew more complicated over the centuries; the crucial features became more unstable and more subject to individual choice (Baumeister, 1987). Modern Western society is trying to erase gender as a determinant of life course. Dozens, even hundreds, of career paths beckon. Fortunate youngsters go to universities, where they select among many possible majors, each of which offers multiple career pathways. Some careers pay more than others, a cause of inequality and friction.

Your identity is not set at any particular point. You may select a career, but that is hardly the end of it. Most careers offer multiple variations and different levels of success. People can be evaluated based on how much money they earn or have. Modern citizens are free to move to new homes and even new countries.

There are more options and more gradients of success—but all these put more strain and pressure on the self to create and define itself. Becoming who you are requires a long series of choices and evaluated performances. The many different roles in society available to you would make quite different versions of your self. Yet, the view has also emerged that you are still yourself regardless of what roles you inhabit.

The historical transformation of childhood reflects this increased burden of self-definition. A classic work by Philippe Aries (1962) proposed that childhood was only discovered in the early modern period (1500–1800). By this he meant later childhood. By age 8 or so, children were seen ready to start taking on adult roles. (Society itself was much younger than today, as life expectancy was much less than now.) Aries emphasized that it was a historical change to recognize that young people had potential to turn out well or badly and could be influenced for the better. This was not necessarily a great benefit to the youngsters themselves. The first application seems to have been increased emphasis on moral training by means of corporal punishment. But in the long run, there was a new understanding that each child had the potential to become a range of possible adults.

Adolescence likewise changed. If Aries is correct (and, not surprisingly, historians have argued about this), medieval teenagers were treated pretty much as adults. The general concept of adolescence was only embraced in the late 19th century (Mintz, 2004), and the concept of a "teenager" wasn't recognized by society until the 20th century.

Adolescents had always been known as a trouble-prone sort. The Freudians interpreted teen problems in a way that has held up through much subsequent research. The young teenager basically still has the child's powers of self-control but now these have to contend with an adult's desires for sex, aggression, intoxication, and more. Self-control is overmatched.

The task of the teen years is to become stronger at self-control so as to manage the adult's impulses and urges. The controlling part has to catch up to deal with the desiring part.

But the idea that adolescents must struggle to define who they are is a modern gloss superimposed on that ancient developmental struggle. Rather abruptly in the 20th century, teenagers emerged as a distinct category of people with peculiar, troublesome tendencies, people who need to be steered toward a respectable adult life, with roles to be chosen and performed in the somewhat remote future.

Thus, the link from the present self to the future self—the second, harder part of the unity project—became more difficult and therefore more clearly something that required attention and effort.

In the middle of the 20th century, Erik Erikson (1950) coined the term *identity crisis* to characterize what adolescents were going through. The term created a sensation and began to be used widely throughout society. As Erikson (1950, 1968) explained, your parents brought you up to be a certain kind of person. You had the option of just following that path and becoming that person, but you could instead become someone quite different. If you decided to be different, you had to decide which person you would be. That was the identity crisis.

In my 1987 book, I offered a concept I still think important: You have to find a way to decide who you want to be. You need some criteria to sort among the many options. It turns out there are many criteria, such as money, work–life balance, enjoyment of the work, and kind of family life. (Single? Dual-income, no kids? Gay marriage with or without adoption? Husband and wife with 3.2 kids?) This presents a historically new sort of problem. You need meta-criteria, higher-level criteria to decide which set of criteria you will use to decide who to be.

Teens are still struggling to develop enough self-control to manage their adult-strength urges, feelings, and impulses. And on top of all that, they need to search inside themselves for meta-criteria for how to decide the course to set for the rest of their lives, in theory at least. Fortunately, some of these decisions can be changed later on. But the difficulty of changing increases sharply the longer one goes down a particular path.

Moreover, the notion that searching inside yourself will enable you to find the answers is dubious. In some cases, this becomes a rationalization for doing whatever you feel like. ("I have to be myself.") If the answer is not inside yourself, does it lie outside you? Except for highly religious people, who believe that their god has dictated what their calling should be, there is not much reason to believe that the answer is out there either. One response to this is to say there is no objective answer and people just make choices to create and define who they are. Still, on what basis do they make such choices?

A Growing Rupture in the Relation
of Individual to Society

One theme of this book is that selves exist to relate the individual, animal body to the social system (society and culture). The relation between individual and society has been a vital driver of how and why selves exist, and how they have taken shape. As the chapter has tried to show, this relation has changed across Western history.

Social mobility obviously detached the individual from his or her place in society, requiring a new concept of the person as existing apart from roles (MacIntyre, 1981). Social mobility was not just vertical, but also horizontal, with similar results. That is, even if you remained in the trade or middle class, you had increasing options for where to live and what work to do—so you had to make choices that would define your identity, much more than in the past. The gradual prying apart of the individual and society was not just abstract discussion among intellectuals. As we have seen, society was fascinated by theaters and acting, possibly indicating an interest in the playing of roles.

Another revealing historical change was the new desire for privacy. There was not much privacy in the Middle Ages (Moore, 1984). In fact, it hardly occurred to people to want privacy, except possibly for a few things such as illicit sex, treasonous plotting, and bowel movements. Phillippe Aries (1962) may have overstated the case when he said that "until the end of the seventeenth century, nobody was ever left alone," but perhaps not by much, and his general point about living constantly surrounded by others was probably correct.

The change can be seen in architecture (Moore, 1984). If you tour a European palace from before the 1700s, you may notice that there are no corridors. Doors just lead from one room into the next. Getting to a back bedroom required passing through several other bedrooms, which may have facilitated nocturnal sexual mischief but reduced privacy for the occupants. Then during the early modern period (1500–1800) buildings began to be designed with corridors and hallways so that one could go to the main areas from one's own private room without passing through other people's rooms. The desire for privacy has grown and spread in recent centuries, to the point at which it is now a coveted luxury. People at the top of society jealously guard their privacy with walls, cameras, remote locations, and sometimes armed guards.

The rise of private life was gradual. Having a bedroom that precluded other people passing through it was one of many steps and indications. Some historians have made a case that the relative value of public and private life shifted around the end of the early modern period (1800; Sennett, 1974). That is, the 17th century placed high value on activities out in society, including work, play, and conversations with strangers in the many clubs, bars, and coffee houses that brought people together. These activities had a higher value than what you did at home with your spouse and children. This became reversed in the 19th century, which placed ever higher value on private life, at home in the family. Today, we take the supreme importance of home and family life for granted, but people have thought differently at other times and places.

SELVES IN CONFLICT WITH SOCIETY

It would be lovely to say that over the centuries, self and society have come ever more into harmony. But it's hard to make that case, and some would argue it's gone the other way. The notion of self and society as enemies has spread, not vanished.

The idea that the individual person could be in conflict with society as a whole, which modern life also takes for granted, was at one point a new idea. It did not much occur to anyone in the Middle Ages. But when the medieval worldview broke down, this idea gradually spread and fostered a wide assortment of responses. Let me summarize them briefly. (Fuller treatments available in Baumeister, 1986, 1987.)

The Romantic period (roughly 1750–1850) recognized the conflict between individual and society. The individual struggled against oppressive social conditions to try to be him- or herself. There was a sense that somehow society had gone terribly wrong, epitomized by Rousseau's assertion that things were far better long ago and that everyone should go back to nature. Princesses at royal courts played at being shepherds and farm maids, even while actual shepherds and farmworkers were moving to the cities to get work in the factories of the industrial revolution. They were escaping from the constraints, poverty, and drudgery of life in farming villages. In literature, when Romantic heroes failed to find a way to make society let them be themselves, they often died. Goethe's *Sorrows of Young Werther* ended with the hero killing himself, and this inspired a wave of copycat suicides.

The Romantic period also capitalized on the Enlightenment, an intellectual movement that questioned and reinvented how society should treat individuals. What were then radical ideas have become commonplace today, so it is hard to appreciate how radical they were. The British Empire was approaching the height of its power. The colonies who tried to seize control themselves by military rebellion were all defeated and suppressed, except one. In that peculiar outlier, American colonists set up a new country and borrowed heavily from Enlightenment ideas. When declaring independence, they asserted, "All men are created equal." Indeed, they declared this to be a "self-evident truth." That idea would have been utterly foreign to the medieval mind.

A key aspect of Enlightenment and Romantic thought was that the religious framework ceased to dominate every aspect of life. Religion retreated from the center of society to its periphery. Christianity had effectively deferred fulfillment to the afterlife in heaven, but that was no longer enough. People wanted fulfillment in this life. Love and work (especially some kinds of creative work) gained prestige as ways of finding fulfillment in this life.

Replacing religious with secular fulfillment suggests a kind of collective impatience. People did not want to wait until they were dead to feel good and reap rewards for their efforts. This reflects a changed view of the individual self. Instead of aiming at fulfillment in the very long run, as in after death, people wanted fulfillment now.

Romanticism's idea of going back to nature gradually gave way to various 19th-century refinements. These included plenty of writings and social movements aimed at changing society. The idea that society was bad remained strong, as reflected in anarchist movements that wanted to get rid of government, complete with early versions of terrorism and the assassination of political leaders.

The 19th century also saw a first wave of Utopian writings, both fiction and nonfiction. These involved thinking of how society could be changed so that individual selves could thrive and flourish rather than simply accepting the often harsh, oppressive conditions that prevailed. Indeed, the Utopian initiative was not confined to writing, and various groups of people actually undertook to create their own perfect societies. Communes and other Utopian experiments proliferated. Most of them only lasted a short time. The clash between the individual and society was acutely suffered, and some people tried to solve it with new kinds of society.

In the mid-1800s, transcendentalism emerged as important in American intellectual life. Emerson was the foremost thinker of the movement, along with Whitman, Thoreau, and others. The idea was that there was no hope for perfecting society. One had to make concessions as needed but should seek fulfillment in private life and by communing with nature.

Neither escaping society (transcendentalism), nor removing government (anarchism), nor starting over to make a new and perfect society (Utopianism) had really worked. By 1900, there was a sense that the individual was hopelessly at the mercy of giant societal forces that did not care about the individual, and which the individual was helpless to control. Images of the person as a tiny, struggling individual caught in a giant machine and cruelly oppressed by it were common. Alienation became a major theme among intellectuals. Given the early 20th century's world wars, flu pandemic, and economic depression, it's no wonder people thought the individual was helplessly gripped by giant, indifferent, or even malicious forces.

At bottom, alienation was a stage in the transition from small to large groups. The closed, narrow society of village life of the Middle Ages was gone forever. In the modern world, strangers were everywhere, reminding people that they occupied only a tiny place in the big dangerous world.

In the second half of the 20th century people moved on under the rubric of accommodation, a form of compromise. One could neither escape society nor simply acquiesce. The project of selfhood involved accepting the reality of mass society but still cultivating one's individuality and personal fulfillment.

PERSPECTIVE

Two of the giants among groups researchers, John Levine and Richard Moreland (1990), have written authoritative overviews of the groups research literature. One of their observations stuck in my mind. Starting with the obvious point, that people like to belong to groups, they added a disturbing qualifier: Most of the things we like about groups dwindle sharply and sadly as groups get larger. Belonging to a small group, like a family, sports team, work group, or amateur rock band, can afford one all sorts of great and small satisfactions. (To be sure, there are annoyances, too.) One takes pride in the group, cultivates relationships with other members, feels validated by working with them, and so on. Belonging to a giant group, such as an army or multinational corporation, doesn't offer the same warmth. Yet, that is the direction in which things have moved—not least because bigger groups can often do more things, better or more efficiently, than small groups.

One problem for the modern self is to adapt its small-group mentality to living in large groups. This is likely to be a cause of friction and stress for a long time. The human self evolved in groups of a few dozen people and by several calculations can personally know maybe 150 people. A city of a million people is hopelessly beyond that—and such cities today are only medium-sized. There are powerful system advantages to large cities, including economic systems, so any impulse to go back to living in small towns and villages is doomed. The modern self is very old wine in a very new bottle, for which it is not quite suited.

KEY POINTS

- In the European Middle Ages, people were equated with the social roles they were born into. There was no separation between inner and outer self. Laws required people to dress according to their social rank.
- By the late Middle Ages, the influence of the clan was weakened, and individual judgment increased the importance of morality.
- In the early modern period, with the growth of cities, insincerity was a common problem. With much of the self seen as hidden, appearance could be deceiving.

- As Puritans scrutinized their thoughts and feelings for marks of sinfulness or virtue, society began to recognize the possibility that self-knowledge could be self-deception.

- Increasingly in the modern era, the individual was seen as in conflict with society as a whole. By the early 20th century, there was a sense that the individual was hopelessly at the mercy of giant societal forces that did not care about the individual, and which the individual was helpless to control.

- In the second half of the 20th century, selfhood involved accepting the reality of mass society but still cultivating one's individuality and personal fulfillment.

CHAPTER 4

Different Societies Make Different Kinds of Selves

America has been the world leader in psychology for most of the past century. As mentioned in Chapter 3, most data about the human self come from studies run in America, based on American citizens (most frequently university students). That increases the risk that one will mistake specifically American traits and tendencies for universal ones. The optimistic, self-flattering styles of thinking that emerge from studies of American students might not be matched in other cultures. The great Shelley Taylor told me of attending an international conference where she explained her findings that normal, healthy people exhibited positive illusions, such as exaggerating their good qualities, and overestimating how much control they have over their fate. An elderly European scholar shook his head, slightly confused, and said, "So are you saying, the normal, healthy person is essentially an American?"

INTERDEPENDENT AND INDEPENDENT SELVES

The cultural component of self moved beyond anecdote in a big way in 1991, when Hazel Markus and Shinobu Kitayama published a landmark paper arguing that Chinese and Japanese people thought of themselves in ways that differed systematically from what research on Americans had found. A flood of research followed that, mostly confirming and extending their basic points.

The new view emphasized that East Asians, such as Chinese and Japanese people, understand the self as *interdependent*, primarily defined by social roles and in relation to other people. They are highly sensitive to the duties and obligations that attend these roles. The interdependent self certainly has its own preferences and attitudes, but these are considered to be of secondary importance. They should be kept from interfering with one's social obligations and with being a worthy, valuable member of the collective group.

In contrast, the form of selfhood flourishing in North America and western Europe can be characterized as independent. This sort of self is defined by its inner attributes, more than by how it is related to other people. Abilities, preferences, desires, attitudes, and traits are centrally important to this form of self. Naturally, roles and relationships are there, too, and even obligations and duties, but the individual self takes priority.

Thus, when the Twenty Statements Test is given to Americans, they complete the 20 phrases "I am _____" with adjectives that describe their abilities and personality traits. Asians respond to the same test with more references to relationships and group memberships. To be sure, the differences are relative, and both kinds of answers are furnished by members of both cultures. Still, the Americans seem to explain themselves more in terms of individual attributes than relationships, compared to the Asians.

In a powerful extension of this view, Steve Heine and colleagues (1999) contended that the self-enhancement motive is largely absent in Japanese society. Americans like to think about how great they are as individuals, and they emphasize self-praise in order to feel good about themselves. Japanese, on the other hand, focus on self-improvement. They emphasize self-criticism in order to highlight areas where they should change. Among other signs, the researchers reported that American professional athletes exult in their talents and gifts, which make them entitled to lavish rewards, whereas Japanese professional athletes remain humble and constantly strive to get better, even when they are already the best.

The idea that the self-enhancement motive is culturally relative, indeed absent in some cultures, provoked a long-running debate. Sedikides and his group (e.g., 2003, 2005; O'Mara et al., 2012; cf. Heine, 2005) argued that Japanese still seek to think well of themselves, merely finding different ways and criteria to do so. If you criticize a Japanese man's work, he may not respond as defensively as an American might. But perhaps his self-esteem is focused on being a good group member and performing his social obligations. If you criticize him for neglecting his family, or being unworthy of his job, or even being a bad citizen, he might indeed bristle.

Thus, there are clearly differences between how Asians and Westerners think of themselves, and the debate is over how deep those go. Regardless, a few points need to be made.

First, the two types, independent and interdependent, are not necessarily the only possibilities. Relatively little work has delved into self-beliefs and relevant motivations in other groups. One tantalizing exception is recent work by Kitayama and colleagues on Arab self-beliefs. Arabs mix the assertiveness that is typical of the independent style of self with the collective spirit that defines the interdependent self (Martin et al., 2018). Why? One plausible answer was that the harsh desert environment required people to be aggressive in defending their group, and to be reliable, trustworthy, respected members of their group. Whereas assertiveness among Westerners is linked to promoting the individual self, the assertiveness of Arabs is about promoting their group.

Second, even within a society, people are different. In today's North America, women are on average more collectivist and more interdependent than men (Cross & Madson, 1997). The individualistic self of the modern era is most fully realized among men in modern, Western societies.

A third key point is that the different styles of selfhood are not simply alternatives. The best guess is that the Western style of independent selfhood is historically recent. Most world cultures probably started out with interdependence. For some of the peculiar reasons associated with medieval European history, discussed in Chapter 3, society changed in unusual ways and began to cultivate a new version of self that was understood as existing independently of its position in society and its roles.

If political and sociological changes favor independent selfhood, then over time, Asian and other cultures are likely to shift toward more independent selfhood. This seems to be happening, as indicated by the worldwide trends toward greater individualism (Santos et al., 2017).

The two kinds of self have implications for how most people's everyday social life is organized. In terms of whom you spend your days with, there is a tradeoff. Some people are better suited to you than others: better companions and teammates. The only way to get the perfect set is to pick and choose, and that includes rejecting and replacing ones who don't work out. The downside is that they can reject and replace you, too; so there is a pervasive anxiety about maintaining relationships. In contrast, it is appealing to have a society in which relationships are permanent and no change is possible; the downside is you might well end up stuck with people you don't like. Social life must resolve the tradeoff, one way or the other. Either allow people to choose and change, and accept the stress and anxiety that accompany ongoing turnover in relationship partners, or else lock in relationships permanently, and accept that people will just have to put up with frequent interactions with people they don't get along with. A vivid illustration of this problem is the question of how easy divorce should be. In some times and places, divorce is effectively impossible, and married couples are stuck with each other for life. At the other extreme, people could divorce each other with minimal hassle, simply going down to the village square and saying, "I divorce you" several times in front of witnesses. Either extreme highlights the costly tradeoff, but there is no perfect spot along the continuum either. Still, the worldwide trends are moving toward easier divorce and greater individualism. The independent self seems well adapted to the kind of social life that seeks well-matched partners even if that means frequent turnover and the anxiety over loss.

Meanwhile, the interdependent self is better suited to a social environment in which relationships are permanent, so you'd best adapt so as to get along with the people around you. Be humble rather than assertive. Understand yourself as part of this group. After all, the clan is rather permanent, and you are just carrying it on during your brief life. That's who you are, and the self's unity project is served by invoking its connections to others (see Chapter 10). This is very unlike the independent self in the high-turnover social environment because for that self, the connections to particular others are not necessarily part of who you will be in the future.

Even among the independent selves of Western society, people identify with social relationships when those are permanent. With the liberalization of divorce, marriage is not as permanent as it was, though people do identify themselves by marriage. Still, the most permanent relationships are filial. The average middle-aged American woman probably could not explain her identity without mentioning her children. Meanwhile, young people may also identify themselves in relation to their parents, but as they grow up and go their own ways, the relevance of parents to self-identity recedes drastically.

Thus, the self operates differently depending on the social environment. Remarkably, the difference is evident even among modern young American students. There is evidence that people present themselves very positively to people they are meeting for the first time—but become quite modest and self-effacing when presenting themselves to friends (Tice et al., 1995). To maintain a relationship over a long period of time, humility and modesty serve better because they will minimize conflicts. If even American students shift toward modesty when interacting with acquaintances, imagine how much more important it is for people in collectivistic cultures to do so. They have to get along whether they like each other or not.

A vivid illustration of this was provided in Thurston's (1987) history of the Chinese Cultural Revolution. In that giant social upheaval, people accused their colleagues, superiors, and neighbors of being insufficiently zealous Communists. In struggle sessions that occurred in public, one person would be humiliated and physically tortured, such as by being forced to "do the airplane" (have arms strapped to a heavy bar resting on the back of the neck and extending on both sides). They were told to confess misdeeds and struck hard when answers were unsatisfactory. A woman described the torments she suffered led by a neighbor she scarcely knew, who caused her intense social and personal pain. After many years, the Cultural Revolution passed, and the survivors went back to their lives from before. The woman came back from the reeducation camp and resumed her life and job as before, more or less. That meant living in the same apartment building, with that same neighbor. Moving to a new home was not permitted. Naturally, they avoided each other. Sometimes she would pass him coming down the stairs when she was going up. He would nod to her briefly and keep going.

No doubt the difference between greater individualism and collectivism has multiple causes. Scholarship has suggested some important ones. One seemingly surprising factor is germs. In areas where there are many pathogens and disease is a constant danger, cultures evolved to enforce conformity, so people act in ways that will not spread disease (Fincher et al., 2008; Park & Schaller, 2009). In contrast, if the environment has fewer pathogens, then society can tolerate letting people do things their own way, so food and hygiene practices can be more variable. Clearly, these differences developed long before people understood anything about how germs transmit disease. The difference was probably accomplished by group selection: The groups that made everyone conform to norms of cleanliness prospered better than the groups that had lax standards that permitted idiosyncrasies.

The start of farming was a big step in human social progress, and different kinds of crops may have shaped how selves were formed in the new, stay-put societies that supplanted the nomadic hunter-gatherers. Recent work finds that even in Asia, areas where wheat was the main crop fostered a more individualistic style of self and society, as compared to areas that grew rice (reviewed by Henrich, 2020). The reason is that farmers can grow wheat on their own, but cultivating rice is inherently a more communal effort. Hence, wheat-growing societies could let people go their own individual ways, but rice-growing societies emphasized cooperating with the group and obeying its norms.

FACE AND DIGNITY CULTURES

Another way to characterize the difference between Asian and Western cultures is the difference between what can be called "face" and "dignity" cultures. Face cultures are defined by those in which a person's worth is heavily dependent on others' evaluations, and private views of self are of minor importance. In contrast, dignity cultures assume that each person has intrinsic worth, independent of others. Face and dignity overlap with interdependence versus independence, but not perfectly. For example, Israel is a collectivistic dignity culture.

The different attitudes are preserved in modern American university students from different ethnic backgrounds. A nicely done pair of studies (Kim & Cohen, 2010) compared how students reacted to getting information about themselves, either based on considering things from their own personal point of view or from the point of view of other people who were important in their lives. The students from Asian heritage reacted strongly when they considered this information from a third-person perspective, that is, involving how their social circle would view them. But exactly the same information considered from their own, first-person perspective had essentially zero effect. The implication is what matters to them is face, namely how others see them.

In contrast, American students with European heritage reacted more strongly when considering their own personal view than considering how they were perceived by others. The effects were in the same direction in both cases, suggesting that the European Americans do still care what others think, but they give greater priority to their own perspective. Other people's views can be rationalized and dismissed more easily than private information, perhaps.

Allport's (1958) term "functional autonomy" denotes how means to an end can itself come to function as an end. A person's view of self is a means to keep track of how one is viewed by others. In the long run, self-regard can attain functional autonomy so that people care about self-esteem and self-regard, somewhat apart from any direct connection to what others think. Perhaps this process of functional autonomy has been carried farther in the European sort of dignity culture than in the East Asian face cultures. Neither is inherently better, but there is a difference in terms of everyday experience of self.

KEY POINTS

- The properties of the typical self are based on what works best in a person's social system.
- The self may develop differently in different cultures.
- The independent self is conceived as an autonomous, self-contained agent, operating on its own, making choices and pursuing self-selected goals, complete with its own inner set of values and preferences.
- The interdependent self is understood as firmly embedded in a network of social relationships, complete with obligations and accommodations.
- In face cultures a person's worth is heavily dependent on others' evaluations and private views of self are of minor importance.
- Dignity cultures assume that each person has intrinsic worth, independent of others.

CHAPTER 5

Four Pitfalls of Self Theories

No Self, Multiple Selves, Authentic True Selves,
and Self-Actualization

The assortment of thinkers who have offered theories about the self is breathtakingly wide and diverse. This chapter addresses a few ideas that some have found appealing and exciting, but that I think ultimately do not work. As always, we should be alert to what positive insights reside even in theories that are ultimately unsuccessful.

IS THE SELF AN ILLUSION?

Is it plausible that selves are not real? There are serious thinkers who deny that there is such a thing as the self. My impression is that these skeptics are mainly found among brain (neuroscience) researchers and cognitive psychologists, as well as some of the more radical fringe thinkers in religion and philosophy. Most social scientists cannot do their work without acknowledging the reality of selves. Imagine an economist, for example, who seeks to describe the workings of a marketplace without the separate selves of buyers and sellers. What would be the point of buying something without a self to own it or consume it? And whose money would the buyer plunk down?

Before we delve into these arguments against the reality of selfhood, a word of caution: The skeptics have some good points.

Religious and Philosophical Objections

Objections to selfhood are famously and thoroughly argued in Indian Buddhist philosophy. They have a "no-self" doctrine, or sometimes, as in

Nagarjuna's thinking, the self is described as empty. A similar argument in Western thought was developed by David Hume (1739), the iconoclastic British philosopher, who found himself unable to be aware of any specific thing known as the self. When he introspected, all he could find was a "bundle of perceptions."

These objections are making a valid point, namely that the self does not exist independently of its social environment. But still, Zen masters who assert "no-self" doctrines still seem to have functioning selves. They don't put their shoes on someone else's feet by mistake because they couldn't tell the difference. (After all, to execute muscle movements based on a difference between "your" feet and "my" feet is only meaningful if you and I have distinct selves.) But as we have argued already, selves exist in relation to a society. The lone creature does not care a fig about selfhood. It does not bother with it except for the minimal animal parts, like coordinating the various leg muscle movements so as to walk.

Hume's point carries things a step further, perhaps. If you try to focus your attention on your self, you can't manage to get a pure experience: "There I am!" But that doesn't demolish the reality of the self, only the ability to experience it directly. Immanuel Kant, one of the greatest minds of the 18th century, devoted a core passage of his epochal *Critique of Pure Reason* (1797/1967) to responding to Hume on this point. As Kant put it, you cannot perceive yourself as an object, like Hume said. But you can perceive it perceiving some other object. To use a modern American idiom, you "catch yourself in the act" of doing, seeing, or thinking something. Put another way, you aren't aware of yourself in quite the same way you perceive a table. But you can be aware of yourself assembling, pounding, or setting the table. The self is perceived in action because it is a process. The mind perceives its own perceiving, and that's how it discovers the self. If the word *discovers* is too strong for your taste, perhaps try *constructs* or *imputes*.

The view that selves are illusory also underpins many spiritual practices, particularly in Asia. Yoga and meditation are supposed to quiet the ego, dispel selfish concerns with acquiring things and gaining status, and help the person see the self as a trivial fleeting thing not worth being concerned about. Many people are drawn to learn these practices in part because of the promise of being able to achieve inner peace by way of dissolving the ego.

Some recent studies cast doubt on this process, however. The intrepid Jochen Gebauer and his team (2018) studied groups of yoga students and meditators for several weeks, measuring their concerns with self before and after yoga class, or before and after meditation. Instead of moving toward loss of self, the meditators and yoga students became all the more concerned with self. They shifted toward greater self-enhancement: their self-esteem and narcissism went up, as did their tendency to rate themselves as above average. In fact, the average student in a yoga class gradually came to regard him- or herself as better at yoga than other students in the same yoga class! Clearly, self and ego were not vanishing as the class went on. The more a student identified with yoga and meditation, the stronger the effects were. These effects were found not just with beginners but with advanced practitioners, too, so they don't just reflect some novice misfire.

Why? Gebauer and colleagues propose that practicing any skill increases your ability, and as that happens, the ability comes to seem more central to your self-concept. As a result, self-evaluation changes by acquiring something new to feel good about. Sure enough, yoga and meditation did come to feel more central to how these individuals understood themselves, and that made them more positively biased about themselves. The researchers concluded that "serious re-thinking" (2018, p. 1306) is required in connection with the long-standing view that these spiritual practices quiet the ego.

Gebauer's explanation fits a key theme of this book: The self cultivates its unusual talents and characteristics because groups flourish with differences among selves. The key for the cultural group is being able to slot people into what they're talented for so that the total performance by the group is improved. This process would be helped if individuals focus on what they're good at and build their self-concepts around how they can be most valuable to the group (including society as a whole).

More remarkable evidence comes from a cross-cultural study by the indomitable Shaun Nichols and his colleagues (2018). They compared choices and values among American and Asian citizens as well as Tibetan Buddhist monks. The monks embraced the Buddhist philosophy that the self does not persist across time, unlike the other groups. (Of the seven samples, the Americans had the highest belief in continuity of self across time, and the monks had the lowest.) In theory, believing that there is no continuous self should reduce fear of death as well as selfishness. After all, "you" won't really be dead since "you" won't exist in the future, regardless of heart attacks.

But the actual result was stunning. The monks showed the highest fear of death. They even specifically showed highest fear of the aspect of death that annihilates the self. It's hard to square this with the theory that selves don't exist across time. The very experts who deny the self act the most self-oriented.

A further set of questions in Gebauer's study asked people whether they would give up some medicine that they needed to survive, to enable someone else to survive. In some cases, the medicine would prolong your own life slightly but would add many years to someone else's life. The medicine gives you an extra 6 months or them an extra 5 years. Regardless, the monks generally said they would not give the medicine, even if it would prolong the other person's life far longer than their own life. The monks were significantly more selfish than the other groups, in this sense.

Thus, the Buddhist no-self doctrine is not what it seems to a casual observer. Nichols and colleagues noted that Buddhist literature contains many autobiographies—but "how can one affirm an autobiography while denying the self?" Like Hume, the Buddhists assert that the self does not exist as a separate, independent thing, fully separable from its surroundings. Nevertheless, within its social environment, the self is quite real and important. Real Buddhists use their selves every day.

Neuroscience and Cognition

Those in different fields study different things, and only some of those things require selves. An anonymous reviewer once made a profound point in response to one of my manuscripts. He or she pointed out that some fields question the self, while others assume its reality. The reality of the self is questioned by researchers who examine narrow aspects of individual mental functioning, focusing on specific thoughts and mental subroutines. Neuroscience (the study of brain processes) and cognitive psychology (the study of thought processes) are prominent among the skeptics of self. In contrast, researchers who focus on social systems cannot dispense with selves. These include economists, sociologists, even researchers who study two-person relationships. (Imagine trying to analyze a marriage without referring specifically to either of the two separate people involved in it.)

The difference among research fields is crucial. If you're down in the weeds examining the details of how one part of a single mind works on specific problems in specific situations, the grand unity of selfhood is a quaint and generally dispensable notion. But anything about human relationships and social systems requires selves—indeed, preferably extended-time selves.

My initial impression is that some brain researchers think that only brain processes are real. When they couldn't find any specific part of the brain that constituted "the self," they shrugged and assumed that self must not exist. After all, as already pointed out, having a theory of self is not all that important to their work.

Then again, I've heard that lately there is renewed interest in the self among neuroscientists. I argue that the self is something the brain does rather than something that is (exists) inside it. It's a process rather than a thing, not unlike life itself. It always seemed plausible to me that neuroscientists as a group might initially dismiss the self, once they could not pinpoint a particular part of the brain that constitutes it, but that they would also start to appreciate and use the self when their research moved from mapping out specific areas to analyzing how the different parts work together to manage behavior in the complex social world.

Let's consider the arguments that the self is an illusion.

The Case That Self Is Illusion

Is the self merely an illusion? One hears it labeled as such by various so-called experts—even some experts on the self.

Bruce Hood's (2012) *The Self Illusion* undertakes to provide a definitive statement of the illusory essence of self. I found Hood's book charming, well written, and well grounded in the scientific literature. I learned plenty from it. Still, it failed to convince me of the nonexistence of the self. Then again, I'm not sure it really tried.

Hood seems to waffle between strong and weak versions of his thesis. At times he denies the existence of the self. But when setting the terms at the start, he quotes Susan Blakemore to the effect that asserting the self is an illusion doesn't mean it doesn't exist. Perhaps, then, an illusory self can be real even if it is partly an illusion. He went on to explain: Saying the self is an illusion is only to say it is not what it seems. He never quite got around to explaining how the self seems to be one thing but is really something else, unless it's "really" just a bunch of brain cells firing. Still, if his assertion is merely that people are mistaken in some of their beliefs about themselves, we are all in agreement, and indeed that is very old news.

Plenty of evidence indicates that people are mistaken about themselves. They do not realize the extent of unconscious influences on their behavior. This is no surprise. By definition, you are not aware of your unconscious processes. Likewise, people have memories that help them know themselves, but memories are sometimes wrong, and indeed memory research suggests that each memory is reconstructed slightly differently each time you remember it. Memories are not a solid, fully reliable basis for selfhood, though I assume memories are somewhat accurate in general. People also underestimate how much they are affected by external, situational factors. So if you believe the self is solely in charge of everything you do, that is an illusion. True enough.

But Hood wants to demolish the self much more thoroughly. Many passages compare the self to various visual illusions, which do entail seeing things that do not exist. He catalogs how various external forces influence a person's behavior and concludes, "If it is a self that flinches and bends with tiny changes in circumstances, then it might as well be nonexistent" (2012, p. 396). He isn't explicitly saying the self is nonexistent, but its properties suggest it is, or "might as well be." This seems a cheap shot. Taken literally, one could try out that argument elsewhere: If a tree or flower flinches and bends in the wind, does that mean it might as well not exist? I am inclined to think that the ability to adapt and change in response to environment is one of the great features of the self, rather than a reason to deny its existence.

Hood does a good job of establishing that people act differently in different situations and even think of themselves differently in different situations. But could this not simply be that the same self adjusts to the situation? He says no: "That is the heart of the illusion" (2012, p. 474). To me, that is one important aspect of the reality of the self. It adjusts to the situation and role, changing its traits (which are just patterns of behavior) accordingly. Your self really ought to exhibit different patterns of behavior, thus different traits, when in church with your mother versus at a bar watching the game with your buddies. You are nevertheless the same person, the same self. In either place, if someone from whom you borrowed $100 last year shows up, you could take the opportunity to pay him back. If you don't, then the next day when you are in the other situation, you still owe him.

Here's the crucial question: If the self is an illusion in the sense that it does not really exist, then what is the reality? Hood offers cryptic metaphors: it is like a spider web without the spider. Yet in the real world, it always takes a spider to make a spider web. Also, he says, "In a sense, who we are really comes down to those around us" (2012, p. 219). But if my self doesn't exist, how can it be explained by the selves of the people around me? I finished his book without understanding what he thinks the reality is. If there are no selves, who owns that smartphone? Who earned that driver's license or master's degree? These are all selves, complete with specific names.

The further question is why this elaborate set of illusions exists. Hood is clear that there must be a good reason: "Why did we evolve the self illusion? Like every other illusion our brain generates, it serves a useful purpose" (2012, p. 517). But when it comes to specifying the purpose, he is less clear. Somehow Hood thinks it is a convenient simplification that improves efficiency. "We have evolved to treat each other as individual selves" (p. 519), he says, and well, that's fine, but doesn't that suggest the self is real rather than illusory? Without the self we would be "overwhelmed by complexity"—but animals get by with minimal selves and are not thus overwhelmed. It seems more plausible to me that we evolved the ability to create and maintain selves precisely in order to make complex social systems possible.

To sum up: With all due respect, the case for the nonexistence of the self does not bear scrutiny. True, there is no specific physical thing. And it is a product of circumstances, and it often fails to understand all the causes of its actions, especially subtle cues in the situation, and unconscious processes. The weak form of Hood's assertion, that your self is not precisely what it seems, is fine. But nothing he says proves the nonexistence of selves.

It is fair to say, "There is no such thing as the self" because the self is not a thing in the physical sense. There is no specific physical item—though one has to be careful because the self starts (at least) with the physical body.

That means in the simplest views, there is a physical thing. But clearly the self is more than the body, and it is not the body plus some other physical thing. It is rather the systems by which the body acts. One sign is death. The body continues to exist after death, but the self does not.

The vital insight from religious and philosophical views is that selves (unlike bodies) do not exist as separate entities but rather exist in relation to others. Selves flourish amid complex networks of social relations. Selves come from a complex conceptual system, like an assembly line in a factory, that organizes different actions by different individuals to accomplish complementary things, cooperation enabled by communication.

THE CASE FOR MULTIPLE SELVES

One idea that comes up every 15 or 20 years, as if newly discovered for the first time, is that each person has many different selves rather than just one. Each time this idea bursts on the scene, it generates widespread enthusiasm for its novelty and creativity . . . but then it fizzles out. Still, the enthusiasm is a sign that there is something important about it. "I am large, I contain multitudes," proclaimed Walt Whitman in *Leaves of Grass* (1855/2013). Or, to quote the seminal psychologist William James, "Properly speaking, a man has as many social selves as there are individuals who recognize him and carry an image of him in their head" (1892/1948, p. 179) More recently, the Yale thinker Paul Bloom (2008) has argued that people have multiple selves. He suggests that people fail to save for retirement because saving money for that purpose is essentially giving the money away to an elderly stranger.

Whitman wrote the above line in a poem to which he gave the title "Song of Myself," not "Songs of Ourselves." James wrote that line above but then immediately backed off to some degree. He said maybe it would be more accurate to propose that the tally of selves equals the number of groups who know him, not the number of individuals. James went on to say that having different styles of action, even seemingly different personalities, amounts to "practically" consisting of multiple selves. Practically, as in, not really.

As for Paul Bloom, whom I greatly respect and admire, I asked him the following one conference evening at the bar: If he really believed that saving for retirement was giving one's money away to an elderly stranger, would he mind putting his retirement savings in my name? After all, one elderly stranger is as good as another, so what's the difference? He laughed. I have not gotten the money. Not that I seriously expected it.

These are highly intelligent people, and their assertions of multiple selfhood deserve thoughtful consideration. Then again, the contradictions quickly reveal themselves, as in the Whitman and Bloom examples. There is something essential about singular unity in the self. More broadly, the idea that people have multiple selves is soon abandoned rather than leaving a lasting foundation or insight. That's a sign it ultimately is not a workable, defensible position. Nonetheless, perhaps we can learn what the key insights and phenomena are that lead intelligent thinkers to entertain the idea of multiple selves.

A recent and impassioned case for multiple selves was made by the remarkably productive psychologist David Lester, whose work in other contexts has influenced and strengthened my own. His book *On Multiple Selves* (2015) quotes many different thinkers approvingly in their various assertions about how each person consists of multiple selves. He presents the best data he can find to support his case. (He also quotes various other writers less approvingly, including me, who have been skeptical of the multiplicity of selves.) Let's get what we can from his strong case.

In most of the book, he talks about "subselves," which are never quite defined but are presumably different parts, aspects, or versions of the same self. The notion of subselves is much less flamboyant than the notion of truly multiple selves. Lester wobbles between the two, falling back to subselves when discussing data or rigorous arguments, but then reasserting multiple selves when on safer ground, distant from the constraints of evidence and proof. This wobbling increases my skeptical assessment that the case for multiple selves is difficult to make in a clear and consistent fashion.

The common underlying idea is that people play different roles in different situations and change their behavior. Perhaps they even change their operative personality traits, as they move from one situation to a very different one. No one will disagree with this. But do those differences really amount to separate selves?

Even Lester cannot maintain a consistent argument for truly separate selves in the same person. As evidence, for example, Lester writes that "an individual may wake up depressed on some mornings and happy on others" (2015, p. 166), and goes on to propose that different (sub) selves are involved. Yet, the very same sentence described the person as being the same self, not least by using the term *individual* (the meaning of which is etymologically related to the word *indivisible*). And so he is saying that it's the same person waking up on different mornings. If it were truly different selves, he would have to say that different persons wake up on different days, some depressed, some happy. Being the same self at different times contradicts the assertion that one is truly different.

The problem comes up over and over. Lester gives the vivid example of Rudolf Höss, the commandant of the Auschwitz death camp. At work, this Nazi sent tens of thousands of innocent people to their deaths. At home, he was reportedly an affable, loving father who was tender with his children.

Different selves, says Lester. But does he mean that? Suppose you were sent to arrest Höss for his war crimes, but he was not in his office signing death warrants. Rather, you found him at home, playing with his children. Would you refuse to arrest him because, after all, those crimes were committed by *someone else*? Indeed, it is hard to see how we could ever prosecute an evil man like this, if he really had multiple selves and managed to remain being one of the nicer ones. If Höss remained his loving-father self, then he could not be condemned for all the killing "he" did because, after all, that was another self, and the loving-father self is innocent. To me, that argument is ultimately unworkable.

Still, let's try to see the positive insights that the multiple-self theorists seek to capture. The most obvious point is perhaps that people do change their styles of action and perhaps even how they feel about themselves in different situations, perhaps especially when occupying different roles.

This is, however, one of the great accomplishments of the human self, not an argument against its singular existence. The human self is remarkably capable of adjusting its styles of action according to situational and role demands. It can be nurturant and emotionally warm in one context, yet consistently cold and ruthless in a different one.

One still knows oneself to be the same person. Even if Rudolf Höss were at home playing with his children and hearing them call him "Vati" (Daddy), he would still almost certainly answer to his name, Rudolf, or even his job title, Herr Kommandant, if someone happened to come in and address him. He may have felt and acted differently at his office in the death camp and at home with his family. But that does not rise to the level of genuinely different selves.

Perhaps the more profound point is that unified self is often stitched together out of these partial selves (or subselves, as Lester calls them). One theme of this book is that the unity of self does not arise out of some inner requirement of the brain, or even out of some ongoing sense of bodily continuity (though that helps). Rather, the self is something the brain learns to create and sustain, in response to external demands. I find it incoherent to suggest that the same person "is" different people at different times. The advantages of human cultural society depend on stable relationships, and so it requires each body to be responsible for what that body has done at other times, and continuity of self is woven into the fabric of society. But it is much more plausible that children learn how to act in different situations and only gradually build those into a coherent, continuous self, including the understanding that I today am still obligated to pay back the money I borrowed last month, and I am still responsible for my misdeeds last week, even if the misdeed and the borrowing occurred in quite different situations.

The theater is a useful metaphor. The same actor plays different roles. The actor may feel differently and think differently and speak differently in the different roles. But the actor's name is the same and the different performances add to the same actor's career.

The unity of self is thus an achievement, and it can be more or less complete. Some people may be less successfully unified than others. There is much more to be said about this in an upcoming chapter.

In presenting the evidence for multiple selves, Lester cites research that has devised scales to measure how much people *believe* in the unity versus multiplicity of their selfhood. The main finding of all that research is that people who believe in multiple selves generally have a variety of psychological problems. They show more neuroticism, report more family problems during their childhood and more bad life experiences as adults, have more depression and lower self-esteem, are less happy, have more anxiety, are more maladjusted in general and less able to cope with uncertainty. (Note that coping should presumably be one of the advantages of having multiple selves, as one can have a different self for different occasions, so it should be easier to cope.) At the extreme, having more multiple selves and believing in them is associated with hearing voices in your head that are violent, critical of self, and hypersensitive to being criticized by others. That road leads to schizophrenia and psychosis, in which the self really does fall apart into multiple pieces. But those are not good states.

To be sure, it is difficult to say whether the belief in multiple selves is a cause or result of all those problems. But regardless, believing in multiple selves is associated with many problems and poor overall adjustment.

What can we take away from this perennial assertion that each person has multiple selves? First, it is technically false. Unity of self (including continuity across time) is part of the essential nature of self (see Gallagher, 2000). Second, it is amazing and impressive that the human self is capable of playing quite different roles and adjusting how it acts and reacts based on the different roles. Third, the ultimate unity of self may be an achievement resulting from merging different role performances. That suggests the single self is somehow stitched together out of the different parts. People who fall short of effectively integrating their multiple strands of self are unhappy and subject to multiple problems. Something fundamental has gone wrong for them.

Lester's notion of "subselves" (though I will not use that terminology in this book) points to something real and correct. The different parts of the self are not different personality traits. Rather, they are nearly unified, organized almost-wholes. The next part of this book will cover the project of creating unity out of these pieces. The human mind is apparently able to think up different versions of the self, complete with different courses of action and different sets of emotional reactions. Some of these are integrated into the person, others are not.

A last point is that people may have multiple conceptions of themselves, associated with different roles and habits. These are not truly independent but rather are different versions of the same self. Although the work-self and the home- and family-self may have some different emphases, habits, and styles, they overlap substantially. The next section will develop this idea further—though starting from a very different point.

THE QUEST FOR THE TRUE SELF

In the Middle Ages, when European Christians wrote about the cross on which Jesus had been crucified, they always capitalized the designation: the True Cross. Pieces of the True Cross were available for a price or other reward, throughout Europe, and indeed some historians have calculated that the total weight of these European fragments of the True Cross far outweighed the original cross. No surprise: Most if not all were fakes.

It is thus out of respect to one of the great memes in the history of our civilization that I capitalize the idea of the True Self. Both respect and skepticism are intentional. How could there exist such a thing as a True Self?

Carl Rogers, Abraham Maslow, and other leading thinkers spoke as if the True Self were buried deep inside and merely had to be brought out. The notion was of an inner self, hidden away and contrary to one's overt actions and appearances. By way of context, from the earliest humans up until the Renaissance, most people lived in small social groups in which everybody knew everybody. The possibility that someone might be different from the person they pretended to be was minimal. But as cities began to grow and social life brought people into contact with strangers, and as social mobility increased, there was increasing recognition that people were not always who or what they seemed. As Lionel Trilling (1971) wrote in Sincerity and Authenticity, the 16th-century world was fascinated with deception, hypocrisy, role playing, and related phenomena. Sincerity came to the fore as a valued virtue. It meant equivalence between inner and outer selves. To be sure, the problem was knowing the selves of others, more than knowing oneself.

Authenticity seemingly has more to do with the True Self than sincerity. But as Trilling explained, sincerity was the opposite of pretending to be someone you're not, whereas authenticity was the opposite of blending into the crowd and just going along with the mass society.

Let's consider the cases for and against the reality of True Selves. There are actually two versions of the question of true selfhood, given the frequent confusion of self with self-concept. First, there may or may not be a genuine entity that qualifies as a True Self, presumably hidden partly inside the mind and different from how the person acts. Second, and independently of that, there may or may not be a true *concept* of self. Is either viable? I think not.

The Case for True Selves

The case for the True Self begins with a fascinating study of modern American citizens' beliefs, by Rebecca Schlegel and colleagues (2013). They showed that people readily understand and use the notion of the inner True Self, and that people are more satisfied with their decisions when these are in accord with the True Self than when not. Schlegel and friends were careful to distinguish the True Self from what they called the "actual self," which is how you behave in reality. The True Self is something different, though presumably having some overlap with reality.

Strictly speaking, there was no proof that people do genuinely believe in True Selves. People were able to answer questions about it—but then, people can probably answer questions about unicorns, despite knowing these do not exist. Still, people seemed to use the idea readily and with gusto. That doesn't mean that true selves are real, but it does mean that the idea of a True Self resonates with something people have experienced.

Is the True Self less like the True Cross and more like the Holy Grail, a quest for ideal perfection that almost always ends in failure? It doesn't have to aspire to godlike perfection; more likely, it's a plausible, best-case version of yourself. That's the inner guide, the person you aspire to be, or to be known as, or both.

The purpose of the ideal self is to serve as a guide. People might call it the True Self, but it does not really deserve the name, especially when distinguished from the actual self, which is how you actually act.

A valiant case for the True Self was recently made by Richard Ryan and Ed Deci (2017), two thinkers whose career was devoted to building self-determination theory. In their career-capping book, they review multiple prior theories about True Selves and come out strongly in favor. They do not think of the self as a thing and are indeed quite insistent that it is a process. (I quite agree.) To them, the notion of a True Self is tied up with autonomy, a central concept in their theory, indeed the one for which it is named. Their views on autonomy will be covered later and indeed seem quite right to me. Their case for a True Self is less convincing.

Ryan and Deci's argument for a True Self starts by noting that the concept has been mentioned in many different forms over the centuries, which suggests that there is an important experiential truth to it. However, rather quickly they shift to "the ever-present possibility for [selves] to be false" (2017, p. 348). People do act in ways they find contrary to their values. But that's about it. That people can refuse to enact a false self somehow suggests there must be a True Self. This has been a tempting argument all along—thinkers infer that if there are false selves, there must be a True Self. But that does not follow logically. It's at least possible that there are just various different possible versions of the self, some of which are more consistent with the ideals and desired reputation than others.

Ryan and Deci review multiple thinkers who have talked about True Selves, though these are mostly psychoanalytic (neo-Freudian) and similar theorists. The grounding in data is not there—not necessarily damning, but overall a bad sign. Still, what do these thinkers have in common? Ryan and Deci (2017) list several elements common to the various theories about the True Self.

- First, it is a "natural endowment" (p. 362), already there at birth, at least as potential. In other words, you are born with a True Self.
- Second, it is not just a concept but also has motivational force. One *wants* to be true to oneself.
- Third, it integrates all aspects of the self, so it is opposed to a part-self. This will be the key to their theory of autonomy, and I think it is profound. But I'm not sure it requires there to be a True Self.
- Fourth, it is one force that competes with others, such as external influences. They note this explains "why the voice of the true self is so difficult to hear and to follow" (p. 366).

In my view, those four themes do not add up to much in the way of true selfhood. The first point seemingly reduces it to triviality. If the True Self is already there at birth, it must be rather minimal. Saying that it is there only as potential hardly improves the case. I think babies have multiple potentialities. A given baby might turn out different ways. To claim that one of them is the True Self while the others are false seems to invoke some notion of destiny or fate, as if each baby is designed by some cosmic force for a very particular future life course, and to make any alternative choice would be false. Are some babies born to be astronauts?

The second point, that the True Self has motivational force, has the same conceptual problem as the first. The baby is supposedly desirous of growing into one particular person, one ideal version of itself. Can a baby be born with a desire to become an astronaut? The innate motivations are generally basic, universal things, like fear of falling, desire for food and pleasure, sex, safety, and the like. Plus, where one ends up is often the result of major coincidences and unexpected changes. Did the baby Roy born in Cleveland, Ohio, in 1953 contain some version of my current adult self as an Australian professor and author? After all, in college I had firmly chosen two other fields of study before I changed to psychology. And what if who I am now is not my True Self? How would I even know?

The third point, integration, is highly relevant to autonomy, and in my view it is one of the major strengths of Ryan and Deci's theory. Authentic, autonomous action occurs when a person ponders the options and carefully, knowingly selects one as the right course. Impulsive actions are more likely to be false in the sense that they reflect only one of the many desires and impulses. Still, there are conceptual problems, as indicated by the fourth point. The person supposedly wants to become the True Self but also wants to become alternative, false selves. How could we possibly know whether someone's wish to take piano lessons, or to read magazine articles, or to have sex with half the football team derives from true or false selfhood?

Ryan and Deci observe that the voice of the True Self cannot easily be heard or followed. That definitely seems to weaken any claim that the True Self has motivational power. If we are somehow created to want to become our True Selves, but also want to become alternative selves, there may be nothing motivationally special about the True Self. It's just one voice in the crowd of possible selves. Apparently, we often cannot hear its motivational directives. If the True Self is a guide, it is a feeble one.

But Is Nothing True?

To be sure, there are true facts about the self. Some of them are listed on your driver's license. You might have a fake license, and indeed some teenagers have fake licenses without true ones (thus, a false self but no true self). Still, most adults have a valid driver's license on which are stated important true facts, such as date of birth, gender, height, and weight.

Still, height, address, date of birth, and hair color hardly correspond to what people mean when they invoke notions of true selfhood. Rather, the notions suggest some inner essence, as well perhaps as some concept of it. Moreover, it is doubtful that a collection of facts, even if all true, add up into a coherent entity that deserves the name of True Self. For example, if Harry bought pants that were too small for him, we could say he was indulging a false self and not being true to his self. He might like to think he is slenderer than he is, but his True Self had a fatter waistline than the self who bought the pants.

The key point is that these true facts about the self do not constitute a True Self. The True Self is often invoked as an entity that differs from how the person acts but that embraces some actions while repudiating others.

Authenticity Raises Further Problems of True Selfhood

The concept of the True Self got a serious and skeptical look from multiple perspectives in a 2019 special issue of the *Review of General Psychology* devoted to research on the topic of authenticity (see Baumeister, 2019, for integrative commentary). This afforded a rare chance to see this problem from different expert perspectives. Many of these experts assumed that authenticity had much to do with the True Self, and that probably people report feeling "authentic" when their actions match what they think is their True Self. (Or at least what they wish it to be.) But unless they know their True Self correctly, these assessments mean little. People would be checking to see whether their behavior matches a True Self that isn't really true.

Hence, a first blow to the idea of true self-concepts is that people's opinions of themselves are distorted (usually in a favorable direction). Essentially, nobody has a fully correct concept of self. (A later chapter attempts a frank appraisal of how accurate people's views of themselves are.) In other words, no self-concepts are genuinely, fully true. In research on authenticity, a devastating problem is that there are no measures other than self-report. There is no way to determine objectively whether someone is being authentic. All the data ever tell us is whether and when people feel like they are being authentic, and those feelings are based on people's partly false understandings of themselves. And they feel authentic when they are doing good things, feeling good, and being approved or admired by others.

A closer look at the authenticity research literature raised further problems for the True Self. It seems that people report feeling most authentic when they are doing what external society values, not when they are acting in accord with their actual personalities. Introverts, for example, report feeling most authentic when they act in an extraverted manner—thus, the opposite of their objective personality (Fleeson & Wilt, 2010). The same was found for all the Big Five personality traits: People high in neuroticism felt more authentic when acting in non-neurotic ways, and so forth. You feel authentic when you do what society values, as opposed to following your own deep inner self. Then again, maybe your deep inner self is just about figuring out how to do what society values, so as to rake in society's rewards.

Yet another problem was that the True Self was more about conformity and harmonious interaction than about standing up for one's unique beliefs. Many researchers assumed that being authentic meant being "impervious to external influence" (Sedikides et al., 2019). But the data indicated the opposite. People feel authentic when going along with external influence.

Several leading thinkers in this area concluded that the True Self is not a reality but a guide, a kind of idealized conception of self that can help the person know how to act (Rivera et al., 2019). That would explain why it is generally positive rather than realistic. As for going along with societal influence, well, that is after all what the self is for: to relate the animal body to the social group and system.

Do False Selves Entail True Selves?

False selves are a genuine part of experience. (To be sure, it sounds funny to say, "False selves are real."). Everyone knows that people can be fakes; indeed, almost everyone has to act in an insincere manner sometimes. This lends plausibility to the idea that there are True Selves. If there are false ones, mustn't there also be true ones? Actually, I think the answer is no, but you can see why it is a seductive assumption.

Indeed, the very notion of inauthenticity has come under criticism. Yes, sometimes people put on a false front in response to situational demands, such as pretending to favor a sober, thrifty, ambitious, self-disciplined lifestyle when meeting prospective employers or in-laws. Still, the deception itself is intentional and thus reflects the person's true inner processes, what Jongman-Sereno and Leary (2019) have dubbed "inevitable authenticity." Everything the person does is in a sense a genuine act by the person. Even actresses and con artists are authentically and deliberately performing their deceptive actions.

Nevertheless, people do have a clear and strong sense that sometimes other people act falsely and conceal rather than express their True Selves—and, moreover, that they themselves do the same. Inevitable authenticity aside, let us grant that people can produce false versions of themselves and false conceptions thereof. If false selves are real, must there be a True Self? My negative answer rests partly on the numbers, on the asymmetry: There are multiple false selves, so why should there only be one true one? A particular person does not have a single false self, so it is illogical to infer that there is a single True Self.

Books provide a useful analogy. Some books are deliberately, openly false. Books of fiction, such as novels and poetry, make no claims for being true; indeed, they often proudly assert that all contents are false and any resemblance to real people or events is unintended coincidence. But the book industry needed to invent the new term *nonfiction*, essentially a negation of a negation, to cover the rest—because, obviously, not everything in every nonfiction book is true. Even textbooks, whose primary purpose is to teach the truth to the next generation, are soon outdated as some of their claims are overturned by the march of science. In the same way, people have non-false concepts of self, indeed multiple ones. So maybe there are false selves, but that doesn't entail a single true one. There may be multiple non-false conceptions of self, even if none of them is impeccably, thoroughly true.

No, false selves do not entail a True Self. But people do have multiple non-false conceptions of self. Again, these are not fully separate selves in any sense. Rather, they are different versions of the same self, rather like the way different jazz artists will perform the same composition.

Which of the Non-False Selves Matters Most?

I spent a month reading the papers for a special journal issue on authenticity and trying to write up their implications (Baumeister, 2019). To recap, there is no True Self, as an entity that is different from what you actually do, say, think, and feel. There is also no single true self-concept—though there are plenty of nonfiction versions. They are not different selves but different versions of the same self.

So it comes down to which of these non-false conceptions of self is the most important? Which one matters, pragmatically? The hands-down winner is the desired reputation. The actual reputation determines how people treat you, and so your actions must be guided to create and sustain the optimal reputation for your roles in society.

Pragmatic importance generally boils down to what should I do, to get the best outcomes in terms of resources? One's social interactions are guided partly by the imperative to maintain a good enough reputation. That's the primary role of the self in human social life. Put another way: How do beliefs about the self matter in choosing how to act? The most important one to keep in mind is the desired reputation. Don't do anything that will ruin that reputation, and capitalize on opportunities to convince other people you are a decent sort of person. Of all the various ideas you have about yourself, that is the one that should have the most influence over your actions.

People feel most authentic when their actions fit with their desired reputations. "That's me!" is what they feel, elated because it is how they want to be known to others.

Final Verdict on the True Self

True Self (as a guiding idea) and decision satisfaction are cues for each other: that's the main conclusion of Schlegel and company's work. But that's the point. The ideal self is how one wants to be and be known, an ideal unmet in reality. The closer your actions correspond to your idealized True Self, the more satisfied you are with the decision.

It may seem contradictory to insist that there is a genuine entity that is the self, while denying that there is a True Self. But the True Self is a guiding idea, not an actuality. The actual processes that constitute the self have ideals and goals, and they strive to bring the person's actions into line with these aspirations.

SELF-ACTUALIZATION: ANOTHER HOLY GRAIL?

"Self-actualization" became a buzzword in psychology after being promoted by the mighty thinker Abraham Maslow (1968). In his early theory, self-actualization was the apex, the ultimate in motivation, the thing one sought after one had taken care of all the more pressing and mundane needs, like food and shelter, and love and self-esteem. The core idea was that some people had fulfilled their potential by becoming something better than they were, while other people failed to achieve that. Maslow's theory resonated with many people who wanted to find fulfillment by becoming their best possible selves.

Maslow interviewed assorted people and somehow classified some of them as self-actualized and others as not. From these interviews he spotted patterns and drew conclusions about what self-actualized people are like. But subsequent research has not taken that very far. After all, the exercise, albeit inspiring, is scientifically dubious. He decided what criteria to use to spot self-actualized people, and then he used their common traits (presumably reflecting those criteria) to say what they are like—but this is circular. If I start by classifying red cars as self-actualized and green ones as not, and then I sort cars on that basis, and then compare the piles, I'll discover that self-actualized cars tend to be red rather than green.

Part of the problem is that Maslow's own thinking remained vague about self-actualization. More recent scholarship (Koltko-Rivera, 2006) turned up some serious struggles in Maslow's later writings, including his personal journal and private writings. He knew that he hadn't nailed down precisely what self-actualization is. In fact, in his later years he decided self-actualization was not the top level of motivation, but rather just another in-between one. He posited self-transcendence as the highest level. Self-actualization is about fulfilling the self in some way, but people who satisfy that move on to striving to transcend the self, which is somehow involved in helping others and abandoning concern with self-interest. He also acknowledged to himself that he had failed to produce a coherent theory of self-actualization (and no one else had stepped forward to do so either).

Nevertheless, let us take the idea of self-actualization seriously. It seemingly requires that each self has a built-in specific potentiality, akin to the traditional notion of destiny—that it may or may not realize. Nobody would say I failed at self-actualization because I didn't win an Olympic medal in women's figure skating, which clearly was not my greatest potential (indeed was not my potential at all, as I am not a woman and don't skate). In an important sense, self-actualization is a conceptual cousin to the True Self. It entails that each person comes equipped not just with a real configuration of traits and acts but also a particular possible and ultimate-ideal version of self, with different traits and acts and attainments.

Perhaps each person does not have a single destiny but multiple possibilities and potentialities. Self-actualization could reside in several of them. A young woman might have artistic talent, and so she could find self-actualization as a painter. But can we say that same talented woman is not self-actualized if, instead of painting, she goes into business and makes a fortune running her own company? What about if she drops out of work and raises three children? That could also qualify as self-actualization, though how do we interpret it if once in a while she wistfully wishes she had time to paint again, or that she had spent a few more years taking her company to a higher level? Are her feelings of fulfillment the only criteria that count?

How could one determine what a person's truly best potential is? The argument drifts back into the same problems as the True Self, with the further twist that it is not even claimed to be real but merely possible. Is there any objective way to define and measure self-actualization, independent of one's own satisfaction with one's life?

These problems may explain why self-actualization has not been a thriving research topic since Maslow's death. It is hard to establish clearly and objectively the boundary line between those who are and who aren't self-actualized.

Self-actualization is perhaps more readily noticed by its absence than presence. This would parallel what we concluded about the True Self. False selves exist in common experience, but the True Self is mostly a conceptual metaphor for the opposite of these false selves. In the same way, people may know it and feel it when they are *not* reaching their potential, but the conceptual opposite, self-actualization, is more a mythical ideal than a definite state.

The fact that science can't measure something doesn't prove that it doesn't exist. There may be something to self-actualization. After all, many people embraced the idea as important, which is one sign that it was meaningful to them. Still, the lack of good ways to measure self-actualization has prevented researchers from storing up a host of facts and findings, so not much can be said with confidence.

The most important and creative treatment of self-actualization in recent years appeared in Eli Finkel's (2017) book *The All-or-Nothing Marriage*. As the title indicates, he is not developing a new theory of self-actualization, but rather using the concept to dissect how modern marriage has changed. He rejects the view that people today ask more than ever from marriage, but what they ask is different from the past. Colonial-era couples struggled to manage the farm and put food on the table. Today, the family is not an economic unit so much as a place where people seek personal growth and satisfaction. Spouses are supposed to help each other improve themselves and find fulfillment, a process Finkel charmingly describes as "climbing Mount Maslow." As he explains, people who treat their marriage that way can find realms of satisfaction and intimacy that their ancestors scarcely imagined—or can become disgruntled and even get divorced for reasons the ancestors would have found unfathomably absurd.

Still, what exactly is the mutually self-actualizing marriage supposed to be like? Finkel's coverage of the research on relationships is superb, but the weakness and vacuity of self-actualization research impede his analysis. The self-actualizing marriage has something to do with feeling good, sustaining love over years of marriage, and expressing oneself. Regarding those criteria, feeling good goes with plenty of positive things. Sustaining love is also a good thing, but again not specific to self-actualization. The same goes for career success.

The other criterion, self-expression, sounds more promising—but what is it? Was Adolf Hitler the apex of self-actualization, given that he was able to put his hopes and dreams into practice, though the eventual end result was not what he hoped for? Still, it is hard to claim that his opportunities for self-expression were blocked during the dozen years when things went his way. Self-expression cannot be a full answer. It requires a self that is being expressed. We cannot celebrate people who express their wicked selves, like Hitler.

The grander problem that self-actualization raises is the nature of human potential. We can provide an objective account of what someone currently is: the person's height and weight, citizenship, record of achievements or failures. These things are real, and the only problem is measuring them precisely. In contrast, someone's potential is by definition not real. Measuring that and even defining it are quite tricky. And where does it come from? Someone's potential is a not-yet-real alternative version of the self, presumably possible and better than the current version. How did they get that specific potential?

That brings up the related question of whether each person's potential self is unique or is instead pretty much the same. For much of Western history, the dominant ideal of potential and fulfillment was to go to (Christian) heaven after death. In contrast, every artist seeks to contribute something unique. Getting an objective handle on someone's unique potential is quite difficult. In particular, suppose someone was born with superb basketball talent but in a culture or historical era where no basketball was played. Hence, no one knew that the person had this terrific potential. Would there be any legitimate basis for saying this person was not self-actualized? What if the person had a happy, fulfilled life anyway, without basketball, despite having that unrecognized talent? Thus, I will not be devoting much space to self-actualization, fond as I am of the notion.

KEY POINTS

- It is fair to say "there is no such thing as the self" because the self is not a thing in the physical sense. While the self starts with the body, it is more than the body. It is rather the systems by which the body acts.

- The idea that each person has multiple selves invokes the correct insight that a person may think, feel, act, and react differently in different situations or with different social groups. People may have different conceptions of self, but they are different versions of the same self rather than wholly separate self-concepts.

- The notion of a True Self develops the important idea that people have goals for themselves, not just in terms of specific achievements but in the sort of person they want to be. The idea that there is a True Self different from the way someone acts is ultimately unworkable.

- Self-actualization builds on the idea that selves have potentialities and gain some sense of satisfaction when they achieve these desirable outcomes. But psychology has not had a great deal of success nailing down what it means and how to get there.

- The most important nonfiction versions of self is the desired reputation. One's social interactions are guided partly by the imperative to maintain a good enough reputation. People seem to feel authentic and true when they do something that helps realize the desired reputation.

- Self-actualization builds on the idea that selves have potentialities and gain some satisfaction when they achieve these desirable outcomes, but there is little evidence that people have a true inner self.

Why Do We Have Selves?

CHAPTER 6

Some Beginnings of Self

Self starts with body. Human children think self is body. A human being is first of all a body, an animal, like countless others across many species. We are animals, but we are more than animals. Why did this particular species of nonhairy ape develop this elaborate structure of a self? It is more than just the body, and so many other animals have gotten along fine without much in the way of self.

Part Two of the book asks a basic question: Why do people have selves? As we have seen, the human self is far beyond what is found elsewhere in nature. So why did human selfhood come to exist, emerge, and evolve with so much greater complexity than its precursors? Humans are animals, too, complete with a full set of animal traits: We need food and water, feel pain, grow, learn, fight, have sex, nurture children, and so on—just like all the other mammals.

In an evolutionary perspective, one assumes the answer has something to do with improving chances for survival and reproduction. But that's hardly a full answer. If having an advanced, complex self improves survival and reproduction, presumably many other animals would have evolved in the same way. Yet, they didn't. What are the specific advantages of having a self that somehow produced those improvements?

BODY AS BOUNDARY OF "ME" AND "NOT ME"

The self did not appear all at once in a giant evolutionary leap, as if there were a clap of thunder and suddenly there it was, the first human self. More likely, the human self is the culmination of a long gradual process involving

65

many smallish steps, some hardly related to others. They are likely a series of adaptations to a changing social environment. Selves gradually evolved more complex powers. Why? Evolution favored selves that enabled groups to benefit from ever more complex systems. Better selves, better systems, more food, more babies. Biology measures success by increasing population. In sober biological perspective, the human self evolved because it raised more and better babies.

The first step was drawing a boundary that would later become me versus not-me. Every living thing, even the tiniest one-celled creature, maintains a precise boundary between *itself* and the surrounding environment (e.g., Gadamer, 1975). This is part of the essence of life: the creation of this boundary between self and not-me (everything else). All the different parts of a living thing are connected to each other, even if they are actually far apart, such as in giant trees with the topmost leaves far above the underground roots. Everything inside the boundary is at least loosely connected in an interactive system with every other part, in a way that it is not connected to the outside world. The tree's roots get water down in the ground, and as a result the leaves and branches grow, far above them. The system recognizes the difference between what is part of it and what is not. Substances pass across this boundary, as nutrients are ingested and waste expelled, but nonetheless the boundary remains intact and precise.

The point is that the boundary between the tree itself and the rest of the universe is a precise, objective reality. This reality is something a self can build on. The tree doesn't bother creating much of a self, but a human baby will put plenty of effort into building a self that starts with the difference, the boundary line, between its own body and the rest of the world.

It's crude but helpful to think of life as an integrated system of chemical reactions, which are linked together and separate from their surroundings. If the reactions stop, the organism dies. Life evolved to prevent this from happening, so as to continue living as long as possible. Life is not a thing—but rather a process inside a thing. *The process includes maintaining the boundaries of the thing.*

Death makes this even clearer. The organism dies as a unity. Yes, all throughout the course of life some cells do die and are replaced by new ones, rapidly in young creatures, more slowly in older ones. But the organism *as a whole* is either alive or dead, period. There are no actual zombies, vampires, or Frankenstein monsters. Everyone is clearly dead or alive, with very few borderline cases (viruses) or other exceptions. The whole self, encompassing mind, body, and whatever else, is all completely dead (or alive), as a unity—and, crucially, independent of whether anything else is alive or dead.

This must be fully appreciated. A key part of the essence of life is drawing a boundary to create a unity inside the boundary. Being merely alive is a long way from having a self, especially in the human sense, but the boundary is the first step. Nonliving things don't draw this borderline, don't care, and don't really have selves. Caring comes from the living creature's goal of continuing life via survival and reproduction.

The existentialist philosophers used this idea in a different way (Heidegger, 1927; Sartre, 1943/1974). They noted the individuating power of death. A living thing is either alive or dead as a whole, and so its death reaffirms its boundaries. When you die, precisely you ceases to exist, and nothing else does. Although someone else may die in your place in a specific situation, you will still die, so your death is uniquely yours. Your death thus marks out the boundaries of your self.

The objective self thus precedes the subjective self—indeed by millions of years. The system that binds together all the molecules in a living being, and separates them from all the universe's other molecules, is the first, most primitive and rudimentary kind of selfhood.

Life is a system that unifies a diverse set of molecules to work together, with a precise boundary between it and the world. The living systems become more complex with evolution, and the human organism's system develops a self that starts with this basic fact of bodily me versus not-me (everything else)—and understands the difference, and uses it to guide action in ways that help prolong life. The self helps the living thing to live longer and reproduce more.

ACTING AS A UNITY

The difference in strategies between plants and animals represents a big step forward toward selfhood. A major difference is that animals have a central nervous system, including a brain, which is its center. The nervous system basically does two things. First, it brings information from all parts of the animal to a central place (the brain) where it is put together and it then decides what to do. Second, the nervous system carries the commands from the brain to the muscles or other parts that move the body.

Animals have more of a self than plants. A plant *functions* as a unity, to be sure. But an animal functions and also *acts* as a unity, in ways the plant doesn't. A primary example is that animals move; the whole organism coordinates to execute movement, all paws taking turns propelling the body in the same direction, in a coordinated system. Plants don't do that. That is a huge step toward having a self. The brain coordinates the whole body to move in a particular direction.

Animals with brains and central nervous systems also have the experience of unity. That may be why Zen masters and other moral vegetarians refuse to eat animals but don't mind eating plants, despite rhetoric about cherishing all of life. The animal has a subjective experience of being alive, and the plant presumably doesn't. The animal who dies to provide you with meat has lost subjective experience and may well have suffered while dying. In contrast, the vegetables on your plate did not lose much in the way of conscious experience in order to be there, and they did not feel pain in dying. Fruits can be eaten without taking the life of the plant that provided them (just pick an apple off the tree, and the tree remains fine).

A few animals seem able to recognize their own faces in a mirror, a simple test of self-awareness. Why did they begin to develop self-awareness? This further development of self probably depended on social context. Social life demands much more of the self than does solitary life. Indeed, the evolution of intelligence may have been driven mainly by social life. Robin Dunbar (1998, 2009) compared brain sizes (relative to body weight) across many animal species (especially primates like us). He concluded that bigger brains were linked to social factors rather than biological or environmental factors. The operative differences between animals with bigger versus smaller brains lay in the complexity of their social worlds, not their relationships to food or territory. Dunbar's conclusion was that bigger brains are linked to bigger social networks. Intelligence evolved to help creatures understand and relate to each other, rather than for solving problems in the physical environment.

GROUPS AND SELVES

Self may thus begin as the biological unity of the living organism, but it soon adds much more. The biological advances in selfhood are driven mainly by the requirements of being part of a social group. The more complex the group, the more complex the self.

It may seem odd to look to groups to understand what is special about the human self. But groups and selves differ even in basic life-and-death ways. One profoundly important difference emerged from research by Sugiyama (2004). To put the findings in perspective, consider our closest relatives, the chimpanzees. We share 99% of our DNA with them. Yet in the wild, their life expectancy is only about 40 years, while humans live considerably longer. Why?

Chimps become able to forage and feed themselves early in life. Each chimp takes care of itself for the rest of its life. It lives with a group, but each is responsible for itself. At some point, it may fall and break a leg, or have some other injury that prevents it from getting food. The poor chimp then starves to death, even perhaps when surrounded by its group.

The researchers interviewed human hunter-gatherers who also live in the wild, and in groups. Over half of them reported that they had had such a serious injury or illness in the past and were unable to forage. Unlike the chimpanzees, however, humans feed each other in such circumstances. The injured or sick human can recuperate, thanks to being fed by others. Thus, half of those people would have been dead—but they survived because human groups share food. Other apes don't. In effect, the practice of sharing food doubled the population in one generation. Chimps were once more populous than monkeys but are now in danger of extinction and would do well to copy this human practice, if they could.

SOCIAL ORIGINS OF SELF

Ownership requires selfhood. Without selves that endure across time and maintain their distinctions and differences, ownership is meaningless. Something can't be mine, without there being an I or you. In practical terms, ownership connects the animal body (unity of single life) to some item in the environment, within a society. As we shall see, though, ownership is more than a link between a person and a thing—it crucially involves other people, too.

Pronouns reveal the importance of ownership. Pronouns are among the most commonly used words in all languages and are second terms for things that already have their own names. You have a name, but you also call yourself "I," and interaction partners designate you not just by name but also by "you," not to mention "he" or "she." Pronouns are an odd innovation, a convenient shortcut for very commonly used concepts. So if there is a pronoun, it is likely for something that is frequently needed in conversation.

Pronouns are also about selves. They refer to various entities, singular and plural: *I, me, you, we, us, his, her, they.* (Note that they are very quick to pronounce: Their function is to make talking quicker and easier. They save time, especially for people with long names.) The fact that pronouns mostly denote selves reflects the fundamental importance of selfhood in social life (and especially in communication, which is a basic and universal feature of human social life). Many interactions are about you and me, how we treat each other, indeed often what we can do that will benefit both of us.

In that context, it is a bit of a shock to see one more self-related term merit a cluster of pronouns: ownership, as in *mine, your, yours, our, his, her, their.* Their presence among the pronouns suggests that they are extremely basic and important concepts, and so are frequently needed in conversation. Here is why it is shocking. Most pronouns designate a thing, an entity, an identity (*her, it*). Possessive pronouns designate a *relationship.* And one side of that relationship is a self. Possessive pronouns thus indicate a practical application of self. Ownership means this is yours, not anyone else's. It invokes a self.

In human cultures, ownership takes the form of shared symbolic understandings of money, inheritance taxes and disputes, property rights, and much more. Animals have much less of any of these things, but there are some preliminary forms. Most notably, some animals are territorial, in the sense that they feel linked to their land and will defend it against others, even others of their own species. They mark it using the only medium available to them, urine, and they attack others who come near. They make a point of urinating where a rival has, to replace the rival's scent with their own. Still, the fact that they do that shows they are not respecting the property rights of others, in the way humans do.

The human mind seems well designed to handle ownership. It learns the rules for ownership early, asserting it aggressively if sometimes incorrectly early in childhood ("mine!"). Ownership information gets an inside track to extra mental processing. A nice program of research from multiple labs has shown that people remember their own things better than other things, even if the things they own were just acquired moments ago and by random assignment rather than personal choice (e.g., Cunningham et al., 2008; Golubickis et al., 2018; Sparks et al., 2006). For example, people in one experiment sorted a huge tray of objects into two baskets, one for their stuff and one for not-their-stuff, all assigned at random and just encountered for the first time. Later, unexpectedly, they were tested for whether they recognized the objects. They remembered the ones that went into their basket better than the stuff that went into another. The same effect is found if they just watch somebody else do the sorting: They still remember their own stuff better. In some ways, this is the more provocative finding because it doesn't involve any kind of bodily movement of taking control.

It is tempting to think of ownership as an individual thing: something is mine, period. At first blush, it seems to designate a simple relationship between a self and a thing. But that's wrong. Ownership is social, not individual. As said in Chapter 2, if you lived alone on an island and never saw another human being, you would not own things. If you happened to have a toothbrush, you wouldn't think of it as "your" toothbrush, it would just be "the" toothbrush. Assuming you had language, which itself requires society and socialization. In a group or society, "mine" means that nobody else should use my toothbrush, at least not without my permission. It's better if we all have our own toothbrushes.

Ownership invokes a social system, indeed a social system of multiple roles inhabited by specific and different selves. Ownership assigns the thing to one self, who has the privilege of using it. If other people want to use it, they have to ask the owner for permission. Ownership has to be recognized by the group, not just the single mind. Economic historians note that in ancient times, before there was much in the way of formal government and official record keeping, land sales had to be public events, with witnesses—so that everyone knew that the land had changed owners (Bernstein, 2004).

Indeed, economic history suggests a key insight into why we have ownership. Bernstein's book *The Birth of Plenty* (2004) undertook to explain why some cultures prosper and flourish, while others languish in backward poverty. He surveyed cultures of each type and identified four vital features of social structure that are conducive to prosperity. The first one (and the only one relevant here) is property rights. Societies that recognized individual ownership of property and defended the individual against arbitrary seizure and confiscation, even by the king (or by a group of peers), outperformed other societies. That fits one of the key themes in this book: The self evolved to perform roles in complex social systems, so as to enable those systems to produce more resources and improve survival and reproduction. Ownership improves those systems, so ownership is one of the foundations and functions of the self.

Without ownership, there can be no economy, no marketplace, no trade. Economic systems can greatly improve quality and quantity of life. Selves likely evolved to capitalize on the benefits of a marketplace. Although today's scholars associate culture with agriculture, trade is much older than farming, and there is some evidence that trade was one advantage our human ancestors had over the other early biological cousins (e.g., the Neanderthals; see Horan et al., 2005; Ridley, 2020).

The beginnings of ownership link it to the self and its actions (Belk, 1988) and to bodily rights. So the notion of "my" shoe or car is akin to early understanding of "my" hand or foot. Furthermore, around the world in many different societies, what the self creates is typically assumed to belong to the self, unless there is some clear alternative agreement. If you build something, paint something, or otherwise create it, it is yours. Likewise, if you bring it into being, such as by cultivating a plant, it is assumed to be yours unless there is another agreement.

The social nature of ownership is also reflected in the fact that it only matters when someone else might want the item. Yes, most cultures recognize your ownership for things you create. But as noted by Russell Belk (1988), people do not feel ownership toward their personal excrement. They definitely created it—yet since nobody else wants it, ownership is irrelevant. Ownership is about multiple people wanting the same thing and about one person having established the right and privilege to decide its use.

Moreover, ownership extends across time. If I create or buy a cup today, it is mine tomorrow, which means you cannot use it without my permission. In contrast, I can use it without your permission because it's mine. This privilege continues until I relinquish ownership of the cup. Ownership is only meaningful in a social group consisting of selves that exist across time. Ownership is perhaps one of the benefits of continuity of self; thus, it is not just a contributor to the unity of self but a motivating factor.

Ownership thus invokes at least two key features of the human self. First, it is embedded in social structures that enable them to become more effective at producing resources. Second, it extends the self across time.

THE EVOLUTIONARY ADVANTAGES OF CULTURE

One scholar who has thought carefully about the differences between humans and other animals, based on a long hard look at the evidence, is Thomas Suddendorf. His 2013 book *The Gap* (i.e., the gap between humans and all the rest of earthly creatures) starts its first chapter with the ominous title "The Last Humans." But he isn't saying we face imminent extinction. The message is something quite different. Evolution produced a whole panoply of hominids, or what can be regarded as different rough drafts of human beings. Did they all interbreed and produce a mongrel offspring? No. Somehow one version prevailed over the others, not just outperforming them but obliterating them. Rather than facing extinction, the "last" humans are multiplying their population, nearly 8 billion and counting upward. Why did this one version of humankind prevail over all the others?

The Neanderthals are a revealing case. One to one, man to man, Neanderthals would have been pretty formidable opponents for our Cro-Magnon ancestors: They had slightly more muscle mass and even slightly bigger brains. But they were unable to create social systems as advanced as the Cro-Magnon. These included economic systems, such as trade, and division of labor (Horan et al., 2005). And so the Cro-Magnons migrated into the Neanderthal's homelands and gradually took over, to the point that the Neanderthals went extinct. Put bluntly, our ancestors moved into their neighborhoods and ate their lunch.

The creation of social systems was key to our success. Animals have social systems, but human social systems do so much more. That brings us to culture.

In previous works I have argued that culture is humankind's biological strategy (Baumeister, 2005). Culture is how human beings solve the universal problems of survival and reproduction. As defined in Chapter 1, culture is an advanced way to organize social life, based on shared knowledge, ad hoc cooperation shaped by communication and joint plans, and participation in systems of interaction with complementary, interlocking roles. All of nature confronts the basic problems of survival and reproduction as the only ways that life can continue. Culture is a highly unusual but powerfully effective solution to those basic, universal problems.

The origins of culture thus lie in ways groups work together. There is some dispute as to the relative importance of group hunting and group fighting. (Chimpanzees exhibit both of those.) Both of these were probably factors, as groups who could use communication and shared understandings to guide their group hunts and group fighting would likely prevail over rivals who could not.

The provocative conclusion from this line of thinking is that the human self evolved to enable groups to flourish. This is not a group selection argument. Individuals benefited by being part of successful groups. In the evolutionary past, groups of hominids who could achieve some measure of culture outperformed other groups who could not. Probably the human self emerged to take the form it did precisely because of those systems, which means that its structures and functions are dictated by social life in a cultural context. The human genes were not selected for long life so much as for social interaction. The social interactions lengthened the life span. The next chapter looks at how social interactions are key to how a child begins to develop a competent adult self.

KEY POINTS

- Selves may begin as the biological unit of the living organism, but they soon become more. Biological advances in selfhood are driven mainly by the requirements of being part of a social group.
- Unlike chimpanzees, who share most of our DNA, humans will share food with the group and feed the injured or ill.
- Ownership enables social systems to become more effective at producing resources, and it extends the self across time.

CHAPTER 7

How Baby Grows Up to Have a Working Self

Does a newborn baby have a self? There is certainly not much of one. The newborn's brain hasn't begun to store information. At some level it does perhaps control movements of arms and legs, but without realization.

STARTING OUT: BRAIN MEETS BODY

Like every living thing, the newborn baby's body has a precise boundary between self and world. But the brain probably does not understand this boundary though it learns fast. My own baby was not much inclined toward crying, so my wife was surprised to hear her wailing one morning. When she inspected, the baby's finger was poking her own eye, and when Mama gently moved the arm, she quickly quieted down. The baby apparently had not realized that the offending finger was on her own arm and under her own control. The brain had not yet imposed systematic control over the arms.

Later developmental steps reflect the brain's increasing understanding and mastery of her own body. Learning to crawl, to walk, to ride a bicycle, and other milestones indicate how the brain becomes ever better at controlling the limbs in a coordinated fashion so that the whole body can move around effectively. The coordination shows the beginnings of self, in the sense of the brain imposing unity on disparate parts. Before long, the control over arms and legs is extended to include speaking, the vocal apparatus. Generally, the arms and legs deal with the physical environment, while the speech apparatus deals with the social environment.

The self imposes unity by means of systems. For me, the most vivid example of this was watching a baby on the day she learned to crawl. She had enough control over arms and legs to turn herself over onto her belly on the floor, but locomotion had eluded her. But on this particular day, it came together. Consider what the brain has to do in order to make the body crawl. It must understand it can control the arms and legs, that there is a left and a right version of each. Crucially, crawling depends on moving the right hand and left knee forward while the other two are firmly planted. Then the weight shifts onto the right hand and left knee, while the newly freed left hand and right knee can move forward. And then back again. This was the same baby who earlier hadn't known enough to move her arm so as to stop poking herself in the eye. Now her brain had a system for moving all four major limbs in a systematic, coordinated fashion, enabling her to move from one place to another. I recall the big self-satisfied smile on her face as she realized it would work.

A helpful perspective is to think of human babies as all being born prematurely, compared to other primates. Human culture requires big brains, and much brain growth has to occur after birth, possibly for the simple reason that a mother's body could not survive giving birth to a bigger brain. Most of the apes can take care of themselves much earlier in life than human children can, including moving around and getting food. The human child remains helpless, vulnerable, and dependent for many more years. But the value of that lies in how much farther the human brain develops. Very young children seem like animals, but during the second year they seem abruptly to develop levels of self-awareness and interpersonal skills that surpass what other animals can do. Studies routinely show things that 4- and 5-year-old human children can do but that are beyond the mental powers of fully grown chimpanzees, gorillas, and orangutans (for reviews, see Tomasello, 2014, 2018).

The baby brain's job is to understand how human society works, what its place is, and how to perform those roles. If we define identity as position in society, then a newborn baby has an identity before his or her brain is able to understand any of this. I knew a married couple who had grown up in different social classes. When their baby was born, the upper-middle-class grandparents opened a bank account for the little guy and deposited $5,000 as a gift. The blue-collar relatives on the other side of the family were gobsmacked to hear that a 1-day-old baby owned more wealth than nearly any of the adults they knew. "A baby has $5,000?" they asked each other incredulously. The money and the baby's ownership were real, reflecting his identity. But of course the baby himself had not the slightest inkling of any of this.

The broader point is this: Identity, as position in society, exists before the brain knows it. Growing up is learning what your place in society is. "Know thyself" is an imperative for every growing child, not in the sense of self-discovery, but of discovering where society has put you and what it expects from you. From this very minimalist start, the typical human child grows slowly into an adult with a fully functioning self.

THE SELF ACROSS TIME

Most animals just live in the immediate present, with no understanding of time or the future. Human social systems extend across time and need people to perform roles that also extend across time. For this to work, the human brain has to understand time—including understanding itself across time.

The right-now self is created first. Like other animals, the human child needs to learn to respond as a unity in the immediate present, starting with coordinated movement (crawling). The past is irrelevant and the future remains a vague, remote prospect. The present, however, is compelling, and the brain slowly learns how to respond as a unity. Also like other animals, it does carry forward lessons, so despite a lack of temporal reasoning, today's actions are different based on how yesterday's actions brought rewards or punishments.

The child's adult companions do think about the future and talk to the child about it. An adult might talk about an upcoming trip, which seems far off to the child, but eventually the day arrives and the child can begin to see the connections.

Progress is a central part not only of the child's development but also of his or her developing awareness of self across time. Susan Harter (2012), who wrote an authoritative account of the self in child development, notes that young children's self-understanding invokes temporal comparisons long before social comparisons. That is, comparing one's own abilities against those of others has to wait. But even the young child acknowledges his or her new skills and abilities with pride. Harter points out that at young ages, improvements stand out because they are frequent and important. A small child's skills and abilities change rather fast, and so it is clear that one can now do something new. Tasks that recently were frustrating or required struggle become less daunting as one performs them with increasing ease and success. The mind can spot these changes much more easily than comparison of self with others, which requires some perspective taking so as to evaluate self and others from a similar standpoint.

THREE KEY ASPECTS OF SELF

There are three key aspects of self: self-knowledge consisting of self-beliefs, the executive self, and the interpersonal self. The development of self-conscious emotions shows how these three aspects of self are intertwined.

Consider pride and shame, two basic and powerful feelings. Both rely on some understanding of the self: What you just did was good or bad, reflecting on your full self and hence evoking these emotions. They are typically also learned interpersonally: The caregivers bestow praise or objections, thus helping the child to know whether to feel pride or shame. And before long these feelings guide the executive so that the child deliberately acts so as to avoid shame and earn pride.

Three steps in the emergence of self-conscious emotions are delineated by Harter (based on Stipek et al., 1992). The earliest, perhaps, is direct pleasure in mastering something new. Spontaneous "mastery smiles" can be observed in young children, as one sign of emerging self-awareness (Kagan, 1981): the child tries to do something, is at first unsuccessful, and then later succeeds. The smile recognizes the change: *Now I can do it.* This does not require social interactions, perspective taking, adult praise, or anything that complicated. Rather, it indicates direct pleasure arising from progress, from being able to do something new. Probably there is not much perspective on the self as a whole there. The right-now self enjoys being able to do something, and perhaps it smiles with the step forward, given that a hitherto elusive success is now attained. But there is perhaps no sense that the global self has changed in any meaningful way.

The second step is about adult reactions. Starting around the second birthday, or shortly before that, the child begins to anticipate receiving praise for mastering new things. The pleasure comes from receiving approval from adults, rather than from the direct pleasure of mastering something. The third step, coming perhaps a year later, can dispense again with the adult reaction. The pleasure is not just from mastering something new, as in the first step, but from an awareness of self as now gaining a new positive attribute. The child at the first step is not dissatisfied with self when unable to do something, but the older child is, and so the mastery denotes a positive change in self. It is not just replacing frustration ("I can't do this") with satisfaction ("I can do it!"), but a change in awareness of self, indeed an awareness of change in self ("I am now better than I was").

As with many things, the child got to the endpoint by way of other people. That is, he or she becomes able to appreciate his or her own mastery as if from other people's perspective, without needing others actually to express their pride. Being able to mentally simulate others' positive reactions enables the child to bask in their imagined approval. This also shows the self coming to understand the importance of reputation. What counts is what others know you can do.

Shame, another self-conscious emotion, shows the same pattern. Toddlers do not perhaps feel shame in the same way adults do, a global sense of oneself as deficient and bad. Rather, some authors speak of "pseudo-shame," which is fear of being punished (Harter, 2012). Such pseudo-shame reactions can be seen in animals, such as dogs, who are presumably incapable of much in the way of advanced self-awareness, but who are smart enough to anticipate punishment based on familiar cues. Harter and others conclude that true shame in children does not appear until about age 5, by which time there is more extensive self-awareness combined with the ability to take another's perspective. The child's pseudo-shame may not involve a genuine negative attitude toward the self—it simply reflects the dawning recognition that an adult will disapprove and probably punish. After a while, the child internalizes this external perspective and is able to feel bad about misdeeds regardless of any direct actions or utterances by adults.

Self-Beliefs

Positive Beliefs about Self

The small child is unable to maintain the difference between what he or she wants to be and what he or she actually is. This was observed by both Freud and Piaget and reaffirmed in Harter's (2012) work. More broadly, Harter notes that children generally have unrealistically high self-esteem, but it differs from the inflated self-esteem found among some adults. Narcissistic adults know the difference between aspirations and reality, and they believe they are genuinely superior beings. Children cannot tell the difference, and so their high opinions of themselves reflect that lack. Put another way, narcissism in adults is often the product of defensive processes, motivated biases, wishful thinking, and other distortions. In a child, it doesn't require all those. The child is simply not capable of knowing the difference between what he or she wants to be and what he or she is.

That has profound implications. Conscious thinking may be more for guiding action than for seeing reality. Our research on how adults think about the future has converged on a similar point (Baumeister, Vohs, & Oettingen, 2016): First, your mind forms a thought of what you want the future to be like, and then, afterward, it adapts to reality (such as evaluating feasibility, acknowledging obstacles, and perhaps making a plan for how to reach that goal).

Indeed, the child's confusion of "who I am" with "who I want to be" adds a new perspective to the pattern of inflated self-appraisals throughout life. People have various nonfiction conceptions of themselves, and the most important of these is the desired reputation: who you want to be known as, by others in your society. One might look at that as suggesting that adults have figured out what's important, namely how they want to be regarded. However, the childhood pattern suggests that the young brain starts off with a notion of the desired self. Some of this probably starts from learning what parents value, such as when they praise someone. The child may lack the capacity to understand fully the difference between private self-regard and reputation, so they are essentially the same to the child. Regardless, the crucial point is that *self-beliefs are inherently aspirational, right from childhood.* In other words, what the self thinks about itself is based on what it wants to be true, especially as generally recognized in its social circle. Developing an objectively correct self-concept, as distinct from what one aspires toward, comes later. No wonder self-knowledge lacks accuracy—accurate understanding of self is a secondary problem. Knowing what you want to be in the social world comes first.

The beginnings of self-esteem come early. Contrary to the prevailing modern view in society, children do not start off with fragile or low self-esteem. On the contrary, children think quite highly of themselves. They know they cannot do some things, but gradually they master these, and they look forward confidently to being able to do more of these. Measuring self-esteem in small children is difficult, given that they cannot read or write or use numbers and probably lack the ability to quantify their reactions on a continuum. Still, researchers have made some progress by observing behaviors that seem to express varying degrees of self-confidence. Initiative, independent action, curiosity, and general confidence are one set of markers. The confident child is eager to try new things and trusts him- or herself. The child with low self-esteem, in contrast, tends to lack self-trust and openness to new experiences. The other set of markers involves how the child responds to stresses, problems, and changes. High self-esteem is indicated by being able to adjust well, accept criticism, tolerate some frustration, and the like. The low-self-esteem child gives up easily, does not handle frustration well.

Harter's research team was most surprised to observe that the young child's self-esteem seems largely unrelated to objective competence. Some children are more capable than others at various things children do at that age—but their degree of self-esteem and confidence is not tied to objective capabilities. The link becomes stronger with age.

The gap between self-appraisal and actual competence fits well with what we shall see about self-esteem. Self-esteem is perception, not reality. (For example, research had found that people with high self-esteem rated themselves as more intelligent, more attractive, and more socially skilled than people with low self-esteem—but objective tests found little or no difference; reviewed by Baumeister et al., 2003.) Some people esteem themselves more highly than others, but these differences emerge early in life and largely independently of objective reality.

I doubt that children are truly indifferent to their objective competence or lack thereof. More likely, it is that, as Harter and others emphasize, small children have not yet mastered social comparison. They only assess their competence in solitary fashion, and if they compare at all, it is to how they were earlier—which yields generally favorable comparisons because children get better at things over time. Objective competence, as assessed by teachers, parents, and researchers, compares to what other children can do. A child who can only count to five may get low marks on competence from researchers, if other children of that age can count to 20 or 100. But the child who counts to five knows only that previously he or she could not count at all, so counting to five may seem perfectly fine.

As children grow older, they engage in more social comparisons, and increasingly subtle and nuanced ones. It's not just whether one can swim—it's whether one can swim the 200-meter backstroke race as fast as other team members, indeed down to fractions of a second. The attributes of the self are carefully measured and ranked.

Self-esteem levels fluctuate over the lifespan (Robins & Trzesniewski, 2005). How they change during early childhood is difficult to assess because it is hard to get reliable self-report measures from children. It does appear that self-esteem drops in adolescence, however, then slowly recovers and continues to rise into middle age. Eventually, it drops (indeed rather sharply) in old age. Crucially, it seems that the rank orders are maintained despite these average rises and falls. That is, if you think you're better than 80% of your peers, you still think so when everyone's self-esteem drops at adolescence, and likewise you're still above the same 80% in middle and old age, give or take a few. We may speculate about the ups and downs for the full population as it grows older. Adolescent mental capacities are much better than children's at adopting other people's perspectives, so they can see themselves as others see them, more or less. The realization that others do not admire them as much as they (as younger children) had assumed is discouraging. That contributes to the awkwardness, self-doubt, painful self-consciousness, and other negative feelings of adolescence—culminating in a drop in self-esteem.

The person recovers from this as he or she marches on from adolescence into adulthood. Plus, of course, most people start to accumulate some legitimate reasons for feeling good about themselves, enabling them to shed the darkest self-doubts. Adolescence is marked by occupational uncertainty and romantic turmoil, but by age 30 most people have found a mate and a job, and as these go reasonably well, self-esteem rises. The decline in self-esteem during old age is also understandable, as people recognize they fell short of some life goals, that they no longer have the mental and physical powers (let alone the good looks) of their prime, and that they have less and less role to play in society.

The Executive Self

Moral Self

Morality is a set of society's rules that define various actions as good or bad. The highly important moral aspect of selfhood requires some important foundations.

• It requires understanding of the moral rules and principles that society values. Society presumably starts with parents or other caregivers. Indeed, Freud placed great importance on toilet training, which is something children struggle to master as a significant step. Freud thought learning to control bladder and bowels was important for psychosexual development, which today's experts probably doubt. Rather, its importance may be more about self-control and an early form of moral rules. Even before the child masters the moral importance of sharing, the child learns to feel pride and shame associated with these societal rules.

• Moral selfhood requires self-control and perhaps a simple version of free will, as in the capacity to act differently in the same situation. Moral rules are all based on the assumption that the person could act differently in the same situation (e.g., you are capable both of lying and of telling the truth, and whereas lying may bring advantage, morality urges you to tell the truth).

• Moral behavior generally requires some motivation to behave morally instead of selfishly. Being capable of virtue is not enough. You have to *want* to be good.

• The desire to be a good person probably derives from the desire to have a morally good reputation and leads to specific desires to act in morally good ways. This requires some understanding of reputation and other people's perspectives, and some understanding of how others will evaluate you.

• Moral reputation is rooted in time. A right-now self would not be fully moral. At most it might have learned that there are moral rules and be able to apply them when making a difficult choice. Automatic moral responses seem to have that nature. For example, people's automatic responses to moral wrongness treat such actions as outside the realm of possibility (Phillips & Cushman, 2017). But it is because of the future that the self eventually decides to obey moral rules, that to do so is appropriate and rational even for the self's own benefit. Immoral actions today are punished in the future, whether by social isolation, or the flames of hell.

• Advanced moral behavior requires moral reasoning, though, as Blasi (1980; Hardy & Carlo, 2011) and others have long pointed out, moral reasoning ability is a disappointingly feeble predictor of moral action.

Moral development starts early, though full appreciation of abstract principles comes later. Very young children prefer others who are nice and who help others. Harming is seen as bad. This seems to be something that children are innately predisposed to learn right away.

Moreover, children seem to grasp quite early that the crucial thing is to be regarded by others as being morally good. Internalizing all this, so one behaves morally regardless of who else might know, comes later. As some scholars have pointed out, children understand the importance of moral reputation long before they can fully appreciate the strategic advantages of building a reputation. In Leimgruber and colleagues' (2012) studies, children were quite fair and generous when others were watching and others could know exactly what the children decided, but if others could not really see what they did, they were "strikingly ungenerous," which is to say, selfish. In this, we see the growing tension between natural selfishness (the brain's first job is to bring benefits to the body that houses it) and the dawning awareness that one's enlightened self-interest depends on being accepted by others.

From my perspective, the early recognition of the importance of moral reputation is not all that surprising. The point is this: Learning right and wrong starts by learning what actions bring punishment by others. I suspect children learn this well, and only later start to think that they should be good even when no one is looking. Even that lesson may arise from an intermediate step, as they come to realize that unobserved misdeeds are sometimes discovered later.

Put another way, children seek a "veil of fairness," that is, an external appearance of being moral and fair even though their private behavior is unfair (Shaw et al., 2014). In other words, they are more concerned with seeming to others to be fair than with actually being fair, again indicating the primacy of self-presentation and reputation. When the adult experimenter would know how they divided rewards between themselves and another child, the children were pretty scrupulously fair. But when they could take more for themselves while the experimenter mistakenly thought they were being fair, they did so.

In another study using children from age 6 to 11, the children saw there were two prizes, one for self and one for another child (Shaw et al., 2014). One of the prizes was much more desirable than the other: a colored highlighter pencil, as opposed to a common pencil. The children were told to choose between two ways of deciding who got what. They could just choose the one they wanted, or they could privately flip a coin to decide who got what. The older children seemed to grasp better than the younger ones that flipping a coin would be the fairest way, and so they were more likely to choose the coin flip. But they reported that they won the coin flip well above the rate of chance. Thus, they secretly cheated to sway the outcome in their favor, while appearing to the experimenter to be fair by choosing the coin flip.

This pattern, "moral actor, selfish agent" (Frimer et al., 2014), may seem and even be hypocritical; it gives the impression of moral virtue while secretly cheating for selfish benefit. However, let me offer a somewhat more benign interpretation. The task of every cultural animal is to take care of self while acting within the rules of the group. The group expects and rewards more virtue, while taking care of self means getting rewards and benefits for self. These studies show that adults and even older children understand both goals. Cheating while pretending virtue may be an extreme and unfortunate example of what is generally the adaptive fashion, which is to pursue self-interest within the rules and norms of society.

The clash between morality and self-interest was illuminated in other studies on how 6- to 8-year-old children reacted to fairness versus favoritism in how others dispensed rewards. Whether you like someone who is fair to all as opposed to someone who plays favorites can invoke both motives—especially if you are one of the favorites! In this work, favoritism meant that someone gave someone else preferential treatment (more rewards) (Shaw, DeScioli, & Olson, 2012). Children preferred fairness when they were merely observers of another child giving rewards to other children. When the children themselves received preferential treatment, then they were divided, some liking the one who gave them extra rewards, others still preferring the equal division. This indicates a clash of moral values: Fairness is good, but gratitude is also a moral obligation, and certainly it is nice to receive extra rewards. In further work, children liked it better when they got bigger rather than smaller rewards (self-interest), but even within that context they preferred that the other child received the same large rewards they did (fairness).

Thus, children like to be given rewards and treated as special, and some children like being treated preferentially, but they also have a general desire for fairness in terms of equal rewards for all. Sometimes they are torn as to which to prefer. One further factor that shifts preferences toward favoritism and away from equal treatment was competition. When the experimenters said it was part of a game and asked them whether they wanted to win, they said yes, and afterward they preferred the child who gave them more (thus helping them win).

Morality is a prime example of what Allport (1954) dubbed functional autonomy: Things that are first done as means to other ends gradually become ends themselves. The small child first learns to obey moral rules as a way to avoid punishment. As we have seen, children readily abandon their scruples when they think no one is looking (and no punishment is risked). But internalizing the rules means wanting to be good for goodness's sake. Many adults feel strong desires to be virtuous, regardless of who may be watching. Guilt, shame, and pride may all be felt in solitude.

Moreover, the innate moral tendencies inside young children are probably designed for learning what is morally valued in their society, rather than having innate morals themselves. Perhaps the aversion to harm, mentioned above, is innate, but fairness takes different forms. In a study that was published with the title "Fair Is Not Fair Everywhere," Schäfer and colleagues (2015) found that children from very different societies all wanted to divide rewards fairly—but used different criteria. Children in modern Western civilization used equity based on merit; the children who contributed the most to earning the prize were given the biggest shares. Children from quite different societies, including a partially hunter-gatherer culture, ignored merit and distributed things equally. Thus, children do have a moral sense, including moral feelings and judgments, but this adapts to their society's morals.

Self-Control

Self-control is one of the keys to the self, as we will see. The brain adjusts its actions, sometimes alongside its thoughts and feelings, based on what the social environment wants and rewards. Growing up is a process by which the child learns how society works, learns his or her own place in society, and learns how to act on a day-by-day basis so as to be a valued member of society. Developing self-control is crucial.

Self-control in childhood predicts (and probably helps cause) a broad range of adult outcomes, including school achievement, career success, money, committing crimes and being arrested, mental health, physical health, problem habits like smoking and drinking, popularity, stable relationships, and even death (e.g., Moffitt et al., 2011). This is important news for parents, teachers, and others who deal with young people: The best thing you can do for them, in terms of helping them toward a happy and fulfilling life, is to improve their self-control.

We know a great deal about self-control in children, and a recent comprehensive work has pulled all the findings together (Robson, Allen, & Howard, 2020). The simple answer is that the better a child's self-control is at any particular age, the better the child's life is later on. The time sequence pattern strongly suggests, though does not quite prove, that self-control is a cause. The consequences start early in life but continue to have impact and value right up into old age.

Children who have better self-control in preschool, around age 4, do better in the early school years (around age 8). They are more competent socially, and also more engaged in school, and they get better grades. They have fewer behavioral problems associated with both "internalizing" and "externalizing" disorders. Internalizing problems mean beating yourself up. In practice these are measured in the form of anxiety, suicidal thoughts, loneliness, depression, and withdrawing from social life. Externalizing, meanwhile, means taking it out on others, such as by aggression, refusing to cooperate, or being disruptive in class or other social settings.

Children with good self-control also are less likely than others to be victimized by bullies and other peers. Self-control enables one to obey norms and interact with others effectively. Children who lack these skills attract negative attention, including from bullies.

Moving along, good self-control in the early school years (around age 8) leads to better outcomes into middle school (age 13). That is, the 8-year-olds with better self-control go on to learn and perform better in school, including doing better in math and reading. They also show fewer problems in their various forms: smoking cigarettes, taking drugs, becoming depressed, getting fat, and getting in trouble with the law (as well as schoolyard fighting).

The link to getting fat was particularly intriguing. Among children in the early school years, low self-control was *not* linked to being fat. But having low self-control at that age was linked to being fat later on, as an adolescent and even as an adult, many years later. Perhaps a child's weight depends on parental feeding practices and other factors. But lacking self-control at age 8 is an early sign, and perhaps a cause, of subsequent obesity. What this means is, some fat kids have good self-control, and as they grow up, they manage their weight effectively (and so aren't fat anymore). But kids who have poor self-control, whether fat or skinny, grow up to be fat.

The benefits of self-control continue. Good self-control around age 13 produces benefits lasting into adulthood, approaching age 40. Teenyboppers with good self-control turn into adults who are more likely to have jobs (lower unemployment), less prone to be arrested or have problems with aggression, lower anxiety and depression, and less likely to smoke tobacco, drink alcohol, and abuse drugs. They even have better physical health (alongside better mental health).

That's an impressive set of benefits for having good self-control starting in childhood. At each rough stage of development, the kids with good self-control do better in multiple ways at the next stage, all the way from preschool to middle age.

The researchers who compiled all these data also compared different ways of assessing self-control in children (Robson et al., 2020). A behavioral test worked best, but teacher ratings were almost as accurate. Parent ratings were notably poorer. Children up to age 11 or 12 often think their parents know them better than they know themselves (Rosenberg, 1979). And they might. But parental ratings of children were consistently the least effective and accurate at predicting actual outcomes. One might think that parents would indeed know their children best because they have had years to observe the child—but parents are not objective observers. Indeed, parents' ratings of their children may be subject to gross distortions and rationalizations, including wishful thinking. A single hour of observation in the lab by a stranger gives a more effective assessment of a child's self-control than what the parent can offer based on having known the child for his or her entire life. This is probably less a testimony to the stunning accuracy of laboratory methods than a sign of how biased parents are when talking about their children.

There are two major tasks for developing self-control. One is to acquire the powers of restraining oneself and altering one's reactions. The other is to learn how to use these powers wisely and appropriately. The first may be mostly an inner process, though of course it can be guided and helped by parents and teachers. The other again depends on the child learning how culture and society work and what they value. This distinction will be important in the chapter on mental illness because some people seem to master only one of these without the other, which is a recipe for problems.

The Interpersonal Self

The self does not appear in isolation but rather comes into being as a member of groups and in relationships. The child's self develops to negotiate the social world. Self-knowledge may develop primarily to help with the social environment. An early study (Damon & Hart, 1982, 1988) asked children to describe themselves and also to elaborate their answers in terms of why these mattered. Their answers generally emphasized the interpersonal context, such as that baseball skills are valued by their friends. These answers suggest children have come to recognize the central importance of reputation: What matters is how others perceive you, insofar as that predicts whether they will accept or reject you.

To be sure, as the children move into adolescence, they refer increasingly to their own standards and values. Thus, they start to evaluate their self-beliefs based on their own values, not just those of other people (functional autonomy again). Still, I suspect the evaluations of others lurk underneath and matter to some extent. By adolescence, the self's unity across time is moving forward and the young person is seeking to create a self that will be useful and appealing in a broad variety of situations. Hence, it feels as if it is one's own values, not those of others, that are the basis for what matters, as with morality. Still, the public self is the key to thriving in human life, which is social life.

Learning How to Interact

Much of upbringing and child development is about learning how to interact with others. Culture enables people to work together so as to create more resources, starting with more food, and so one has to behave properly to get along with others. One learns about one's immediate society, its status hierarchy and rules, its risks and opportunities. Plenty of social animals do this. For human children, there is also the task of mastering the group's body of shared information—its doxa—that includes the shared understanding of how the physical and social worlds work.

The child has many lessons to learn and seems reasonably well oriented toward learning them. Learning to share and take turns is difficult at first, but such things soon become second nature. Adults in many societies automatically form queues to facilitate turn-taking in almost any setting. Perhaps the most revealing example is British rioters lining up to take turns looting stores, which was reported in the 1980s and periodically thereafter (McArdle, 2011).

A particularly revealing pattern has been dubbed overimitation. It seems irrational and wasteful, yet human children do it more than apes—so it seems human evolution added a penchant for irrational silliness. Many animals have social learning, which means that they see another animal do something and as a result do it themselves. The crucial difference involves steps that are irrelevant to the goal. Suppose you were hungry and you saw an adult come in, approach a box, turn around twice, tap the top of his head, open the box, and get some tasty food. If you were a chimpanzee, you would learn that the box contains food, and you would go open the box. A human child learns the same outcome but will also copy the double twirl and head top tap. In fact, even children who have already interacted with the box and figured out how to open it to get food will incorporate the ritual after watching an adult. These patterns have been found in widely different cultures, suggesting a strong evolutionary or innate basis (McGuigan et al., 2007; Nagell et al., 1993; Nielsen et al., 2014; Nielsen & Tomaselli, 2010).

In a sense the chimpanzee's action is smarter. But it shows that the chimp's mind is essentially solitary. It just uses other chimps as a useful source of information. The human child already wants to participate in the group, and so doing what others do for the sake of being like the others is an end in itself. In a sense, the child is not just learning how to do something—he or she is learning how *we* do something.

Overimitation shows that the human child is learning more than how to deal with the world. Part of becoming a human adult is copying and mastering the way things are done in one's community. The human child learns about culture as much as, or more than, about nature. That's why he or she copies the rituals.

The learning of culture is also evident in teasing, which seems a minor thing to adults but is a much bigger aspect of children's lives. Adults tease each other, often as part of flirting or playful interaction. To children, being teased is often acutely unpleasant, though it seems to hurt less as the children get older. The generally innocuous nature of adult teasing means that we tend to have forgotten how painful it was to be teased as a child. Multiple psychological theories have tried to explain why children tease. A major review of the evidence was provided by Keltner and colleagues (2001). No one theory can explain all teasing, from flirting in the workplace, to the dozens of exchanges of insults leading to gang fights, to children's making fun of each other's names or clothing.

One clear theme in teasing, however, is that it often focuses on norm violations. That is one reason children do it aggressively and suffer when it is done to them (Shapiro et al., 1991). Children are learning norms, as in the implicit rules for how to act that make up some of the shared knowledge in their society. When one has violated a norm, other children (or teenagers) will point this out, sometimes helpfully (and in that case usually privately), but more often in a "gotcha!" public manner. (Think of the various ways of letting a young man know that the zipper on his pants is down.) Many schools have adopted anti-teasing policies because teasing can be a form of bullying. This focuses on the unhappy target (as victim) and ascribes purely hostile (bullying) intent to the teaser. But I think teasing is often done because it is a way of showing off. The teaser remarks on someone's norm violation and thereby shows to all who are present that the teaser is well aware of the norm. As children strive and compete to master the norms, teasing is a way of winning: *I know what's right, and you don't.* This may extend into cruelty and bullying, but such motives may be faint or absent. When someone objects, the teaser often says, "I was only teasing!" Sometimes this may be a cover for meanness, but other times it is probably quite correct and sincere.

Teasing reflects the difficulty of following all the complex and unclear rules of society, as well as the competitive urge to show oneself to have mastered some rules better than someone else.

Information Agent

The human child becomes an information agent, that is, one who traffics in information. The child learns that there is a doxa, that is, a set of shared knowledge. Growing up means gaining access to the doxa. It is not just acquiring information. It is finding out things that everyone else supposedly knows, as well as understanding that everyone supposedly knows them, too. Overimitation reflects the urge to master the shared information, including how things are done in one's group.

The discovery of sex, later in childhood, is not just a solitary insight. Rather, it means coming to understand what many other people are talking about, what those jokes mean, what people argue about, and how others might misinterpret one's innocent comments or acts. It enables one to take part in conversations and debates about sex. Those assume some degree of shared understanding.

Several early signs of becoming an information agent have been noted by researchers (for a review, see Baumeister, Maranges, & Vohs, 2018; Shteynberg, 2015). A first is joint attention, the practice of focusing attention on the same things others are focusing on. This appears quite early in life. "Look!" is a simple command to focus attention where someone else is looking, and it is commonly heard both from (even small) children and from those who communicate with children. Babies seem to sense when others are attending to the same thing. They also show heightened interest in something if others are also looking at it. Very young brains already keep track of what is being looked at by multiple people, and such things get more attention and more processing, leading to superior memory. Later, shared attention improves effort and performance. Emotional reactions are intensified.

Joint attention comes much earlier than sharing attitudes or values. Thus, one of the first elements of the social brain is learning to pick up on what others are attending to, and redirecting one's own attention to the same thing. Having the same attentional focus presumably helps group coordination and shared activities.

NARRATIVE SELF

As we have seen, children acquire self-knowledge in multiple forms, and these beliefs are kept somewhat separate from each other. The self gradually comes to understand itself as having various attributes, such as traits and abilities. Meanwhile, it also develops a narrative understanding of itself. Its life comes to be understood in story form, indeed as a cluster of stories, some of which comprise only a few minutes, others spanning and integrating multiple years.

The development of the narrative self has been a central focus of McAdams's (e.g., 2013, 2019) work. The beginnings of the narrative self involve becoming an actor. The child learns from others how to act in various situations. Like professional actors, children learn to perform their roles properly, doing the tasks assigned to them. Sometimes their actor training involves reciting scripted lines. Children are taught to say "please" and "thank you," sometimes prompted with "Now what do you say?" The patterns of overimitation are part of this: the child seeks to know how to be and act in these social situations. The agentic powers of the inner self are sufficiently taxed merely to perform the appropriate actions without mistakes.

Older children move from mere actor to agent. They are not just following a script to do what is expected. Instead, they are making choices that shape the course of events. Choice requires much more of a coherent self, unless it is merely choosing at random, or just following the strongest impulse as a right-now self would do. Choices are guided by the extended-time self, including its goals and long-term values. Other than totally right-now choices, such as what to eat, choices require integrating some thoughts of the future (and perhaps the past).

During the teen years, the self adopts a third role, as author of the narrative. The person continues to act agentically within the story but now, with greater wisdom, greater understanding of society, and more integrative understanding of self across time, the self can choose and change the story line. This is quite important because the adolescent's task is to lay the foundations for adult life. That involves making choices of career and mate, and the different options often promise very different stories for one's life and thus cast the self in somewhat different roles.

LEARNING HOW TO PLAY ROLES

Identity typically means holding and playing a role in a group or system. When one asks children, "What do you want to be when you grow up?," their answers refer to roles that interlock with other roles. A role does not exist in a vacuum but rather in relation to other roles. Performing a role (father, teacher, police officer . . .) means interacting with others in a particular, prescribed fashion.

The child develops in part by learning to perform these roles, typically in relation to others who hold the complementary roles. Some of this process can be observed in children's games. Nearly all games involve multiple roles. By examining how children's games change as children grow older, one can get a powerful glimpse into how the child acquires the capacity to perform roles. One young researcher took that to heart and interviewed several hundred children, ranging from 2-year-olds to teenagers, as to what was their favorite game and how it was played. She also interviewed teachers for different age groups as to what games were favored by their pupils (Baumeister & Senders, 1989). These data were collected before video games became such a prominent part of childhood.

For young children, just adopting and performing a role continuously is a challenge. They might play house, in which several children take on the roles of mother, father, and child. Often the game starts with some dispute because several children want to be the mother, which is flattering to the real mother if she observes this—until she realizes that to the children, the main point of being the mother is being entitled to boss the other kids around. Nevertheless, such games are popular with the youngest children, and it is instructive to notice what these games lack as compared with other games. There are often no rules, no competition, and no success or failure (no winners and losers). The role is stable, in the sense that the children do not exchange roles (at least not as part of the game; they might take turns being the mommy). The roles have no particular goals, nor is there a clear endpoint to the game. To the extent that the several players interact, they support each other's role performance, as compared to adult games (e.g., chess) in which the players seek to thwart each other's performance goals. The first step, apparently, is simply understanding how to adopt a role and play it continuously. Young children favor noncompetitive games, such as house, presumably because role performance is difficult enough for them without having someone else trying to thwart them. Noncompetitive games were favorites around age 5.

A few years later, games based on role transformations or exchange become popular. This is a transitional stage in which roles are opposed to each other but outcomes are decided by chance (e.g., rolling dice). These games, which became favorites starting around age 7, introduce the child to the idea that different people have different goals that go against each other, so not everyone can be successful. But insofar as the result depends purely on chance, the self's executive does not have to make choices or perform successfully. The self's activities may be limited to moving one's marker a randomly determined number of spaces along the board.

The most familiar example of these types of games would be playing tag. There are two roles in that game, and players switch from one to the other—indeed, switching is the point of the game. To be able to play tag, the child must have already mastered holding down a role and performing its functions (as in house), plus the additional step of understanding that one's role in the game changes. Clearly, you are the same person when you are "It," trying to touch other players, as when you are not "It" and someone else is trying to touch you. But your identity within the game has changed. The notion of a continuous self that performs different roles and switches among them is an important step forward because adult selfhood also requires one to be able to do both. Moreover, tag has rules, unlike house, so these games require the child's self to have reached the point at which it can perform its role despite constraints.

The games in this second stage define roles by fixed criteria: You are "It" if the previous "It" has tagged you, and you hold that role until you succeed in touching someone else. The roles have goals, and, crucially, the different goals are opposed to each other. The goal of "It" is to tag someone, while everyone else's goal is to avoid being tagged. This introduces the child to competition and opposition, but in a simple and safe manner. True failure remains impossible, except if someone becomes "It" and remains unable to tag anyone else. (This may happen to the smallest, slowest child in the group, especially if there are age differences.)

Also briefly popular are games based on struggling to follow the rules. Simon Says is an example: One must mimic the leader's motions, but only if the leader says, "Simon says" first, and to mimic otherwise is to lose. These games show the child's agentic self learning to adapt its actions based on seemingly arbitrary and tricky rules. No doubt much of life confronts the child that way, as an accommodation to seemingly random and whimsical rules.

Later on, games assume that children know how to follow rules, and so the rules cease to be the point of the game and merely enable it. These games, like the games based on role switching, are only popular with children around a certain age (in this sample, around 8 years old), suggesting that these challenges are specific to that age range. However, it is a bit risky to assume that the games are popular precisely when the child is most struggling to master that role-switching aspect of self. The games may become popular as the child nears the end of that struggle. That might be when they are most fun because they exercise a new skill. The arbitrary rules games like Simon Says appeal after toilet training, which has long been treated as confronting the child with confusing rules.

Competition makes role performance more difficult because other players are trying to prevent you from performing your role successfully. Competitive games involve opposing roles, and the outcome depends on the choices and skills of the respective selves. The games played by the oldest children, and indeed by adults, often combine stable roles with switching of subroles, thus indicating a high level of competence and complex role playing. In volleyball, players remain on the same team but alternate as to who serves and who stands at the net. In baseball and cricket, too, players split into different fielding positions and then take turns batting. Maintaining a continuous self while still switching roles may be especially challenging so that games depending on that process are delayed till later.

With age the self comes to measure itself more and more precisely. On this too, games show the pattern. No one keeps score on a simple game such as house or tag. But many games involve scores. (Obviously, numerical scoring only works for children old enough to understand numbers.) In terms of development of self, this means that the self is learning to evaluate itself and its performances not simply as good or bad, but along a continuum—and often one that allows for precise social comparison, down to fractions of seconds.

FROM ADOLESCENCE INTO ADULTHOOD

The adolescent phase requires making important choices that will define your place in society as an adult—or else accepting the place that parents and society have already prepared for you. Teenagers are famous for erratic, mercurial behavior. Some of this may stem from the intensity of teen emotions. Not having yet fully mastered how to subdue and control one's feelings, they react strongly to new developments. But some of this behavior may be simply role experimentation. The teenager tries out different ways of relating to the world and dealing with life's challenges. Changing friends can expose one to different social groups with different norms, or different ways of dealing with norms.

Another core problem of adolescence has already been mentioned: The person enters it with a child's powers of self-control but begins to have adult-powered impulses and feelings. Alongside that, the teenager is better able to see self from others' perspectives, which is initially troubling and daunting.

Over time, however, the person's self-control gains in capacity to exert control, and it modifies the self's actions so as to be acceptable to others. It resolves the big questions of mating and career, at least tentatively. The need to experiment with different lifestyles passes, as one settles into dealing with the demands and opportunities of the life one has chosen.

KEY POINTS

- The human baby initially has a right-now self. The child needs to learn to respond as a unity to the immediate present starting with coordination of the body.

- Harter's three steps in the emergence of self-conscious emotion are spontaneous "mastery smiles"; anticipating adult praise for mastery; and awareness of self as gaining a new positive attribute.

- Children's self-beliefs are inherently aspirational right from the beginning and largely unrelated to objective competence. As they grow older, they engage in more social comparisons. Attributes of self are carefully measured and ranked.

- Morality in children is an example of Allport's functional autonomy: Things that are first done as a means to other ends gradually become ends in themselves.

- There are two major tasks for developing self-control: (1) restraining oneself and altering one's reactions and (2) learning how to use these powers wisely and appropriately.

- Good self-control in childhood predicts a broad range of adult outcomes including school achievement and career success.

- Much of upbringing is learning about one's immediate society, its status hierarchy and rules, its risks and opportunities.

CHAPTER 8

Human Groups Need
(and Shape) Selves

Why do human beings need to construct and maintain a distinctive (even unique) identity at all? The answer may lie not in individuals but in groups. Yet, the benefits of groups don't need individual selves. As Moffett (2019) has documented, ants have highly effective societies, but an ant cannot recognize a particular other ant, even one who has toiled beside it for a long time. Ants only recognize the difference between their own colony and other colonies. It's as if you couldn't tell your spouse or best friend apart from any stranger on the subway but you always immediately spot a foreign tourist as different.

For me, the crucial insight emerged from an accident of other duties. When writing a textbook on social psychology, my coauthor (Brad Bushman) and I divided up the chapters as to who would write the first draft of each. Neither of us had ever had much contact with the research on groups. When the writing of the chapter on groups fell to me, I set out to read the research literature. As I read, I looked for big themes that came up repeatedly, so I could use those to organize the chapter. I found two big themes.

One theme running through the research literature is the basic wonderfulness of groups. People like being in groups. Groups can do things that lone individuals cannot do, such as surrounding an enemy or prey, or lifting heavy loads. If a group and a lone individual both want the same resource, such as a fruit tree, the group will likely get it. Modern corporations, universities, governments, and other groups accomplish things that would be impossible for a single person to do, and these mostly make society better.

The second theme was the destructive, nasty, even evil consequences of group life. When people form into groups, they become extra-hostile toward outsiders, less likely to compromise or to find mutually beneficial solutions. Group members skimp on effort, leaving the hard tasks to others. Committees sometimes make stupid, self-defeating, irrational, destructive decisions. In warfare, genocide, oppression, and the like, groups do far worse damage than lone individuals.

So, I had two important themes; the only problem was that they contradicted each other. How can groups be both wonderful and terrible? In groups, people accomplish more good than they could do alone, but they also do awful things that loners would not and could not do. Put simply, sometimes groups are more and better than the sum of their parts—but sometimes they are less and far worse. What makes the difference?

Grappling with this problem led me and some colleagues to compare the lists of good and bad aspects of groups, searching for a key difference. The decisive factor, we found, was the individual, responsible, differentiated self.

The bad side of groups generally emerged when individual selves became submerged in the group. The next section addresses some of the main ways research has shown groups to be underachieving or positively destructive (for a full review and sources, see Baumeister, Ainsworth, & Vohs, 2016).

WHEN GROUPS ARE BAD

Groupthink

When members all embrace the group's views and values, and especially when some group members maintain the dominant view by suppressing dissent, groups become prone to make blunders, ranging from minor to catastrophic. Everyone thinks alike, no one questions the plans and decisions. Even very smart and well-intentioned groups fall into disaster in these ways.

Mob Violence

People merge into an angry, violent group that is prone to break laws, damage property, and even kill people seen as enemies or wrongdoers. The mob mentality is more destructive than most of the participants would be if they were acting as single, responsible individuals. Individuals stop thinking of themselves as autonomous moral beings and simply act along with the mob.

Selfish Practices

Selfish practices destroy commonly owned properties. The *tragedy of the commons* referred to how public grasslands were ruined by herdsmen who let their cows or sheep eat so much of the grass that there wasn't enough left to grow back, so the resource ran out instead of endlessly replenishing itself (Hardin, 1968). Today, this is happening worldwide in the oceans, as individual fishermen (and presumably fisherwomen) catch as many fish as they can so that there are not enough left to reproduce the stocks, and fish populations dwindle. Many other natural resources show similar patterns. What is owned in common gets used up, whereas what is owned individually sometimes gets carefully husbanded and preserved.

Social Loafing

What happens when people all put their muscles together to do a big task? The answer has been labeled "social loafing" (e.g., Karau & Williams, 1995; Latané et al., 1995). Abundant laboratory experiments show that people reduce effort when part of a group, as long as their individual performances are merged into the group. Making individuals accountable eliminates the effect. For example, swimmers swim more slowly when part of a relay team than when competing as individuals. But if the times of individual swimmers in the relay team are posted so everyone knows how fast each individual swam, suddenly the loafing stops and they perform at their best.

Information Loss

Committees are supposed to be wiser than lone decision makers because different members can contribute their unique knowledge and perspectives. Unfortunately, what often happens is that the committee members get together and talk about what they all know in common. Beautifully designed experiments by Stasser (1999; Stasser & Titus, 1985) show that committees fail to bring up all their information and therefore make poor decisions because they focus on what they all know in common. If you can get them to contribute their own individual knowledge, they start to find the best answer more often.

Collective Brain Fog

So-called brainstorming sessions bring members of a creative team together to stimulate each other by tossing out ideas. When this technique to enhance creativity was first discovered (by advertising agencies in the 1950s), it was greeted with terrific excitement. But careful studies gradually showed that brainstorming groups produce fewer and less creative ideas than the same number of people working alone (Mullen, Johnson, & Salas, 1991).

WHEN GROUPS ARE GOOD

In contrast to the foregoing, the powerful successes of groups capitalize on the differences among individuals (again, see Baumeister, Ainsworth, & Vohs, 2016). Some revealing examples follow.

Division of Labor

Early factories, called "manufactories," consisted of multiple expert crafts-men working in the same place but each producing an entire product by himself. Over time it was discovered that quality and quantity of produc-tion could be sharply increased by splitting the process into parts and hav-ing different people perform different parts. The modern social science of economics was launched by Adam Smith (1776/1991), with his famous description of a pin factory. Each man performed a different task, making the production more efficient and cheaper. A huge bonus was that the level of expertise required of each worker was much lower, saving enormously on labor costs. As a classic example, in 1900 each automobile was made by one or two men, who had to know pretty much everything about how to make a car. As a result, their labor was enormously expensive, and it took them the better part of a year to make a single car. Plus, they had to be paid at their high rate even when tightening screws or sweeping up, so the whole process was a money trap. Only very rich people could afford these expensive cars—paying two super-expert mechanics for a year, plus all the materials.

But by 1915 the Ford assembly line had revolutionized the process. Each man on the assembly line only had to be able to perform one task, a limited skill, so the labor was much cheaper than that of an expert mechanic. And he could become an expert at his small part of the job so that the cars were actually better in quality. Plus, they were made much more rapidly. Thus, division of labor produced more and better cars, faster, and at much less cost, than the old system of having an expert mechanic do the whole job.

A more recent study compared two flute factories (West, 1999). One only employed expert craftsmen, each of whom made the entire flute him-self. The other used division of labor, with each worker doing only one part of the job, and proficient only at that. But the second one produced more, better, and cheaper flutes. Capitalizing on the differences among cooperat-ing selves produced the best result. That's a key clue to what the human self evolved for.

Accountability

Holding people responsible for their actions, identifying who does what, and asking people to explain and justify their actions all lead groups to perform better (e.g., Lerner & Tetlock, 1999, 2003). Incentive structures can reward and thereby increase good actions, and can punish and thereby decrease bad actions. I strongly suspect that all human societies do this. Indeed, making people identified individually to the group counteracts some of the negative effects of groups listed above. People who are indi-vidually accountable to other group members behave better and perform better than people who aren't.

One could go on, but these are enough to make the crucial point. *Groups go bad when individual selves merge into the group. Groups flourish when they capitalize on individual selves each different from the others, individually accountable and responsible, thinking for themselves.* This is a vital point, especially in the context of assuming that humans evolved their specific traits, including selfhood, in order to capitalize on the advantages of groups.

There is one qualification that is a technicality, relevant for the most skeptical and critical readers. Anonymity is not quite the same as merging into the group, and in fact sometimes being anonymous enables people to think and choose as individuals. For example, secret ballots enable voters to express their opinions freely, without fear of being punished for not conforming to what other people prefer.

Sometimes, anonymity protects individuality. Sometimes, it interferes with it. Anonymity prevents the group from controlling the individual. If the goal is to make people do something that is a sacrifice to them, such as putting forth hard work or contributing money to the joint project, then identification works better because the lazy loafers and free riders can be identified and punished, while the virtuous contributors are recognized and rewarded. In contrast, when it's a matter of getting informational input from multiple sources, then anonymity protects the individual from pressure to conform. It lets people think for themselves, and that's what helps the group succeed.

In both cases, what matters is that the person participates as a distinct individual. Groups do best when different individuals contribute as best they can, based on their different knowledge, abilities, and other resources. A distinct, autonomous, unique, responsible self is a great boon to a productive social system.

All of this is tremendously important for understanding the human self. We evolved our unique human capacities in order to capitalize on the advantages of groups, indeed a new (as far as nature is concerned) kind of group based on sharing information, collective planning, and coordinating different individuals. Human beings took over planet Earth not by virtue of being the most ferocious animals, with fearsome claws or fangs, but instead by virtue of being able to work together in small groups. Recent work (see Tomasello, 2014; von Hippel, 2018) suggests, for example, that early human groups collected stones and developed collective stone-throwing skills that would drive away other animals.

Many social animals hunt together, and it is instructive to examine the case of our closest animal relatives, the chimpanzees. Chimps do hunt as groups and do manage something akin to division of labor. But, as Tomasello (2014; Tomasello et al., 2012) explains, each chimp is really out for himself. (Pronouns here are male: Female chimps do not work together as much as males.) For example, if a group of chimpanzees finds a monkey, they want to kill and eat it. But they don't share deliberately. The one who catches the monkey will eat as much as he can, while the others will come over and try to grab a piece of the meat.

Suppose the monkey climbs a tree, and the nearest chimp follows it up the tree. The other chimps are smart enough to realize that they won't be able to get to the monkey ahead of their colleague who is already halfway up the tree, so some of them might try to predict what will happen if the monkey manages to escape that chimp. They might spread out to block the possible escape routes. This looks like group coordination, and it is a step in that direction. Still, whoever catches the monkey will eat as much as he can before the others converge. There is no consensus of working as a group and sharing the rewards. A human group will spread out so as to be sure that someone will catch the prey—but then they share it.

What is the big point here? The individuated human self exists, not because the individual brain or body needs it, but because groups need it. People can only make complex systems work if they have selves who are up to the task of performing their roles in the system. They have to be both willing and able, and they have to consent to do what is best for the group even if not immediately best for the self. The individual, differentiated human self exists because of the requirements of a functioning society. As noted above, division of labor improves performance and increases the total resources, so there is more to share, and lots of people (thus the group as a whole also) are better off.

Society is a big group composed of little groups. The groups flourish better if the individual members are differentiated and participate as distinct, individual selves. Differentiation of individual selves is what makes human social systems superior to all other animal social systems.

As Chapter 3 emphasized, full cultivation of individuality is a modern phenomenon. For most of history, and even today in many cultures, social life was and is heavily organized around extended families and other kinship groups (see Henrich, 2020). These benefit some from individuality but Western history started weakening those ties, which enabled European society to surge ahead of other world cultures and achieve economic, military, and scientific dominance.

PRECISELY HOW DO DIFFERENT SELVES HELP GROUPS?

Thus far we have seen abundant evidence that human groups are at their best and have the most success when they capitalize on the different identities of their various members. To some extent, this flies in the face of much conventional wisdom. After all, the very idea of a group means sameness: all the members have the same identity as a member of the group. To be an Italian or a Rotary Club member or a Floridian is to have an identity as a member of a group who all identify themselves that same way. There is a marvelous body of theory and research on what's called "social identity theory" (e.g., Hornsey, 2008), all based on the essential assumption that what the self gets from being in a group is sameness. The defining fact about a group is how they are all the same.

In contrast, the emphasis here is how group members are different from each other. The more the group recognizes that and takes advantage of it, the better it fares. Ideally, selves emphasize how they are different, special, unique. Ideally, too, each self finds a niche where it can contribute to the group effort as well as thriving itself. Often those are linked, such as when people who perform valuable and difficult jobs in society get paid high salaries. Their work enables the group to thrive, and they are well rewarded so they can thrive individually.

Do selves indeed seek to be different? Certainly, there is always plenty of conformity. But perhaps conforming is the easy way out when one is uncertain. Perhaps people conform in lots of ways but still cultivate some kind of uniqueness or specialness in particular domains. Just being chosen romantically by someone else is a huge affirmation of your uniqueness: He chose you instead of another woman because he thinks you are special. *You're the one he wants.* (Or she, of course.)

Back in the 1970s two psychologists developed a "need for uniqueness" scale to measure that personality trait (Snyder & Fromkin, 1977). It proved useful and valid. The idea was to capture the motivation to be different from everyone else. Because there is a scale to measure differences among people, it is assumed that this desire is stronger among some people than others. So yes, people do seem to have some desire to be different, but some people have more of that desire than others.

If the self is designed to capitalize on its individual traits and talents, then people should be extra-interested in those. Sure enough, evidence indicates that people identify more with their distinctive (unusual) traits than with the traits they share with many others (Miller, Turnbull, & McFarland, 1988). After taking some tests, research subjects were told they had one trait that was fairly common and another that was unusual. When given the opportunity to gain more information about these traits, they were much more interested in learning about the unusual one. That is, they wanted to know how they stood out from the group. In other studies, they sought to learn how they compared with other members of their group, even if they could learn just as much about themselves by comparing with someone else not in the group.

The desire to learn how one differs could mean multiple things. In theory, it could mean that people want to find out how they are different so they can change, so as to be more like everybody else. But, more likely, it reflects how groups use individuals. The most effective group capitalizes on each person's unique talents and capabilities. Your value to the group may lie in what you can do that nobody else can. Hence, you are eager to learn what makes you special within the group.

To be sure, these studies were run in North America (Canada), which is an individualistic culture. Possibly people with a more collective style of self-definition would identify more with what makes them the same as others. Some cultures emphasize individuality more than others. Much has been written about that (see Chapter 4). The gist is that the collective generally comes first, as in historical and evolutionary precedence. The shift toward greater individualism emerged somewhat recently in Western history. Asians tend to be more collectivistic even today, while Westerners have become increasingly individualistic over the centuries. But what is better?

The assumption is that competition among societies and cultures will favor the superior ones. The weak ones will fade in competition with others. The better system will defeat the dysfunctional system, in the long run, by and large.

So what is the long-term trend? There is a global increase in individualism (Santos et al., 2017). Over time, the cultures and societies all over the world are drifting toward more and more individualism. That's the macro trend. It suggests that individualism (i.e., emphasis on the unique single individual person, respecting difference more than sameness) has advantages over collective systems.

The Miller and colleagues (1988) findings fit the view that groups capitalize on differences among members—so the self is motivated to find out what sets it apart from others. Your opportunities, even your value to the group (indeed to society as a whole), rest on what makes you a little different from others. The things you know that others don't, the abilities you have that others don't, the perspective or charm or other traits that set you apart are precious and important.

Even studies on the influence of stereotypes on self-concepts have found that people form self-concepts to emphasize how they are better than the stereotype of their group (von Hippel, Hawkins, & Schooler, 2001). Women and African Americans formed strong impressions of themselves as intelligent if they performed well, more so than White men. Meanwhile, the White men identified with athletic skills if they excelled at sports. The things that set you apart from your group in a good way become central to your self-concept—and, no coincidence, these are also the things that contain your value to your group. These are what you're good for, in terms of contributing to the group benefit.

Thus, one take-home message is that many people do seek to define themselves with an emphasis on how they are different from others. Now let's look back at the evidence on groups benefiting from having lots of individually identified, different selves. What other patterns emerged?

The self has to want to be integrated into the group. It certainly has that desire. As psychology researcher Warren Jones once remarked in a major symposium, "In many years of doing research on loneliness, I have met many people who say they have no friends. I have never met anyone who says they don't want to have any friends."

When we surveyed all the research literature about groups and selves, we pushed ourselves to articulate the ways groups benefited from having individualistic selves (Baumeister, Ainsworth, & Vohs, 2016). There were several themes that came up repeatedly in different areas of study. These will be key clues to the essence of the self, going forward into future chapters:

- *Do your part.* Many group projects depend on total effort, but that is maximized if the individuals heed the pressure or responsibility to contribute their effort or other resources, for example, money. For example, any country has an advantage if its citizens willingly pay their taxes, as opposed to dodging and underpaying. Society can use the culpable individual self as a tool to increase and stabilize its revenue.

- *Moral responsibility.* The group functions better if the individual members understand their moral responsibility to act in ways they can justify to the group. Groups perform best if people are esteemed and respected for their prosocial actions. Likewise, groups benefit when individuals are dissuaded via punishment and ostracism from performing antisocial actions. People must know that what they do today will affect how others treat them in the future, perhaps for years to come. All of this will help motivate people to participate constructively in the social system. And when most people do that, the system helps society to flourish so that the group as a whole is better off. Moral reputation is such an important foundation of the self that the next chapter is devoted to it. It, too, extends across time.

  Moral responsibility is related to the first point, doing your part. The group can morally condemn individuals who fail to contribute their fair share.

- *Information agent.* Groups build up collective stocks of information. They share many understandings—the doxa, "that which goes without saying," of which there is a great deal. But individuals must operate in relation to this collective stock of information. Research found that groups who let people think and judge for themselves, collecting information from individual and different perspectives and then pooling it, performed best in the long run (e.g., Janis, 1972; Surowiecki, 2004). Ideally for the group, each individual self will collect information, share information with others, critique new information carefully, and help build the collective body of knowledge. The self is partly an information agent.

● *Specialized performance.* Breaking up the group task into parts and assigning different parts to different people, who become specialists, creates a huge advantage. (We saw this in the flute factory study, and the assembly line generally.) The self will be most helpful to the group if it can operate a specialized role in the system. Toward that end, it helps if people perform distinct, even unique roles in the group. Everyone can specialize and thereby become expert at his or her part of the group job—and because everything is done by experts, the total group achievement is improved. The downside is that one individual can accomplish nothing unless the others do their part.

To conclude: What matters is how you are different. Groups work by having people specialize in different things, and so different talents could, if matched to social roles, improve the efficiency of society. Individuals come to understand themselves based on what they have to offer the group in the way of unusual, positive capabilities.

More broadly, the lesson is that human brains evolved to capitalize on advanced social systems. These systems work best with differentiated selves. Societies with such selves have better, stronger social systems that enable them to wipe out the competition.

KEY POINTS

- Groups go bad when individuals' selves merge into the group.
- Groups flourish when they capitalize on different individual selves, individually accountable, responsible, and thinking for themselves.
- Groups need the individuated human self. The most effective groups capitalize on each person's unique talents and capabilities.
- Many people seek to define themselves with an emphasis on how they are different from others.
- What matters is how you are different. Groups work by having people specialize in different things so different talents, matched to social roles, improve the efficiency of society.

CHAPTER 9

Moral Reputation as a Foundation of Self

Morality is a centrally important aspect of the self. It took psychology a long time to get around to realizing this, but it's nevertheless true. Morality is a set of rules and criteria that define various actions as good or bad. The self is fundamentally a moral agent. One of the self's important jobs is to make behavioral choices while making sure that they stay in the morally defensible realm. Getting a reputation as selfish or dishonest will damage your social prospects, so it behooves you to heed those rules when choosing your actions. Morality is often most relevant when there are temptations to be selfish or impulsive, but one's reputation depends on resisting those. In those cases, it's important to have potential actions reviewed by the whole self before being executed. Morality thus helps the self achieve unity across time.

MORALITY AND COOPERATION

Simple notions of what is good or bad go back far in evolution; animals feel good when they do things that contribute to life (like eating and having sex) and feel bad when things jeopardize life (like danger, cold, hunger, poison). But morality defines good and bad in ways that go far beyond physical benefit to self and sometimes in ways that work against direct physical benefit.

Societies can be seen as vast systems of cooperation. By working together, people can achieve things that individuals cannot. Humans adopted morality to help the cooperative process. Indeed, the moral self begins with cooperation, as detailed in Tomasello's *Natural History of Morality* (2016).

Like many scholars, I had casually associated religion with morality. Many religions enforce moral codes. One day I had the chance to talk about the emergence of morality with a group of researchers who had just published a major work on it (Norenzayan et al., 2016). I asked them my burning question: Which came first, religion or morality? I wanted to ascertain which was derived from the other.

Their answer surprised me. They said religion and morality were both present in the earliest known societies—but they were separate. The historical change was thus not what I had thought, that either religion or morality gave birth to the other. Rather, the change was the two joining forces, with religion supplying a context and rationale for moral rules, and morality becoming a vital means of spiritual advancement.

This led me gradually to the view that religion and morality have psychologically quite different origins. Specifically, *religion was invented, whereas morality was discovered*. (If you believe there is one true religion, it can be exempted from this analysis—but my point still applies to all the others.) Invention means creating something new, while discovery means finding something that already exists. Religious views were invented to offer explanations of life's mysteries, such as how the universe began, and why various things happen. In contrast, moral principles were discovered as our ancestors parlayed their newly evolved capacity for cooperation into cooperative societies.

For present purposes, the key point is this: Morality is derived from what enables a social system to flourish so that its members have the resources to sustain and increase the population. Most of the Judeo-Christian Ten Commandments are moral rules that help social systems to function better. Imagine a society with the opposite rules, so people felt it morally obligatory to lie, cheat, steal, murder, and the rest. It would be a disaster.

Indeed, recent research has found broad similarities in moral rules across 60 different societies, scattered around the world (Curry et al., 2019). Reciprocate favors, obey commands from superiors, take care of your family, don't steal others' property, support the group, be fair in dividing resources, and similar rules—these were found essentially everywhere. Why are they the same everywhere? Because societies function better when people follow these rules. As the researchers noted, these rules promote cooperation, and societies are essentially large-scale exercises in mutual cooperation for the collective good.

All of this fits beautifully with the previous chapter's point that the human self evolved in order to make groups function better. The properties of the human self are based on what enables groups to flourish so that members can survive and reproduce. Morality is a prominent case. Groups do best when people support each other, obey authority, reciprocate favors, take care of their families, and so on. The moral dimension of the human self is based on what enables their groups to thrive.

Competition and cooperation have quite different histories (Tomasello, 2016, 2018). Most animals know some forms of competition, which goes back very far in evolution. But animals do not need much self-awareness for competition, and certainly not much morality. Cooperation, in contrast, is much more complex and creates evolutionary pressure for self-awareness. In other words, the brain's hardware has to be much more sophisticated to do cooperation than to do competition. Almost all social animals and many solitary ones have competition. But humans have gotten cooperation to work in ways none of the others can even imagine. Self-awareness is part of the reason.

Cooperation often requires trusting each other: each makes a sacrifice or effort, leaving oneself vulnerable to exploitation by the other. But once cooperation becomes a preferred strategy for survival, it becomes necessary to induce others to cooperate with you. If you betray people, soon you will have no cooperators, and you will be in trouble, even in danger of starving. In order to live in a cooperative social network, you need to be concerned about how others perceive you. You need to maintain a reputation for being trustworthy and reliable as a cooperator. That is, when tempted to eat all the fruit of the cooperative food-gathering expedition yourself, you need to stop your self from doing so. Knowing that there is a moral rule against selfishness isn't enough to make you do that. You stop yourself because you realize that selfish, greedy action will be bad for you in the long run, despite the immediate gain.

This crucial step forward to cooperation thus brings several more features of the self into play. The cooperative self needs public self-consciousness (knowing how one is perceived by others) and extension across time. It also has to be able to alter its behavior, to do what is best for the long run rather than taking immediate gain. To be sure, all these advances remain incomplete, even among humans. People sometimes fail to understand or to care about how others perceive them, and they do succumb to short-term gains at long-term cost. But they are far more successful at cooperating morally than other animals.

Most apes do not really cooperate, and so they have little or no sense of morality. Some researchers have tried to make a case that some monkeys have a rudimentary moral sense by highlighting cases in which monkeys protested when another monkey received a treat better than what they got. But these are ambiguous; they could just reflect violated expectations and frustration, as indeed follow-up studies have suggested (Tomasello, 2016). And even if they were able to think in terms of unfairness when things go against them, the other half of the moral sense is missing; they are not bothered by unfairness in their favor. Many people feel guilty when they receive rewards or good treatment better than what other, equally deserving people get (e.g., "survivor guilt"; Brockner et al., 1985; Lifton, 1967).

But if animals have any sense of fairness, it's only linked to how they can get more for themselves. It's a selfish idea of fairness, not a moral one. Most likely it's not even that.

An important precursor to a true moral sense is found in some apes, according to Tomasello. This occurs in connection with the other important cooperative activity they have: fighting. As he explains, two chimps may form an alliance to fight together, which enables them to take down bigger chimps for whom neither would be a match one-on-one. If such a fighting partnership forms, then each partner has a vested interest in the other's welfare. That's the big step forward toward morality because one cares about someone else. The chimp might even give some food to his partner, especially if the partner has been hurt and cannot take care of himself as well as normally. It's rare for an animal to give food to an unrelated other adult, but the chimp seems to understand that he will be worse off if his ally fails to recover.

Still, a huge difference between humans and other apes is the ability to work together and share the rewards. Remember, humans evolved to live in small groups. A modern big-city dweller can get away with cheating or betraying someone now and then, especially a stranger. But in a small group, people will remember what you did. Plus, crucially, you need somebody to cooperate with you and a small group offers only a few options. If your immoral actions result in several people being unwilling to cooperate with you anymore, you may soon run out of friends. Compounding the problem, humans talk and gossip, so a few selfish actions can turn off even people who were not directly affected. They know your reputation.

The moral self thus begins with reputation. It is not a private, inner sense of fairness or guilt or the Golden Rule. The pragmatic human animal realizes that its very survival depends on how it is viewed by others—with moral judgments based on past actions. You may want to eat today, but you also need to eat in the future; being selfish today could seriously cost you in the future. Above all, you need to connect with others and be accepted by them. Morality is the blueprint for how to act so they will accept you.

In modern society, the moral self is important in that it enables the system to function well. When people do their respective jobs and are honest and fair with each other, the system works very well for creating surplus resources. Everyone gets a share of the pie. When the pie is much bigger, the shares are bigger. Humans evolved to make groups function better, which means having a group system. Immoral behavior undermines the system and prevents it from creating more resources. For example, counterfeiting money weakens the ability of buyers and sellers to trust each other and can even distort the value of money (adding the counterfeit money means there is more money chasing the same amount of goods). Without trust, buyers and sellers fail to make the deals that would have benefited them both.

MORALITY RESTRAINS AND CONSTRAINS THE SELF

Morality introduces a different set of reasons to feel good and bad—indeed, some that compete with the basic motives to sustain life. Morality promotes actions that benefit the group, rather than the individual. A society cannot put a positive moral value on having members steal from each other because that would undercut the benefits that come from having property.

Crucially, moral rules often come at the expense of the self. To refrain from stealing food when one is hungry is costly to the self, in at least two ways. First, one does not get the food one needs. Second, the individual has to overcome the natural impulse to take food when one is hungry—so more psychological work is required in order to be good.

Morality, Reputation, and the Self

Undoubtedly, morality imposes costs. You can't do everything you want, or that might bring you benefits. Breaking the Ten Commandments may bring joy, as you steal desirable things, lie your way out of trouble, have sex with an exciting but off-limits partner. Then why do people behave morally? Is it merely from fear of punishment?

No. Behaving morally is a good strategy in the long run. It attracts others to cooperate with you. It gains you status in the group.

Morally virtuous behavior can raise your status in your social group. A series of experiments by Hardy and van Vugt (2006) confronted people with choices between benefiting themselves and benefiting the group. These are moral choices: Possibly the main social purpose of morality is to make people act so as to benefit the group, even at cost to short-term self-interest. In a lab game context, people were given money and could decide how much to keep for themselves and how much to invest for the group's benefit. Whatever they invested was doubled by the experimenter and divided equally among the three members of the group. Thus, the best for everyone was for everyone to invest all the money for the group, in which case everyone would receive a double payout. But if the others declined to invest, you'd be a sucker, enriching the other members while taking a loss yourself.

Altruism was found to improve a person's status in the group. That is, the people who did the most to help the group (invested the most money) ended up being regarded most favorably by others. They were also the people chosen first and foremost when people had to choose a partner for a subsequent cooperative game. Insofar as the purpose of the moral self is to get others to cooperate with you, it works.

Reputation was the key driver. After the first round, people were informed what everyone in the group had done. This made it clear that decisions were public knowledge and could influence reputation. Once people realized that others would know what they decided, they became much more virtuous and generous.

All of this confirms the view that morality supports cooperation by way of reputation. People know they need a good reputation in order to get others to cooperate with them. Behaving in a virtuous manner to help the group is a reliable path to getting that good reputation.

Morality is therefore important to the individual self because one is judged by society on the basis of these moral rules—and these judgments improve or reduce one's prospects. Much research has examined how people make moral judgments, usually by presenting them with a description of some action and asking whether the person's action was morally right or wrong. A powerful critique of this vast body of research said that in practice, morality is for judging people, not isolated actions (Uhlmann, Pizarro, & Diermeier, 2015). Yes, we judge specific actions and sometimes use those judgments to punish people for objectionable misdeeds. But the more basic and important use of moral judgment is to evaluate the *people* as good or bad, rather than just their specific actions. This is because pragmatically, what matters is predicting what the person will do in the future. Can that person be trusted? Should I undertake a joint venture with that person? Will that person cooperate at first and then screw me over? Pretty much everyone needs to find partners for joint ventures. That's who we are as a species. So everyone has to choose which potential partners are best. And moral reputation is a key basis for choosing.

Indeed, morality is central to how people form impressions of each other (Goodwin, Piazza, & Rozin, 2014). When people perceive and evaluate each other, they put great stock in moral traits. Any clear indication of good or bad moral character gets noticed every time and has a big effect on the overall impression, more so than other kinds of information.

What is important is not so much how the human being regards him- or herself, but rather how the person is regarded by others. First and foremost, human beings need to know how they are regarded by other people, and their mental powers are devoted to keeping track of that. This is not a passive process. They realize that they want others to regard them in particular ways (as morally trustworthy, honest, reliable, unselfish), and they bend their actions to promote that sort of desirable reputation. Thus, we have the beginnings of both an ideal self and an actual self-concept, all driven by the vital importance of knowing one's public self. You are free to think whatever you please about yourself, but what matters is what other people think of you. If you engage in flattering self-deception to convince yourself you are a paragon of virtue, but other people regard you as wicked, selfish, and untrustworthy, you might starve. Your shining, magnificent self-concept won't help. It is vital to know that and adjust your actions accordingly. If other people doubt your virtue, you need to be extra-careful. This fits what was said earlier: The most important inner concept of self is the desired reputation.

How much do people realize the importance of moral reputation? A fascinating study compared adult apes and human children (Engelmann et al., 2012). They were all given a temptation to perform a selfish, immoral act. Some did it, and some didn't. The experiment manipulated randomly whether there were other adults (of the same species) present. Human 5-year-old children adjusted their behavior accordingly: They behaved more virtuously when others were watching and more selfishly when alone. The nonhuman apes failed to make any adjustment. Their rates of selfishness were identical, regardless of whether someone else would see.

The difference between apes and humans reveals the differential recognition of the importance of moral reputation. By age 5, human children know that it really matters whether others see you as good or bad, and so they protect their good reputation by behaving extra-virtuously when others are present. The other apes either don't know or don't care. They do not change their behavior for the sake of a good moral reputation. *In this important respect, at least, human selfhood has leapt far ahead of what our nearest animal relatives have.*

Moral reputation thus integrates all three major aspects of the self, as the coming chapters will develop: the interpersonal, self-knowledge, and the executive self. The importance of reputation, the image of self in other people's minds, invokes the interpersonal aspect. The person's mental record keeping to update and maintain a conception of self (even if just focused on how one is regarded by others) invokes the self-knowledge aspect. And the periodic adjustment of behavior, including decision making and self-regulation, invokes the executive aspect.

My best guess is that human beings acquired morality to help them solve the problem of knowing how to act in a society that is based on cooperation. (After all, we have to explain not just where moral rules come from—but also why people elected to obey the rules once they knew them.) Think of the dilemma of the early human beings. Each one has begun to realize that its survival depends on attracting partners in cooperation, which in turn depends on how other people evaluate its past actions. Some may be furtively selfish anyhow, but to some extent they all recognize the need to sustain a positive moral reputation. But how? Morality furnishes a blueprint for how to act in order to have a good reputation (and on that basis to assure oneself of a steady stream of potential partners). It may seem paradoxical that humans evolved to follow rules that require them sometimes to act against their own immediate self-interest, such as by not taking food from a weaker person. Yet, these rules show the way to advance one's self-interested goals in the long run.

MORALITY AND TIME

A groundbreaking study of morality and time by Eugene Caruso (2010) began by pointing out that moral rules are generally assumed to remain constant. An act that was morally wrong yesterday will be morally wrong tomorrow, and to the same degree, assuming the circumstances have not changed. Yet, his work found that people condemned identical misdeeds more when set in the future than in the past.

In general, people seem to "moralize" the future. That is, they apply stricter moral rules to the future than the past or present and show greater moral concern. In various studies, thinking about the future made people condemn misdeeds by others more intensely, as opposed to thinking about the present. They even called for more severe punishment for themselves for future misdeeds than in the past. So it is not simply a matter of selfishly wanting everyone else to obey the rules and exempting oneself. People will make greater sacrifices for their reputation when focused on the future than the present (Vonasch & Sjåstad, 2020). People are even more virtuous and generous in their own actions, or at least they say they would be, when they are thinking about the future and the present (Sjåstad & Baumeister, 2019). That's because thinking about the future makes them worry about having a good reputation.

Morality is oriented toward the future, and a moral reputation is built for the future.

MORALITY IS ESSENTIAL TO THE SELF

Not only does morality take priority when people form impressions of others. Morality is widely seen as the essence of the self. The superior importance of morality was shown in a creative research program by the indomitable team of Nina Strohminger and Shaun Nichols (2014, 2015). They instructed people to perform various thought experiments, such as imagining that someone named Jim had a brain transplant, or was reincarnated. Afterward, the person was the same in some respects and different in others, and the researchers asked whether the new person "is still Jim." People were willing to see sameness of self despite loss of ability to recognize things, despite loss of desires, and despite even loss of his memories. But loss of his moral conscience made him no longer Jim. Across many such studies, morality stood out as the most central change. (Personality came in second.)

Memories were important, but only some memories—specifically, memories about important relationships and other experiences highly relevant to one's place in the world. People did not think someone losing their memory for how to do math problems, or how to play the piano or ride a bicycle, meant loss or change of self. These findings support the view that the self is about how one relates to society, rather than just storing any sort of useful information.

A provocative further study by the same team surveyed families of people who had brain disease, such as Alzheimer's and dementia. They asked crucial questions such as, "Do you feel you still know who the patient is?" and "Does the patient ever seem like a stranger to you?" Again, it was changes in morality that were seen as producing the biggest changes in the patient's identity. The families tended to regard the patients as still the same person despite memory loss, personality change, impaired speech, and increasing difficulty with moving the body. But moral changes—honesty, integrity, trustworthiness, generosity, loyalty, and the rest—caused the family members to say they did not know the patient anymore. In fact, as the disease slowly degraded the relationship between patient and family, it was moral changes that determined how much and how fast the relationship deteriorated.

Thus, morality is central to what makes you who you are. Other people, whether casual acquaintances or close relationship partners, will continue to think that you are yourself despite various changes to personality, memory, and abilities. But when your moral traits change, those people start to regard you as having changed into someone else.

Beyond Moral Reputation

As human societies evolved into social systems far beyond what other animals have, the role of the self expanded. Moral reputation is one crucial aspect of this newly expanded self. The self as moral agent has its roots in the requirements of culture as a large, organized system of cooperation. Moral reputation rewards people who cooperate fairly and punishes those who shirk or betray, and the need for a good reputation motivates people to behave in ways that enable the social system to flourish.

Moral reputation is, however, not the only motivator. Let's briefly note a few others. Societies have systems for getting work done, and so a reputation for competence matters. The self seeks to be competent at tasks, so as to appeal to others. Being competent is helpful, but being *regarded as* competent is also vital. Other people will want to cooperate with you all the more if you can be relied on to do things well. Indeed, respect is generally composed of both morality and competence.

Many societies have systems of economic exchange. Money is only about 3,000 years old (Weatherford, 1997), but barter and other forms of exchange are considerably older. The modern self has to be economically competent, at least in terms of understanding money, knowing how to get it, and spending it appropriately.

Societies also build up a shared body of knowledge. It includes a shared understanding of the physical environment and shared assumptions about social relations (e.g., how a family is formed and what its privileges are). It includes moral principles and values, often some sense of history, religion, and ways of doing things. The self must operate in relation to this information (Baumeister et al., 2018).

In short, participating in a human society requires the self to function in multiple ways. It has to be a moral agent to protect its good reputation. It has to be competent at some tasks (and be recognized as competent). It has to be an information agent and an economic agent. The human brain evolved to be able to manage all those tasks, and the self is a combination of those functions.

You can't get the benefits of human society without a self. That's the short answer to why we have selves.

KEY POINTS

- Morality is a set of rules and criteria that define various actions as good or bad.
- The moral dimension of the human self is based on what enables their groups to thrive.
- To live in a cooperative social network, you need to be concerned about how others perceive you. You need to maintain a reputation for being trustworthy and reliable as a cooperator.
- Morality supports cooperation by way of reputation. A moral reputation is built for the future.
- Possibly the main social purpose of morality is to make people act to benefit the group, even at a cost to short-term self-interest.

CHAPTER 10

The Unity Project

The Unfinished Business of Stitching the Self Together

How many molecules in the body of a newborn baby are still part of the body of the 70-year-old man into whom the baby has grown? Certainly not very many and quite possible none, like the ship of Theseus from Chapter 1, where every piece of the ship, has been changed. There seems no plausible basis in physical reality for saying that the 7-pound baby and the 200-pound old man are the same person. Yet socially and culturally, the two are inextricably linked. Whenever the 70-year-old fills out government forms, he states where *he* was born (as that baby). Society officially recognizes him as the same person, notwithstanding the wholesale gradual replacement of all his molecules. The molecules come and go. The meaningful organization endures even while the physical substance is replaced. The new molecules just continue doing the same jobs in the system that the old (departed) ones did.

The ancient Greek parable, the ship of Theseus, is a useful metaphor for understanding one of the core issues of the self: the problem of unity. The self means being a single entity, a unity. The very idea of multiple selves contradicts the essence of selfhood as discussed in Chapter 4. Indeed, life maintains a strict boundary between self and world. Biological unity is the forerunner and *foundation* of selfhood.

TWO KINDS OF UNITY OF SELF

There are two main kinds of unity, and they have quite different bases and processes (Gallagher, 2000). The first and simpler one is the unity in the present moment. We can call it right-now unity of the right-now self. This has its roots in the essence of life. To be alive means in part to define a boundary between self and environment. When the experiencing brain begins to work with this fact, it creates experience and guides action as a unity. Pain is not experienced as a fragment—*au contraire*, the whole self is aware of pain and responds to it. Yes, the pain is felt specifically in the knee or back, for example—but the whole self is aware of the pain and reacts. If you step barefoot on a hot coal or hill of fire ants, the pain is in your foot but your whole body takes action. The unity of self in the moment emerged far back in evolution and is probably why we have a central nervous system in the first place. The nervous system brings information to the brain and carries its commands to the moving parts. Very early in evolution, living things adapted to the usefulness of operating as a unity in the present moment.

Return to the ship of Theseus. All during its journey, it clearly had right-now unity. A ship out on the sea acts as a single thing and system. When it moves, it moves as a unit. Sinking means the destruction of the entire ship, though it may come apart so not all parts sink together. But it's the end of the entire ship.

The second kind of unity extends across time, and that's where the ship of Theseus poses its challenge. Not only are you one being, one person in the present moment—you will be the same person tomorrow and in 30 years, and you were the same person many years ago, even though some of your attributes, attainments, and reputational aspects will have changed. Social identity is always a work in progress, at least until death. Even after that it remains forever incomplete.

Most animals have right-now self to some degree. In contrast, the unity of self across time is something that other animals do not much need. Why then do humans need it? It is a requirement of the more effective cultural systems. What you do today, in terms of morality and achievement, affects how people (and society generally) will treat you tomorrow, and possibly for years to come. The college degree you collect at age 22 is still on your résumé when you are 50. It may show up in your obituary. The social system functions better if people have long-term consequences for the good and bad things they do. When people understand that telling a lie today to help them avoid punishment or get some reward could lead to long-term problems, like still being regarded as a liar 20 years from now, they avoid lying. And societies function better with honesty rather than pervasive lying.

The unity of self across time is a project that people must work to create, unlike the unity in the present. The unity of self across time is vital for human culture, but that very fact entails that it moves beyond nature. Evolution furnished the hardware, but much of the content (software) is gained from culture. A unity of self across a lifetime is not an issue for nature.

If you say something today that contradicts what you said 10 years ago, nature just shrugs. It's very hard to imagine any gorilla or hyena or insect caring a whit about being consistent with something it did or expressed a decade earlier, or even a week earlier. Survival and reproduction are negotiated in the present, and comfort, too. If it serves your interests to change your abstract opinions, nature probably doesn't see any problem. The adaptive course is obvious: do what's best right now. *Objections to inconsistency are cultural, not natural.*

The unity of self across time is not a given. It needs to be created and sustained. To appreciate it, let's step back and again consider the simpler, right-now kind of self.

Right-Now Unity

The unity of self starts with unity in the present moment. The self acts as a single entity, an *individual*, and it tends to feel as one also. As we have seen, unity in the present moment is part of the essence of life, starting with the very simplest one-celled organisms maintaining a boundary between self and environment.

The folks who advocate multiple selves are generally speaking about unity across time. As Lester (2015) said, people feel different on different days, and they act differently in different situations. That could mean that in each moment, the person still feels and acts like a unity, albeit a different unity on different occasions. But presumably, the psychological makings of these different selves are all there inside the person all the time. Hence, unity in the present could be a problem, too. How does the body decide which of the various versions of self gets to dictate how it acts?

Here is where the brain and central nervous system come into play, and even consciousness. I have rejected the idea of multiple selves, but there is no disputing the fact of inner conflict. Diverse impulses and inputs can compete for precedence. Torn between going home and going to the store (or church vs. brothel, in the classic hypothetical dilemma), there is no compromise that involves having one foot walk home and the other to the store. The inner conflict is settled internally, and a single winner is chosen, and then both feet walk to the same place.

Autonomy means self-government. Living things are all somewhat autonomous, but humans remain dependent on parents for many years, so full autonomy is not realized until adolescence or adulthood. As emphasized by Ryan and Deci in their magnum opus *Self-Determination* (2017), autonomy means acting as a whole person, as opposed to acting on just one impulse. Indeed, one influential theory of consciousness holds that its primary function is to get the whole self involved (e.g., Baars, 1997; Humphrey, 1986). That is, the mind contains much information and many desires, scattered in many different locations. Having a conscious thought is akin to putting the idea up on the big screen, for all of one's mind and memory to see, so that it activates associations to all these different thoughts. A person might see some exquisite dessert on offer and have an impulse to eat it. Many animals would just go for it. But the human mind can hold the thought in consciousness for a moment, whereupon other thoughts are activated, such as one's resolve to lose weight by eating less, or health warnings, or the fact that the food belongs to someone else, or even just that one should not spoil one's appetite for dinner. The resolution of the inner conflict is not that part of the self eats and part abstains. Rather, the self acts as a unity, having resolved the competing impulses. This sort of process helps sustain unity in the moment. Self eats, or it doesn't, though a human mind might integrate both impulses by resolving to have only a few bites. (We know how that turns out.)

Remember, underneath the veneer of civilization, humans are also animals. Animals learn without much self. They learn simple associations between stimulus and response. The animal mind, and by extension also the human mind, has stored many of these associations: When X happens, so does Y. The rat in the Skinner box learns: When the light is on, press the bar and watch for the food treat to drop. When the light is off, don't bother. But the rat does not have to integrate a wealth of social considerations into that decision, such as moral rules, economic calculations, long-term plans, promises and commitments, symbolic implications. All of these are part of the human self, and so to act as a unity, the human self should give consideration to all of them.

Unity across Time

The term *free will* is controversial, mainly because people define it in different ways and therefore argue past each other. As usual, though, there are genuine and important phenomena associated with the notion. Making a choice deliberately, with input from the full self, is an important aspect of this. Free will is understood here not as random action but rather as *responsible autonomy*: choosing how to act based on inner processes that allow the full self to be involved (Baumeister & Monroe, 2014). One decides and acts as a unity, a self.

To illustrate, consider the difference between an impulsive crime and a carefully planned one. The impulsive criminal did break the law but did so on the spur of the moment, while overcome by anger. He did not stop to consider the consequences and implications. Many murders are like this. The part of the self that considers the future failed to contribute to the action. The right-now self was angry and lashed out, and that was that. Although this is definitely a crime and deserving of punishment, many judges and juries impose lesser sentences on such impulsive murders than on other killings that are carefully planned in advance. The advance

planner was already thinking about the future and had ample opportunity
to consider how his future life would be affected—but he went ahead and
killed anyway. There is thus more free will in the premeditated crime than
in the spontaneous one.

One of the lively debates in current social psychology is whether everyone is prejudiced. People's expressions of racial (and other) prejudice have
dwindled precipitously over the last half century. Some researchers have
suspected, however, that people secretly harbor prejudices and have simply
stopped admitting to them. Some psychologists developed the Implicit Attitudes Test (IAT), which is hard to fake because it just looks at reaction time
differences pairing good and bad with different races (Greenwald & Banaji,
1995; Greenwald et al., 1998). By this measure, the vast majority of Americans of all races show a bias, suggesting negative unconscious attitudes
toward Black people. However, the IAT has not had much success predicting actual discrimination; it is mostly useless for predicting bad behavior.

The unity of self explains the discrepancy between unconscious prejudice on the IAT and actual behavior. People have associations, but they do
not act on them. (Indeed, some scholars have concluded that the IAT measures media portrayals, not personal antagonism.) Devine's (1989) work
on the difference between prejudiced and nonprejudiced people found that
pretty much everyone is familiar with the stereotypes and thinks of them
in relevant situations. The difference lies in whether one puts these into
practice or refuses to do so. Living in America today, watching television,
and so forth, it is hard to avoid having an association that connects Black
men to crime and danger. That link is in everyone's mind. But the modern
citizen acts as a whole self, and one does not have to use that association as
a basis for discriminating against specific Black people in work and social
life.

There is a wide gap between having stereotyped or prejudicial thoughts
in one's mind and embracing them, let alone acting on them. One part of
the big brain generates some thoughts and thrusts them into the stream
of consciousness. Another part of the brain is constructing the unity, and
it considers but rejects those thoughts. The unity project operates amid
a complex brain and mind with plenty of thoughts and feelings, some of
which contradict each other. The need to maintain a coherent identity in
society prompts the brain to attend to consistency, so as to act as a unity, an
individual character in a coherent ongoing story of one's life.

Three-quarters of a century ago, the philosopher Jean-Paul Sartre
(1953) used the idea of integration in his theory of existential psychoanalysis. One of his examples, probably more suited to his time than ours, was
of a woman letting herself be seduced into sex, during which she fails to
integrate certain meanings into her experience. When a man compliments
a woman on her dress, he does not mean it the same as if he saw the dress
hanging on a rack in a store. Rather, he is probably noticing how her body

looks in the dress. But the woman might skip over that aspect and react as if he is merely praising her taste in fabric and design. By not acknowledging the sexual undertone, and by responding as if his compliment had nothing to do with her body, she can avoid recognizing herself as someone cooperating in a sexual episode.

Thus, even the unity of self in the present moment can be a partial or incomplete fact—especially for humans, whose right-now self has to work with multiple layers of meaning. Unity in the moment may be an achievement rather than a given, at least for complicated human beings.

QUITTING ADDICTION:
ONE CHALLENGE TO UNITY OF SELF

The self's unity project can be seen among people who struggle to quit addictions. The addict's body has discovered an important source of pleasure (the drug) and wants it frequently. In Harry Frankfurt's (1971) famous formulation of second-order desires, the addict wants the drug but also wants to *not* want it. Or, to put it slightly differently, the addict wants to use the drug but later will want to *not* have used it. Pleasure now, sorry later. Thus, both unity in the moment and unity across time are challenged, by conflicting desires.

A popular theory has analyzed addiction as a disease of free will (Volkow, 2015). Many people and a few experts think addiction involves some loss of free will. Yet, the evidence for that is peculiar. Hardly anyone disputes that most people who smoke many cigarettes every day are addicted, but society still assumes they have free will. As one colleague remarked, many signs proclaim, "No smoking" but not "No smoking unless addicted." After all, if one lacked free will, one would be powerless to resist the urge to smoke. In that case, it would be unfair to punish them for smoking because they couldn't help it. Apparently, though, smokers are quite capable of resisting the urge to smoke. Even just based on a sign on the wall.

My own extensive reading of the research led to the conclusion that cigarette addicts retain full control over their actions, as in how to move their hands and feet—but they lose control over their desires (Baumeister, 2017). They cannot help having many desires to smoke, each of which they can resist. But the resistance takes its toll. Someone who quits smoking may wish for a cigarette dozens of times a day and have to resist all those temptations. The frequent resistance gradually depletes their willpower, in that sense reducing their capacity for free action. Hence, the moment of weakness, and the relapse.

Instead, the case for loss of free will is made not in regard to unity in the present but rather unity across time (e.g., Ainslie, 2001). Many smokers resolve to quit but fail. To be more precise, most of them do quit for a period of time—but later they resume smoking. Still, does that argue against free will? If free will means anything, it surely means that you can change your mind. The smoker decided to quit, then decided to smoke again, and then regretted the latter choice. A person with totally free will could certainly do that.

Unity across time is the problem for the addict who wants to quit. On the occasion of quitting, typically, he or she is firmly resolved. *Never again!* But then on other occasions the person feels differently, misses the pleasures and in some cases the activity of imbibing. Even deciding to quit may invoke a problem of unity across time. As Ainslie (2001) pointed out, even for the smoker who worries seriously about the long-term health risks, it is always rational to have one more cigarette. One more won't kill you, and meanwhile it will provide the familiar and welcome pleasure. One more cigarette means a definite, clear gain and a miniscule risk. It is only the accumulation across time of a great many of those small, rational decisions that leads to the destructive results: cancer, emphysema, impotence, and the rest.

The same problem of unity of self is found in many other behaviors. Dieters want to eat the tempting food but will later want not to have eaten it. Many people want to spend money on current pleasures but also later wish they had saved their money. Gamblers love the thrill of gambling but regret their financial ruin. As one couple memorably explained to their therapist, "Gambling is not our problem. We enjoy gambling—both of us do. Our problem is this $100,000 debt" ("Look Out, Vegas," 2000, p. 31).

To quit addiction, it is usually necessary to push harder so as to forge a unity of self across time. The smoker (or dieter or would-be saver) has to treat the present moment as if it will be the same choice he or she makes every time. Yes, one more cigarette won't kill you, and one small dish of ice cream will not make you fat. But you have to make each decision as if it sets the pattern for all future choices.

This is essentially the psychological version of Immanuel Kant's (1797/1967) "categorical imperative" formula for moral action. He said, to know what is morally right to do, you must act as if your action would set the universal principle for how everyone would always act in similar situations. To quit addiction, or to succeed at your diet or exercise program, you should act each time as if your action were the basis for how you would always act. The present action should embody the self as it will be henceforth. That's one of the most effective ways that the self forges unity across time.

To forge that unity of self, the mind connects the present moment to many other moments in past and future. What the body does in the present moment is organized by a meaningful, intentional pattern that connects across time. Even with the best of intentions, abstaining from one cigarette once doesn't do you any good. Success requires that you make the same decision on many occasions. The self in each such moment has to acknowledge its connection to the other occasions and consistently stick with abstinence. That's unity across time.

SOCIETY WANTS A SELF WITH CONTINUITY

Unity across time is thus cultural, not natural. It's cultural, as Chapter 8 emphasized, because the human self took its shape so as to be suitable for effective social systems.

Social systems are more effective when selves are consistent and continuous over time. There are multiple aspects to this. Moral and (later) legal culpability mean that people can be punished for things they did in the past. As a result, they have to behave better in the present so as to avoid punishment in the future. When everyone behaves better, the society flourishes more. Economic systems likewise depend on continuity of self. Trade and economic activity have greatly increased wealth. That means increasing the resources and quality of life for individuals. But it all depends on continuous selfhood. Ownership also enables individuals to store up tools and other resources, and in modern life money and housing, to provide for their own future.

Performing a role in a social group also benefits from continuity of self across time. If people perform the same role over and over, they can become more skilled at it. Because this is true for many different roles, many tasks are done by specialists and experts. Even in the present moment, there are some advantages from division of labor. But these advantages are multiplied across time.

Plenty of animals mate and raise children, but the continuity of the human self across time has improved even that basic, natural process. Male apes hardly ever provide food for their offspring or for the mother of their offspring. By forming long-term attachments in which the male performs a provider role, humankind has been able to raise multiple children who remain dependent for a much longer time than other young apes. The long dependency may seem like a disadvantage, but it allows more time for the large brain to develop and for the youngster to be socialized into the knowledge and practices of the group.

A self that combines responsibility and autonomy is powerful and most beneficial to a social system. The self must knowingly perform its roles in society, without being directly compelled by others (autonomy), so the system can function to produce more resources. And people must understand and accept the future consequences of their actions. Society holds people responsible for their good and bad deeds, and people understand this—and that understanding greatly increases the proportion of good deeds, acts that help the system to thrive (responsibility).

My friend Bill von Hippel has captivated many audiences with a moving tale gleaned from the great Jane Goodall's observations of chimpanzees in the African wild (and covered in his 2018 book *The Social Leap*). It is an example of some of the earliest forms of social cooperation, especially among females. One young chimp mother, whom Goodall had named Melissa, was sitting with her little baby. Two other adult females in the group, a mother–daughter pair, approached Melissa and her baby. The older one pulled Melissa down and held her to the ground, viciously biting her face and hands, while the younger one tried to grab the baby away. Melissa fought back but had little chance, given two against one, and with only one hand available for fighting. Badly beaten up and bleeding from multiple wounds, she eventually let go. The other two took the baby away and ate it, while Melissa watched.

Remarkably, Melissa quickly reconciled with the other two females. Within an hour she was seen holding hands with one of them, even while the other was still devouring the scraps of the baby, and while Melissa was still bleeding from the fight. Soon, the daily life in the group of chimps went back to normal (albeit minus the baby).

It is possible to admire Melissa as a paragon of forgiveness, though as my iconoclastic colleague Jim McNulty (2011) has shown, granting forgiveness to partners who are mean or abusive tends to increase their bad behavior. Sure enough, the pair of females repeated this sort of behavior over the months so that this particular group of chimps lacked a younger generation. Nor is this a unique pattern. Michael Tomasello's (2016) book on the evolution of morality reports that social connections among adult female apes are largely limited to this sort of temporary female bonding to kill another female's baby. Groups of humans whose women killed each other's young like that would have had trouble competing with other groups. Goodall realized that the tribe of chimps she was observing would not have a future. That mother–daughter pair was eating all the babies.

Melissa's response seems to reflect a totally present-oriented pattern. The baby was no longer part of the group, but the two females who killed it were, and she had to get along with them. She did not think of retaliating in the future for the past crime, nor even of allying with other mothers to prevent future, similar atrocities.

What enabled humans to break free of this seemingly natural pattern of female aggression? Melissa the chimp seems not to have held a grudge. By definition, grudges forge unity across time, connecting present anger and future retribution to past offense. Unlike apes, humans hold grudges. At some point the bereaved mothers would join together to avenge their dead babies and prevent further incidents like that. Killing someone else's only child would be a crime that would stain the killer's reputation for a long time and make lasting enemies. Human responsibility extends across time. Moreover, cooperating to plot revenge in the future seems beyond the mental powers of chimps, much unlike human beings.

Thus, the human self connects past, present, and future in far more elaborate ways than other animals—and for good reason. Grudges and forgiveness are uniquely human concerns, precisely because the human self extends across time. Holding a grudge versus forgiving is a choice that rests on an ongoing self, both past and present and usually future, too. Animal selves don't have that dimension.

UNITY OF SELF REMAINS INCOMPLETE

The self comes to exist as the brain learns to operate a role in the social system. In the process, it learns that today's actions have consequences in the near and even the distant future. It should therefore choose actions in the present moment with some consideration of what the consequences and implications will be for the future self. Will what I do today matter for what happens to me in 3 years? Or 30?

People differ as to how future-oriented they are. As an obvious example, some people spend their money as fast as it comes in, but others save. Saving money sacrifices the present self for the future. Note that in our evolutionary history, there was little opportunity to save. Hunter-gatherers possessed few objects, such as clothing and tools, and their main resources—the food obtained by hunting and gathering—could not be preserved. When cultures began to use money, this extended the self into the future (and somewhat into the past) because money earned today could be used to get something one would want in the future, whenever that might become important. Modern citizens save for their retirement, thereby connecting their selves across many decades.

Here, however, is the crucial point: The self's integration into unity across time is purely a conceptual fact, not a physical one—and it remains incomplete. No life achieves perfect integration, perfect consistency.

In fact, social psychology in its formative years during the mid-20th century devoted considerable effort to understanding people's strivings for consistency (e.g., Festinger, 1957). The aspect of unity across time was not discussed very explicitly, but it did underlie the main theories. The assumption was that the person held the same values and attitudes and beliefs across time. If at one point in time the person did something that was inconsistent with those values, it created a problem for later.

For social psychology's first couple of decades, the desire for consistency was assumed to be something wholly inside the person. Theorists simply posited that the human mind came equipped with an urge toward consistency. The idea was, people became distraught at catching themselves in inconsistencies, so they sought to resolve these. If they had done something that went against their beliefs, such as describing an experimental procedure as fascinating when in fact they had found it boring, they resolved this by revising their opinion. Maybe it was not so boring after all, they told themselves (Festinger & Carlsmith, 1959).

But why would people care about consistency? After all, our animal relatives don't seem to have compunctions about consistency. Why did this one weird species of almost hairless apes suddenly become concerned with being consistent across time?

Society benefits from consistency—so society encourages consistency. Society can thrive better if people are consistent. Lab studies found that people were much more concerned about consistency when others were watching than when alone. If the inconsistent behavior was known to others, then people changed their attitudes to fit what they had done, so as to be consistent. If they performed the same behavior in a confidential manner that no one else would know, then they did not bother to revise their opinions to improve consistency (Baumeister & Tice, 1984; Schlenker, 1980; Tedeschi et al., 1971; for a review, see Baumeister, 1982). Moreover, the inconsistency did not bother people if it had been forced by external circumstances, but if it was seen as reflecting their personal (individual) free choice, then it did motivate change (Linder, Cooper, & Jones, 1967).

The implication is highly relevant. *Consistency across time is something that society expects,* not an inner craving of the individual mind independent of whoever might be watching. People strive to create a consistent *public* identity. There is no reason for a biological organism to care a whit about a logically or philosophically elegant issue such as abstract consistency—except that other members of the cultural society care about it. A good man is expected to keep his promises and maintain his commitments even when he is tempted to do otherwise, but no dog or bear or bug is even capable of such principled sacrifice. And the human expectation arises mainly because social systems function better, and produce more rewards to benefit their members, when individuals are consistent.

Moreover, the project of creating a consistent self across time remains incomplete. Unity across time is a conceptual achievement, not a physical fact. It is made out of meaning, not of physical forces acting on inanimate matter. That was the point of the ship of Theseus's story.

The multiple impulses for how to act should only be enacted if they are consistent with the identity the person seeks to establish across time. Some responses may seem appealing in the moment—to tell your boss what you really think, or to climb into bed with the wrong person—but for best results in the long run, they should be resisted. The project of creating a self that has continuity (unity across time) dictates that only some of these impulses should be enacted. The others should not be embraced by the self as actions consistent with the single, unified self.

Nowhere is this more apparent than morality. Moral reputations extend across time, indeed fairly long time frames, and for good reason. Moral inconsistencies create serious problems for individuals and have done so dating back to our evolutionary history.

Another revealing version of incomplete unity occurs when people must conceal some aspect of themselves. Sedlovskaya and colleagues (2013) called this "internalizing the closet," adapting the term (*closet*) associated with homosexuals who dared not reveal their sexual orientation for fear of severe reprisals from a highly intolerant society. They write, "A double life may lead to a divided self" (p. 695). A broad variety of people fall into the category of needing to conceal some important aspect of themselves, including people whose sexual desires stray into forms disapproved by their society, people whose religious or political beliefs clash with what their social groups enforce, and people who may have some social or legal status that they must conceal (e.g., criminal history, illegal immigrant status, record of mental illness). Sedlovskaya's research showed that people who conceal something about themselves have a clearer sense of divided identity. For example, gay men can classify attributes quickly as to whether the attributes fit them at work or at home—they conceal their homosexuality at work but not at home, and as a result they maintain two different concepts of self.

Having a divided self was not a good thing, though it may prevent worse things, such as being found out, persecuted, and prosecuted. The people who concealed their stigma, and therefore maintained a stout separation between public and private versions of self, were prone to depression and other forms of distress. As usual, maintaining a divided self is costly and stressful. A divided self is an unhappy, dysfunctional self. Unity is better. But unity remains inevitably incomplete. It is a continuum. The better your brain integrates your self across time, the happier and better adjusted you are.

There is an additional point here. The evidence in Chapter 5 linking belief in multiple selves and distress (as Lester, 2015, presented) was correlational, so it's hard to know what causes what. It could be that people suffering from psychopathology and mental illness are responsible for the correlation—such people are both prone to unhappiness and to experiencing a divided self. In contrast, the stigma problem studied by Sedlovskaya does not derive so much from an inner pathology as from living in a disapproving society. That means a divided self is not just a symptom of problems but a *cause* of them.

KEY POINTS

- There are two kinds of unity of self: right-now unity and unity across time.
- Social roles require not only unity in the moment but also across time, such as moral accountability.
- Being consistent across time is something society expects, not something the brain evolved to care about. People who fail to achieve this unity across time suffer consequences in society.
- Thinking before acting enables the whole self to own or disown the possible action. The brain knows its actions today will have consequences tomorrow and years hence.
- The unity of self over time typically remains incomplete. Human selves are forged from many parts, and they do not always mesh very well or easily.

PART THREE

KNOW THYSELF

CHAPTER 11

Self-Awareness

Part Three focuses on the three main aspects of the self. These are based on three fundamental experiences of selfhood. The first one is self-knowledge. It invokes the fact that human consciousness can turn toward its source and become aware of, and construct elaborate banks of information, about itself. Part Four features the executive self that exerts control, changes itself, and guides action. Part Five is devoted to the interpersonal aspect of self.

Many years ago I read about a company that was struggling with complaints from its own staff. It seems the elevator was slow, and people on the higher floors were grumpy about the long waits. The top brass wanted their employees to be happy, but this is a tough problem to fix. There is no way to speed up elevators, nor can new ones be installed in an existing building without enormous cost. But someone came up with a creative solution that reduced the complaints substantially: floor-to-ceiling mirrors were installed in the elevator waiting area. Instead of standing around annoyed, people could look at themselves, check their clothing and grooming, make minor adjustments, or even just enjoy the image of how good they looked. Apparently, focusing on oneself can be an effective antidote to impatient boredom.

Does a self have to be aware of itself? Perhaps not. But a self-aware self can function better than a self that lacks self-awareness. To understand the self, it will be important to understand the advantages and mechanisms of self-awareness.

People are aware of themselves. But the contrast between human self-awareness and that of other creatures is remarkable. The question of animal self-awareness has been debated over the years. For the most part, the answer seems to be that animals have little or no self-awareness. A few of them do pass some simple tests. These few show scattered, preliminary signs of self-awareness. Most animals don't even get that far.

The best data come from the so-called rouge test, which is a way of assessing whether an animal knows that its image in a mirror is of itself. The lab test works like this. The researcher sneakily dabs a bit of red makeup (rouge) onto the animal's forehead and then lets the subject wander around until it sees a mirror. Does it then reach up to touch its own forehead, thereby showing that it knows that the mirror image of the red-foreheaded animal is of itself? A very small human baby can tell that something is amiss with the image, but typically it reaches out toward the mirror. By the second birthday, however, the human child will react to the mirror image with visible surprise and consternation, reaching up to touch his or her own forehead (Amsterdam, 1972; Bard et al., 2006).

Researcher Gordon Gallup (1970, 1982) created a big splash by showing that some of the great apes can pass this test: they touched their own foreheads rather than the mirror. But only some of them did this. Only the smartest of the great apes, such as chimps and orangutans, ever pass this test. And not even all of them pass it, so it's limited to the smarter individuals among even those species (Suddendorf & Collier-Baker, 2009; Swartz et al., 1999). Most gorillas do not pass it, though Koko (of psychology fame) did. The chimpanzees and orangutans need time to get used to the mirror and figure out that it's a reflection of self. In contrast, all humans do, and they do it while still very young. Thus, even on this very simple test of self-awareness, humans are far ahead of all other primates. Five-year-old humans seem to have more consistent self-awareness than fully grown-up apes.

An intriguing theory about the origins of self-awareness in animals was put forward by Povinelli and Cant (1995). They noted that the so-called great apes (including humans) evolved to live in trees yet were rather large. This creates practical problems: a big, heavy animal wants to live high above the ground, possibly standing on weak or thin branches. The ape could see a branch within reach—but what if the ape grabbed the branch and broke it off, sending itself plummeting downward to a dangerous injury or death? So Povinelli and Cant thought the beginnings of self-awareness involved having some understanding, some self-concept, of one's own body and how heavy it was—all for the sake of judging whether it is too heavy to swing to that branch.

I have told this theory to various other psychologists, and in general they immediately rejected it. They were confident that the origins of self-awareness must lie in social life. Povinelli and Cant must have encountered this objection, too, and they readily acknowledged that social life creates many more demands and opportunities for self-awareness. But as they point out, there are diverse kinds of social animals, most of whom show no sign of self-awareness. Social life alone is not enough. It may well be that self-awareness first evolved to help solve the problem of heavy bodies dealing with uncertain tree branches—and then self-awareness began to pay off in social life and so became co-opted to serve complex social demands. I think that's the best guess based on what we know now.

THE EFFECTS OF MIRRORS

Social psychologists have used mirrors to study self-awareness in ways far beyond just checking whether people can recognize themselves. Mirrors provide a cue that stimulates self-awareness. Early experiments by Shelley Duval and Robert Wicklund (1972; Wicklund, 1975; Wicklund & Duval, 1971) had college students perform a standard task, the same for everyone. By flip of coin, half the students did these tasks in front of a mirror (its presence was briefly explained as something left over in the lab for another experiment and thus ostensibly irrelevant). The other half did the tasks with no mirror. The coin flip is a standard part of designing good experiments. Every human being is unique, so one can never draw a strong conclusion from a single person's action. If the researcher randomly assigns people into the different treatment conditions, however, the differences average out pretty fast, so the two groups end up being similar in all key respects even though the individuals are all different and unique.

The students acted differently when the mirror was present versus absent. Some of the main findings about the effects of sitting in front of a mirror were these (see also Carver & Scheier, 1981):

- *Effort.* They worked harder. They got more done.
- *Virtue.* The moral quality of their actions improved. Behavior came more in line with their values or with whatever moral values had been made salient. They cheated less, stole less. In short, they were better people when the mirror was present. The mirror put a damper on immoral acts.
- *(Non)Aggression.* They were less aggressive, unless aggression was presented in a positive light (such as if the research assistant wore a karate club jacket.) This mostly goes along with virtuous action. The mirror makes people want to be good, and that includes refraining from physically assaulting other people, which is generally reprehensible unless done in service of a worthy cause, like protecting children.
- *Consistency.* They were more consistent across time. Their descriptions of themselves fit better with objective behavior. That is, they answered questions less in line with wishful thinking and more in line with the way they actually were (Pryor et al., 1977). If they were caught being inconsistent, those facing a mirror changed their attitudes more to make themselves consistent.
- *Emotion.* They felt their emotions more intensely.

SELF-EVALUATION

The early researchers had proposed that being aware of yourself was essentially the same kind of awareness that one used for seeing the external world—merely pointed in a different direction. Inward rather than outward, as it were. But the accumulation of findings indicated that self-awareness was different, special, more *evaluative*. I can be aware of a plant or a table without immediately comparing it to some kind of ideal. But to be aware of myself is almost always to consider how I measure up. When people look in the mirror, they don't just think, oh, there I am, hmm. Rather, they wonder: Is my hair a mess? Do I look good today? Does this shirt look right on me? What will other people think when they see me?

In a word, self-awareness almost always involves *standards*. Standards are ideas about how one should or shouldn't be, such as moral rules, goals, role or job demands, norms, fads (which are temporary norms), sports records or qualifying cutoffs, and laws. These may be personal or social or moral ideals. They may be other people's expectations. They may be how I have been in the past or aspire to be in the future. Regardless, self-awareness is less about oh-there-I-am and more about how-do-I-measure-up? It compares how you are with how you should or could be.

Comparing to standards is part of the reason that people behave better when they are self-aware. This idea continues to spread. It has been used to explain why religious people tend to be better behaved than other people. As Norenzayan (2013) explains, "Watched people are nice people." Religious people often think their god is watching them and judging them all day long, and so they had better be good.

One might object to the idea that religious self-awareness promotes good action. After all, what about religious persecution? What about religious terrorists? But the idea that morality means being good toward all humankind is a recent notion and not universally accepted. Morality appears to have evolved to promote good treatment of members of one's own group. Our hunter-gatherer ancestors managed to share, cooperate, and help each other in diverse ways, while still being ruthlessly violent toward outsiders. Indeed, Norenzayan's book *Big Gods* (2013) emphasizes that the transition from early religion, with plenty of different gods, into the more modern, monotheistic pattern having a single god for everyone, helped enable people to trust and cooperate with people other than their immediate relatives. This was partly because the common idea of "god the father" (or sometimes mother) meant that you and I are in a sense family and should treat each other as such, even if we had very different parents.

Self-awareness helps explain why people misbehave more when they wear costumes. In a memorable demonstration (Beaman et al., 1979; see also Diener et al., 1976), Halloween trick-or-treaters were told to take only one piece of candy but were left alone with the opportunity to take more.

They all wore costumes and masks, but for half of them, the host asked each child's name and where the child lived. The children who had identified themselves and who saw their reflection in a mirror while taking their candy obeyed the instructions about taking only one candy. In contrast, children helped themselves to more when there was no mirror or when they did not first state their name. Indeed, among the oldest children (past age 13), the majority of them stole extra candy when there was no mirror, as compared to none when the mirror was there. Among young children, self-awareness is less developed and less evaluative, so the mirror had little or no effect. In other studies, children stole more when anonymous, when someone else had been designated as responsible, and when they were part of a group instead of alone. The presence of any adult reduced stealing: Watched people are nice people, at least watched by adults!

Likewise, the link between self-awareness and standards helps explain many of the effects of alcohol. Even small doses of alcohol reduce self-awareness, as shown in a fine program of research by Jay Hull and his colleagues (1981). Slightly inebriated people are less self-aware than others, as indicated even by markers such as how often they use first-person pronouns such as "I" and "me" when speaking. Alcohol, of course, has been linked to all manner of misbehavior. Intoxicated people are more aggressive than others, getting into fights and arguments. They say and do things without reflecting. Alcohol is also well known to contribute to sexual misbehavior, or failing to take precautions against pregnancy and disease.

In fact, one study showed that raising the liquor tax in a community led to a reduction in the rate of sexually transmitted diseases (Staras et al., 2016). When alcohol costs more, people drink less. As a result, they are less likely to have unprotected sex with someone they do not know very well, who may be carrying such a disease.

Comparing oneself to ideals and goals can also be depressing. After all, hardly anyone lives up to his or her ideals all the time. The original theory of self-awareness concluded, quite reasonably, that self-awareness would be inherently unpleasant. If self-awareness means comparing what you are against what you ideally could be, you'll always come up short. But this hardly squares with the observation that people seem to enjoy looking at themselves and thinking about themselves (as in the anecdote about the slow elevators).

This problem was solved by noting that people sometimes compare themselves to low standards. For example, they may compare themselves not to perfection but to the average person (Carver & Scheier, 1981; Taylor & Brown, 1988). As we shall see, the average person tends to think of him- or herself as above average. In that context, self-awareness is pleasant: It is gratifying to reflect on how good one is.

Many of us get little or no pleasure from looking at our reflections but still do consult mirrors as a way of making sure we are presentable to others. Prior to giving a presentation, going on a date, or entering a party, it is useful to check one's appearance so that one can avoid making a bad impression. Comb the hair, straighten the tie, adjust the makeup or jewelry. These may seem small actions, but they are part of a bigger pattern; being aware of self is useful for making changes to the self. Human beings self-regulate to a much greater extent than any other creature, and self-awareness is a vital part of that (Carver & Scheier, 1981, 1982, 1998).

In recent years, the idea of self-awareness has been extended in a creative direction by noting that people can reflect on themselves and their experiences in different ways (Kross, 2009; Kross & Ayduk, 2011). One way is from the inside: You recall the experience from your own perspective, as it happened. This tends to bring back the feelings and concerns that you had at the time, effectively reviving and almost reliving the experience. In contrast, some people manage to reflect on the experience from an external perspective. Doing that, which is called "self-distancing," is powerfully useful for reinterpreting. When people advise you to "get some perspective" on your troubles, they are giving the valid advice to reflect on them in a self-distancing manner. Fewer emotions are evoked. Instead, you can view yourself as if what happened was to someone else. With the benefit of that distance, you can see other ways of making sense of what happened to you. Remarkably, teaching people to do a bit of self-distancing about their marital conflicts improved marital satisfaction across a 2-year study (Finkel et al., 2013).

Self-distancing is a useful way to relax biases, wishful thinking, and emotional distortions that inevitably crowd into direct experience. Often people feel as if what they are suffering must be unique in world history, but when they try to describe it as if it were about someone else, it starts to sound familiar, even banal.

SELF AS CONSCIOUS OR UNCONSCIOUS

Another endless argument in the social sciences is about whether conscious or unconscious processes drive human behavior. Here, too, I argue that pitting them against each other as competing explanations will only take us so far and will ultimately miss much of what is really important.

The question of whether the self is fundamentally conscious or unconscious is misconceived. It is both. They work together, often cooperating and complementing each other, sometimes clashing. This is true not just for the self but for conscious and unconscious processes generally. A prominent conclusion from studying conscious and unconscious causes of human action is that almost all human behavior is the product of both conscious and unconscious processes (for a review, see Baumeister, Masicampo, & Vohs, 2011). Hardly any actions are carried out without some conscious participation, and yet conscious processes themselves rest on unconscious ones.

The idea of unconscious self-concept has been most thoroughly developed in connection with self-esteem. The possibility of assessing self-esteem by measuring unconscious processes has plenty of appeal, not least because the usual measures can be faked. That is, self-esteem is typically measured by asking people to rate how good they are on various attributes, such as competence and likability. People seeking to make a good impression may rate themselves more favorably than they really believe. Other people may have deceived themselves into thinking they are great, even though way down deep (in the unconscious) they know otherwise. Researchers are tantalized by the tempting possibility that they could get closer to knowing someone's true self-esteem if they could measure unconscious attitudes, thereby bypassing faking, impression managing, and self-deception.

Alas, progress has been mixed at best in terms of getting at the truth via these measures of unconscious or "implicit" self-esteem. A painstaking series of studies by Bosson, Swann, and Pennebaker (2000) compared seven (!) different ways of measuring it. The different measures did not match up well at all. Some pairs were negatively correlated so that *in general* people who scored higher in self-esteem on one measure scored lower on another. That is really bad news for measurement: Different measures of the same thing should furnish similar answers, not opposite ones. The best positive correlation among all seven measures was a dismal .23, and that was between two quite similar ones (liking the initials in your name, and liking the numbers in your birthday). The authors compared this to the fable in which various blind men touched different parts of the elephant and drew completely different conclusions as to what an elephant is like. In contrast, when they compared several of the standard questionnaire measures of self-esteem, these were quite strongly correlated with each other.

A further blow was that the implicit measures fared poorly in predicting various behaviors, such as grades in college, and overall positive and negative emotionality. Again, the old-fashioned questionnaire measures did better at predicting behaviors. The hope had been that the implicit measures would be better than the questionnaires at predicting actual behavior because scores were not distorted by trying to make oneself look good and similar motives. But they didn't—if anything, they did worse.

Some theorists have held that people might hold different attitudes about the self. The idea of dual attitudes has had some success in other contexts, so why not the self? If conscious and unconscious concepts of self are really different, then they might hold different levels of self-esteem. But this view, too, has run into trouble. It seems the implicit and explicit measures are getting at the same thing. The most important case for researchers consists of people who score high on the explicit questionnaire ("Yes, I'm terrific") but score low on the implicit measure (e.g., not liking the numbers in one's birthday). But researchers have found that these people are aware that they are inflating their answers on the questionnaire in order to look good. When they are instructed not to do that, they furnish similar scores on both measures (Olson, Fazio, & Hermann, 2007).

Therefore, let us discard the idea that people hold plenty of attitudes about themselves of which they are unaware and are at odds with what they consciously think. People may have feelings of self-glorification or self-loathing that they conceal from others, but they do not conceal them from themselves.

The unconscious mind can have multiple sets of information about the self that would not all be consistent with each other. In the unconscious they rarely bump against each other and so the contradictions are not noticed. Only when both are relevant and send their input into the conscious mind that is contemplating a decision, only then, does it become apparent that these different networks of information contradict each other in some relevant, clear way.

Moreover, the conscious self is decisive when choices are made consciously. Automatic and unconscious processes certainly influence many decisions and may be decisive in some, though it's hard to imagine an automatic impulse prevailing over determined conscious opposition in a single contest. Over the long run, to be sure, automatic impulses can exploit a moment of weakness in conscious control. But I'm pretty sure consciousness evolved to be able to override automatic impulses in the moment. Otherwise, what's the point? You could figure out the best thing to do but then wouldn't be able to do it, so all you'd gain is seeing how stupid you are.

The Conscious Self Overrides

Let us assume for a moment that the conscious self strives to impose unity on the diverse welter of impulses, feelings, values, and the rest. Let us also assume that the process remains incomplete and unfinished. What will then happen is that there will be thoughts, impulses, emotions, desires, and more that will be created for the self by unconscious processes but that will be refused integration into the self. One will have a thought or feeling or impulse but respond by saying, "That's not me."

One of psychology's classic papers made this point in relation to prejudice. Modern American citizens have prejudices, some of which are prepared by evolution and nature, others learned from experience, and others as a combination. Yet, the prevailing modern values condemn prejudice, and so people seek to overcome it. Patricia Devine (1989) conducted a series of experiments to investigate the difference between prejudiced and nonprejudiced people. Her first idea was that prejudiced people know stereotypes but nonprejudiced people don't. She tested this theory, and it was a complete flop: everybody knows the stereotypes. Her second idea was that nonprejudiced people may know the stereotypes, as a kind of abstract knowledge, but when they meet someone, the stereotype does not leap to mind as it does for prejudiced people ("Aha! Here's another Polack, Black person, homosexual, police officer. . . ."). This, too, was a spectacular failure. Nonprejudiced people think of the stereotypes just as readily as prejudiced ones when they encounter someone from that group.

The key finding was that nonprejudiced people override and suppress those thoughts. When encountering a Black person, they might think, this person is probably lazy, violent, unintelligent, and so forth, but they reject those thoughts: "I don't believe those stereotypes." That's how they differ from the prejudiced people—the ones who don't override and reject those thoughts.

For present purposes, the point is that the unconscious generated the reactions, so indeed they were present in the psyche—but because they clash with the unified self-concept the person seeks to create, they are disavowed. *I have those thoughts, but I don't endorse them. They're not me.*

The idea that the conscious self can reject the products of its unconscious mind is an important key to how the self operates. We shall find it repeatedly. There is a movement to hold people responsible for their unconscious reactions. But as Devine showed, no one can avoid thinking of stereotypes. What separates the tolerant person from the bigot is whether the person "owns" those automatic products of the unconscious mind. It's not the unconscious reaction but the conscious override that defines the nonprejudiced person. The self exists most importantly at the level of integration and unity. The relevant implication for the self is that you probably have thoughts, desires, feelings, and impulses that you refuse to accept as part of you—and there is room for lively debate as to whether those should count as part of you. To be sure, acting on them and then regretting or apologizing is not entirely convincing. If you acted on them, then at least for a moment your entire self did embrace and endorse them.

The rejection of one's own mental life in service of unifying self was brought home to me in a different kind of experience. Mostly I've been an easygoing, happy person. At one point, however, a convergence of misfortune was so overwhelming that, surprisingly, thoughts of suicide started popping into my head from time to time, unbidden. I never acted on those thoughts nor even really endorsed them as reflecting "me." The thoughts were alien, intruding into my stream of thought as I went about my daily life amidst the assorted ongoing disasters. I'm not a closed-minded person, and indeed I make a point of considering alternatives, so I did contemplate rationally the prospect of self-imposed death, but it never carried the day. There was a reasonable case to be made, as suicide would create a permanent zero in terms of further experience, which is better than a net negative. I realized, too, that people miss the point when they tell the suicidal person that things will get better. I knew they would get better eventually. But the relevant question is whether I wanted to endure all the unpleasantness that awaited ahead before things got better. Oblivion, as in zero further conscious experience in my life, is rationally superior to a lot of negative experience, even if positives were conceivable in the remote future. Another factor was that it was not enough to just endure the future, but it would require active coping, many meetings, decisions, initiative, all of it unpleasant and stressful, all supplanting the few good things remaining in my life, like intellectual work.

Clearly, those suicidal thoughts originated inside my mind. Yet, I refused to integrate them into my unified conception of who I am. Indeed, I mocked them a bit. I like good champagne and at the time kept a small wine cellar with a couple dozen bottles. As a joking response to the intrusive thoughts of suicide, I would tell myself that I certainly wasn't going to kill myself while I still had good champagne to drink. After all, the appeal of suicide was to escape from misery, and the drawback was missing out on pleasure—so it would be stupid to kill myself while I still had immediately available pleasure in those bottles. The mocking attitude reflects the fact that I never really owned those suicidal thoughts—though I had a lot of them.

The point, then, is that the unconscious contains plenty of material, information, impulses, and more—but the conscious mind can disown them. Full integration into the self requires the conscious part of the self, which is where unity is constructed.

KEY POINTS

- A self-aware self can function better than a self that lacks self-awareness.
- Most psychologists believe that the origins of self-awareness lie in social life.
- Self-awareness is evaluative and almost always involves standards. How do I measure up?
- Self-awareness encourages better behavior; people behave better when they know they are being watched.
- People can reflect on their experience from the inside or gain perspective by self-distancing. The latter is a useful way to relax biases and emotional distortions.
- The self is both conscious and unconscious, but the conscious self can override and reject impulses that emerge from the unconscious in the service of unity of self.

CHAPTER 12

What Sort of Knowledge Is Self-Knowledge?

People are generally eager to learn about themselves. The pursuit of self-knowledge has taken many forms over the years. People consult horoscopes (with scant validity) in the hope of learning about themselves and their feelings and prospects. Students sign up for psychology courses, sometimes hoping to learn about themselves. People are often intensely eager to hear what others have thought of them. Ancestors can be traced back by centuries through online records. Genetic testing can illuminate past and future.

A prominent and prestigious early source of knowledge was the Oracle at Delphi in ancient Greece, where "Know thyself," in Greek, was carved in stone in the temple. The injunction to "know thyself" is variously attributed to at least half a dozen different ancient Greek philosophers. The wide usage of that phrase suggests that the ancient Greeks were already concerned with knowing themselves.

However, many scholars believe that for the ancient Greeks "know thyself" meant something more like, "know your place," which would have suited the society at the time. It may have been used to admonish braggarts and overconfident individuals to understand their limits and curtail their undertakings, for there were far fewer safety nets back then. It may have meant to know one's abilities so as to perform one's duties in society. Almost certainly, it did not mean that you should strive for high self-esteem or engage in ruminative inward-looking ramblings to discover some hidden true self.

The idea that "know thyself" meant "know your place" meshes well with the idea that selves evolved so as to fit into groups by performing distinct roles. Nowadays everyone believes in vast, complex inner selves, including some that may turn out to be quite different from visible behavior and public impression. But previous generations did not have such a rich mythology of hidden selfhood. Maybe "know thyself" did not mean that the animal body should learn to introspect, but rather that it should learn and master its position in the large social system.

The self comes into being as the brain learns to operate a set of roles, an identity, in the social system. "Know thyself" is precisely what that brain needs to hear, to spur it on its way to know its proper place, the duties that come with it, and its capabilities for performing those duties. Knowing yourself was a very pragmatically useful aid to knowing how to make choices and execute performance as your animal body moves through its typical day.

The rise of cities full of strangers was a major transition for humankind. Learning to adapt to bigger and impersonal social systems was a huge further step (Moffett, 2019). "Know thyself" could mean, know your position in this new and bigger system, understand how what you do contributes to how society in general should work. As already explained, the human self evolved partly to make larger social systems possible. Those systems function best when individual people understand their roles and perform them accordingly. In that sense, "know thyself" was vital for the success of human society. But that sense is vastly different from knowing yourself in the modern sense of getting in touch with your deepest feelings and discovering inner traits that make you special.

What then is the self that needs to be known? Knowing your role and duty may have been the early version, to keep the naked ape focused on participating in society rather than indulging its more natural, baser impulses. But in modern life, self-knowledge means discovering all the inner things that make you special, little quirks, likes and dislikes, hidden talents, limitations and vulnerabilities, perhaps above all your feelings, hopes, and fears and dreams.

No doubt you have a mass of information about yourself. It is a jumble of different kinds of things: your name, your attitudes about money and how much you have, memories of your high school sweetheart(s), your sore ankle, unfair things people have said about you, what you worry about, how long it's been since you had sex, what foods you dislike, and on and on. To begin tackling the problem of self-knowledge, we must first decide how to sort this information and what kinds of it to emphasize.

THOUGHTS AND FEELINGS VERSUS ACTIONS

One researcher who tried to sort through the various types of self-knowledge is Susan Andersen. Her conclusion was that the inner life counted for more than actions. People said that knowing their innermost thoughts and feelings was better than knowing how they acted, as a basis for understanding the self (Andersen & Ross, 1984). Andersen provided some objective evidence that that assumption was correct. In one of her experiments, people listened to taped interviews that spoke about inner thoughts and feelings, or about past actions, or a mixture, and then rated their impression of the person being interviewed. The listeners' ratings matched the interviewees' own self-ratings best when they heard the discussion of thoughts and feelings (Andersen, 1984). To be sure, as we shall soon see in abundance, people's self-ratings are hardly the gold standard of accurate knowledge. Rather than saying knowing feelings is the best way to know someone accurately, it is probably safer to conclude that knowing people's feelings enables you to see them as they see themselves. Indeed, participants thought that other people would understand them better knowing their inner thoughts and feelings from a single day than from observing their behaviors across a couple of months, which is startling. As a social scientist, if I wanted to know somebody, I would want to have months of behavioral data rather than a single day's thoughts and feelings.

Furthermore, Andersen's line of work provided important evidence that different kinds of knowledge about the self matter to self as opposed to others. Experimental subjects were instructed to discuss positive things about themselves, emphasizing either their private, inner reactions such as feelings, or their overt behavioral reactions (or, in the control group, no instructions). Half were told this was for private reflection, while others were told their answers would be taped and played for others, who would form judgments. All of this was intended to boost people's self-esteem, and it did, but to different degrees. Discussing inner reactions and feelings had the most impact (for raising self-esteem) when people were privately reflecting on themselves, but it had the least impact in the public situation, when they were taking other people's point of view (Andersen & Williams, 1985). Other people care about how you act, not just how you feel.

Still, that's a matter of predicting other people, not yourself. Self-knowledge does not have the same purpose and hence may follow different rules.

Why do people think their inner thoughts and feelings are more revealing than their actions? Almost certainly, they recognize that one's actions can be influenced, even forced, by external factors. To be sure, they ought to know that external factors can influence their inner thoughts and feelings, too. There are two possible explanations. One is that they think the goal is to know the inner self, and their inner thoughts and feelings are more directly linked to that than their actions. Actions are often ambiguous and can be easily misunderstood, whereas thoughts and feelings are less vulnerable to this. After all, people use actions to infer the thoughts and feelings, starting with the question of whether the person intended the action as it happened (and intended for the consequences it achieved) (Malle, 2006). If you know someone's thoughts and feelings, then you already know his or her intentions. "That's not what I meant" is often heard in connection with actions, but if someone understands your inner thoughts and feelings, they do know what you meant.

The other explanation is that their thoughts can paint the picture of themselves they prefer, even if it departs from reality. For example, someone who thinks of herself as generous but in fact is stingy would not be recognized as stingy from her thoughts and feelings—but her actions would reveal the truth.

SELF-BELIEFS: PROPOSITIONS, NARRATIVES, AND VALUES

Nobody seriously questions the idea that people have self-knowledge— using the term loosely enough to include some false beliefs, exaggerations, convenient omissions, and wishful thinking. But if we want to map out self-knowledge, we must first ask, what sort of thing is being mapped? What is the form of self-knowledge?

Let us start with the two kinds of knowledge: *narrative* and *propositional*. These correspond roughly to stories and facts. Water boils at 100 degrees Celsius (212 degrees Fahrenheit). That's a proposition, a fact. Saying that water boils at 36 degrees would also be a proposition, albeit a false one, thus not a fact. Most people do have false beliefs about themselves. Hence, it won't do to call this kind of self-knowledge facts. "Propositions" include both the true and the false. Stories are a different kind of knowledge, involving a meaningfully interrelated series of events, usually organized around some purpose, with various events causally related to others. Stories can include facts, but that does not mean that facts are more basic. With self-knowledge, it is the other way around. The stories come first, and generalizations about the self (the propositions, true or false) come later, deriving from the stories or inferring.

Back when I was just finishing my PhD, the "self-concept" was the general way that psychologists talked about self-knowledge. The term has gradually gone out of fashion. In part, that's because the term *self-concept* implies there is a single, coherent view of self; with the progress of research, that view has become impossible to sustain. People have a great deal of specific information about themselves, both factoids and stories, but these do not necessarily add up to a coherent whole. It is even possible that a person would have beliefs about him- or herself that contradict each other. In that case, a coherent whole would be impossible because of the internal inconsistency.

Remember, the unity project is perpetually unfinished business. The discarding of the term self-concept recognizes that. If the unity project were complete, someone could have a single, coherent self-concept. But all the bits of information about the self never get fully assembled into a coherent, consistent whole.

Going to the opposite extreme, the trailblazing Hazel Markus (1977) put forward the notion of "self-schemas." Each schema is one piece of information about the self. There is something fundamentally right about this because people do have lots of single particular beliefs about themselves: "I'm tall," "My birthday is in April," "I'm bad at statistics." But it misses something. Self-knowledge is not just a collection of unrelated beliefs, without some systematic organization. It strives toward a coherent organization, an integrated conception of self, even if that striving remains incomplete. The various self-schemas were always meant to be eventually incorporated into a coherent whole. Each individual's unity project is never completed, but it does go a long way toward integration.

The term *knowledge* avoids the problem of suggesting that self-knowledge is a single concept. But there is a different problem. Calling it "knowledge" implies that the knowledge is correct. There is a long tradition in philosophy of distinguishing knowledge from belief. A belief may be mistaken, but as philosophers like to say, "You can't know what ain't so." I will use the term *self-knowledge* but with the caveat that correctness is not implied. It's abundantly clear that many people have beliefs about themselves that are not correct, as we shall see. A more precise term would be *self-beliefs*.

One advantage of the self-schema approach is that it meshes well with how some psychologists study self-knowledge—that is, as if it is a list of traits and attributes. One classic procedure is the so-called Twenty Statements Test (Kuhn & McPartland, 1954), in which research subjects get a questionnaire that has 20 lines reading "I am _____," and they fill in the 20 blanks.

True, people can probably answer questions about themselves by listing traits. Do you have a list of traits in mind? Probably you could name a couple, but I find I have to stop and think in order to come up with them. It's not how my information about myself is stored. In contrast, people can readily tell stories from their lives.

The conventional wisdom is that self-knowledge has two forms, a list (or organized set) of attributes, and a collection of stories. The first can be subdivided into a few kinds of attributes. The one most studied by psychologists comprises personality traits. Some would also emphasize roles in society: daughter, husband, police officer, surfer, accountant, Giants fan. The last of these (specific sports fan) invokes interests and preferences, which differs from both roles and personality traits. Interests, preferences, and values do constitute a useful and common type of self-knowledge, albeit long underappreciated by researchers. Let's consider each of these types of self-belief.

Self-Knowledge as a List of Personality Traits

Lucy asks Pete, "What kind of person is George?" In reply, Pete rattles off a list of George's personality traits. This may be how people think of other people. Still, is it how they think of themselves? And is it the *main* way people think about themselves?

It would be simple and efficient if knowledge about self took the same form as knowledge about others. But we can't assume they are the same, and in fact there are good reasons to assume that they are different. Self-knowledge is subject to all sorts of wishes and wants, while other people may be coldly appraised so one can decide how to interact with them. One example comes from a study on the so-called planning fallacy (Buehler et al., 1994, 2010). This fallacy is that people tend to be unrealistically optimistic about their plans and prospects. The researchers asked students when they would finish their theses, and their estimates were way off. (Guess in which direction.) The researchers also asked each subject's roommate to predict when the subject would get the thesis done, and the roommates were pretty spot-on accurate. Accurate prediction of meaningful human action is quite possible. Just not accurate prediction of oneself!

We're accurate at predicting other people because that's what our information about them is supposed to do, and we have no strong biases to make us embrace false assumptions. Indeed, the importance of predicting people accurately means we cannot afford to be all that wrong. But self-knowledge is different. You don't need to predict your own future behavior because you can decide your future behavior, for the most part. Therefore, you don't need to form a list of your own personality traits.

So maybe traits are something other people have. A classic paper by Jones and Nisbett (1971) proposed that people see each other in terms of traits but see themselves in terms of values. It is tempting to see traits as causes of behavior, and research on personality tends to operate that way—measure the trait, and then provide a situation to see how people behave. Still, even if researchers do manage to find that measures of personality traits accurately predict behavior, they do not prove that there is something inside the person that could be called the trait responsible for producing that action.

Traits are patterns. Patterns are helpful for predicting the future, so one can prepare for it. That's why traits are useful for describing other people, more than oneself. Everyone is in the business of predicting how other people will act in the future, so everyone wants to see the patterns in other people's current and past behavior. You can use those patterns to extrapolate, so as to know what to expect next time. A widely repeated truism in psychology is "the best predictor of future behavior is past behavior." With yourself, this is irrelevant. You can decide how to act in the future, and there is not much to be gained by trying to predict how you will act in the future based on how you have acted in the past. With everyone else you don't have control, so you need to predict. Having a set of beliefs about your own personality traits has only a little pragmatic value.

As one example: Imagine yourself walking into battle, carrying a spear. You want to know whether the man standing next to you will fight or flee. If he runs, your own safety is jeopardized because while you're fighting the enemy soldier in front of you, another can spear you from the side, where your comrade was supposed to be. Predicting what he will do is very important. But you do not need to predict your own behavior because you can decide on the spot whether to advance or flee.

The Jones and Nisbett paper mentioned earlier posed a major challenge to the idea that self-concepts consist of traits. They said, essentially, that personality traits are seen in other people, not in the self. One sees one's own behavior as flexible and dependent on the situation. A trait is in a sense limiting because it means that the person consistently acts this way rather than that way. People know their own history in detail and know they have acted both this way and that way at different times. They also want to retain the belief that they are free to act in different ways.

Jones and Nisbett's idea that people use traits for thinking about others, but not about themselves, received a stiff blow when researchers started counting (Monson, Tanke, & Lund, 1980). People ascribed more traits to themselves than to others. The view that the self-concept lacks traits was replaced by the opposite view, that people attribute more traits to themselves than to others. Yet perhaps this wasn't entirely the opposite view. It preserved Jones and Nisbett's insight that people see themselves as able to act in different ways. They might check both "quiet" and "talkative" when describing themselves, not because they are contradicting themselves, but because they know sometimes they are happy to be silent while other times they chatter on in lively fashion. They are saying that they are capable of both kinds of behavior. (In a later study, people explicitly chose "both" when rating themselves; Sande, Goethals, & Radloff, 1988.)

There was a catch. People mostly attribute more traits to themselves when these are good traits. If the opposite traits are "starts fights" and "cowardly," people tend not to pick either one. Was this all a mere cover for self-enhancement, that is, simply trying to claim as many good traits for the self as one can get away with? Careful studies by Cheung and colleagues (2014) said no; there really is a sense in which people attribute more traits to themselves, even when these are bad. They offered people the chance to protect their self-esteem from bad labels by saying, essentially, "Occasionally I do these things," and then people again rated themselves as having more traits than other people. Even when asked to describe themselves in free form, people would mention negative traits—but laden with qualifiers such as "sometimes" or "a little bit" or "possibly," and so on.

Cheung and colleagues tried giving people pairs of opposite traits that were framed as both good or both bad. Half rated themselves, while the rest rated an acquaintance. Crucially, they rated each trait separately, rather than being forced to choose a spot along a continuum between them. When both traits were good (serious vs. playful, energetic vs. relaxed), they claimed both for themselves more than for others. Thus, the sum of the good traits was higher for self than for others: I'm both serious and playful, while George is mostly serious and not that playful. When both traits were bad (e.g., gullible vs. suspicious, or stingy vs. wasteful, submissive vs. domineering), there was no difference between rating self and others.

But the researchers then took another step and looked at the difference between the ratings of opposite traits. If you rated yourself as 4 on domineering and 3 on submissive, you'd get a difference of 1. Difference scores were smaller for self than others. In principle, this effect could arise because one rates oneself as having neither trait—but as we know, overall people rated themselves higher on both traits, and especially the good ones.

How can we pull all this together? If traits are assertions that a person acts one way rather than the opposite, then yes, traits are something we ascribe to others. It is helpful to predict how other people will act because one cannot control how they act, and one has to anticipate in order to decide how to deal with them: trust them, form an alliance with them, stay away, go along but keep on guard? With oneself, there is less need to settle on traits because one wants to preserve the freedom to do either.

That's the conclusion if we see traits as limitations, as meaning that I generally act this way rather than that way. But if instead we see traits as kinds of behavior, then one sees the self as full of that. You have more potential and more diverse history than other people, as far as you know. Almost certainly, you know more about your own actions than about anyone else's.

Any given person is one or the other, but I am both.

A further twist is that people care a great deal how they are perceived by others. So if everyone sees everyone else as having traits, then other people see you as having traits, and so you want to know what those are—and ideally manage that list. That means you need to have some ideas about your traits. You have to see how others regard you and know what traits they think you have. Wherever possible, you want to help them see you as having some traits rather than others. Most likely, interest in knowing one's own traits derives from concern with how one is perceived by others, rather than being able to predict one's own behavior.

What happens when people disclose things about themselves to each other? I find it hard to imagine that people on a first date exchange lists of the traits they ascribe to themselves. Now and then someone might mention a trait term, true. But most of the information exchanged when two people are getting to know each other would take a different form. Two of these are particularly worth keeping in mind: stories and interests/values.

Self-Knowledge as Narrative

Much information about self and about other people is retained in stories (McAdams, 2001, 2019). If someone asked you to tell something about a friend of yours, as in "What's he like?," you might give a couple of standout traits, whether the person is nice or intelligent, but probably pretty soon you'd tell a story about the person. This is a bit of a puzzle to researchers: Why tell the story, if the story is only to make a point that could be summarized by naming a trait? You could say, "He's honest" rather than telling a story about the lengths the fellow went to one time in order to return money that he was overpaid. This puzzle is hardly limited to the psychology of self-knowledge. Why sit through a 2-hour movie when you could read a one-paragraph summary of what happens, or even just get a one-sentence summary of the message (e.g., "crime doesn't pay," "racism is bad," "love conquers obstacles and brings happiness")? There are a couple of answers.

- *Stories provide proof.* Stories provide a kind of proof. It is easy to claim to be honest or say someone else is honest. A story describing an exceptional feat of honesty is more persuasive and impressive. The trait is the conclusion, but the story is the evidence, and people are more persuaded by evidence. And certainly a story about someone behaving dishonestly would make a deeply negative impression.

- *Stories provide narrative continuity.* Stories correspond more closely than lists of traits to how people think. Indeed, life is lived in story form. A trait is an abstract term to describe a pattern, and so it has to be inferred from the story. The person may or may not bother doing that. The event is in memory as a story.

After all, who do you think would really know you? Someone who read a carefully prepared, accurate list of your personality traits (and nothing else), or someone who listened to a long set of (true) stories about your life? Some evidence for the importance of stories emerged from research on neurosurgery patients. A report on several such cases by Jecker and Ko (2017) grappled with the following question: In what sense was the person the same person after neurosurgery as before? They concluded that the continuity of the story was the most important factor. Indeed, in some cases the continuity emphasized connecting to a much earlier version of the self, rather than the self immediately prior to the surgery. This may sound odd, but often that was the therapeutic goal. After all, people do not typically have brain surgery when everything is going great for them.

In their first case, for example, a man descended into epilepsy and as a side effect developed intense motivational responses. He had overwhelming rages, such as getting so upset when another car cut in front of him that he accelerated to catch up, cursed at the other driver, threw his coffee cup and hit the other car. He developed huge appetites for food and would eat everything edible in sight. (Even his definition of "edible" broadened: He remarked that if someone had put a car on the dinner table, he would have eaten it.) Worst of all, he developed huge sexual compulsions, constantly wanting sex with his wife, and becoming obsessed with child pornography, which led to his arrest and imprisonment. After brain surgery, however, he "reclaimed his story," becoming the relatively gentle and restrained person he had been earlier in his life. The continued existence of the body is not enough to mean that one remains the same person.

In a previous chapter, I noted that the moral self was seen as essential to the unity of self. Now I am emphasizing narrative continuity. Moral narratives are central. The example of the man whose brain tumor caused him to have destructive rages and pedophilic sexual desires is a good example of how both morality and story are central to the unity of self.

The Narrative Self

The importance of the narrative self has been a career theme in Dan McAdams's research. It provides a refreshing alternative to the simple view that the self is a list of traits. McAdams describes the self as "an internalized and evolving life story" (2001, p. 117). This story does not fully take shape until adolescence. And as the story keeps changing, it is not ever quite in final shape, at least until death. Children take preliminary steps in this direction, as is covered in the chapter on child development of self. But adolescents and adults understand themselves as actors in a set of ongoing events that can be readily told as stories. Their actions and decisions shape the way the story unfolds. In fact, most of the world's great literature consists of stories about how individuals' actions and choices shaped the sequence of events, leading to some outcomes rather than others. That's what the self does: it acts within these ongoing stories.

Clearly, self-understanding as acting in a story requires a self that extends across time. I doubt that nonhuman animals can have a narrative self-understanding. But nearly all humans do.

The problem with regarding self-knowledge as a collection of stories rather than a collection of traits is that stories are about the past. The reason people want to know about each other is to know how they will act in the future, so as to decide whether to trust them, follow them, avoid them, marry them, and the rest. The stories about someone's past are mainly of interest as guides to how the person will act in the future. Traits, as patterns, are readily extended into the future, so knowing someone's traits enables one to predict future actions. Knowing stories about the past is only useful if one can use them to predict future actions—and that typically involves inferring some kind of stable trait in the person, as the reason the person acted as he or she did in the story.

Yet, McAdams's (2013) analysis gets past the problem that one's stories are backward-looking. Life is lived in story form, and for most people the present moment is somewhere in the middle of a story (indeed perhaps several separate, overlapping stories). The story self has several levels, which human beings master one at a time. The first is to play a role: one learns what role is assigned to the self, and one performs it. Small children focus on this. Next, one learns to take a more active role (as a motivated agent), making decisions, performing well or badly, meeting challenges. One is more than an actor playing a role.

And then, as one moves into adolescence and adulthood, one takes on an additional job, as author of the story. One chooses themes, story lines; settling on a spouse or job is stepping into a new story, usually a major one. This subsumes the others because one is still playing a role in the story one has helped to script, and one can perform well or badly, can choose effectively or ineptly. The grownup self combines all three roles: It writes the general story, plays its part in it, but also makes choices to get what it wants in the context of the story.

The narrative and propositional selves both have pragmatic utility, but in quite different spheres. The narrative self is what gets you through the day, making choices and performing tasks. Daily life is filled with meaningful sequences of events, which is what stories are. Meanwhile, though, reputation is created and sustained, and reputation is mostly propositional. You want to be seen as having certain stable attributes, particularly moral ones, but also competence. Even when stories become part of your reputation, it is mainly because the stories indicate what your traits are, so people can predict your future actions.

Self-Knowledge as Interests and Values

A third form of self-knowledge involves interests and values. Let's revisit the first-date test for self-knowledge: How do people communicate about themselves on first dates? Do they exchange lists of trait terms? They might however tell each other what interests them and what their important values are.

Psychologists have not lavished nearly as much effort on studying interests as on traits. When they do study interests, however, they are often surprised and impressed. A sweeping tour of the research literature by Rounds and Su (2014; Su, Rounds, & Armstrong, 2009) made a strong case for the importance of interests. Interests are more stable than personality traits. Interests far outperform personality when it comes to predicting career success. To be sure, abilities are also important, and they predict career success pretty well, but interests are a worthy rival. If success is measured in things like occupational prestige and grades at university, ability is the strongest predictor, with interests in second place, far ahead of personality traits. If one simply measures success by how much money the person earns, then interests are the strongest predictor, higher even than ability. (That difference is quite impressive because capable people earn more than incompetent ones.) Rounds and Su conclude that "interests affect the direction, vigor, and persistence of goal-oriented behaviors" and hence predict whether people reach their goals or not.

SOME OF EACH?

People do have multiple kinds of self-knowledge. We can debate which is most important, but none is likely to be completely absent. Still, my take is that much self-concept research has overemphasized self-beliefs about personality traits and underappreciated the importance of interests and values. (Abilities may have gotten roughly their due.)

There is some evidence that different kinds of self-beliefs are stored separately in the brain, though we do not know why that would be. Some fascinating clues come from people who suffer sweeping amnesia. They are unable to remember any part of their lives, all the events and stories that made them who they are (McAdams, 2013). Indeed, they cannot remember a single thing they ever did. Yet despite not being able to recount any of their past experiences, they could still rate themselves on personality traits and scales. Moreover, their self-ratings seemed surprisingly accurate. In one case, the person recovered memories later and took the same tests, getting the same results as during the period of amnesia. In others, people's ratings of their personalities during amnesia still matched how others who knew them well (including knowing them before the amnesia) rated them. Apparently, then, (propositional) knowledge of one's personality is stored separately from (narrative) memories of specific experiences and events. You can lose the entire memory of your life, everything up to this particular minute is a blank—yet you can still rate your personality traits as well as someone with a normal memory.

The self has important jobs, and it uses knowledge about itself to help it do those jobs. The self has to keep abreast of how it is perceived by others, so as to maintain good reputation. It also has to make decisions so as to function in its ongoing narrative-style life. For the latter, its interests and values are paramount, as well as some knowledge of its capabilities and limitations, all in relation to goals. For the former, it is the never-ending process of creating a stable image marked by positive traits to appeal to others. The reputation is propositional.

All of that brings up the issue of why people seek self-knowledge. The next chapter sorts through the data and disputes on this.

KEY POINTS

- Personality traits are patterns and important facts about the social world. Inferring other people's traits helps you predict how the others will behave and adjust your actions accordingly.

- You don't need a mental list of your own traits, apart from wanting to know how others regard you.

- Traits are mainly for predicting other people. One does not have to predict one's own behavior because one can choose how to act.

- The *desired reputation* is the most important of the various concepts of self. The desired reputation likely contains personality and moral traits, and of course mainly good ones.

- In addition to traits (including abilities), self-knowledge can take two other forms: (1) stories and (2) interests and values, as they guide behavioral choices.

- Much self-knowledge is contained in stories, not in propositions. People experience life in story form.

CHAPTER 13

Why Know Thyself?

$\mathbf{A}$ scientific theory of self must explain why it is helpful to know yourself. Given the widespread prevalence of the advice to know thyself, one would expect there to be several answers as to why this is important. Knowing your place, your capabilities, and your obligations would all be conducive to performing your part in the system. The assumption is that you develop self-knowledge to enable the self to perform its function better, namely to perform its role in the social system. If that's what the ancient Greeks meant by knowing oneself, it would have been solid advice for how to play your part in the system and not make trouble.

From a practical standpoint, knowing yourself is also useful for managing yourself so as to get the most out of life. This fits the idea that self-awareness is for self-regulation (Carver & Scheier, 1981). Indeed, what else would it be for? Creating highly self-aware beings through natural selection was a huge and remarkable step, far beyond what most living things are capable of. What benefit made it worth it? What was its selection advantage? The ability to adjust and change oneself so as to fit into the group better would be the most plausible theory. Social self-regulation would be hugely beneficial for a species that is experimenting with new, advanced, complex social systems as its biological strategy. The argument, then, is that the capacity to build self-knowledge evolved mainly for the purpose of participation in social systems.

In this chapter, we consider what people's motives for self-knowledge are. These have far-reaching implications, for they not only motivate the quest to know oneself; they also guide what sorts of self-knowledge are sought. The biases that distort self-knowledge away from hard truths have their roots in the reasons people seek to know themselves.

Understanding what motivates the quest for self-knowledge will shed light on how self-knowledge takes shape—what it emphasizes, what it downplays, and what it distorts or systematically omits. The human self is more curious about itself than about plenty of other things, though not all.

Self-knowledge is useful for diverse practical reasons. Will I pass this course if I sign up? Can I do this job by myself? Will that person agree to date me, or marry me, if I ask nicely? Can I afford that car? In short, self-knowledge has considerable practical value, and so it is not surprising that people seek it. But there's a twist. The practical value is based on the assumption that the information is accurate. You want to know whether you can successfully manage that course, that car, that tree branch. But it did not take psychologists long to discover that people's views of themselves are often far from accurate. The way they seek self-knowledge is often detrimental to accuracy. We shall soon focus on the question of how accurate self-knowledge is, but for now let's remain focused on motivation (i.e., what people want).

THE SELF-ENHANCEMENT MOTIVE

If people sometimes seek inaccurate self-knowledge, then we need to reconsider the question of why self-knowledge is sought. The pragmatic usefulness of inaccurate self-knowledge is dubious. To be sure, there are further twists. People cannot knowingly cultivate false self-knowledge. If you wish to believe that you are a musical genius or a soon-to-be movie star, which is objectively false, you do not say, "I choose to believe false things about myself." Rather, in your mind at least your self-knowledge is true and accurate.

The distortions in self-knowledge are hardly random or balanced. They err overwhelmingly on the side of the favorable and positive. So it seems fair to propose that self-knowledge is sometimes motivated by the wish to think favorably of yourself and to get information that will enhance that shining image. This is generally called the "self-enhancement motive" (e.g., Sedikides & Gregg, 2008).

Indeed, the idea that people wish to hold a positive view of themselves, that they desire high self-esteem, is a foundational assumption in many psychological theories. It is one of the four basic needs in cognitive–experiential self-theory (CEST; Epstein, 1998). It is the central foundation of social identity theory (e.g., Hornsey, 2008). It is not one of the three basic motivations in self-determination theory (Ryan & Deci, 2017), but it is often invoked when they explain why people pursue needs in this or that way. It is hard to find any theory about the human self that disputes or dismisses this view. I have seen it casually invoked in papers in other fields as well.

So people desire self-esteem. Yet one must ask, why would humans have evolved with a desire for high self-esteem? As we shall see later in the book, self-esteem has very little direct practical value. After all, evolution instilled good feelings to encourage the animal to do things that bring pragmatic benefits, such as improve survival and reproduce. Thinking well of oneself, especially when not justified by objective qualities, does not do much by those criteria.

CONSISTENCY AS MOTIVE

There is a second motive contestant: consistency. Here, the assumption is that people seek to gain information that confirms what they already think about themselves. This is most commonly known as self-verification, based on the rich career of William B. Swann Jr.

Because people generally hold favorable views of themselves, self-enhancement and self-verification often overlap, at least to the point at which it is tough to tell them apart in laboratory work. Nevertheless, Swann (1985, 1987) has studied the fascinating minority of people who hold strongly negative views of themselves. Sometimes they show a clear preference for negative feedback.

Preference is an ambiguous word, and Swann's research has elucidated in what sense people "prefer" bad feedback. If one distinguishes emotional from cognitive reactions, then self-enhancement tends to win on emotion, while self-verification and consistency prevail on cognitive ones (Shrauger, 1975). When someone tells you that you are much better than you thought, your emotions say yes, yes, while your sober calculating mind is skeptical. A classic paper by Swann and colleagues called this the "cognitive-affective crossfire" (Swann et al., 1987). Thus, people prefer verifying over-flattering feedback in the sense that they believe it more, not in the sense that they like it more.

Another useful difference is between automatic and controlled mental processes. Self-enhancement seems to be automatic. The rejection of favorable feedback in order to maintain negative views of self requires controlled processing, which is a slow and laborious kind of thinking (Kahneman, 2011; on self-verification in controlled vs. automatic processing, see Swann et al., 1990). Hence, the self-enhancement response ("Yes, I am indeed wonderful and talented!") comes automatically and easily, while the self-verification response ("Uh, wait a minute, there are ample objective signs that I'm not really that great") takes time and effort for the mind to override the automatic reaction with a more sobering, judicious appraisal.

The fact that the quick, automatic response leans toward self-enhancement fits another theme of this book: The desired reputation is the dominant and most important of the various concepts of self. Your mind automatically embraces any evidence that you really are the way you want others to know you, which is generally more positive than the reality, or at least a best-case version of you.

Thus, the preference for consistent information is not deeply rooted in basic desires and feelings, but rather is combined with the more advanced mental processes. Consistency is after all part of the unity project, and it is a late addition to the self-system. The simple self wants to preserve freedom to do whatever is most appealing in the present moment and not be constrained by consistency pressures. It wants to embrace the most positive versions of self because these will promise the most wonderful future.

Swann sees the desire for consistency in self-concept as rooted in the general desire to achieve a stable understanding of the environment. He is quite right that people want their world to be stable and predictable because that is adaptive and comforting. Some of those reasons do not apply to the self, however. One wants the environment to be stable so one can know how to deal with it, but one does not have to deal with the self in the same way. Indeed, as was clear in the evidence about attributing contradictory (but good) traits to oneself, people prefer to reserve freedom to act in different ways. Most of the time there is no need to predict how you yourself will act. So there is no pragmatic reason for you to be consistent for your own sake.

Instead, the desire for consistency in self-concept is rooted in other people's expectations. People desire a stable environment. To other people, you are part of their environment—so they prefer you to be stable and predictable. People exert pressure on each other to be consistent. Morality is part of it: keeping your promises is fundamentally a kind of consistency. Even apart from explicit promises, morality condemns hypocrisy in the form of expressing some value on one occasion and then violating that value on another. But even apart from morality, people expect consistency, and they will often ask for an explanation when you change.

Thus, we have a tentative understanding of one of the motives to gain self-knowledge. People strive for consistency, not because of some innate motivation in the brain, but because other people want them to be consistent. Other people want to understand you and predict you, and they cannot do that very well unless you are consistent. Consistency is also useful in society. When group performance and cooperation depend on people performing their roles reliably, consistency is important. Consistency is also expected in moral domains, as in keeping promises and being fair.

If the motivation to be consistent is based on other people's expectations and social pressure, then people should be more consistent when others are watching than when alone. Are they? That question was a major battleground among researchers for a decade or more, and the answer was an overwhelming yes. In particular, researchers studying attitudes and cognitive dissonance observed how people would adjust their attitudes to be consistent with some action they had been manipulated (some would say almost tricked) into performing. Clearly, they did this much more when other people were watching. For example, a standard pattern in research on cognitive dissonance enticed participants to record a brief speech arguing for some position to which they were personally opposed. Afterward, they would shift their opinion to be more consistent with what they said, and away from their original attitude. This happened much more when the speech was a videotape with name and face than an anonymous audiotape. Just getting people to sign their names was enough to increase the shift in attitudes (for reviews, see Baumeister, 1982; Schlenker, 1980; Tedeschi et al., 1971).

The desire for a positive view of self (self-enhancement) likewise may be rooted in other people's opinions. Others do not expect positivity in the same way they expect consistency, but how they treat you is based on how much they like and respect you. Remember, one of the core functions of the self is to garner approval and acceptance from others. Your self naturally wants others to regard you favorably.

ACCURACY AS MOTIVE

In contrast, the desire for accurate information is relatively indifferent to how others see you. Accurate information is useful in making your own decisions. People get clear pragmatic benefits from accurate information, and distortions for the sake of favorability or consistency carry risk. Whether to pick a fight, ask someone out, or take out a big loan are tough and consequential decisions that are most safely guided by highly accurate information.

BEHIND THE THREE MOTIVES

Let's review the bases for the three main motives to answer the question, why people seek self-knowledge.

The desire for accurate information is well grounded in pragmatic utility. Knowing your strengths and weaknesses, your charms and your flaws, will help you make better decisions and thereby will lead to a better life. This is the clearest and strongest prediction, so this should be the paramount motive.

The other two motives, for consistency and positivity, lack any clear or direct pragmatic usefulness for the self. They are however central to how people want to be regarded by others. That makes them indirectly useful to the self: If you want other people to accept you and cooperate with you—which is a central goal in social interaction—then you want to be seen positively and as consistent. You want people to trust you, like you, respect you, feel comfortable around you, and so on. Being good and consistent will help that come true. Consistency and positivity are features of the desired reputation.

We have three reasons that people might seek to learn about themselves. They are the respective quests for accurate knowledge, for positive knowledge, and for consistent, confirming knowledge. A classic paper by the august Constantine Sedikides (1993) pitted them against each other in a variety of experimental tests. We can leave the painful details of his many studies for the zealous scholar. Here, I will feature his conclusions.

First, and most important, he concluded that all three motives were genuine. He could not reduce any of them to the others or conclude that any one of them was too feeble to matter. All three reasons guide the search for self-knowledge. This is profoundly important: The quest for self-knowledge is not based in a single motive but is driven and steered by three different motives.

Second, in terms of relative power, the three seemed to operate in the opposite rank order from what you would assume based on pragmatic usefulness. *A priori*, one might assume that accurate information is the most useful, while consistent or self-verifying information is somewhat useful, and flattering information might feel good but has the least informational value. But Sedikides found that people most reliably and earnestly sought positive information about themselves. Confirming what they already believed came in second. The desire for accurate information was real, but it came in a distant third place.

Possibly in another setting, when pragmatic concerns were paramount, accuracy would have fared better. Still, it seems that under ordinary circumstances, people mainly wish to hear favorable things about themselves.

Thus, we have a winner in the contest of theories about why people seek self-knowledge. Or rather, we have three winners, but one was the biggest winner, namely self-enhancement. People seek and prefer favorable information about themselves.

The relative weakness of the accuracy motive is puzzling. Accurate information is clearly the most useful kind of information, especially for making decisions. Why does that come in third place?

The answer may lie in social relations rather than pragmatic decision making. Consistency and positivity are rooted in how one wants to be viewed by others. Forming an accurate inventory of your own strengths and weaknesses may be of some use, but it is not the primary goal of self-knowledge. Human beings learn about themselves to help them relate to their social group.

IS SELF-ENHANCEMENT HEALTHY?

The strongest motive to seek self-knowledge is the desire for favorable views of self. Is that healthy? Insofar as evolution selects in favor of patterns that improve life, one is tempted to conclude that self-enhancement must be adaptive. On the other hand, nobody likes people who are boastful or otherwise obsessed with constantly proving their superiority. Plus, of course, there are risks that go with thinking you're better than you are.

There are strong arguments, backed up by plenty of data, on both sides of the question. Hence, I do not think we can agree on a simple answer as to whether flattering oneself is good or bad. Instead, the resolution may depend on how the person goes about satisfying the self-enhancement motive.

The Negative Case

The negative case was made most forcefully in a classic paper by Jennifer Crocker and Lora Park (2004). They summarize much evidence indicating that people who are primarily concerned with maximizing their self-esteem (and/or their favorable public image) suffer costs in terms of distress, disregard of learning, and damage to interpersonal relationships. When self-esteem is threatened, people react in especially dysfunctional ways. They become so focused on rationalizing or avoiding threats that they fail to learn, to think, and to do other constructive things. For example, students who are mainly concerned with getting a good grade sometimes neglect actual learning. Efforts to minimize the impact of potential bad grades are even worse, such as when students fail to study enough, so that a low grade can be dismissed as indicating lack of preparation, rather than the more serious flaw of lacking intelligence.

The Positive Case

The positive case for the self-enhancement motive has been a theme of Sedikides's further work. In particular, a major meta-analysis (Dufner et al., 2019) combining results from almost 300 studies and 130,000 participants found far more benefits than costs, especially for the individual. In general, successful self-enhancement was linked to many positive signs of good adjustment, including more good and fewer bad emotions, less depression, and higher overall life satisfaction. Indeed, tracking people over time suggests that self-enhancement comes first, bringing higher happiness and better adjustment in its wake. That indicates self-enhancement is a cause, not just a consequence, of good things.

The Interpersonal Effects

The interpersonal effects of self-enhancement were more mixed. Self-enhancers were liked better than other people at zero acquaintance, that is, in first impressions. But this disappears entirely over time, and may even reverse. In one well-known study (Paulhus, 1998), ongoing discussion groups were tracked over several months. The narcissists and other self-enhancers were rated most favorably in the group at the first meeting, indicating that putting one's best foot forward is helpful for making a good impression. Months later, however, these same people were actively disliked relative to the rest of the group. This fits some themes that come up repeatedly in later chapters. Thinking you are better than others is hard on a relationship, and maintaining a cooperative partnership with an ego-maniac is difficult.

Another theme is that thinking well of yourself is generally quite nice for you, but it has costs that are borne by the people around you. If you've lived or worked with someone whose self-regard was inordinately high, you probably know what I mean. To avoid conflict, you have to tiptoe around to respect his or her egotism, and that makes everyday life more difficult.

Can we reconcile the Crocker and Sedikides positions? Pursuing self-esteem can certainly cause problems, especially for relationships but even for the self. Perhaps these problems arise when the pursuit is done to the exclusion of other goals, when it is done to excess, and perhaps when circumstances are bad or threatening.

Mostly, though, the tendency to see oneself slightly better than reality is healthy and normal. Appraising oneself with uncompromising accuracy can be useful, especially when deciding whether to accept a challenge. But the rest of the time, it is pleasant and even good for you to put a positive spin on your self-appraisal.

SELF-IMPROVEMENT: A FOURTH MOTIVE?

Not long after Sedikides published his definitive work on the three motives for self-knowledge, I was able to have lunch with him, and I asked him which of the three motives was the most helpful for getting through life effectively. He answered immediately that none of them was. Instead, he said, self-improvement yielded the best results. People who go through life trying to improve themselves end up better off, by and large, than people whose top priority is any of the other three: trying to think really well of themselves, trying to find out the truth about themselves, or trying to confirm what they already believed (Taylor et al.,1995).

Self-improvement has not been as much studied as the other motives, perhaps because the view of self is not the goal or endpoint. Rather, it is a means. One useful sign comes from seeing whom people compare themselves against (Buunk, Kuyper, & van der Zee, 2005; Taylor et al., 1995). When you want to feel good about yourself (self-enhancement), you use downward comparison. That is, you focus your attention on people who are doing worse than you are, and you dwell on how you are superior to them. In contrast, a focus on self-improvement brings upward comparison: noting others who are better than you and where you have room to improve.

Upward comparisons provide useful information. Downward comparisons make you feel good about yourself. Self-improvers favor upward comparisons.

Self-enhancement also tends to emphasize the past, whereas self-improvement is future-oriented. Improvement means changing the present to make a better future. The other motives are based on how the self is now, or at least how you like to think of yourself now. Self-improvement sees the self as it now is in relation to what it could and should be, in the future. It also elicits a greater focus on objective information than the others, though of course self-assessment also seeks objective information.

In terms of honesty and accuracy, self-improvement has the advantage that it accepts current imperfections in order to envision a better future in which those have been fixed. When research subjects are primed with the self-improvement motive, they do not show some of the self-deception patterns such as ignoring or dismissing negative feedback. When you are focused on self-improvement, you are open to acknowledging your faults because these are the areas in which you want to get better (Green, Sedikides, Pinter, & Van Tongeren, 2009).

Self-improvement is often the purpose of self-regulation. This is covered in some depth in future chapters dealing with the executive function part of the self, the part that makes choices and gets things done.

MORE ON SELF-KNOWLEDGE AND SELF-ESTEEM

When it's a matter of seeing and sizing up other people, mostly you want to see them accurately. (There may be some exceptions made for loved ones and idolized leaders, and probably detested enemies.) Overestimating or underestimating other people leads to poor decisions about whether to partner up with them, which is one of the main reasons to form impressions. In contrast, you want yourself to be perceived favorably by others because that will open up the best opportunities. Accurate self-knowledge is at best a mixed blessing. When you think about yourself, therefore, the primary focus is probably on the impression you want other people to have of you.

Thus, self-knowledge is not just a collection of factoids and stories. Rather, it is heavily laced with evaluation. You want to know not just what your traits are but whether these are good or bad.

Hence, our inquiry into self-knowledge must also address the striving for self-esteem. Self-esteem is the good–bad dimension of self-knowledge. Self-esteem actually has two major roles in self theory. One is the quest for high self-esteem, the desire to think favorably of oneself. We have already addressed this to some degree because the self-enhancement motive includes the striving for high self-esteem. The other involves variations among people: Some people have higher self-esteem than others, and the difference shows up in a broad assortment of actions, reactions, and emotions. A later chapter covers personality differences, including how to understand the key differences between people who have high versus low self-esteem. Here, we focus on it as a motivated dimension of self-knowledge.

Having some knowledge of oneself can be useful for dealing with the environment. Should you go up to that group over there and try to join in? Will you be accepted or rejected? Can you help steer events toward a good outcome? That kind of self-knowledge is important.

In human social life, you create a public self that is basically propositional though informed by narratives. Events can alter it, like if you achieve something great, get a major award, or do something disgraceful. The private self may be essentially narrative, though informed by propositional knowledge.

The key point is that the human social being finds it useful to maintain an inner model that tracks how it is perceived by the group. It's useful to know your place in society, know what others expect of you, indeed know how well they think of you—which is largely based on how well you perform your role(s) in the social system.

SELF-ESTEEM: GLOBAL OR SPECIFIC?

Thus far we have seen that people are motivated to build and maintain a positive view of self. The most likely reason for this is that humans evolved to live in a cooperative society, and so their reputation matters. The self-concept is useful as a person's way of keeping track of his or her reputation. The self-concept may take on a bit of functional autonomy here, which is to say, people start to act as if the self-concept is an end in itself, independent of reputation. People may therefore sometimes deceive themselves. It feels good to reassure oneself that one is loaded with positive attributes, even if the reality and reputation do not justify that happy conclusion.

One debate that has raged over the decades is whether thinking well of oneself is a global matter or is mainly about specifics. Researchers have split over whether what matters is your total, overall view of yourself (e.g., "I'm a good person") or domain-specific evaluations ("I'm good at playing piano sonatas"). Herbert Marsh's research program (e.g., Marsh, 2006; Marsh & Craven, 2006) has shown that global self-esteem has fairly little relationship to school performance, whereas domain-specific self-esteem is often linked to performance: Children who think they are good at math actually do better at math (see also Marsh et al., 2006) . To be sure, it is tough for a researcher to separate the effects of being good at math from thinking oneself good at math. Some of Marsh's best evidence comes from studies based on social comparison. The same children, with the same math ability, do better when they are a big fish in a small pond (i.e., surrounded by other kids whose ability is less than theirs) than a small fish in a big pond. That suggests the favorable view of self, based on fortuitous comparisons, helps cause the better performance.

To be sure, thinking you're good at math when you're not is more likely a problem than an advantage. But thinking you're bad at math when you're not is also a problem, and perhaps a more common and serious one. If the rest of the class gets the new concept right away while you need a second try, you might get discouraged and fail to make the second try.

The global and specific forms of self-esteem are not entirely unrelated. A person fits into a society by being useful in some key fashion, perhaps by honing one fine skill. In evolutionary history, perhaps being good at tracking animals for game, or being good at finding and digging edible roots, was valued by the group. This specific skill led to being accepted by the group, so that the self was good enough overall based on being good enough at one thing.

THE MYSTERIOUS EFFECTS OF SELF-AFFIRMATION

In 1988, Claude Steele put forward a theory of self-affirmation. His view was that people wish to have an overall positive view of self. Stellar perfection was not necessary. Being generally good enough was the primary and crucial goal. Steele thought there would be palpable consequences of merely thinking about one's good qualities.

Does the goal of having a globally positive self-view work like important goals in general? Given this drive for a globally favorable self, one could look for two patterns that are found with many motivations, namely satiation and substitution. Satiation means that when you get what you want, you are satisfied for a while and therefore stop wanting it—like not being hungry after eating a big meal. Normally you love steak and fries, but after a big meal of those delicious foods you don't want any more.

Substitution means that you are content with different, alternative sources of satisfaction. If you normally have a sandwich for lunch but one day find your favorite sandwich shop closed, you can be satisfied with something different instead, like some pizza.

Would the desire for a positive global view of self work like this? Steele thought so. He said that if people experienced self-affirmation, such as reflecting on something good about themselves, they would be satisfied enough to dispense with protecting self-esteem in other domains.

Over the years, an impressive body of research findings has built up to support Steele's theory. An interesting twist has been that self-affirmation procedures have not been confined to thinking positive thoughts about oneself. In many studies, people simply reflect on their most important values, or they write a brief paragraph about why these values are important to them. It's not entirely clear just how doing that constitutes a "self-affirmation," though it does allow the individual to express important values that presumably guide his or her actions.

A series of reviews by the fabulous team of Dave Sherman and Geoff Cohen (2006, 2014; see also Moss, 2016; Sherman, 2013) has documented the many benefits from these simple affirmations. For example, when people fail at some task, they often feel bad and may ruminate about what went wrong—but if they have engaged in self-affirmation, they do not have such a negative reaction. Likewise, interpersonal rejection sometimes makes people feel more prejudiced toward members of other groups, but, again, self-affirmation eliminates this reaction. There is even evidence that self-affirmation enables students from minority groups to do better in their schoolwork.

The general conclusions are these. Self-affirmation reduces all manner of defensive responses, by which is meant negative, hostile, or distorting reactions to anything bad (or even possibly bad) about the self that happens to come up. This fits the satiation aspect of the motivation: Self-affirmation satisfies the drive to think well of self, and so for a while one can be more accepting of criticism and setbacks. Self-affirmation promotes a kind of resilience that we shall later see associated with high self-esteem: "This failure does not demolish me because I know I have many good traits, and so I can bounce back."

Three general conclusions are emphasized in Cohen and Sherman's (2014) overview. First, the basic concern is with global self, less than with specific aspects. That is, the goal is to establish oneself as a good person overall, with morally valued traits and competencies. (Hence, substitution works well.)

Second, the drive is toward adequacy rather than superiority. The person wants to be good enough rather than needing to be better than everyone else. This also fits well with human evolutionary history, in which hierarchy was actively discouraged and people were not supposed to set themselves above others. Rather, the group would accept you if you were good enough. As Sherman and Cohen put it, self-affirmation is "an act that demonstrates one's adequacy."

Third, the point is not praising yourself but rather acting in ways that are worthy of praise or esteem. This suggests again that fitting into the group is what matters, rather than simply thinking well of yourself in the privacy of your own mind. Thinking well of yourself is not the ultimate goal, most likely because self-love is not sufficient to maintain your acceptance in the social group. For acceptance, actually doing positive things (and having others recognize and respect them) is crucial.

Many people associate self-affirmation with simple habits of self-praise. In the early decades of the 20th century, there was a fad promoted by Emil Coué (1922), who advised people to recite to themselves frequently (at least 20 times per day) "Every day, in every way, I am getting better and better." This was thought to help unconscious processes function well and bring positive changes.

The self-affirmation findings from the research labs do not entirely correspond to this simplified version, but the resemblance is palpable. The emphasis on being good enough (rather than superior) and on the global self is correct, as is Coue's link to unconscious processes. (Studies found that self-affirmation boosted unconscious/automatic self-esteem responses but not conscious self-esteem.) Again, however, simply praising yourself to yourself is not enough. Instead, reflecting on core values helps prepare the self to act in estimable ways, should the occasion arise.

KEY POINTS

- People are motivated to seek self-knowledge for self-enhancement, for consistency, for accurate information, and possibly for self-improvement. The self-enhancement motive is the strongest, at least in American samples, but all are real.
- The self seeks to build a positive, consistent reputation.
- Self-knowledge is heavily laced with evaluation. You want to know not just what your traits are but whether these are good or bad. Self-esteem is the good–bad dimension of self-knowledge.
- Self-affirmation reduces all manner of defensive responses so, for a while, one can be more accepting of criticism and setbacks.

CHAPTER 14

Building Self-Knowledge

How People Learn about Themselves

The self is something that is created and re-created. There are certainly some definite facts about one's identity, such as name and birthplace. But in general self-knowledge is information about an entity that is in flux, and it is gradually built up and refined.

People desire self-knowledge, and they wish it to be somewhat accurate, though as we have seen, they also prefer it to be positive. They acquire it by multiple means, which is itself an indication of how much they want it. This chapter is about how self-beliefs are formed and accumulated.

INTROSPECTION

Some self-knowledge comes from looking inside. Self-awareness means being aware of yourself, and presumably it yields some useful information. People know their thoughts and feelings, and of course they have been front-and-center witness to their own lives and experiences, so they do have plenty of available information about themselves.

The reliability of introspection has been an ongoing debate for almost the entire history of psychology. The first psychology laboratory, headed by Wilhelm Wundt in Germany, relied heavily on introspection as its main source of data. The wider population's view of psychology was long dominated by Sigmund Freud's approach. Freud certainly included introspection but regarded it as seriously deficient and always suspect. In Freud's view, much of the important stuff was unconscious, which by definition is out of reach of introspection. Decades later, American behaviorist labs revolted stridently against introspection, focusing their main efforts on studying white rats (who are not much given to introspection) and measuring objective movements, while dismissing the mind as a "black box" impervious to proper scientific inquiry. Later, social psychology took off with the study of attitudes, for which introspection and self-report were central: the best way to know somebody's attitudes is to ask. The reliance on having people report their thoughts and feelings as the main way to do psychology has gained ground in recent decades, partly because it is much easier than observing and measuring actual human behavior (Baumeister, Vohs, & Funder, 2007).

Still, modern psychologists remain skeptical of introspection. A huge blow to the prestige of introspection was delivered in the 1970s by two thoughtful psychologists at the University of Michigan, Richard Nisbett and Tim Wilson (1977). They noted that people spend plenty of time explaining their actions and feelings to other people—but often they are unable to know the true causes of these. Nisbett and Wilson concluded that introspection is mostly a sham. People have a stock of standard explanations for why they do things, and they dip into this stockpile to explain themselves, rather than having any genuine understanding of what goes on in their mind.

As often happens, the initial article had a huge impact by making a profound and important point but taking it to an extreme. Wilson, at least, continues to believe that conscious thinking is relatively misinformed and useless. His innovative research has shown that when people try to analyze their reasons for something, they tend to mislead themselves. Their immediate gut reactions are often closer to the mark than what they say after a period of introspective analysis. In one of his books (Wilson, 2002), he advises readers to dispense with introspection. If they want self-knowledge, they should take classes in psychology that cover research studies on general patterns of human behavior. Trying to know yourself through introspection is doomed and futile, in Wilson's view.

Others pushed back. Introspection remains a popular method in psychology and, as I said, it has been gaining ground in recent decades. As psychologists gradually abandon methods that involve observing actual behavior, they rely ever more on asking people to report what they are thinking and feeling. Psychologists cannot focus their research on asking people what their thoughts and feelings are while simultaneously believing that these self-reports are hopelessly invalid.

As usual, my approach seeks to identify what is right on both sides, and integrate. People do know what they are thinking and feeling, so introspection works very well as far as that goes. Meanwhile, those thoughts and feelings are partly the result of unconscious, automatic processes, and introspection cannot get at those. By definition one is not conscious of what happens unconsciously! When the conscious mind seeks to explain itself, it must therefore impute, even guess, what the unconscious processes contributed. It may get some right but probably not all.

In other words, introspection can describe better than it can explain. The contents of consciousness can be observed and reported accurately. The reasons and processes behind them are sometimes shielded from consciousness, so introspection cannot reveal them. Moreover—and this is an important aspect of the Nisbett and Wilson contribution—the conscious mind seems not to know that it doesn't know these things, so it guesses, and then mistakes its guesses for valid truth.

Self-knowledge based on introspection is therefore partly valid and partly mistaken. The mistakes are not likely to be the opposite of the truth. Rather, unconscious biases will systematically distort self-knowledge, without your knowing that distortion has happened. This will prove to be a key part of the self-deception process.

THE SELF-REFERENCE EFFECT: THE GOLDEN FOLDER

I turn now to the idea of building self-knowledge using a simple, even minimalist approach. Let's try a mundane and simple metaphor. The self is like a folder, into which things can be inserted for storage and from which they can be retrieved for later use. It also has extra importance, so whatever gets put into that folder automatically gains impact and value.

The core idea is this. Information processed in connection with the self gets extra attention and mental processing and is stored in memory better than other information. This has been called the "self-reference effect," which means that anything that refers to the self gets noticed and remembered better than most other information.

The classic study that opened up this way of thinking was published in 1977 by Rogers, Kuiper, and Kirker. Their experiments used a deceptively simple procedure. Research subjects saw a word flash on the screen and had to answer one question about it. Different words got different questions. The crucial question was "Does the word describe you?" Other questions were whether the word was printed in large print, whether the word rhymed with another word, and whether it had the same meaning as another word. These were all randomly mixed and interspersed. Different participants answered different questions about the same words.

Later in the experiment, after all the words had been seen and all the questions answered, there was a surprise test: The experimenter asked people to write down all the words they remembered. The researchers could then count up which words were remembered and match those with what question had been asked. The crucial finding was that people remembered best the words that had come with the question "Does the word describe you?" Somehow that question boosted memory, compared to other questions. That was the self-reference effect.

The self-reference effect may give the impression that people mainly remember things that fit their self-concept. In fact, Rogers and colleagues had to correct that in their own work. When they first tried to publish their findings, they had concluded that people mainly remembered words for which they responded "yes" to the question about describing themselves. Fewer words that got a no answer were recalled. However, the journal editors noticed a statistical problem because people said "yes" to that question far more often than they said "no." (This fits what we have already reported as a general pattern, that people think they have lots and lots of traits, even ones that seem to contradict each other, as long as they aren't bad traits.) So even though there were more "yes, that describes me" words than "no, that doesn't describe me" words among the ones people recalled on the final test, it wasn't that the yes answers were remembered better. When the researchers corrected for the statistical problem, the "no, that's not me" words were remembered just as well.

The important point is that briefly thinking about a word in relation to the self makes the word extra-memorable. It was the question, not the answer, that made the difference. Just thinking about whether a word fits you, even if you end up deciding that it does not fit you, causes it to stick in memory better than other words. That brief association, caused by thinking of the word in connection with the self, boosted memory.

If we think of the memory process as putting things into folders, the self has an especially important folder; hence, the "golden folder" in this section's title. The human mind is alert to things that are relevant to the self. Even the act of denying that something describes you is enough to make it sink in.

The self is not the only golden folder. A subsequent paper (Greenwald & Banaji, 1989) concluded that the self is "powerful but ordinary." Yes, the self adds importance to other things so that they are remembered better, but other important cues also enhance memory. Other folders, perhaps including sex and money, would also enhance memory.

Not everyone shows the self-reference effect, and one reason may be that the folder is not so golden for them. People who suffered childhood traumas are an important exception, apparently because they tend to have mental dissociation, a failure to connect different thoughts in general. These early traumas attach bad feelings to the self, and so the unity project keeps bumping into them. When new information relevant to the self comes in, they do not do the elaborative thinking of additional connections and implications that normally solidifies these mental connections (Chiu et al., 2019).

The self is also much impressed by its own activity. In particular, making choices improves memory. A series of studies by the incisive Brandon

Schmeichel and colleagues (in press) showed that people remember things best when they put forth mental effort to choose them. This goes beyond the self-reference effect because even when other people choose things for you, you do not remember those things as well as when you choose things for yourself.

Another related pattern is the endowment effect, which is that owning something makes people value it more (Kahneman et al., 1990). The original experiments showed some people a coffee mug and asked how much they would pay for it, while other people were given the coffee mug to keep and then asked how much they would sell it for. It was the same mug and moments earlier they had never seen it, nor did they choose it, but the mere fact of owning it made them assign it a higher price. This is usually discussed in terms of economic rationality and financial decision making, which is fine, but it is also relevant to the self. As we have seen, ownership is one of the important social foundations of selfhood.

Ownership connects an item to a self. The implication is that value flows from the self to the item. The mere fact that something is mine makes me value it more. This is part of the more general self-enhancement effect; people overestimate the positive value of the self, and so they overestimate the positive value of things that belong to the self (Beggan, 1992). The golden folder makes its contents seem a bit golden.

One pathway to self-knowledge is extra information processing. The self pays extra attention to information relevant to itself, thinks more about that information, and therefore gives it an extra-strong memory trace. Its thinking and choosing activities leave extra-strong memory traces. The self also pays extra attention to and confers extra value on things that it owns. These patterns of basic information processing contribute to self-knowledge.

THE LOOKING-GLASS SELF

Undoubtedly, people learn a great deal about themselves from others. Interacting with others gives you plenty of information about what kind of person you are, what things you do well or badly. It may seem funny that you have to rely on others to find out about yourself because you can observe yourself directly. But though you can observe the physical facts of yourself, you don't know how they measure up to what is valued in society. You can run a mile by yourself and have direct experience of how hard it was and how long it took, but you need to engage with others to conclude whether your run was Olympic potential or a disgrace.

So there is at least one radical alternative to the simple view that you know yourself from direct experience: your self-knowledge is acquired from others. Your self-concept is the product of feedback from other people. Your knowledge of yourself originates in other people's views of you. Remember, too, that what others think of you has enormous pragmatic importance. What you think of yourself is of much less consequence, at least in terms of directly contributing to your success or failure in life.

My favorite example of this is now slightly dated, thanks to the widespread availability of Internet porn. But prior to that, I used to provoke people by claiming that a man's knowledge of his own penis size was basically hearsay. This seemed a joke because a man can simply look down and see exactly how large his penis is, so there's no hearsay about that. Crucially, he has no way of knowing whether that is good or bad—something that depends entirely on comparison with others. And it was extremely rare for a heterosexual man to see an erect penis other than his own. Self-knowledge depends on social interaction, including feedback from others and social comparison.

The idea that self-knowledge is derived from social interaction was central to a major intellectual movement in the middle of the 20th century, symbolic interactionism. George Herbert Mead (1934) and others wrote about the "generalized other," a compendium of interaction partners who knew you and who taught you to know yourself. Carried to an extreme, this approach dispenses with navel-gazing introspection and other sorts of inner experience as the foundation of self-knowledge. People interact with each other and through those interactions acquire information about themselves, partly from explicit statements about you but also in how they treat you. Knowing others comes before knowing the self.

In one of the earliest statements of this view, Cooley (1902) spoke of the "looking-glass self." His idea was that other people function like a mirror (a "looking glass"), enabling you to see yourself. Without others, you would have no self-image.

Self-knowledge thus comes from looking outward, not looking inward. One popular small-group exercise is to give everyone a number and tell everyone to pair up with as high a number as possible. The catch is that people do not know their own numbers. Instead, the numbers are shown on cards attached to each person's forehead. Even though people cannot see their own number, they figure it out pretty fast. If everyone is approaching you, your number must be high. Conversely, if everyone shuns you, you're probably low.

There is something right and important about this. Information about the self is only meaningful in relation to others. Even when there are objective measurements, like how fast you can run a mile, the numbers only matter in comparison. Many traits refer specifically to how you interact with others. In the Big Five dimensions of personality, at least two of the five (extraversion and agreeableness) are entirely about styles of treating other people, so social input is decisive. (You can't be agreeable if nobody thinks you are.) Even more important, other people tell you how they see you, and self-knowledge is largely distilled from this input.

These powerful ideas got a bucket of ice water in a sweeping review article by Shrauger and Schoeneman (1979). Those two scholars combed through dozens of studies that provided data on a key prediction of the symbolic interactionist view. If your concept of yourself is based on what other people think of you, then it should match pretty well with how other people rate you. The small mountain of data compiled for this project yielded a fairly dismal conclusion. People's self-concepts did not match up very well with how others viewed them. The looking-glass self didn't seem to be functioning very well.

Digging deeper, Shrauger and Schoeneman took a hard look at one of the ostensible middlemen in the looking-glass process. In between Betsy's opinion of herself and Betsy's acquaintances' opinion of her was a hybrid: Betsy's understanding of how her acquaintances viewed her. It generally emerged that this matched up pretty well with Betsy's view of herself, and not so well with how others viewed her.

That helped locate the problem. The looking-glass process was operating just fine as far as Betsy knew. That is, her self-concept is quite close to the way she thinks others see her. The mysterious gap lies between how she thinks they see her and how they actually see her.

Two Problems with the Looking-Glass Self

Two problems prevent people from forming an accurate impression of how others view them (Felson, 1981, 1989). One is that people do not tell you bluntly and fully what they think of you. In particular, they avoid pointing out your faults and failures to you. Even when the occasion calls for it, they may make excuses or prevaricate. Actress Bette Davis, looking back on her stellar movie career in a 1987 interview, said that her favorite line in all her films was "I'd like to kiss you, but I just washed my hair." Obviously, such a line is much harder for the unkissed suitor to make sense of than "I think you're ugly" or "You don't have enough money to get a kiss from me." It even might give hope that she would kiss him if he managed to ask again at a more propitious time, when her hair was dirty or at least dry.

The other problem that prevents people from knowing how others see them lies in their own defenses. When others do manage to say what they think is wrong with you, you might well dismiss or rationalize what they said. People's psychological defenses will be covered shortly. For now, the point is that the failure of the looking-glass self is not entirely due to people's reluctance to criticize. Rather, it is a kind of conspiracy of silence. When the news is bad, one doesn't want to say it and the other doesn't want to hear it. The chances for well-rounded effective communication are slim.

Moreover, defensive self-deception aside, some skepticism about feedback from others is probably a good thing. If you changed your opinion of yourself every time someone complimented or criticized you, it would be hard to have any sort of stable understanding of yourself. The unity project would be almost impossible. And many criticisms are ambiguous: Sometimes other drivers honk at you when you've done something wrong, but sometimes they honk because they are grumpy and rushed and you happen to be in the way. The first chapter discussed the question of whether people are a product of their environment or can create themselves by their own choices and efforts, and the answer had to be a dialectical mixture of both. Here again, we see that people are affected by feedback from others, but they are not just passively shaped by it. They actively and selectively take in feedback from the social world to build a stable understanding of self.

INFERENCES FROM BEHAVIOR

One more theory of self-knowledge is that some of it is acquired by processes largely similar to how we learn about other people. You observe someone's behavior, note patterns, and make inferences and conclusions about what kind of person is there underneath.

This deceptively simple theory was proposed by Daryl Bem (1965, 1972). For years it was the sparring partner for cognitive dissonance theory, as both sought to explain why people changed their attitudes to fit their sometimes weird recent actions. Dissonance theorists proposed that people want to be consistent and so seek to justify their actions by affirming that their actions did indeed express their attitudes. Bem wondered if a simpler explanation would suffice: People see themselves doing something and infer their own underlying motives, much as one would when observing other people. Many studies undertook to test competing predictions for the two theories. Cognitive dissonance won most of the battles, but self-perception won some of them.

On the surface, Bem's theory seems like another rejection of the idea that people get self-knowledge directly by introspection, somewhat reminiscent of how the behaviorists rejected studying mental processes, or how Nisbett and Wilson disparaged self-reports. But Bem was no fool. In stating his theory, he had not claimed that introspection was useless or ineffective in general. He merely said sometimes it does not work, and in some cases people fall back on these self-perception processes.

Suppose I think I like good-tasting healthy foods. Yogurt is one, and I approve of fruit flavors, so I should like peach yogurt. On that basis, several times I buy peach yogurt and install it in my refrigerator. But then I never eat it and end up throwing it away each time (though I then buy a new one). I might at some point conclude that I don't really like peach yogurt, contrary to my introspective assumption. I should stop buying it so I don't have to keep throwing it away.

Moreover, as we have seen, the purpose of knowing others is different from the purpose of self-knowledge. No doubt self-knowledge can occasionally borrow methods from how one learns about others, but given the discrepant goals, we should expect there to be ample differences.

There is enough evidence to affirm that some self-knowledge is acquired through these self-perception processes. But probably it is a fairly minor source.

THINKING GROWS SELF-KNOWLEDGE

Once there is a coherent foundation of self-knowledge, new information about the self continues to come in. The new information is then slotted into the existing body of information, depending on how the already-there understanding of self is organized and what the new information means.

A major principle is that while people are often eager to learn about themselves and frequently add new information, once that knowledge is formed, it becomes resistant to change. Once people decide they are a certain way, they are reluctant to revise that. They are especially reluctant to revise in a negative direction, so upward revisions are embraced a bit faster. This, after all, is what underlies self-verification (consistency) patterns: People prefer to confirm what they already believe about themselves. And of course they are more willing to change something negative to positive than the reverse. People may be initially skeptical when hearing that they are smarter, or better-looking, or more charming than they had previously thought, but they are willing to be persuaded. It is harder to persuade them that they are stupider, uglier, or more obnoxious than they had believed.

What do we know about people accepting new information about themselves? Since the 1960s, at least, researchers have recognized that people are often surprisingly willing to accept information about themselves, though this may just mean that self-knowledge is flexible and diverse enough to accommodate vague, general characterizations. I began my research career working with the "P. T. Barnum effect" (Meehl, 1956), named after the famous showman. It means that ordinary people are willing to accept a wide range of characterizations of themselves, including a generic and randomly assigned one, as a highly meaningful, personal, and accurate account. A famous version (from Aronson & Mettee, 1968) randomly gave people feedback that they were stable or unstable, did or did not have "compulsive tendencies," were selfish or unselfish, were good at remaining calm or tended to get excited under pressure, and the like. People were inclined to believe whichever version they were given.

The Barnum effect may explain the perennial appeal of horoscopes, fortune telling, and other sources. If we throw some randomly generated personality descriptions at you, probably you can think of something you've done or felt that fits each one. Here are a few of the horoscopes I recently saw while riding public transport: "You may have to put a lot of effort into making something right"; "You may be feeling as if you have a million things to attend to. Make a list!"; "You may have to accept the right of someone to be different, or to hold a different opinion"; "Find ways around the limitations being imposed on you currently."

Did you react to any of those by thinking, "That could be me"?

People can view themselves in various different ways. As we have seen, they tend to see themselves as having all (good and neutral) traits, even seemingly contradictory ones. But if they do make up their mind that they are one way and not another, that view resists change.

KEY POINTS

- Self-knowledge is important, and you get it through multiple routes and processes, including introspection, self-reference, seeing how others react to you, and inferences from your own behavior.
- Self-knowledge based on introspection is partly valid and partly mistaken.
- Information processed in connection with the self gets extra attention and mental processing and is stored in memory better than other information. This has been called the "self-reference effect."
- Your knowledge of yourself partly originates in other people's views of you, but this is likely to be distorted.
- None of the ways people learn about themselves is entirely reliable, which raises the question of how accurately people understand themselves.

CHAPTER 15

Self-Esteem

Self-esteem is the good–bad dimension of self-beliefs. People with high self-esteem have favorable beliefs about themselves, along with positive feelings ("I like myself"). Low self-esteem is rather more difficult to pin down, but it is in some way the opposite of those good feelings and positive beliefs.

Self-esteem is one of the most widely studied personality traits. There are genuine differences between people who score high versus low in self-esteem. Good measures of self-esteem were available relatively early in the history of psychology, and so data began to accumulate by the middle of the 20th century. At the end of the century, when the Association for Psychological Science commissioned several of us to search through the literature and come up with a conclusion about the benefits (or lack thereof) of high self-esteem, our first computer search yielded 18,000 publications. The number is probably more than twice that today.

IS IT BETTER TO HAVE HIGH SELF-ESTEEM?

Suppose a young man has an IQ of 115: above average but no genius. What ideally should he believe his IQ to be? To think it is 130 would certainly qualify as high self-esteem because 130 is good, and it is certainly better than the objective truth. Yet, is it wise or helpful to encourage people to believe they are smarter than they are? The debate over the value of boosting self-esteem has fascinated scientists as well as society at large. That was indeed the focus of what the Association for Psychological Science assigned a team of researchers to evaluate, and the report covers much of the work on which the early part of this chapter is based (Baumeister et al., 2003; Baumeister, Campbell, Krueger, & Vohs, 2005).

To be sure, making people raise their opinion of their talents and abilities is not the only pathway to higher self-esteem. Perhaps the young man with high self-esteem knows his IQ is 115—but thinks that is perfectly fine. That might be called "self-acceptance": He knows his limitations but also appreciates his good qualities. Such a case is harder to make if the man's IQ is 85, thus below average. Perhaps he can be satisfied with his low intelligence and value himself for other traits.

AN EPIDEMIC OF LOW SELF-ESTEEM?

The so-called self-esteem movement drew international public attention to self-esteem. Starting around 1970, several leaders began to write and speak about the importance of self-esteem, the dangers of low self-esteem, and the need to bolster it across the population (e.g., Branden, 1969). There was a general sense that people were suffering from an epidemic of low self-esteem. Some groups, such as adolescent girls and minorities, were especially seen as prone to "plunging" low self-esteem (discussed and refuted by Kling et al., 1999). Programs were developed to bolster self-esteem. There were school classes devoted to self-esteem, in which, for example, students might be assigned to make a collage depicting their good traits. There were self-esteem coloring books, self-esteem blankets, self-esteem car seats. Entrepreneurs developed programs to come to schools for a couple of days to help build students' high self-esteem.

Social scientists seized on self-esteem as a potent explanation for many of society's ills. Perhaps women have failed to flourish in society because they have low self-esteem, and indeed a popular book argued that when a girl reaches puberty, her self-esteem plummets downward (Pipher, 1994). Likewise, many writers explained how African Americans were held down by their low self-esteem, which had its irrational and unfair origins in the larger society's prejudices against them. Their high crime and violence rates, poor school outcomes, unstable family relationships, and the like could all be explained as stemming from low self-esteem. If only self-esteem could be raised, these problems might diminish sharply or even disappear.

The State of California appointed a task force to encourage self-esteem across the state, with the hope that it would reduce social problems such as crime, violence, drug abuse, mental illness, unwanted pregnancy, and unemployment (see California Task Force, 1990). John Vasconcellos, the state representative who spearheaded this initiative, waxed optimistic that raising self-esteem would help solve the state's money problems (Winegar, 1990). He explained that people with high self-esteem do better work, earn higher salaries, and therefore pay more taxes than people with low self-esteem. After some years, the task force was disbanded, its goals unrealized. The state's budget problems continued.

Several crucial questions were shunted aside. First, was there really an epidemic of low self-esteem? Second, is boosting self-esteem to higher levels an effective way to improve lives and make society as a whole better? Third, and most fundamentally, does high self-esteem really cause good things to happen?

When researchers looked at how people scored on self-esteem measures, they never found scores clustering at the low end. *Au contraire*, most people scored somewhere from the middle to the high end, with very few truly low ones (see Baumeister, Tice, & Hutton, 1989). This was true for all the different measures of self-esteem that different researchers developed.

Perhaps most surprisingly, African Americans generally scored higher on self-esteem than White people (Crocker & Major, 1989). All those lavish theories about how low self-esteem lay at the root of African American citizens' problems were suddenly irrelevant.

As for the distaff deficit, well, a massive review of evidence by Kling and colleagues (1999) concluded that there is a consistent but quite small difference between men and women on self-esteem, and it reaches its peak around adolescence—the peak being about a quarter of a standard deviation. Kling and colleagues explicitly rejected the alarmist arguments of Pipher and others who spoke of a crisis in teen girls' "plummeting" self-esteem. Even there, it does not seem that girls' self-esteem drops, but rather teenage boys get a spike in egomania. Some writers have speculated that this has its roots in evolution. The young male ape needs confidence to challenge the alpha male, which determines whether he will have plenty of babies or none.

My impression is also that the small gender difference in self-esteem is mainly due to body image. I do not see that young women think they are less intelligent than young men, or less socially skilled, or less moral. But many young women think their bodies have flaws, whereas young men, for whatever reason, generally think their bodies are just fine. The quarter standard deviation difference could well be mainly tied up in that discrepancy.

Looking back, psychology's support for the self-esteem movement was an honest mistake. Low self-esteem was correlated with all manner of personal problems, including poor school performance, unemployment, and unwanted pregnancy. So, if there were fewer low-self-esteem people, there should be fewer of all those various unfortunates. But as the researchers had all supposedly learned in their methodology class, correlation does not prove causation. In the long run, the extravagant promises of the self-esteem advocates were not filled. Self-esteem is more a result than a cause. Sure, unemployed people have lower self-esteem than people with great, high-paying jobs. But low self-esteem is not the reason they ended up unemployed. Rather, unemployment caused the low self-esteem.

School performance matters to many people. Plenty of studies found significant albeit modest correlations, such that kids scoring higher in self-esteem got better grades. Some of these relied on having the children report their grades, which makes things easy for the researchers but introduces a major problem, to which we shall return shortly, namely that maybe those with high self-esteem just claim to have better grades rather than really having them. But other researchers did the due diligence of getting school transcripts, and the correlation was still there. High self-esteem really did go with better grades.

Americans in particular have long sought ways to make kids smarter and better educated without their having to do all that homework. Wouldn't it be lovely if you could become a math whiz on the strength of believing in yourself to be a math whiz? But, in the long run, it turned out that you really have to do all those homework problems if you want to be a math whiz. Believing yourself to be a budding genius is little or no help.

The truth began to emerge in studies that tracked children over time. One major study looked at self-esteem and grades over several years. Self-esteem in 10th grade failed to predict school performance in 12th grade—a serious blow to the idea that self-esteem causes grades. In contrast, grades received in 10th grade did significantly predict self-esteem in 12th grade. So, it's not that thinking well of yourself causes you to earn high marks. Instead, earning high marks makes you think well of yourself (Bachman & O'Malley, 1977, 1986). The high marks came first, then the high self-esteem.

PERILS OF BOOSTING SELF-ESTEEM

What about school practices aimed at raising self-esteem—might they not still do some good? The people who made gobs of money from visiting schools to raise children's self-esteem were not often eager to obtain scientifically strong data about whether their programs were effective, quite possibly because the data showed that the programs accomplished little other than encourage idle self-praise. One pair of researchers who combed through the available data concluded that these programs were ineffective at producing real improvements in behavior (Scheirer & Kraut, 1979).

Properly designed research is extremely rare, however. What is needed is random assignment of children from the same population so that some of them get self-esteem boosting and others don't. (Random assignment evens out all the ways that people differ from each other.)

Only one study has really done a proper job, and it is unlikely to be repeated. Professor Don Forsyth conducted it in his own introductory psychology class (Forsyth et al., 2007). All the students who received poor grades on the midterm exam received weekly emails the rest of the semester.

The emails contained a review question and, by random assignment, possibly something else. For some, the emails also contained a message aimed at boosting self-esteem (e.g., "Remember to hold up your head and your self-esteem"). Shockingly, the self-esteem boost caused students to perform worse on the final exam. Apparently, students took the message to heart in the form of "Why should I bother with working hard on this course? I'm already a wonderful person."

These days psychology tends to insist on replicating experimental results, and a one-time finding, provocative as it is, is viewed with skepticism. Unfortunately, it is almost impossible to conduct a replication of Forsyth's study. He honestly thought that the self-esteem boosting would improve grades, and the ethics committee agreed. Once he found that boosting self-esteem made students get lower grades, it became seriously unethical to try that again. It's a bit like doing a study to try out a new medicine that was expected to improve health, only to find that it made people seriously sick and killed a few of them. No one would repeat that experiment.

Another bit of useful evidence comes from one of the traditional issues for schoolteachers and administrators, namely whether to flunk a student who does poorly. When I was young, before self-esteem became a policy issue, some students simply accumulated too many failing marks and had to repeat the year in the same grade level. The self-esteem movement brought this practice under fire, as it was deemed detrimental to a student's self-esteem to make him or her repeat the year, left behind by friends and peers and thrown in with the younger kids. The practice of *social promotion* spread: Advance the child to the next grade, perhaps with a bit of extra help and encouragement, so as to avoid damaging self-esteem.

The practice of social promotions received a telling blow in studies by Herbert Marsh and colleagues (see Marsh, 2016; Marsh et al., 2017). The socially promoted students don't bounce back. They have not mastered the material for the third grade, and now they have to start fourth grade without being adequately prepared. (Plus, all the other kids think/know the kids are dumb and struggling.) In contrast, students held back for a year improve dramatically. It turns out third grade is easier the second time around (and especially if the kid was not quite intellectually mature enough a year ago but in the interim has grown capable of mastering the material). Crucially, the gains are sustained. In one study, Marsh and colleagues (2017) followed up with the children 5 years later. The ones who had been held back had continued their improved performance, unlike the socially promoted ones, who were still struggling.

Much of Marsh's work bears out his theory that it's better to be a big fish in a small pond than the reverse. The socially promoted child remains the smallest fish in the same pond; as I said, all the other kids decided long ago that he's the dummy in their group. Plus in the new year he has to build on knowledge he's supposed to have already but doesn't have, never got. In contrast, the held-back child now holds an advantage because of having already been through the material. She meets a new, younger group of children and can even be a bit of a leader. In short, the child is now a much bigger fish relative to the new, smaller pond than before. And these children continued to do well in ways that could be objectively measured 5 years later.

How Psychology Got Fooled

The data were flawed, but all social science data are flawed. The convergence of evidence was reasonably impressive. When results were significant, people with high self-esteem were found to be doing better on all sorts of things than people with low self-esteem. Often the results were small or not significant, but such results don't get much publicity, whereas the significant results did get noticed.

Over time, however, the fatal flaws in the evidence began to emerge. We've already seen one of the big ones, linking self-esteem to school performance. Yes, higher self-esteem went with better grades. That's what got everyone's hopes up. But when they tracked kids over time, good grades came first and led to high self-esteem. Not the other way around.

Another problem is even more fundamental but easily overlooked. It has to do with how people fill out questionnaires. Self-esteem is measured by questionnaire. You get classified as high in self-esteem if you answer questions about yourself in a positive manner, giving yourself high ratings on various good things. Researchers assumed that they were tapping into some powerful inner trait. In many studies, they would then give people another questionnaire, such as asking them how good their health is, or their relationships are. People who had just finished giving themselves positive ratings on the self-esteem scale would then go on to give their relationships positive ratings, too. Researchers would then compute the correlation and conclude, wow, people with high self-esteem have better relationships than other people. But perhaps it is just how they think of themselves and how they rate themselves. *One needs objective measures.* One can't trust the questionnaires alone.

Dramatic evidence of the fallacy of relying on how people rate themselves emerged from a study of five major relationship skills among college students (Buhrmester et al., 1988). Those with high self-esteem rated themselves as significantly higher than other people on all five skills. They were better at initiating relationships, as in striking up a conversation and starting a friendship. They were better at bringing up problems, at providing emotional support, at disclosing personal information about themselves, and even at managing conflict. All of these findings made conceptual sense and provided the sort of evidence that tempted researchers to conclude that high self-esteem has many benefits—in this case, making the person more competent socially. What made this study impressive, however, was that the researchers also obtained ratings from the roommates of the subjects. After all, who is better positioned to evaluate your social skills than someone who lives with you in a small space for many months? The roommate ratings failed to confirm the benefits of high self-esteem, however. The only finding that was still significant was initiation. The initiation benefit was dramatically weaker with the roommate ratings than the self-ratings, but still significantly above zero. It seems that people with high self-esteem are a bit better than others at initiating contact and making friends. Apart from that, zilch. The roommates didn't see the high self-esteemers as having any of the other social skills.

Other findings fueled the suspicion that high self-esteem is more a matter of inflated self-views than genuine superiority. One study found that self-esteem was significantly correlated with intelligence, based on self-rated intelligence. But when the researchers administered an actual IQ test, it showed no correlation with self-esteem (Gabriel et al., 1994). Crucially, self-esteem was significantly correlated with what the researchers called "self-illusion," meaning the discrepancy between self-rated intelligence and actual IQ score. Put more bluntly, high self-esteem has nothing to do with how smart you actually are; it goes with overestimating your intelligence.

Once I attended a talk by Susan Harter, the foremost expert on self-esteem in children. She reported that children's self-esteem depends heavily on their physical attractiveness. Indeed, the correlation was a whopping .85 (out of a maximum of 1.00). Wow. If we assume some degree of measurement error, that meant children's self-esteem is entirely based on how good- or bad-looking they are, with almost zero room for anything else to make a difference. Maybe children really are that shallow, and biology certainly rewards good looks. I was stunned by those results and repeated them to various colleagues, who were equally impressed. However, when I recounted them to Jenny Crocker, another superb researcher on self-esteem, she pointed out that Harter's research relied entirely on having children rate how attractive they were. So high self-esteem goes with thinking you're gorgeous—but not necessarily with actually being gorgeous.

A painstaking study of college students by Ed Diener and colleagues (1995) cleared this up. Yes, students with high self-esteem rated themselves as better-looking than others. Diener successfully replicated the previous findings. However, the researchers took pictures of each research subject and had the photos rated by other students. The correlation vanished. The most rigorous measure focused only on facial features. The researchers thought, perhaps people with high self-esteem are more likely than others to comb and style their hair, wear makeup, and so forth, so they got photos with no makeup or jewelry and with hair cropped out. Other students' ratings of these photos' attractiveness correlated with self-esteem at .00—which means absolutely no relationship whatsoever! High self-esteem is not about actually being gorgeous. It's about thinking you're gorgeous, even if you're not.

There is one more problem with self-esteem. Even if it could be shown that higher self-esteem measured early leads to genuine benefits on objective measures measured months or years later, self-esteem might still lack causal power. I call this "the reality confound." Suppose Sam the Star is truly handsome, brilliant, kind, and charming, while Dismal Doug is ugly, stupid, mean, and creepy. Suppose those differences lead Sam the Star to be accepted and admired, while Dismal Doug is widely rejected and scorned. Suppose, quite reasonably, that Sam the Star develops higher self-esteem than Dismal Doug. (Remember, e.g., that doing better in school did lead to higher self-esteem.) And then suppose that researchers come along and verify that later in life Sam the Star does objectively better than Dismal Doug, in terms of having a higher salary, more sex partners and stronger relationships, a larger social network, and better health. Such a finding would encourage the researchers to say that high self-esteem does indeed predict and perhaps cause better outcomes.

But is self-esteem really the operative cause? Self-esteem concerns how people appraise themselves. Did Sam the Star really flourish because of how he appraised himself? Or was it simply the fact that he was objectively more blessed to begin with? The sex partners chose him because he was gorgeous. The higher salary came from being smarter. The stronger marriage resulted from having more romantic partners to choose among and from having more money, and from being kinder. The friendship network, from his charm. The better health came from the stronger social network and more money. The key point: In terms of research design, it would look as if high self-esteem led to good outcomes, but how Sam evaluated himself was actually irrelevant. Indeed, if his self-esteem actually became too high so that people saw him as arrogant and conceited, then he might have lost some of his advantages.

SELF-ESTEEM AND AGGRESSION

A particular reason for interest in raising self-esteem was the widespread view that low self-esteem causes violence and aggression. When I was writing a book on evil and violence (Baumeister, 1997), I decided to feature self-esteem, given that I had published multiple papers on self-esteem. I had read in various places that low self-esteem causes aggression. Yet, my knowledge about self-esteem made me skeptical. People with low self-esteem tend to be shy, modest, averse to taking chances, unsure of themselves, ready to go along with what other people tell them (e.g., Baumeister, 1993). That doesn't sound like someone who is prone to turn violent.

As I started reading, I found many authors who cited the prevailing view that low self-esteem causes violence—but provided very little evidence of it. Each article would state it as fact and cite a previous source, but when I looked up that previous source, it again was just someone saying it was true (and usually citing someone else, who turned out again just to state it). I never found any original or authoritative source. And I never found anyone who had provided empirical evidence. It may have been that interviews with female victims of domestic violence had proposed that their violent boyfriends and husbands might have had low self-esteem, as a way of making an excuse for the man (and for her staying with him).

When I began reading about violent people, there was no sign of low self-esteem (for a review, see Baumeister, Smart, & Boden, 1996). Most famously, the murderous Nazis styled themselves the "master race," which is hardly a low-self-esteem slogan. They didn't describe their mass murder campaigns as eliminating elite, superior enemies, but rather as exterminating vermin, or terminating "life unworthy of life." Their invasion of Russia was one of the most colossal and costly mistakes in history, and it clearly was based on overconfidence and an inflated view of their own capabilities. It was their high self-esteem that made them wicked *and* brought them down.

A study of rapists in prison found that they described themselves as "multitalented superachievers" (Scully, 1990). Research on bullying started by assuming that bullies had low self-esteem but found the opposite (Olweus, 1994). Indeed, bullies have high self-esteem, as do the children who joined with the bully to pick on a victim. The youngsters who stand up to the bullies and defend the victims also have high self-esteem. Who, then, has low self-esteem? The victims.

Abusive husbands, supposedly lashing out from a position of low self-esteem, turned out to think pretty well of themselves. They tend to think that the world is not respecting their superior qualities, so they have a grievance against the world. They take it out on their wife, as she is available. But it's their unwarranted high self-esteem that is the problem.

After I started publishing the findings that low self-esteem was not the cause of aggression, my friend Brad Bushman wrote to me that we should do lab studies. Self-esteem is easy to measure, and there are plenty of lab procedures for measuring aggression. You'd think there would have been plenty of lab studies showing that folks with low self-esteem are more aggressive, but there weren't, which makes one suspicious that researchers tried them and they flopped. Bushman is an expert aggression researcher, and he agreed to run some large, definitive studies. At my suggestion, he measured narcissism as well as self-esteem because I had come to think that the cause of aggression is thinking you're better than others and then encountering someone else who disputes or threatens that view. Sure enough, narcissism predicted aggression much more than self-esteem, though high self-esteem was a contributing factor, too (boosting the effect of narcissism). The narcissists, full of self-love, were the most aggressive. We found no hint of evidence linking low self-esteem to aggression (Baumeister, Bushman, & Campbell, 2000; Bushman & Baumeister, 1998, 2002; Bushman et al., 2009).

Violence and Threatened Egotism

How favorably someone thinks of him- or herself is thus relevant to aggression, but not in the way psychologists had assumed. Low self-esteem is not a factor. Instead, the cause seems to be *threatened egotism* (Baumeister et al., 1996). The aggressive person is someone who regards him- or herself as superior to others but encounters someone who questions or disputes that. It's not that narcissism leads directly to aggression. If you treat narcissists with respect and praise, they are lovely people. They lash out at someone who criticizes them. In fact, narcissists who are criticized or insulted don't turn aggressive toward just anyone—their wrath is directed very specifically at the person who has disrespected them.

There was a rare chance to get data on violent prisoners who had been convicted of murder, assault, forcible rape, or armed robbery. Presumably, being in prison would be a humbling experience, but these men had the same average level of self-esteem as people who are not in prison. On narcissism, which taps into feeling superior to others, the prisoners actually scored higher than other people (Bushman & Baumeister, 2002). So violent prisoners are not suffering from low self-esteem. They have a sense of superiority and entitlement.

Up to today, the only thing approaching support for low self-esteem as a major cause of aggression is that people with low self-esteem are very slightly more willing than others to admit to having acted aggressively (e.g., Donnellan et al., 2005). But the effect is probably tied to the general tendency that high-self-esteem people rate themselves positively on all questionnaires, compared to low-self-esteem people. All the behavioral data, including labs and real life, point toward threatened egotism.

One theme of this book is that desired reputation is the most important of the various conceptions of self. The aggression data fit this beautifully. It's not what someone privately thinks of him- or herself that dictates aggression. Rather, aggression (sometimes) arises because someone thinks highly of him- or herself and wants others to share that view (desired reputation). When others show they don't concur, the desired reputation is thwarted. That's the essence of feeling disrespected. Aggression is one common response to damaged reputation.

There is a bit of illogic here. Beating up someone who insults your intelligence hardly proves that you're a genius. Why, then, is aggression a common response to insult, disrespect, even criticism? Quite possibly the roots go far back in evolution. In ape society, one's rank in the hierarchy is decided by fighting, and so aggression is the *natural* response to any challenge to your social status. We are still apes underneath all the rest, and so sometimes we respond like they do. When someone tries to take you down a peg, the natural impulse is to hit him or her. Some people act on this.

There may be a gender difference. Female apes do not fight as much as males. The quality and quantity of their offspring—nature's measure of success in life—do not depend much on the female beating up others, whereas it does for the male. Among humans, women are more egalitarian than males, whereas males readily establish hierarchies. Hence, we should assume that evolution oriented human males more than females to be sensitive to status threats and to be inclined to respond aggressively. This line of analysis thus applies to men more so than women.

THE ACTUAL BENEFITS OF HIGH SELF-ESTEEM

The Association for Psychological Science commissioned a panel of experts to wade through the research literature and write a report on what the real benefits of high self-esteem are (Baumeister et al., 2003, 2005). They asked me to head the panel, partly because they knew I had revised my opinions already about self-esteem, and they wanted someone who would clearly be open to revising again based on the data.

Mindful of the various problems, we restricted our search to objective measures. High-self-esteem people report they are doing great on all sorts of things; if you take those self-reports at face value, there are myriad benefits. Most of those melt away if one looks for objective evidence. That's what the roommate, IQ, and attractiveness studies showed.

Two clear advantages of high self-esteem emerged from the thousands of studies we examined. These were patterns that showed up in multiple places and different spheres of activity, including school and work performance, interpersonal relations, problem behaviors, stress and coping, and more. These are the two definite benefits of thinking well of yourself: initiative and good feelings.

Initiative was the first. High self-esteem lends confidence that you know what is right and appropriate, so you can act on it. Low self-esteem fosters self-doubt, and so one doesn't trust one's own impulses and instincts. People with high self-esteem will take charge, will speak up when they think the group or committee is moving in the wrong direction, will seize the chance to pursue success or greatness, will resist external influence, will ignore advice (even good advice, thus ignored at their peril) when they are otherwise inclined, will confidently approach strangers and strike up relationships, and more. All of these are in contrast to the hesitant, yielding, passive, self-doubting approach of folks with low self-esteem.

The second benefit was good feelings. On this we had to bend our rule of objective measures a bit because it is quite difficult to get objective measures of whether someone is happy. Still, the evidence persuaded us, including the widely replicated link between low self-esteem and depression. Things that boost self-esteem bring good feelings, while things that lower self-esteem usually feel quite bad. Some studies show that high self-esteem buffers one against stress so that one can stay positive and function well even when things are going badly. Low self-esteem is a kind of vulnerability, and people with low self-esteem may be devastated by failures and setbacks.

These two advantages are important, but of course they are far less than many of us had hoped for during the heyday of the self-esteem movement. High self-esteem does not make one more competent, more moral, more attractive to others, more successful, and so on. A great many findings fit that point (reviewed by Baumeister et al., 2003). People with high self-esteem rate their performance better than others, but they didn't get any more answers correct. After meeting someone new and talking for a while, they think they made a great impression on the other person, but the other person's ratings show no sign of that great impression. Hopes that high self-esteem would help young people resist temptations to smoke cigarettes, take drugs, drink alcohol, or engage in early sex were not borne out, and indeed sometimes the opposite emerged: Kids with higher self-esteem were more likely to experiment early with drugs and sex.

Around the time our report came out, there was an international scholastic competition, in which thousands of students took math achievement tests. At this point, American schools had been teaching self-esteem, while other countries had not yet adopted that approach. The results were mixed. American students scored the worst of all the countries in the competition, in terms of getting correct answers. However, after taking the test, students were invited to rate their own performance on it, and on that measure, American students scored the highest of any nation.

We published this report in 2003, and it elicited some consternation and backlash, especially among people who devoted much of their careers to promoting the importance of self-esteem. That's fine: it's how science is supposed to work. Since then, there have been some other contributions seeking to extol or at least rehabilitate the ostensible value of high self-esteem.

Some of the most creative work comes in relationships. The chapter on relationships covers the problems coming from low self-esteem: Individuals feel insecure and therefore often test their partner's commitment, but the endless testing and suspicious vigilance take a toll on the relationship (e.g., Murray et al., 2008). Subsequent work has found small effects indicating that people with high self-esteem are rated better by their relationship partners (Cameron & Granger, 2019), though their relationships do not last any longer. If people with low self-esteem ruin their relationships by testing and withdrawing, apparently people with high self-esteem do other things that cause the relationship to end. A more upbeat conclusion was reached by Harris and Orth (2020), though this fell back on relying on self-reports. They found the benefits of self-esteem are biggest when people rate their own relationships in general ("I get along really well with plenty of people!") and diminish substantially when one focuses on specific relationships and/or gets objective measure or partner ratings.

Another promising line of work links self-esteem to health. There are some impressive data linking high self-esteem to better health (Stinson et al., 2008), although most such data rely on self-report. Even self-reports of visiting the clinic might reflect subjective bias rather than objective health. People with low self-esteem feel badly more often than others and therefore might be faster to head to the clinic. It is plausible that high self-esteem improves health. It is also plausible that the reality confound explains this, such as the fact that having more friends and loved ones is good for both your health and self-esteem. Indeed, Stinson and colleagues (2008) found that poor-quality relationships linked low self-esteem to physical illness.

A few have even challenged our central conclusion, that self-esteem is more a result than a cause. The most impressive of these is an investigation by Orth and colleagues (2012), who used a longitudinal study that tracked adults across 12 years. They proudly trumpeted their results as showing that self-esteem does cause important outcomes later on, refuting our skeptical assessment.

They do have the best results I have seen on early self-esteem predicting what comes later. Yet in my reading, they fall far short of showing that self-esteem causes objective advantages. The significant effects they found were mainly on subjective outcomes, while objective ones remained stubbornly indifferent to self-esteem. For example, having higher self-esteem early in the study predicted being more satisfied with your career later in the study—but had no effect on objective outcomes such as your salary or occupational status. To me, this confirms that the value of self-esteem lies particularly in enabling the person to feel good. It doesn't help you achieve more, but it helps you be more satisfied with what you do achieve. That would be quite consistent with the picture emerging from what we have already seen, such as in the roommate ratings, intelligence ratings, attractiveness, obesity, and the like.

THOSE WITH LOWER SELF-ESTEEM

Is high self-esteem better than low self-esteem? The answer, thus far, is yes, though only slightly and only in a few respects. But beyond the quest for the elusive benefits of high self-esteem, what are the differences?

People with high self-esteem are reasonably easy to understand. They are confident and self-assured. They expect to succeed, to be liked, to rise and flourish. But what about those with low self-esteem? Theories have been widely scattered. Maybe they loathe themselves and seek self-harm. Or maybe they seek to confirm their negative opinions of themselves. Or maybe they are afraid of success.

The emerging answer seems rather more mundane than such bold, counterintuitive notions. People with low self-esteem desire success, love, and other good things just as much as other people—but they don't expect them as much, so they tend to focus on muddling through and avoiding disaster. In particular, their first dominant impulse is to protect themselves (including protecting their self-esteem against loss).

The self-protection orientation guides how people with low self-esteem approach life, including career and relationships (for a review, see Baumeister et al., 1989). One year I was walking across Amsterdam with a colleague and we came to a public square that had a giant chessboard built into the pavement. Two men were playing chess with figures that were almost as tall as the men themselves, while a crowd watched. As we walked on, my colleague remarked with genuine mystification, "Why would anyone do that?" I said that it was a good way to challenge oneself and prove one's skills. My colleague remained unmoved and explained that one might end up making a fool of oneself in front of anyone who happened to walk by. Her response reflected the low-self-esteem outlook: recognize chances for bad things to happen, and avoid them. The men playing presumably adopted the high-self-esteem response: seek out opportunities to shine, and never mind the risk.

In an important sense, low self-esteem is not the pure opposite of high self-esteem. High-self-esteem people love themselves and think they are great. But do those low in self-esteem hate themselves and think they are terrible people? If you look at what they actually say about themselves, the answer is no. Low is only relatively low, not absolutely low. If the range of possible self-esteem scores runs from 0 to 100, a large sample of people does not usually yield an average of 50. More likely, it will be 65 or 70. The people high in self-esteem are indeed claiming to be great, but the low-self-esteem responses are more along the lines of "somewhat," "sometimes," "maybe," and "not sure." The range of actual scores might run from 40 to 95. Hardly anyone ever scores at the extreme low end.

Low self-esteem is thus not typically a firm conviction that oneself is a horrible person. Rather, it is a mixed, conflicted, uncertain view of self. This was elaborated by researcher Jennifer Campbell. In some of her best work, she characterized a key dimension of low self-esteem as "self-concept confusion" (Campbell, 1990). She showed that people with low self-esteem lack a clear, consistent set of self-beliefs. They will contradict what they said elsewhere about themselves, change their minds, and favor "don't know" or "unsure" responses when asked about themselves. No doubt this lack of self-certainty contributes to their tendency to go along with what others advise or argue.

Put another way, low self-esteem is the absence of a positive rather than the presence of a negative. But it goes hand in hand with the self-protective orientation. This may be the most costly flaw in the low-self-esteem psyche: the failure to start or pursue good outcomes because of the fear of possible bad ones. *Nothing ventured, nothing lost*—that seems to be the unfortunate motto of low self-esteem.

WHY DO PEOPLE CARE ABOUT SELF-ESTEEM?

The biggest puzzle about self-esteem is why people seem to care so much about their self-esteem, despite the fact that it confers relatively few advantages. Endless evidence shows that people strive to think well of themselves. They resist criticism, reinterpret ambiguous evidence in self-flattering ways, and even behave aggressively toward others who disrespect them. But as we have seen, the benefits do not extend far beyond more initiative and feeling good. One might object, people do plenty of things to feel good, so maintaining high self-esteem is just another instance of that—but that just raises the question of why high self-esteem feels good. Nature instilled the emotions generally to promote adaptive behavior, but what is so adaptive about thinking well of yourself? Indeed, thinking you're better than you really are is one hallmark of high self-esteem, and it seems a recipe for trouble rather than a helpful approach to life. So why do people crave that?

A powerful solution to this puzzle was proposed by the cautiously brilliant Mark Leary, in what he dubbed "sociometer theory" (see Leary, 2004c, 2012; Leary et al., 1995). He invented the term *sociometer* to combine the notions of an internal mental measure (meter) of one's attainments and prospects for social life. Self-esteem may not be all that important in itself, but it is the brain's private way of keeping track of something that is quite important, namely social acceptance. Humans evolved to be part of groups, and so one needs to become the sort of person who will be accepted into groups. Toward that end, the mind keeps track of how well it measures up to these standards. That's what self-esteem is.

An alternative theory has been proposed by a group of men who built on Ernest Becker's thesis in *The Denial of Death* (1973), a book that said the key human trait is awareness that we are going to die. This has been elaborated into terror management theory, which holds that most human activity is basically a defense mechanism against realizing one will eventually die (e.g., Pyszczynski et al., 1997). They have proposed that self-esteem is a key part of this defense (e.g., Greenberg et al., 1992).

While I admire the research program of the terror management people, I have not been convinced by their explanation for self-esteem. Indeed, esteeming yourself might make the threat worse—because it elevates the value of what is lost when you die. In terms of objective data, measures of death anxiety correlate almost zero with self-esteem (see Leary, 2002, 2004b), whereas social anxiety has a huge (negative) correlation— suggesting self-esteem scores are much more linked to social acceptance than death fears. More broadly, people hardly ever think about death but frequently think about their relationships with other people.

Sociometer theory also meshes well with how self-esteem is measured. Self-esteem scales have four types of items, asking, respectively: Are you popular and likable? Are you competent at your work? Are you good-looking? And are you morally good? These correspond quite well to the criteria people use for including and excluding each other. People like likable people, by definition, and work groups want competent performers. Everyone likes good-looking people. And groups exclude those who break the rules and undermine moral trust. So there you have the four types of questions that measure self-esteem. It's all about being accepted.

A profound and promising variation on the sociometer theory, dubbed "hierometer theory," has proposed that self-esteem is about social status (Mahadevan et al., 2019). People do not simply wish to be accepted into groups but also (and perhaps even more) to rise in the social hierarchy. Self-esteem is thus an inner measure of how one is doing in relation to that hierarchy. Hierometer theory shifts the emphasis from getting along to getting ahead.

Very likely, self-esteem recognizes both getting along and getting ahead, so both sociometer and hierometer theories are on target. They also overlap, insofar as higher social status reduces the risk of being excluded. In a corporation, for example, the lowest-ranking employees are much more vulnerable to being fired than the top bosses. Regardless, the broader point is that self-esteem is how the mind assesses its own social prospects, and people care about their self-esteem because humans evolved to participate in social groups—and individuals' survival and reproduction depended on their social success.

Using self-deception to maintain self-esteem is a bit like indulging in addictive drugs. It exploits some processes that are meant to reward adaptive behavior, only skipping the part about actually performing the adaptive behavior. The rush of happy chemicals that comes from great sex or personal triumph can be produced by drugs. The satisfaction of knowing one's place in the group is secure can be produced by affirming one's self-esteem.

Instead of becoming a better person, you merely convince yourself you're already a better person.

KEY POINTS

- There is no epidemic of low self-esteem.
- Success in school and life leads to high self-esteem, not the reverse.
- The two main benefits of high self-esteem are greater initiative and feeling good.
- Measures of self-esteem align with criteria people use for social acceptance.
- Self-esteem is a continuum with a normal distribution. It is how the mind assesses its own social prospects.
- Those with lower self-esteem tend to lack faith in their own goodness. They are prone to seeing the best outcomes as out of reach.

CHAPTER 16

Accuracy and Illusion
in Self-Beliefs

Thus far we have seen how people begin to collect and integrate information about themselves, thereby helping to create self-knowledge. We have also seen why they do it: the strongest motive is apparently the desire to learn and believe positive things about oneself. But indulging that motive would not generally lead to accurate self-knowledge. Moreover, most pathways to self-knowledge are unreliable and may even promote error. Hence, it is vital to ask, how accurate is self-knowledge?

A broad assortment of evidence suggests that people hold self-views that are somewhat accurate but also biased in a positive, favorable direction. That is, the self-concept is a mixture of reality and self-flattering illusion.

An early sign that people hold inflated self-beliefs was a report by Svenson (1981), based on a survey of adult drivers. Ninety percent of them said they were above average as drivers. This seemed implausible: One would expect that only about half the drivers would be above average.

Technically, though, it is possible for 90% to be above-average drivers. Suppose 100 people answered the question about their driving ability simply on the basis of whether they had ever had an accident, and suppose 10 of them had had one accident each. Dividing 10 accidents by a hundred drivers, the average driver quality would thus correspond to 0.1 accident per person, and 90% of the people would be better than that (because they had zero accidents).

But soon there was too much other evidence of self-enhancement to be explained by statistical flukes. The College Board each year surveyed many thousands of high school seniors. One researcher looked at their ratings and found that none of them rated themselves as below average in terms of the ability to get along well with other people, while a whopping 25% of them rated themselves as being in the top 1% on that dimension (College Board, 1976–1977; see Gilovich, 1991). Realistically, only 3 or 4% would qualify for being in the top 1%. (This is because people can use different criteria; Dunning et al., 1989.)

Similar biases were found on other items, such as leadership ability. There is no way to make those numbers statistically plausible other than by concluding that people rate themselves more favorably than the objective facts would warrant.

Perhaps high school seniors are naive or full of youthful enthusiasm. Would mature, wise adults be different? One researcher polled university professors as to how they compared with the average professor, and the self-enhancing bias was rampant there, too: 94% rated themselves as better than the average professor (Cross, 1977).

A memorable demonstration of inflated self-beliefs studied convicted criminals in prison (Sedikides et al., 2014). Clearly, guys in jail should have gotten the message that society holds a low opinion of them. But these men rated themselves quite highly, even on moral traits and socially desirable tendencies. They rated themselves not only as better than the average prisoner but better than the average person in the community outside of prison, on traits such as honesty, compassion, kindness, and trustworthiness. Thus, these men are in prison based on a criminal conviction, but they still think they are more virtuous than other people! The closest thing to an exception to the general pattern of self-flattering illusion is also revealing. Asked to rate how law-abiding they were, the prisoners rated themselves as more law-abiding than other prisoners, but as merely equal to the average person in the community. In other words, prisoners think they are just as law-abiding as the average citizen. But even that rating of equality indicates the extent of self-illusion. After all, the average citizen is not serving time in prison for having violated the law. Notice the prisoners rated each other as not law-abiding. They agree that convicted prisoners have some shortcomings. They just made an exception for themselves.

THE MYSTERY OF LIMITED EXAGGERATION

Let's concede that people do inflate their self-appraisals. However, they do so only to a limited degree. Obviously, if self-flattering illusions flourished unchecked, most people would soon regard themselves as semi-divine or super-human beings. This is not what the data show. Most people see themselves as just somewhat better than they are. An early paper of mine suggested that people find an "optimal margin of illusion," enabling them to draw the benefits of thinking well of self without distorting reality so much that they make judgment errors and get into trouble (Baumeister, 1989b). The optimal margin might be 10–20% overestimation, or the best-case version of the real you. That also corresponds to what a reasonable goal or aspiration level would be: You could be a little better than you are, but cosmically perfect superiority is out of reach.

When you meet and talk with someone, how would you like that person to regard you? A series of studies on these preferences fit the optimal margin idea: People want partners who see them as slightly better than reality ("reality" in the sense of how people see themselves, thus already a bit inflated) (Morling & Epstein, 1997). These partners were preferred over partners who regarded you super-favorably as well as those who regarded you the same as you saw yourself.

Why the limited inflation? The standard way of regarding it, which I think is at least partly right, is that it is a compromise between reality and aspiration. You'd like to regard yourself as genius-level brilliant, A-list celebrity charming, and movie-star sexy, one of the very best people, but you see enough of the objective evidence to know you're not there. An early version of this was Barry Schlenker's (1975) studies on how people described themselves to others after they received explicit feedback. He concluded that they present themselves as favorably as they can get away with. So the accurate self-concept is just a starting point, and people claim to be better than that—but they don't exaggerate so much that they are likely to be shown up by the facts.

Still, evidence piled up that the 20% inflation is not just how people present themselves while knowing the reality is less wonderful. It seems to fit how they actually think about themselves. They may exaggerate a bit more to impress others, but mostly they seem to believe the mildly inflated version.

My thinking on the optimal margin of illusion added that exaggerating puts you at risk for bad decisions, so you keep your self-appraisal close to reality and just allow yourself to feel good by letting it inflate only moderately. Another variation on this way of thinking was by Morling and Epstein (1997), who said these only slightly inflated self-views reflect a compromise between self-verification and self-enhancement motives. Self-verification pulls you back toward what you think is right, while self-enhancement pulls you upward, and so you prefer to spend time with people who see you in between—just slightly better than you see yourself (which in turn is slightly better than reality).

There may however be a simpler explanation for all this. The 10–20% inflated self-concept is not necessarily the result of some complex calculations that compromise competing pressures and constraints. Instead, it may just be the most important conception of self: the way you want others to see you. It may not be the ideal self in the most refined sense (how you would be if you were perfect). But that's an idle abstraction. Instead, it's the reputation you're working to create and sustain, day in and day out. It's what you are trying to make true, the real you, as recognized in the minds of other people.

A fascinating twist on the optimal margin of illusion emerged from studies on dishonesty (Mazar, Amir, & Ariely, 2008). When given a chance to get extra money by cheating, and seemingly safe from being caught, people will indeed cheat—but only a little. In their studies, people rolled the dice in private and reported what the outcome was. This dictated how much money they would get. People did not typically claim the maximum possible amount, but they claimed more than was statistically plausible. Ariely's conclusion was that people will seek advantage by cheating but wish to maintain a view of themselves as honest, so they will limit their cheating to an amount that can be rationalized without damaging the view of oneself as basically honest.

The conclusion that self-concepts mix reality and illusion gains credence from evidence that people respond to reality checks (Sweeny & Krizan, 2013). Optimism is common with regard to vague, general predictions, for example, such as whether one is likely to be happy or successful in life. It dwindles as the questions become more specific, such as whether you will get a promotion next year or win a particular game of chess. Other reality checks have to do with timing. People express confidence about distant future events, but as the time draws near, they abruptly sober up and make more realistic or even pessimistic predictions. For example, a student might predict that he will do well on the test in 2 weeks, but these optimistic predictions are muted when the day of the test rolls around. When the tests are about to be handed back with grades, the same student might genuinely be expecting a low grade. Some of that involves bracing oneself for a possible bad outcome: if you expect the worst, you at least cannot be disappointed.

A cleverly designed experiment by Taylor and Shepperd (1998) examined how predictions changed with the time frame of reality. The people were told they were being tested for "TAA deficiency," a condition marked by a lack of an important enzyme, thioamine acetylase. In reality there is no such medical condition, but the research participants did not know this. It was just a useful fiction invented by the researchers. The experimenter explained that she was supposed to have test strips but the delivery was delayed, and so she would collect a saliva sample and send the results by mail in 3 to 4 weeks. Participants were asked to rate the chances that they would have TAA deficiency. In general, they were fairly optimistic that the test would give them a favorable result, by the end of the month.

Then came the twist. While the research subject was filling out a medical history questionnaire, the experimenter left the room and returned to say that the test strips had just been delivered after all—so she could administer the test and give results right away. And people made another prediction. They were much less optimistic about their test results when they expected to get them right away. Nothing had changed, and there is no logical reason that the same test based on the same data should yield different results today than after a month. What had changed was people's confidence. It is apparently comforting and easy to predict that things will turn out fine next month. It is much harder to be breezily optimistic as one faces the moment of truth, right now.

A medical test result is objective and hard to dismiss. Much other information is more slippery, however. As we already saw with the looking-glass self, people's views of themselves do not typically match up well with how they are actually perceived by others, partly because others do not tell you all the things they dislike about you.

The Limited Accuracy of Self-Beliefs

People definitely have many beliefs about themselves, and these bear considerable resemblance to the truth—but also depart from it in systematic ways. Most commonly, people rate themselves better than is plausible, though not wildly better.

As I mentioned earlier, the autobiographical essayist Montaigne said, as if it were obviously true, that he knew his topic (himself) better than any author had ever known his topic. Most adults probably have the same impression, that they know themselves extremely well. They do have plenty of information, but they are not aware of the omissions and distortions among those self-beliefs. Although others may have less total information about you than you have about yourself, they mostly do not have the same motives to twist things into a pleasing picture. Self-knowledge is biased. That brings us to the problem of self-deception.

Self-Deception

Do people fool themselves? Most people would answer yes to that question. Yet, the impression of widespread self-deception could be mistaken. There are several objections to the idea of self-deception. One is that it is generally inferred about other people rather than observed in oneself. Almost by definition, you cannot know whether you are deceiving yourself.

Moreover, strictly speaking, self-deception requires the self to play two incompatible roles, namely the deceiver and the deceived. John can deceive Max, which means that John knows something that Max does not know. For a time, rigorous psychology researchers insisted that the reality of self-deception could only be established if one could prove that the same person was both John and Max: the self-deceiver both knew something and did not know it (Gur & Sackeim, 1979; Sackeim & Gur, 1979; see also Sartre, 1953). That may sound impossible, but given the split between conscious and unconscious parts of the self, it is conceivable that some knowledge would be present in the unconscious while the conscious mind is unaware of it. But this sets the bar of proof very high. Imagine trying to prove that someone knows something unconsciously but doesn't know it consciously. The requirements of this very strict definition left rather little in the way of evidence for self-deception.

Self-deception poses a profound challenge to the psychology of self for reasons that go beyond the hurdle of simultaneously knowing and not knowing. We have seen that people strive for self-knowledge; self-deception is not ultimately compatible with the quest for self-knowledge because self-deception perpetuates false self-knowledge. I entitled this part of the book "Know Thyself" to highlight its focus on the accumulation of self-knowledge. But perhaps people do not seek accurate self-knowledge exclusively. Sometimes they cultivate favorably distorted or even false beliefs about themselves. Hence, the first question is whether people really do deceive themselves.

A conceptual breakthrough was to abandon the idea that the self has to know something and also not know it at the same time. Instead, try the popular concept of wishful thinking. As we have seen, much of self-knowledge does not consist of objective, immutable facts but rather inferences, comparisons, and construals. These leave plenty of wiggle room. Self-deception could flourish in the wiggles. There may be no single objective measure, or evidence may be mixed or incomplete. Hence, people can reach favorable conclusions by focusing on favorable evidence. There may be a range of possible truths, and people choose one that lies toward the favorable end of the range. The self-deceiver is perhaps more like a lawyer making the best case for her client than a charlatan trying to sell snake oil.

It would indeed be a masterpiece of self-deception if you could somehow convince yourself to believe something that you knew for sure was not true. But it's perhaps more realistic that you convince yourself about something that might be true but probably isn't. Boosting the subjective odds a bit is easy and plausible; turning night into day, or a chronic loser into chronic winner, not so much.

Three Self-Deceiving Illusions

Once the idea of self-deception was freed from the constraint of having to prove that the same person knows something and doesn't know it, evidence for self-deception was abundant. An early and influential paper by the sage Anthony Greenwald (1980) spoke of the "totalitarian ego," comparing the self to an all-powerful regime that seeks to bolster its legitimacy by means of propaganda and other forms of thought control. Like a totalitarian government, the self seeks to be seen as benevolent and capable, perhaps along with a few other positives.

A hugely influential work on self-deception was a review article by Shelley Taylor and Jonathon Brown (1988). They positioned their article as an attack on conventional psychological wisdom about mental health. A long tradition of that work had held that accurate perception of reality characterizes the healthy mind, and mental illness involved distortion. Taylor and Brown proposed, instead, that some mental illnesses see the world too accurately, while the happy, well-adjusted person embraces a set of what they called "positive illusions."

Three positive illusions were highlighted. These indicate three common types of inaccuracy of self-knowledge, that is, three kinds of bias that prevail over any quest to know the truth about oneself. First, people think they are better than they are. Second, they overestimate their control over events. Third, they are unrealistically optimistic about their future prospects. Each deserves comment.

Overestimating Good Qualities

The first illusion, self-enhancement, has already been mentioned. People hold higher opinions of themselves than would be justified by a strict reading of the evidence. People exaggerate their good traits and minimize or underestimate their flaws. They magnify their successes and downplay or rationalize their failures. We look at the mental processes behind these beliefs shortly. For now, it is sufficient to note that people's selves are generally inflated. To be sure, they are not just recklessly or indiscriminately positive. Some positive self-appraisals are correct and objectively justified (see Church et al., 2014), but others are clearly inflated. Illusions are often kept to a modest degree so that they remain within the realm of plausibility. They are more akin to stretching the facts than to making things up wholesale. They stay within the optimal margin of illusion.

Why might people want to hear positive, favorable, flattering information about themselves? There is an obvious but inadequate answer: it feels good. Hearing others say that you are brilliant, charming, gorgeous, capable, trustworthy, reliable—who does not feel a thrill of pleasure at hearing oneself described in these ways? Some might object that people with low self-esteem reject such feedback, as it conflicts with their negative self-views. There may be some such cases, but when I ran experiments, I remember being struck by how the people with low self-esteem really loved hearing favorable feedback that they were fine human beings.

So why does self-enhancing feedback feel good? Or rather, why did people evolve so that they take pleasure in learning positive things about themselves? Thinking well of yourself and feeling happy about positive self-images have no apparent advantage in terms of survival or reproduction. At best one can make out a few possible, sketchy ideas of how they might help a little. (If you think well of yourself, you might be happy, and others might be more willing to climb into the sack with you if you're happy rather than bitter or grumpy, so maybe this would slightly boost your reproductive success.) Still, there has to be more to it than just feeling good.

Overestimating Control

The second illusion is an overestimate of how much control one has over events. People clearly like to have control. Even illusions of control are appealing (Glass, Singer, & Friedman, 1969; Langer, 1975). It does seem that people are prone to exaggerate how much control they have. One of the most influential papers leading to a rethinking was a 1979 article by Lauren Alloy and Lynn Abramson. These two experimenters measured how much control people thought they had on a laboratory task, while they also manipulated how much control the people actually had. (Sometimes the person got what he or she chose; other times, the outcome was random.) Normal, healthy people systematically overestimated their control. Depressed people did not, however, and in fact the depressed ones were remarkably accurate. This led to the pattern of what came to be called "depressive realism," the idea that depressed people see the world as it is while happy and mentally healthy people systematically distort.

Other work has likewise pointed to the general conclusion that people overestimate control. Supposedly one of the factors that lead to lasting trauma in crime victims is the loss of this illusion of control. Police and crime victim advocates have long known that victims' suffering is often far out of proportion to the physical or material harm. Having a purse stolen or an apartment burglarized can leave the victims upset for a long period thereafter, even if the losses were relatively minor and insurance restores most or all of the value. A thoughtful explanation of this by Ronnie Janoff-Bulman (1989, 1992) proposed that people operate on the basis of several positive assumptions about the world, which are related to the positive illusions we cover here. These include that the world is fair, that mostly people are nice and benevolent, and that oneself is a good person. That combination of beliefs furnishes a sense that one has control over one's fate. Crime victimization undermines those beliefs: People aren't nice, the world isn't benevolent, perhaps the self is not a good or deserving person, and self does not have full control. Recovery from crime thus may have less to do with replacing the stolen items than with rebuilding a positive outlook on self and world.

There are limits and boundaries to the overestimation of control. Again, people do not inflate their sense of control recklessly. Rather, they just increase it somewhat. Sometimes they even underestimate control—mainly when their objective control is nearly complete. This tendency to rate one's control a bit less than it is may be a kind of hedging one's bets or allowing for unforeseen possibilities. The updated conclusion seems to be that people overestimate their control when it is low but underestimate it when it is high (Gino, Sharek, & Moore, 2011).

Believing that you are helpless is hardly inspiring, and perhaps it detracts from motivation to do anything. When control is genuine but low, it may help to overestimate control so that you are motivated to try. In contrast, when control is very high, it might help to underestimate control so that you avoid overconfidence and remain vigilant. Outside the laboratory, you do not usually have complete control over events. Indeed, believing that you are fully able to dictate what happens has often been a recipe for failure, as indicated by the appalling failure rate of business start-ups. Even if someone has carefully prepared and arranged everything, there is usually the potential for something else to disrupt the plans, such as subtle machinations by a rival, a natural disaster, or even war. As an obvious example, in a major professional sports championship, both sides have planned and prepared as thoroughly as they can—but only one will win.

Perhaps the optimal attitude is to believe you have some control over events, but it's incomplete. When control is lower than that, people overestimate control, which helps motivate them to do the best they can, thus enabling them to avoid the vicious circle of hopeless, helpless passivity. When control is higher than that, people underestimate control, which keeps them on their toes and avoids the traps of complacency and overconfidence.

Irrational Optimism

The third illusion is optimism. Many studies have shown the pattern by which the average person thinks that good things are more likely and bad things less likely to happen to him or her, as compared to the average person (Weinstein, 1980). Part of this discrepancy can be chalked up to thinking that the average person is a doofus, to whom bad things will happen. But still, people are optimistic about their own prospects. This illusion is not that relevant to self-beliefs, but we will consider it again when considering how the extended-time self makes choices about its future.

Why Deceive Yourself?

There are plenty of reasons that people might want to deceive *other* people. There is even abundant evidence of deception in the animal world. Social life is based on the fact that one creature's opportunities for survival or reproduction can be increased by getting others to cooperate and do one's bidding. Deception can help get someone else to share resources with you,

Accuracy and Illusion in Self-Beliefs

cooperate in a joint venture, trust you, have sex with you, lend you money, and plenty of other benefits.

In contrast, deceiving yourself has far fewer apparent benefits. You are already inclined to do what is best for you, so deceiving yourself is not likely to improve that. Meanwhile, there are large potential downsides to fooling yourself. Among other risks, deceiving yourself means that your decisions and actions are based on false assumptions.

Hence, it seems that an adaptive, well-adjusted, good functioning person would never lie to self. But people do.

The human psyche is set up to prosper by participating in social groups. So the first thing it needs is to get itself accepted into these groups. Self-esteem is based on the major criteria by which groups accept or reject individuals. These are as follows. First, being competent, able to get the job done, perhaps get resources for the group, like food. Second, being likable, easy to get along with—that will be a big factor as to whether others keep you around and work with you. Third, being moral, trustworthy, obeying the group's rules. And fourth, being physically good-looking, as people like good-looking people, probably for reasons that go way back in evolutionary history and therefore are not based on rational thought.

All this means that if you are that sort of person (competent, likable, virtuous/trustworthy, and good-looking), you should feel good. People have an internal monitor to keep track of how they fare on those traits because it is important to be good. You don't need everybody to like you, but you probably do need *some* people to like you. And if you're not that likable, maybe you can get by with being really competent at something. If you're the only one who can do some vital task, like find water or talk to the gods or kick a field goal, they will keep you around.

But suppose you are not high on all those traits. Then you need to change. This takes work. Until you succeed, others may not like you, hire you, marry you. So this feels bad.

The optimal solution, of course, is to do the hard work and change yourself to become a better person. Then you will be able to feel good again. There is, however, a short cut. You can just convince yourself you are a good person, and save all the trouble and tiresome exertion of actually changing.

That is one root of self-deception. Nature has instilled a system to enable you to feel good when you see that you are a good person because this will encourage you to be a good person. If you are a good person, your chances for survival and reproduction improve, which is all nature cares about, so to speak. It is what nature rewards via natural selection. It is what makes you an ancestor of future generations, instead of a dead end. So you have an internal monitor that watches yourself and keeps track of how you are doing. When you do well, it rewards you with happy feelings, and when you do badly, it warns you with bad feelings. You can fool the monitor,

however, by convincing yourself that you are doing well. That enables you
to enjoy the good feelings and avoid the bad ones.

Self-deception in that context is a bit like taking drugs. The brain is
wired to feel pleasure when certain things happen that contribute in a big
way to survival and reproduction. You can skip the achievement of those
things and make yourself feel good by drugs.

By the same token, you feel good when you realize you are a highly
appealing person that everyone will want to connect with, work with, sleep
with, party with. Instead of becoming that person, self-deception lets you
convince yourself you are.

Yet, that is not a fully satisfactory explanation. Why should nature let
you get away with just thinking you are good? If lots of people did that,
they would fail to become good people and take themselves out of the gene
pool. There must be some other benefits.

A popular idea, especially in America, is that believing is helpful for
achievement. Starting early in the 20th century, popular self-help books in
the United States began to hammer home the theme that positive, favorable thoughts can cause good things to happen. The preceding century had
focused on self-control and hard work as the pathway to success. A popular
19th-century saying, sometimes emblazoned on wall hangings, was "Blessed
be drudgery." In contrast, the 20th century's favored slogan was more along
the lines of: *Believe it, achieve it.* (See Baumeister & Tierney, 2011.)

Perhaps the most famous advocate was minister Norman Vincent
Peale. In 1952 he published *The Power of Positive Thinking*, which spent
several years on the *New York Times* bestseller list and sold millions of
copies. Growing out of his early collaboration with a psychoanalyst (who
later repudiated the collaboration and sharply criticized *The Power of Positive Thinking*), it advocated a kind of self-hypnosis with instructions to
focus exclusively on pleasant, optimistic thoughts.

There is popular support for the possible benefits of positive self-talk,
but experts and researchers have been more skeptical. Still, on balance,
many researchers have found reason to be optimistic about positive illusions, even if they doubt that much lasting good comes from meditating on
self-praise on a daily basis. As already noted, Taylor and Brown concluded
that positive illusions are a hallmark of mental health. Taylor's (1983) earlier research on breast cancer had found that women eased their suffering
and coped with disease better insofar as they embraced positive illusions.

Many athletes find it helpful to "psych up" for a major contest, that is,
they try to get into a confident frame of mind that will supposedly produce
optimal performance. Much of this probably revolves around imagining
oneself performing successfully. There is evidence that this sort of "mental
practice" works. Indeed, a report from the National Academy of Sciences
concluded that mental practice was one of the few performance-enhancing
methods that actually does enhance performance (Druckman & Swets,

1988). Just imagining the activity is not enough. One well-designed study on college golfers had them visualize a putt and then actually try it (Woolfolk et al., 1985). By random assignment, some were instructed to imagine a successful putt, with the ball ending up in the hole. Others were told to visualize just barely missing the hole, and a third group was instructed just to imagine putting, without being told anything specific about how to visualize the outcome. The ones who had visualized the successful putt were in fact most successful at actual performance. The ones who had visualized the near miss went on to do worse than average in their actual performances. Such findings provide encouragement to those who embrace the value of positive illusions: imagining success led to success, while imagining failure led to actual failure.

Other work has provided at best mixed evidence for the efficacy of illusions. Part of the difficulty lies in the fact already mentioned: Positive self-views contain mixtures of reality and illusion. As we saw in the chapter on self-esteem, there is ample evidence that high self-esteem is correlated with a range of good, positive outcomes, such as better grades in school—but that's mainly because doing well in school boosts a student's self-esteem. It does not mean that increasing a student's self-esteem will lead to better grades (and in fact most evidence suggests it does not).

Optimism was recently subjected to a similar critique (Tenney, Logg, & Moore, 2015). Optimism is the expectation that good things will happen. If there were no illusion involved, then of course optimists would fare better than pessimists. It makes sense for people to count on optimists more than pessimists, insofar as both are being accurate and realistic. The fact that optimists experience more good things than pessimists tells us nothing about whether unrealistic, illusory optimism has any benefit. A series of experiments by Tenney and colleagues (2015) found that people believe in the value of optimism (even when illusory or unfounded) but that illusory optimism had no actual benefit for performance.

Think of it this way. Suppose you are an adult about to engage in a chess or checkers game, or even arm wrestling, with an average 6-year-old child. You are optimistic that you will win. And you do win. Statistically, your optimism will be correlated with your victory. But did the optimism actually help? Maybe you just recognized the basic fact that you had big advantages and were bound to win, being bigger, stronger, smarter. Had your child opponent been more optimistic, it would not have translated into beating you.

In short, the advantages of optimism lie in the fact that people who have good reason to expect good outcomes are likely to get those good outcomes. The advantage is in the reality part, not the illusion part. Staying optimistic regardless of the facts has little or no pragmatic value, though perhaps it keeps one feeling better for a short time.

Let us look elsewhere, then, to explain self-deception.

Fooling Myself Helps Me Fool You

This subsection began by questioning why it might be helpful to deceive oneself while readily conceding that it is often advantageous to deceive others. An impressive work led the theory of self-deception back to the firmer ground of other-deception (von Hippel & Trivers, 2011). Its core argument was that deceiving oneself is indeed useful—precisely because it increases one's success at deceiving others.

The starting point is that deceiving others is useful but difficult. People understand that others might say whatever is useful, as a means of influence, and so listeners are on guard. People try to ascertain when others are lying instead of telling the truth. They watch for signs such as nervousness or vacillation or difficulty in specifying details in response to questions.

It is after all not easy to tell an outright lie, knowingly, and it is even harder to sustain it over time. Consider first the mental effort required. You know the truth and then knowingly construct an alternative. At minimum, you have to keep both in mind. You have to be persuasive; otherwise, the other will not accept the lie, and so you have to simulate how you would tell the lie as if it were true. You may be afraid of getting caught, which gives rise to nervousness, with all its little tics and giveaways.

The difficulties increase considerably if you have an ongoing relationship with the target of the lie, as opposed to lying to a stranger as a one-time act. With a relationship partner, the lie has to be maintained, so you need to remember both the truth and the false belief that you communicated. With a relationship, there is a body of shared knowledge, so the lie has to be integrated into a larger system of beliefs and maintained there. You need to be ready to embellish the lie as needed. More is at stake when lying to a relationship partner than to a stranger. If the person catches you lying, the relationship could be damaged or even ended. Last, but not least, a relationship partner may over time become more skilled at discerning whether you are telling the truth, such as by learning the signs of what you do when you lie. This will in turn increase your nervousness about getting caught.

All these help explain why people lie to strangers more than to close friends and family members (DePaulo & Kashy, 1998). (There are exceptions: DePaulo found that college students lied roughly every other time they spoke with their mothers; see Ritter, 1995.) People can easily and effectively deceive strangers or casual acquaintances, but lying to a partner in a close relationship is a much riskier undertaking.

Most of these problems are solved if you can believe what you are saying. That is, if you can fool yourself, it is easier to fool strangers. You are not nervous or worried about getting caught. You do not have to maintain separate mental files for the truth and the lie. You can deliver it with a straight face and earnest demeanor.

Method actors have known this for a long time: The better you can become your character in a play or movie, such as by having the same feelings and thoughts that the character would really have, the more convincing your performance would be.

Remember, too, that self-deception is not usually an outright falsehood, but a best-case scenario, a slightly edited version of reality, something better than reality but within the optimal margin of illusion. So when you are convincing others of something about yourself, you are not really being a phony or impostor. You are being the best version of yourself, something you genuinely want to be. You just get yourself to believe it, and it is sort of plausible—and believing it helps you convince others that it's true.

Why deceive others, especially about one's own good traits? There are multiple answers that come back to the self's basic jobs. The self seeks to gain and maintain social acceptance. As we have seen, your chances of being accepted improve to the extent you have socially desirable traits, such as competence, likability, and trustworthiness. And if you do not entirely have them, you can still attract people insofar as you can fake them.

At times I have believed that convincing others was the means to an end. You can only believe it about yourself if others validate it. You're only a great artist if lots of people think you're a great artist. It's hard to sustain the belief that you're a great artist if nobody else thinks so. Constructing your own identity, your ideal self, was the ultimate goal, I thought.

That's probably wrong, but I can understand why I succumbed to that mistake. The inner system in the self works that way. It will be satisfied if it can believe what it wants, even if others don't really believe it. The mistake is failing to realize that the inner system is there for a reason. *Inner processes serve interpersonal functions.* The ultimate goal is not some private, inner experience, or state, or feeling. It's connecting to others, so as to survive, reproduce, and flourish. In terms of what happens to you in your life, what matters is not whether you regard yourself as a great artist, but whether other people regard you as such.

The reason we want to be a good person is because that's the ticket to social acceptance. To be sure, people may not make the connection, but nature did: Natural selection favored humans who were socially connected, as opposed to antisocial isolated types. People who wanted to be good had an advantage, and we are descended from them, more than from people who were indifferent or downright evil. Still, insofar as the biological goal is to be attractive to others rather than to yourself, you desire to persuade others that you are a good person. The better you seem to them, the better your chances of social acceptance. Therefore, it is natural that people want to impress others that they are as good as is plausible. (We shall see evidence for this in the later chapter on self-presentation.) Again, though, as von Hippel and Trivers explained, one will be most successful at persuading others of one's good qualities insofar as one can believe in them oneself.

As we said, people favor people who are likable, competent, trustworthy, and attractive. People may cultivate positive illusions regarding all of these, and if they can get others to see them as high on those dimensions, their chances of social acceptance rise. Self-enhancement, the first of the positive illusions, is thus socially appealing. The other two positive illusions are also appealing. People who have control over their fate appeal to others because the others will not have to take care of them. Indeed, your ability to exert control can be beneficial to others.

Optimism is also interpersonally appealing. Again, the mixture of reality and illusion makes this difficult for observers to sort out. If all expectancies were objectively correct and firmly grounded in reality, then it would be utterly rational to affiliate with optimists (because they are headed for good things) and avoid pessimists (who are headed for disaster). And even though people know that others may exaggerate, they do not correct adequately for this and therefore are drawn to optimists.

Leaders in particular appeal by means of optimism. A leader who says, "Our future is bleak and I will try to steer us so as to minimize the damage and suffering," is hardly inspiring, compared to one who says, "We are headed for greatness and I will guide us there." A classic study analyzed American presidential elections of the 20th century, going over major speeches and public statements to assess the degree of optimism. Time after time, the voters favored the more optimistic candidate (Zullow, Oettingen, Peterson, & Seligman, 1988). Martin Seligman, the most established author of that article, relates how he was in Europe when the study came out showing that being optimistic was the key to winning presidential elections. He says he returned home and sorted through the mail. It contained letters from the Republican and the Democratic national committees—both seeking advice on just how to give the most optimistic speech! Apparently, they wanted to cultivate illusions rather than just letting their candidates speak for themselves.

Another sign of the interpersonal appeal of positive illusions is that depressed people are unpopular. As we have seen, depressed people lack the positive illusions that normal people embrace, and presumably they present themselves to others with that same realism.

In short, positive illusions are useful not just to make yourself feel good but to accomplish the self's main jobs. If you can project a positive view of yourself, including good traits, high control over fate, and optimism about the future, you can increase your chances of being accepted by others—of being liked, of being hired, of being loved and married, of being chosen for leadership.

Cognitive Strategies for Self-Deception

How do people manage to deceive themselves? How do they create and sustain these positive illusions, both in their own minds and in those of other people? The interpersonal strategies are covered in a later chapter, so we postpone that issue. For now, the issue is how people fool themselves (adapted from Baumeister, 1998).

The goal of self-deception is presumably to fool the conscious mind into embracing a positive view of self. The processes that accomplish this have to be partly hidden from consciousness, or else the conscious mind would spot the trick and not be fooled.

Take Credit, Refuse Blame

An early trick that psychologists documented quite thoroughly long ago was called the self-serving bias (for a review, see Zuckerman, 1979). Early analyses of how people infer the causes of behavior sorted these causes into two categories, internal to the person and external. The self-serving bias focuses specifically on one's own successes and failures. For successes, one makes internal attributions, thereby giving oneself credit. For failure, one makes external attributions, thereby escaping or minimizing blame. Most human lives have plenty of both successes and failures. To the extent you can interpret these with a self-serving bias, you can base your self-concept mainly on the successes and not be pulled down by the failures.

Similar patterns have been found for moral transgressions. People make external attributions for their misdeeds (Baumeister, Stillwell, & Wotman, 1990). Even when they acknowledge that they did something wrong, they tend to play up the role of external factors that contributed to it and that mitigate their guilt. Meanwhile, they interpret other people's misdeeds internally, blaming the person rather than the situation.

A recent review of over 200 studies found plenty of support for the self-serving bias (Mezulis, Abramson, Hyde, & Hanking, 2004). Even in the lab, it's consistently a large effect—and nearly always there, they found. To be sure, some do it more than others. Children and old folks show the most bias. Asian samples show it less than others, consistent with the view that Asians embrace modesty and do not seek to feel superior to others as much as Americans and other Westerners do (Heine et al., 1999). The self-serving bias was smaller (though not entirely absent) among people with attention-deficit/hyperactivity disorder (ADHD), anxiety disorders, and in particular depression. That fits the view that positive illusions are a mark of healthy functioning. The depressed folks were the closest to having no bias.

Perceptual Defense: Don't Ask, Don't Look, Don't Know

Even more basic processes can aid self-deception. The first line of defense is attention: what you don't notice won't get into your mind, and hence will not affect your understanding of yourself.

It may not be possible to protect your mind from any hint of bad news or negativity. But you can keep those hints to a minimum. This would be the mental analog to how people look away or close their eyes when the film presents something frightening or disgusting. Lab research has shown that people spend more time reading feedback about their personalities when it is favorable and flattering than when it is unfavorable and critical (Baumeister & Cairns, 1992). Defensive people with the so-called repressive personality style are especially prone to this. Likewise, investors spend more time looking at their portfolio when the market is generally rising (so the news is mostly good) than when it is falling (Karlsson et al., 2009; Sicherman et al., 2015).

Why does this work? The more you think about something, the stronger the memory trace. Something that just gets a brief scan is less deeply encoded into memory, as compared to something you linger over and ponder and replay mentally.

Searching for information is a basic activity of the human mind. Sometimes, you find exactly the answer or evidence you need. Other times, there is no clear point at which the search is done, and so you have to make an executive decision about when to stop looking. This can be adjusted so as to help your case. When you have information that makes you look good, you might be inclined to stop searching for more. When the information is not so favorable, you might keep looking (Ditto & Lopez, 1992; see also Baumeister & Newman, 1994).

The simple avoidance of potentially disturbing information is thus one effective strategy for self-deception. One form of this was labeled "strategic self-ignorance" by the researchers who demonstrated it (Thunstrom et al., 2016). They started from the standard economic assumption that a rational person would always accept free information relevant to an upcoming choice. However, they said, some information might not cost money but could have other costs, such as guilt, or disappointment with self. They noted that America's Affordable Care Act (aka Obamacare) required chain restaurants to post calorie counts of the foods they serve, hoping that this information would steer people away from fattening, unhealthy foods, thereby reducing obesity. But apparently many people simply avoid looking at that information, especially if they are hungering for pizza and french fries. In their experiment, diners at a restaurant were offered a choice between two equally priced meals. It was not obvious which one had more calories, but one actually had nearly double the calories of the other. In the main condition, diners first chose between two folded sheets of paper and were told that one (on the left) was blank, while the other had the calorie contents listed. Thus, they could decide whether to find out which meal had more calories. Over half (58%) preferred the blank piece of paper. Basically, they deliberately elected not to know which meal was more fattening. And sure enough, those people ate more calories.

Selective Memory

Bad news is remembered better than good news, all else being equal. But all else is far from equal. Sometimes people try to minimize bad memories, such as by not thinking about them or by rationalizing them. The mind has some automatic defenses so that bad memories are walled off in the mind—present but rarely visited. People often cultivate happy memories, by telling others about them, by indulging in nostalgia, or by reminding each other of shared happy experiences.

One of the most dramatic signs of selective memory comes from research on parents (e.g., Campbell, 1981). Various researchers have asked parents whether they *ever* regretted having had children. The probability that something has ever happened can only go up over time, never down. Yet, parents' responses showed the opposite, impossible pattern. Young parents said, absolutely, I do feel regret for how much of my life I've lost, how many sacrifices are required, and so forth. Older parents increasingly said, no, I have never regretted it, not for a single minute. By the time their offspring had grown up and moved away, the parents couldn't remember any regrets. Again, these results are logically impossible, as if more football games were scoreless in the final minutes than in the opening minutes: If you once felt regret, then forever afterward your answer must be that, yes, I have felt regret. But the mind kindly erases these regrets and allows itself to think the whole parenting episode was lovely.

Selective Criticism: There Must Be Something Wrong

When a test brings a favorable result, people are happy and don't question it. A bad result is however immediately questioned. *How can that be?* Perhaps the flaw lies in the test, not in oneself. Unwelcome feedback is scrutinized more rigorously than good news. In the long run, of course, a one-sided critical attitude will distort the body of self-beliefs. After all, positive information is not inherently more accurate than negative, but people don't search out its flaws and toss the conclusions from their self-knowledge.

One of the most dramatic illustrations of this bias was in studies by Crocker and Major (1989). They had discovered, contrary to decades' worth of conventional wisdom, that African Americans on average had higher self-esteem than White Americans. How could this be? Anti-Black prejudice certainly exists, and African Americans in general have not attained higher status than Whites (otherwise, their higher status might explain their higher self-esteem). Part of the answer was that African Americans can dismiss or ignore negative feedback as motivated by prejudice. In a clever experiment by Crocker and colleagues (1991), African American students wrote an essay, which was then roundly criticized by a White student. The experimenters manipulated whether the African American thought the White student was aware of the African American's race. If yes, then the criticism had no effect on self-esteem. If no, then the African American's self-esteem was temporarily lowered by the criticism. Thus, African

Americans are the same as everyone else in that bad evaluations from others can dent their self-esteem. But if it is possible to attribute that evaluation to racial prejudice, then it does not affect them. Armed with that protection, they can end up with higher self-esteem by dismissing some criticism.

Selective criticism is a very different defense from simply ignoring bad news. One has to pay attention to it, perhaps replay it multiple times, in order to search for its ostensible flaws so as to dismiss it.

Compared to What, or Whom?: Downward Comparison

Self-beliefs depend on comparing yourself to others. By judiciously choosing whom to compare yourself to, you can keep your self-esteem high. This was another factor contributing to the higher self-esteem of African Americans, according to Crocker and Major. A particular person may know that her educational level or income is lower than that of some people, but if she mainly compares herself to other Blacks from a similar background, she may conclude she is doing quite well.

The strategy is known as *downward comparison*. You make yourself feel better by comparing your situation with others who are worse off. One sign that this strategy works is that it is widely used in social support for people who have suffered some misfortune. "It could have been worse," the supporters say, and they invite comparisons to people who do have it worse. A classic example appeared in Shelley Taylor's (1983) research on how women coped with breast cancer. As she put it, women who had a lump removed compared themselves with those who had lost a breast; those who had lost a breast compared themselves with those who had lost both breasts; women who suffered cancer at an advanced age compared themselves with younger women, for whom the loss was more costly; those with severe problems compared themselves with those who were dying or in great pain. Hardly ever was the reverse pattern observed (i.e., women comparing themselves to others who had less suffering or lesser losses).

Elastic Criteria

Another way of fooling yourself into a more flattering view of yourself involves shifting criteria. It may be difficult to delude yourself as to how tall you are, how old, or how much you weigh because there are objective measures. (You can use perceptual defense and avoid finding out, such as by not weighing yourself!) In contrast, there are far fewer objective criteria for measuring how good a husband or wife you are, how creative you are, or what your capacity for leadership might be.

Most people want to be a good relationship partner, and they want to believe they are one. They can use different criteria to persuade themselves they are good. One is a good listener, the other is devotedly loyal, another is good in bed, another has a fine sense of humor, another makes a high salary and can provide for needs.

A memorably pithy way of making this point was Tom Gilovich's (1991) observation: "That's how every kid can think they have the best dog on the block." The research was conducted by his erstwhile colleague, the astute Dave Dunning (e.g., Dunning et al., 1989). People do bolster their self-esteem by using slippery and alternative criteria. When the trait itself is vague, there are often multiple possible criteria—and you can probably find one that makes you look good.

Freud's Defense Mechanisms

The idea that the human mind employs strategies of dealing with information to support preferred views of self was famously elaborated by Sigmund Freud. His observations focused on dealing with sexual and violent impulses, which were widely disapproved in his day. He proposed that people avoid acknowledging thoughts and feelings that diverged from the respectable version of self they want to believe. Projection, reaction formation, displacement, and other mental gymnastics were ways of disguising bad aspects of the self so that the person could maintain the desired view.

Half a century after Freud's death, colleagues and I reviewed the modern psychological research literature for experimental findings relevant to his theory of defense mechanisms (Baumeister, Dale, & Sommer, 1998). We settled on seven major defenses. The old man did reasonably well. After all, how many scientists today would be confident about having their theories tested long after their death, using methods that no one had even imagined yet?

Three of the defense mechanisms were well supported. These include reaction formation, as in going to the opposite extreme. When people are accused of being prejudiced, for example, they try extra-hard to prove they are not prejudiced. Isolation, another defense, consists of keeping the unwelcome thought isolated in one's mind, in the sense of not forming associations to other thoughts. As we have seen, that is what repressors do: they have bad thoughts and memories, but these are not mentally linked to other thoughts, so the person is rarely reminded of them. Denial, the third defense, is probably not a single defense mechanism but a category of them. Some of them, such as refusing to acknowledge physical facts, are quite rare among mentally healthy people. But others, such as refusing to accept the implications of failure (even refusing to accept a medical diagnosis), seem fairly common.

Two of the more complex mechanisms were also evident, though somewhat differently from the way Freud thought of them. Projection, in particular, seems not to protect the self by mentally assigning one's own bad traits and thoughts to someone else. Rather, it is a side effect of the effort to suppress negative thoughts about oneself (Newman et al., 1997). When one suppresses unwanted thoughts, they tend to linger around the edges of consciousness and find ways to emerge again (what Freud called "the return of the repressed"). Lingering in the mind, these traits shape how one views other people's relevant actions. If you don't want to admit that you are sloppy, or have sexual feelings you disapprove of, you become hypersensitive to any hint of sloppiness or sexual deviance in others.

Thus, Freud's idea of projection was roughly right but needs revision. He thought seeing your faults in other people enabled you to conceal them from yourself. Instead, projection is a by-product of trying to suppress some thought about yourself. In a similar vein, the defense mechanism of undoing was something Freud got partly right. Undoing, in the limited sense of mentally replaying negative events but imagining them going differently, is probably a useful learning technique, and it does not prevent you from recognizing something bad. That is, if you miss your flight or train, you may mentally replay the day's events differently (e.g., leaving home half an hour earlier). It doesn't defend you from recognizing that you were indeed too late, but it may help you learn a lesson that will prevent future mishaps.

Last, we found essentially no support for two of his mechanisms. One is sublimation, by which basic animal instinctual energies can be redirected into socially approved pursuits. For example, Freud thought that intellectual and artistic pursuits use energy from the sex drive. That assumes that people who abstain from sex will be the most successful artists and intellectuals. But universities and artist colonies have not been paragons of chastity. We found no convincing evidence whatsoever of sublimation.

Displacement also fared poorly. Displacement changes the target: You're angry at your boss, so you go home and yell at your spouse or kick the dog. Since our review, some researchers have made a case for displaced aggression (Marcus-Newhall et al., 2000), but it is a very limited case, and it does not serve any defensive function. If your boss chews you out for being disorganized, and then you go home and your spouse also complains about your disorganization, you may react extra-negatively to the spouse. But this is a carryover of bad feelings, which are then triggered by a new person. It does not prevent you from knowing that your boss criticized you, and that you are upset about that. And the displacement has to be triggered by explicit similarity, such as both criticizing you for the same fault.

Nevertheless, Freud scored with five of the seven defense mechanisms, which is hardly perfect, but pretty good. There was one more important twist, however. Most of the modern evidence for defense mechanisms was focused on protecting self-esteem. For example, modern Americans feel terrible if they think they are prejudiced, and today's young people have been brought up to regard prejudice as one of the very worst traits or sins. Freud thought of defense mechanisms as protecting against unwanted sexual and aggressive thoughts.

Yet even in this, Freud may have been more than half right. In his day, inappropriate sexual and aggressive thoughts may well have been seriously threatening to self-esteem and reputation. He was born in the middle of the Victorian period, which was highly moralistic overall and sexually prudish in particular. Obviously, today's members of Western civilization are generally accepting of their sexual thoughts (and of anger, and aggressive impulses albeit not actions). If anything, many people consider a lack of sexual impulses to be a threat to their self-esteem.

Defense mechanisms may therefore have always been about protecting a positive view of self. In Freud's day, self-esteem depended partly on not having sexual desires beyond a few narrowly defined and widely approved ones. He mistook the means for the end, in thinking that defenses were there to protect against sexual thoughts. But when society came around to accepting, even encouraging sexual thoughts, defense mechanisms did not become obsolete. Instead, they merely shifted to protect against the currently highlighted threats to self-esteem.

KEY POINTS

- People have multiple reasons for seeking self-knowledge.
- Beliefs about the self depart from objective accuracy in systematic ways, typically being mildly (but not outrageously) more favorable.
- People engage in various self-deceiving mental maneuvers to produce and sustain those inaccurate beliefs.
- Self-deception is not quite the same as deceiving others. Yet, self-deception is useful for helping to create the desired reputation.
- Multiple mental tricks contribute to self-deception. People are skilled at processing information to help them support the conclusions they desire.

PART FOUR

THE SELF
AS ACTIVE AGENT

CHAPTER 17

The Self in Action

We shift now from knowing and thinking to doing. Beliefs cannot perform roles or make choices. Part of the self is a doer. The self performs a role in a social system. Performance requires making decisions and initiating actions—but within the constraints, demands, and opportunities of the role, as specified by society. The part of the self that carries these things out must therefore act partly on its own but also in relation to external demands. It's one of the most important things the self does. Self-knowledge is mainly useful insofar as it helps the executive know what to do.

One of the classic psychology experiments was run by Ancel Keys, late in World War II. The Allied leaders realized that after the war ended, Europe would be a chaotic mess, and feeding millions of people would be difficult. It was desirable to get some data on how the human body and mind changed when enduring months of inadequate food. Three dozen conscientious objectors were recruited to spend the better part of a year in the study, which included having a near-starvation diet for almost 6 months (Kalm & Semba, 2005).[1]

These men had to cope with a severe diet. They lost an average of a quarter of their body weight. Imagine having your weight drop from 200 pounds to 150, or 120 to 90. In an odd psychological shift, they failed to see themselves as skinny; instead, they came to regard normal people as fat. They used the executive control powers of the self to resist one of the most basic and universal urges, which is to eat when hungry. Not that they were entirely successful. Cheating was a problem throughout, and many men

---

[1] Sources also include Wikipedia, other online sources (*www.madsciencemuseum.com/ msm/pl/great_starvation_experiment*).

were found to sneak-eat food when they could, such as when away from the base.

Hungry they were. Food took over their mental life. The study was run at the University of Minnesota, so the objectors could take classes. Many signed up for classes but gradually gave up and dropped out. They just thought about food, as in borrowing recipe books from the libraries, reading cookbooks as if these were page-turner novels or pornography. Most young men think about sex frequently, but sex receded from their minds as food took over. These men tended to have strong political views, but during the study they lost interest in politics. Apparently, when you're hungry enough, other human desires and concerns recede into the foggy background.

One theory about self-control is that it uses the body's basic energy supply, which makes dieting especially difficult. Many men in the Minnesota study became irritable, disliking minor things about life and each other that normally would not have bothered them. Another sign is that they complained about the inability to concentrate and other mental problems, though mental tests found no problems, indicating their brains could function just fine.

The conscientious objectors in Keys's study probably had not understood what they were getting into when they signed up. Some regrets would hardly be surprising. Yet when the men were interviewed about the study many decades later, when they were in their 80s, they were emphatically positive about having taken part. They said it was one of the most meaningful experiences of their lives. They said absolutely they would make the same choice again in the same circumstances. They knew their peers were fighting and dying to make the world a better place, and they were glad to do their part, too. They refused to kill for their country, but they wanted to do something heroic and self-sacrificing to contribute.

This study was chosen to introduce the executive aspect of the self, that is, the process that controls action, makes decision, and regulates its own responses. The story reveals some key aspects of the human self and its executive function:

- Self-control is used to restrain desires.
- The conscientious objectors invoked abstract ideas to guide their behavior. Incorporating abstract ideas into the causation of behavior is a distinctively human trait.
- Individual action was guided by collective influence. They made enormous personal sacrifices for the sake of their culture.
- Desires changed. Motivation (desire) is the basis for the executive function: The self's executive powers exist to serve desires.
- Self-control is based on energy and starts to fail when energy is lacking.
- The self's executive operates as if it has limited energy, and in some ways it seems to be overly cautious to conserve.

WHY AN EXECUTIVE AGENT?

The human self has remarkable powers to make decisions in complex ways, integrating information relevant to the decision in novel ways, imposing control on the physical and social world, even altering and regulating itself. What are the advantages?

Agency goes back far in evolution and does not require anything like a human self. One of the earliest and simplest forms of agency is found in the bacterium *E. coli*, a tiny creature with nothing we would call a self, except that it acts as a unity, a single system. The bacterium has a row of tiny hairs around its outside. All these can do is occasionally stiffen up and wiggle so as to spin the bacterium around in a circle, which causes it to move randomly (Abbott, 2018).

The *E. coli* thus lives in the immediate present. It senses whether its immediate environment is providing nutrients or not. If so, it stays in place and absorbs them. If not, it spins around and veers off to another place, where it goes through the same decision process again. The goal, though it has no concept of the goal, is to blunder into food before it starves.

How much of an agent is that? The bacterium has no brain. It only performs the simple acts of reading its present situation and choosing between stay-put and spin-away-at-random. If it moves, it has no idea at all of where it is going. Here or away-from-here are the only choices. But this is adaptive, enabling the bacteria to survive because enough of them manage to end up where the food is. Moreover, by discovering the advantages of moving around, they evolve down the animal path rather than the plant path. Most animals do have an agent, in the sense of a brain that takes in information about the environment and then tells the body what to do.

Thus, I have several points about agency. First, it presumably evolved because it extends life (survival), in this case by moving the organism around until it finds food. Second, its goal is a kind of harmony between the organism and the environment, in which the organism can get what it needs to sustain life. Third, it is based on being in a situation with more than one possibility. Its purpose is to produce the more advantageous outcome—that is, being where there is food so it can go on living.

DOING SERVES WANTING

Will computers take over the world, such as doomsday movies (e.g., *The Terminator*) vividly and excruciatingly depict? As Steven Pinker (1997) drily remarked, why should they? What would they demand? Better surge protectors?[2]

---

[2]Pinker's original joke used floppy disks, now an obsolete piece of technology.

Pinker's point is that agency serves motivation. Your ability to control what you do is based on the fact that you want things. Computers can think better and faster than humans, but they do not have wants. Without wanting, there is no reason for them to turn on their masters and programmers, no reason to conspire to rule. A computer doesn't want, doesn't care.

Doing stems from wanting. Living things do want and do care. Each life is temporary, and evolution heavily favors life that seeks to continue living. That's part of the essence of life, which is why computers, being not alive, don't have it. Survival and reproduction, the keys to natural selection, are based on continuing life. The organism has to self-initiate the behaviors to produce those. That's where motivation comes from, originally. The most basic and powerful desires are linked to sustaining life: desires for self-preservation, food, sex, and so on. As with the E. coli, agency serves the goal of continuing life. The powers of the agent increased with evolution, always based on what was good for prolonging or reproducing life. Natural selection is a powerful process, and it has made sure that creatures who walk the earth today are descended from ancestors who strove to sustain life rather than be indifferent.

The brain is the center of the central nervous system. Essentially, that system transmits information from the eyes, ears, nose, and so on to the center, where it is processed, and from which commands are sent to the muscles, to guide movement. It is generally agreed that the origins of the central nervous system are associated with moving and eating, concerns already present in the E. coli, which has no such system. Animals have agency, with a central nervous system, first so they can move around to get food, and second to avoid being eaten by other creatures. They have agency precisely because they want things.

Hand in hand with wanting things is living in an environment in which different outcomes are possible. The agent exists to steer events toward the more desirable outcomes and away from the undesirable ones. Evolution gave you an executive self to try to do your best to guide events toward the good outcomes.

Thus, a key feature of the self is that it has to be able to initiate and control its actions and reactions, so as to produce benefits, based on what it wants. Voluntary behavior is self-initiated, to some extent. The organism must adjust itself and choose its actions so as to pursue enlightened self-interest in the context of complex society. The human self has advanced this voluntary control to levels beyond those in the animal world.

CONTROL AND HARMONY

Let's return to the key point that all living things seek to create and sustain a kind of harmony with their environment, whereby they can get the nutrients and safety they need to survive, in a sustainable manner (i.e., without ruining the environment). Control is initiating change so as to improve that harmony.

Control: First Body, Then World

One of the brain's first tasks in life is to learn how to exert control over its own body. Indeed, many have said that that is one of the key initial steps toward a concept of self, as the brain sorts the world into parts that are always there (its body) and over which it can exert direct control, as opposed to parts that are external, as indicated by being there only sometimes, and at best indirectly controlled.

As the body is brought under control—not a linear process—the brain can use its control over the body to start to control the world. Controlling one's own body so it can act on the environment is fundamental to almost everything that the advanced human self does, including shopping, marrying, voting, driving. Even talking and writing depend on muscle movements under central (brain) control. Choice and control are vital functions of the human self.

A classic paper by Rothbaum, Weisz, and Snyder (1982) explained that there are two fundamentally different ways the self goes about creating harmony with the environment. The first, which they called "primary control," involves changing the environment to suit the self. The other, called "secondary control," involves changing the self to suit the environment. The sequence is not arbitrary. The assumption is that organisms would start with primary control; if that failed, they would switch to secondary control. The sequence has not held up, however, and often people start with so-called secondary control. Indeed, Weisz (personal communication) wrote to me that his subsequent data indicated that secondary control was the more important kind for producing good long-term outcomes. Adapting to life successfully is more about adjusting yourself to fit in than about changing the world to suit yourself, though both are helpful. Regardless of sequence, the distinction is profound and important, as is the fact that despite seeming like opposites, they are both in service to the same goal, namely establishing a harmonious relationship between self and environment.

Primary Control

Primary control is quite familiar and is reflected in the progress of civilization. Where once human beings roamed the fields and forests on foot, looking for each day's food, sleeping outside exposed to the elements, and so on, now the environment has been transformed into people-friendly forms. Houses keep us warm and dry, stores provide food and other items, cars and even airplanes move us easily from place to place, roads make travel comfortable, and signs help us find where we want to go.

Secondary Control

Secondary control takes various forms, reflecting the different ways that the self can accommodate itself to the world. Simply knowing what to expect is a form of predictive control. Even if one cannot change the event, one can prepare oneself for it. Illusory control means convincing oneself, falsely, that one can do something about it, such as via superstitious behavior. In vicarious control, people align themselves with leaders or other powerful people who are thought capable of controlling events, and so even though the person cannot directly accomplish anything, he or she is satisfied by being on the side of someone who can. Last, interpretive control refers to the appeal of understanding events even if one cannot really change them.

The self clearly engages in both primary and secondary control. It engages in the outward directed sort, making decisions and influencing other people so as to get the world under control. Moreover, it also engages in self-control, which adjusts the self to fit the external world's demands.

WHAT THE SELF ACTUALLY DOES

The self evolved to help the animal body participate in complex social groups, the social environment. That insight can help flesh out some features of the self.

To make groups function well, selves first have to integrate themselves into the group. That requires both the desire and the wherewithal. The desire to belong to groups is well established, and indeed the need to belong is one of the most widely invoked ideas in all of social psychology. Still, wanting to belong is often not enough. The rest of this chapter focuses on the wherewithal: what the self does to earn its place in a social group. There are five key activities: being a task performer, following orders, being an economic agent, an information agent, and a moral agent.

Task Performer

Plenty of creatures perform tasks. The human self enables a higher, more advanced, and powerful way of getting things done. Unlike other animals, humans can make themselves toil for hours on end at an unsatisfying chore, like cleaning the garage or preparing a tax return. The human self can work toward distant goals while keeping them in mind and even adjusting the work so as to best reach the goal. It can take a break for an hour or a week, can remember just where things stand, and can then resume the task at the right point. It can also work with others, adapting its efforts to complement and mesh with theirs, sharing a collective understanding of what the goal is, and how their various efforts fit together to get the job done.

The most basic contribution to task performance is to put forth the effort and make whatever other sacrifices are required. A group of people can build a structure to ward off the rain, but it will get built better and faster if everyone helps, rather than some just watching. If the group can exploit division of labor, their shelter will get built faster and better.

As a way to cement one's position in a productive group, being able to perform a unique role is helpful. Successful groups capitalize on the differences among their members, ideally with everyone performing a different task to which he or she is extra well suited. The self therefore needs to know its talents, abilities, and preferences, as well as scouting out a niche in the social system where those would be most productive.

Following Orders

Another extremely important and powerful aspect of human task performance is following orders and instructions. Humans work together in groups in which a leader oversees the process and commands different people to perform specific aspects of the job. The leader is responsible for the system by which people work together, and the followers perform their individual roles, none of which would be of much use without the separate performances of others in other roles. For example, an assembly line can make cars rapidly and cheaply, but each person's job is only useful as part of the whole; without the rest of the assembly line, one guy's skillful and diligent exertions for installing the back seat would not amount to much. Individuals can contribute to the group success by following orders, even if they do not fully understand how all the different jobs and roles fit together.

The human self evolved to work with others, and its success depends on the cooperative efforts of others. The self by itself is pretty useless.

Economic Agent

Another important way that the individual self participates in society is as an economic agent. This has become important, complex, and demanding in modern society, partly because money is so widely used. Some researchers think this is all a side effect because in evolutionary history there were few possessions and so there would not have been much economic activity. Money itself is only about 3,000 years old (Weatherford, 1977), so it did not play a role in human evolution. On the other hand, trade is much older than money (Ridley, 2020). Some scholars estimate that long-distance trade dates back 150,000 years (far beyond farming and even the wheel), and local trade would be even older.

One of the reasons scholars give for why our Cro-Magnon ancestors ousted the Neanderthals was that our species had trade and economic activity, which was one key part of the superior social system that enabled them to prevail over the Neanderthals (Horan et al., 2005). And one sign of economic activity is that there was trade. Relics found in Neanderthal burial sites are mostly of local origin, whereas Cro-Magnons were sometimes buried with items originating far away—thus suggesting a trading network.

Here, let me explain something simple and basic that eluded me for a long time. I'd heard economists claim that trade makes everyone better off by increasing wealth, but it didn't make intuitive sense to me. If Fred and José trade shirts, how are they better off, how are they richer? Each still has a shirt, and indeed the new one might not fit as well as the old one. But that's the wrong model. An expert fisherman may catch more fish than he (plus his family) can eat, and the extra fish have no value to him—but he can trade those extra fish for something else, such as perhaps a clay pot. The fellow who creates the clay pots makes more than he can use, but again he can trade them for fish. He needs food for his family, who cannot eat clay pots, so for him that leftover fish is really valuable. After trading, the fisherman is now better off with a couple of new clay pots, and the potter is also better off for having some nice fish dinners for his family. The increased wealth comes not from creating new stuff but from moving the stuff around to where it's most wanted.

Even in the modern economy, when one person sells a used car to someone else, both are better off because the one wanted to get rid of the car and the other wanted to acquire one.

There's no disputing that trade increases wealth. If you look through history, over and over the societies that were at the center of a major trading network became rich and powerful, while societies that avoided trade gradually withered (Acemoglu & Robinson, 2012; Bernstein, 2004). As other important evidence, wars are usually won by the society or country with the bigger, stronger economy (Beckley, 2010). That's what funds the bigger, stronger army.

Thus, being able to participate in an economy is perhaps one of the key factors that enabled our version of humankind to take over the planet instead of the Neanderthals, who populated Eurasia first and therefore had home field advantage.

The economic agent requires certain things, which have become important parts of the self more generally. Obviously, ownership is vital to trade, and that requires continuity across time as well as abstract connections between selves and objects. There would be no point in buying something without a stable self to own it. Hence, it is no wonder that genuine economic markets only exist among humans because only humans understand selves as existing across time. The right-now self would only "buy" something for immediate consumption, if that.

Trade may also require the self to use numbers, or at least something that almost amounts to numbers (as in quantities and values). How many fish are worth how many clay pots? The modern self is often measured out in numbers: salary, body mass index, years of schooling, number of sex partners or children, years of marriage, cholesterol level, and so on. The habit of measuring the self may have some basis in the need to measure items for trade.

There may even be some innate or innately prepared desire to trade. Children do develop little marketplaces where they exchange things. In my childhood, the most traded items were baseball cards and comic books. Possibly this is simply a means, but some children do seem to like the trading itself.

Economic activity brings up several other crucial aspects of self. It creates the possibility of prospering over time, if one does it wisely. Marketplaces reward and thereby promote rational thought, including planning and calculating. Buying in bulk can bring lower prices, precisely because the seller can make the requisite profit from a few sales and can then afford to unload additional ones at a much smaller profit margin—but only somewhat lower, and so precise calculations are helpful. This fits the general pattern of bringing more careful, rational thinking into the processes by which the self guides behavior. It pays to be smart.

Although money is familiar as a cause of immoral behavior, starting with robbery and going through fraud and cheating, it also can actually promote moral behavior. An economic marketplace depends on trust (Arrow, 1974; Fukuyama, 1995; Wilson & Kennedy, 1999). An unscrupulous opportunist might sell defective goods at high prices, effectively swindling customers, now and then. But to operate a business in a community over a long period of time, a reputation for dishonesty can be disastrous. Economists also have long acknowledged that trust is vital to economic trade, even to the extent that every transaction requires some degree of trust. Understanding trust and the need to be trusted is a requirement for the economic agent but may also be useful for other of the self's activities. More broadly, economic systems and marketplaces promote obeying rules.

Information Agent

Trafficking in information is a major part of what the human self does, and it's something that's rare and circumscribed in other species (for a review, see Baumeister et al., 2018). Humans know and indeed prioritize exactly those communications. They also routinely exchange the contents of their minds. The common greeting, "How are you?," requests a report on the other person's internal overall state. What do people do when they get together, most commonly? Above and beyond all, they *talk*. Talking is almost certainly the single most frequent thing people do when getting together. Even when they get together to do other stuff, they talk while they are doing it. Usually, talking enables them to do it better, whatever it is. Talking is sharing information. It's one of the central things that humans do.

Let us run through the nuts and bolts of how the self operates as an information agent. The relevant context is this: The human self was shaped by evolution to be an information agent. What are the results of that, in terms of how the self is put together, how the self operates and functions?

Getting Information

First, and least relevant, the self seeks information. But almost all animals seek information. Curiosity is not specific to humankind. Still, it is the first step toward being an information agent; you want to get information. After that, the rest is mostly specific to humankind (Baumeister et al., 2018).

Telling Others Your Information

Second, people have an innate desire or impulse to tell the contents of their minds to others. This was featured by Suddendorf (2013) as key to the "the gap," the big difference between humans and other animals. Unlike almost all other animals, humans have an ongoing drive to communicate their thoughts and feelings to others. This motivation helps get information moving.

Circulating Information through the Group

Third, people pass along information, which helps things circulate through the group without the person who discovered something having to tell every single person in the group. Passing along is easy to overlook, but it is probably crucial. The first groups to do this would have had a decisive advantage over their competitors.

Questioning Information to Improve It

Fourth, the information agent is critical and skeptical. Sometimes the agent raises questions, is openly skeptical or even adamantly contrary. Without this, false information would spread through the group just as readily as true information. Skepticism helps refine the information, so it's more accurate. Thus, the human self doesn't just acquire and share information. Rather, the self operates on the information, questioning it, checking the evidence, embracing some parts more than others, and discussing problems with others.

Goals of Information Sharing

It appears there are three goals to sharing information. Accuracy is certainly a goal sometimes. Some groups will have a better stock of shared information than others. This is the stuff that *goes without saying* when members of the group interact with each other. What makes one shared view of the world better than another? To be sure, accuracy is one of the criteria. Correct information has advantages over false information.

Another goal is coherence. Is the information complete and largely free from contradictions very much, including inconsistencies with what we currently all assume to be true (the shared outlook)? New facts must be integrated into what is already known.

The third goal is consensus: How much do all the members of the group know about and agree on this information? If everyone agrees, and everyone knows that everyone agrees, then it goes without saying. A typical conversation can skip all that, taking the shared beliefs for granted, and using them as a foundation for discussing what's new.

When these goals clash, such as when the majority seems to embrace something false, it is not clear which goal will routinely prevail. Often people seem to want to embrace what the group thinks, even if their own information indicates that that is false. This was a key point in one of the investigations that launched modern social psychology, namely the famous Asch conformity studies (1955, 1956). In those studies, participants sat in groups and took turns making simple perceptual judgments, such as which of three lines was the same length as a fourth line. In reality, there was only one genuine research participant, and others were actors (confederates) pretending to be subjects but working with the experimenter. From time to time they would all state a wrong answer. Frequently, the real participant would go along with the group, stating the wrong answer rather than the one he or she could see to be correct. Consensus trumped accuracy.

Thus far we have covered the basic activities of an information agent: getting information, telling others what one has learned, circulating information through the group, and questioning or criticizing the information so as to improve it. There are several additional kinds of activities that information agents engage in. One is withholding information.

Withholding Information

Sometimes when someone asks you something, and you know the answer, you might refuse to disclose it, for various reasons. Promises of secrecy would be one such reason but also sometimes people enjoy advantages from having information others do not, such as by being more valued by their employers. Another form of withholding is lying. People will express information that they know to be false, for various reasons such as personal advantage. (Used car salesmen have a reputation for doing this.)

More broadly, in society, groups of information agents may work together to manipulate and maintain the common stock of information in a way that brings them advantages. For example, assuming that most religions are false (something that most religions assume about each other), governments that require all citizens to support a particular religion are doing precisely this.

The Doxa

Where all this leads is to the construction of a common stock of knowledge. The *doxa* is a term for this: The doxa is the group's shared beliefs, the ones that go without saying and that are assumed by all to be known and shared. Millions of people will all understand that when a speaker mentions "huddled masses yearning to breathe free," he is referring to a verse engraved on the American Statue of Liberty, or that "Christmas shopping" means participating in the annual ritual of purchasing gifts for loved ones; such things indicate the central importance of information in human social life. Each self has to be an information agent in order to participate in society.

The marvelous program of research by E. Tory Higgins (2019) and his colleagues has mapped out some of the important features of the doxa, which they call "shared reality." It includes some ways that the shared reality is not reality at all. People seem to believe what they share with others, even if this is different from their own information. In an effect Higgins dubbed "saying is believing," they showed that people remember what they said better than what they originally learned (Higgins & Rholes, 1978). If you have some information to tell but, knowing that your listener already has a strong opinion about the matter, you alter the information so as to fit the listener's preferences and prejudices—you end up remembering the distorted version that you expressed, rather than the correct information you started with.

Crucially, these processes support the construction and maintenance of similar beliefs. They occur more with members of one's own group than outgroup members: I'm more likely to alter what I say to suit you if you are one of my group rather than an outsider. Remarkably, too, if I later learn that you did not understand or otherwise receive the message I sent to you, then my memory goes back to what I originally learned, rather than what I said. That shows that the original, more accurate information remains buried in the mind, subverted to make way for the shared reality.

Still, the mind seems to prefer the version that it shares with others. Clearly, consensus is powerful. Coherence may wax and wane in importance. Accuracy in a sense remains the supreme goal officially, and there does seem to be some tendency for "truth wins" in the long run, but sometimes that is very long.

Moral Agent

A final but powerfully important way the executive self relates to society is as a moral agent. Societies need morality to control behavior (e.g., Hogan, 1983). Without morality, we are just a gaggle of animals pursuing our animal impulses. Morality imposes rules that enable society to function (Curry, 2016). If people would just walk into restaurants and eat what they liked off other people's plates and leave without paying (as most other apes would), restaurants would cease to exist. Modern society is better with restaurants than without, and so people need to obey the moral rules to enable restaurants to exist. And obviously, it's not just restaurants. The same goes for many other institutions.

So, let's be clear how this works. Prosperous, rich societies prevail over poor ones. We are descended from the winners, but we should know what enabled them to win. The selves that could follow the rules enough to let the system increase total resources, to enlarge the pie, flourished. Moral rules subvert animal self-interest to what is required, so society can increase the pie (Tomasello, 2016).

Fundamentally, the job of society is to help its members survive and reproduce. It contributes in several ways, such as by offering mutual protection, by sharing information, and by increasing the amount of resources (starting with food) available to members. To accomplish those purposes, people have to work together in coordinated fashion. The coordination is often accomplished by a system. Sometimes this requires that they do things that conflict with their immediate personal self-interest—indeed, even sometimes with their long-term self-interest, such as when young men must risk their lives in battle, to defend the society against its enemies.

Morality is largely a set of collective rules that help society function well, so it can operate its systems and thereby improve and prolong the lives of (most of) its members. The most famous set of moral guidelines, the Ten Commandments, are mostly prohibitions against doing things that might satisfy selfish impulses but that undermine the ability of society to function. Killing other members of society, spreading false information, stealing others' property, having sex with other people's committed partners, and similar actions weaken a society, and if they become widespread, the society will collapse.

Moral principles encourage people to restrain themselves. To be effective, the moral principles must be understood by the individual agent and incorporated into the decision-making process.

Of course, the self would ask, what's in it for me? Denying one's impulses and desires seemingly does not offer the self much. But those sacrifices bring the benefit of belonging to the group because groups need members who (mostly) obey the rules. If one obeys the rule not to steal, one deprives oneself of ready access to other people's possessions, which is a cost—but the associated benefit is that one's own possessions will not be stolen away by others.

A possibly more urgent and salient benefit is that morality provides guidelines for how to succeed in a crucial aspect of human social life, namely getting other people to cooperate with you. Human beings evolved to cooperate, even among non-kin, a style of social interaction that can bring immense benefits but requires individuals to be able to convince others to cooperate with them. Whether people will cooperate with you depends on how they evaluate you. People judge each other heavily based on their moral traits. If anything, moral judgments are the single most important dimension on how people evaluate each other generally (Goodwin et al., 2014). (Admittedly, sex appeal may come close in some specific instances. But good moral character even boosts sex appeal [Farrelly et al., 2016].) Therefore, you need to convince the group of your good moral character— otherwise, at least in the evolutionary past, you might well starve. Thus, functioning well as a moral agent was helpful, even vital, for well-being and survival.

KEY POINTS

- The executive aspect of the self controls action, makes decisions, and regulates its own responses.
- Desire (motivation) is the basis for doing, that is, executive function.
- Self-control is used to restrain desires.
- Control is initiating change to improve harmony with the environment.
- The self engages in two types of control: primary control is changing the world to fit the self; secondary control is changing the self to better fit the world.
- The self performs five main roles to earn a place in the group: task performer, following orders, participating in an economy, being an information agent, and being a moral agent.

CHAPTER 18

Self-Regulation
and Self-Control

Starting in the 1980s if not earlier, major thinkers about the psychology of self converged on understanding that self-regulation is central to much of what the self is and does. Understanding how self-regulation works in the human mind is central to understanding the self.

The moral agent invokes moral principles of right and wrong in deciding how to act. Often that requires overriding some impulse or desire, in order to do what is right. Good self-control is one of the most powerful keys to success in life. Indeed, it is fair to say that intelligence and self-control are the two main traits psychology has studied that bring a wide range of benefits across the majority of human endeavors. People with good self-control do better than other people in many respects as described more below.

In what follows I use *self-regulation* and *self-control* interchangeably unless otherwise noted. Scholars who use them differently consider self-regulation to be a broader concept than self-control. Self-control is typically limited to conscious, deliberate processes, whereas self-regulation can include processes outside of conscious control (such as how the body maintains a constant temperature). The unconscious and automatic regulation processes are important in some contexts, but not so much for the present analysis.

BENEFITS OF GOOD SELF-CONTROL

Good self-control is positively correlated with a broad range of positive outcomes. These links remain strong even when researchers measure the personality trait first and then assess objective outcomes several years later, in some cases decades later.

Early evidence came when Walter Mischel followed up his famous "marshmallow test" studies from the 1960s by getting back in touch with those children as they reached adulthood. His group had measured children's self-control behaviorally at age 4: Were they able to resist a tempting treat in order to get an extra treat some minutes later? Mischel's own children attended the school where those studies had been run. When they told various stories about this or that classmate, he sometimes looked back to see how the classmate had done in the marshmallow test. The ones who had done better in the lab were also faring better in the children's gossip. Eventually, he and his colleagues wrote to everyone who had taken part to get life updates. It seems that the children who had shown the best self-control at age 4 went on to have better lives: be more popular, more successful in school and work, and have better relationships (Mischel et al., 1988; Shoda et al., 1990).

A New Zealand study measured self-control (among many other things) in childhood and then tracked people into adulthood. Again, the children who had shown better self-control grew up into adults with more successful lives (Moffitt et al., 2011). If you're a parent, or thinking of becoming one, I suggest you spend 15 minutes reading their article. The range of effects is stunning. Children with poorer self-control went on to have diverse problems. Their overall health as adults was worse, though the problems clustered in some areas more than others. Their lungs were fine though they were more likely to be smokers—but effects of smoking do not show up for a long time. They had more dental problems, probably because they neglected to brush and floss. They were more likely to be overweight and have various metabolic problems. They had more sexually transmitted diseases, presumably because they took more risks and neglected precautions. They took more heavy drugs. They were more likely to drop out of school without getting a degree. They were more likely to create an unplanned pregnancy, more likely to have their children raised in a one-parent household. (This was true for both men and women, i.e., single mothers and absent fathers.) They had lower incomes and less savings. They were more likely to have been convicted of a crime.

Some of these problems came from messing up as adolescents. Dropping out of school, taking up smoking by age 15, or unintentionally becoming a teenage parent can derail the best of plans, and all these were more common among people who had scored low at self-control. Yet even when the researchers controlled for these stumbling blocks, low self-control continued to contribute significantly to adult problems later on. In other words, even if a teenager manages to avoid such adolescent missteps, low self-control will haunt and stunt his or her prospects in adulthood.

Collecting data about large numbers of people over many years is difficult, expensive research to do, and we should not be surprised that such evidence is rare. The New Zealand study is an impressive exception. As luck would have it, the British government collected a large amount of data on most of their nation's children at a couple of points in time and followed them over decades (the 1970 British Cohort Study and the 1958 National Child Development Study). Students' self-control was rated by their teachers between the ages of 7 and 11. Although that was not the focus of the research, bad self-control early in life led to various misfortunes in adulthood. Being relatively bad at self-control at that young age increased the odds of becoming an adult smoker, and even of being unemployed (Daly et al., 2015, 2016). These differences held up even after correcting for age, gender, social class, and other factors.

Other advantages of self-control have been confirmed in other contexts (reviewed by Baumeister & Tierney, 2011; Baumeister & Vohs, 2016). People with good self-control have better mental health. They have better physical health. They even live longer. Nor are their lives a kind of joyless, puritanical slog through duties and discipline: People with good self-control are genuinely happier than others (Hofmann et al., 2014; Wiese et al., 2018). This is true of both kinds of happiness that researchers measure: the bird's-eye view of "How satisfied are you with your life as a whole?" and the moment-to-moment tally of "How do you feel right now?" Furthermore, other people find high self-control folks more trustworthy (Righetti & Finkenauer, 2011) and rate them more highly as work supervisors. Their relationship partners are happier, too: The higher the total amount of self-control two people have, the more satisfied both of them are with their relationship (Vohs et al., 2011).

A fresh look at the data yielded new insights as to how self-control was related to aggression and crime. The turning point was a book by two criminologists titled *A General Theory of Crime* (Gottfredson & Hirschi, 1990). Their theory was refreshingly simple: Low self-control was the key to understanding the criminal mind and personality.

Gottfredson and Hirschi (1990) noted that criminologists had not spotted this previously because criminology researchers tend to specialize (just like most social scientists do). Researchers would collect data and publish studies specifically on one type of crime. What these datasets missed was that many criminals get arrested repeatedly—but for different crimes. Hollywood movies often reinforce the stereotype that criminals themselves specialize, becoming expert in one type of crime (e.g., jewel heist). Out in the real world, however, criminals break one law after another in search of illicit, easy profits. It is a lifestyle marked by low inhibition and disregard for rules. People with good self-control do not usually adopt that lifestyle, but people lower in self-control are more prone to do so.

The two criminologists made a convincing case for the link between poor self-control and crime. One line of evidence that persuaded me was that even the law-abiding behavior patterns of criminals betray their lack of self-control. Criminals have more traffic accidents, more unplanned pregnancies, and the like, compared to other people. They are more likely to smoke cigarettes. When they hold jobs, they miss more days of work. The authors noted the relatively high rate of crime among children raised by single parents. That can have multiple causes, but it does fit the view that those children probably have lower self-control than others. Most single parents work hard to raise their children well, but it is a struggle just to get them fed and clothed and off to school on time. Enforcing a regime with strict rules is easier to do with two parents than one, and that's the kind of parenting likely to instill good self-control. To be sure, it is highly plausible that simply inheriting the genes of a parent who deserted the family would predispose a child to poor self-control. If a father doesn't stick around to raise his son, the son has some of those irresponsibility-producing genes. It's hard to know whether genes or parenting produce the dismal outcomes of children of single-parent families, but low self-control could be central either way.

The crime book inspired criminologists to start collecting data on self-control. The basic point linking low self-control to higher crime was resoundingly confirmed (Pratt & Cullen, 2000). About the only complaint was a predictable one: Low self-control is not the only factor, and other relevant causes must be accepted, too. Complex phenomena rarely boil down to a single cause or formula, and it was an overreach to think self-control would be a complete explanation of crime. Nevertheless, it is clear that low self-control leads to crime. Those big data are correlational but show the pattern across time, which supports causal inference. Low self-control now leads to more criminal action later. Experimental findings confirm the causal link: Experimental manipulations that produce a state of low self-control also produce heightened aggression.

Even among convicted prisoners, variations in self-control make a difference. Those higher in self-control do better than others when they get out of prison. They are less likely to be arrested again. They are more likely to get and keep jobs, they integrate better into the community, and they are less likely to get addicted to drugs and alcohol (Malouf et al., 2014).

All in all, the record is remarkable. High self-control produces a wide range of benefits, some of them quite large with hardly any downside. Over the years I have known many researchers who tried to show some negative effects of good self-control, but in general these have not yielded much. For example, when asked to imagine themselves going to a party, people think it could be more fun to go with someone with low rather than high self-control (Röseler, Ebert, Schütz, & Baumeister, 2021). But this is only in imagination, and we do not know whether actual choices and enjoyment fit that pattern.

SELF-AWARENESS: CHECKING AGAINST STANDARDS

The process of self-regulation can be analyzed in terms of three basic features: standards (ideas about how one should or should not be), monitoring (keeping track of how one is acting in comparison with standards), and the capacity for change. A problem with any of them can undermine the entire process. People who exhibit good self-control generally have all three working together effectively.

The term *regulate* means change based on standards, which are ideas about how things should or should not be. The government regulates industries by establishing standards and telling industries to conform to the standards. Crucially, effective governments do not simply issue commands but also keep track of how well each company is obeying them. It is very difficult to regulate something without closely monitoring and keeping track. This is as true for individuals as for societies.

Self-awareness is therefore central to self-regulation. The hugely influential work by Carver and Scheier (1981, 1982) proposed that the basic purpose of self-awareness is to enable you to change yourself. That's why self-awareness typically compares the self as perceived with various standards, such as ideals, morals, personal goals, and other people's expectations. The central purpose of self-awareness is to identify aspects of self that need to be adjusted, whether this means combing your hair or trying harder on your homework. Self-awareness also helps you monitor the process of change, so you can check progress and see how far you still have to go.

The self-aware process for monitoring progress is quite sophisticated. Early psychological theories assumed that good feelings came from reaching goals. That's correct, they do—but good feelings can come long before that. Carver and Scheier (1990) concluded that the feelings respond to *progress* toward goals. As long as you are moving in the right direction and roughly on schedule, you can feel good, long before you actually reach the goal. This is a powerful improvement in the human mind, which enables people to work toward goals over long periods of time, punctuated by interruptions and other activities but then always resuming. The unity project of connecting the right-now self to the extended self is helped by being able to feel good about what you are doing while the goal is still far off. After all, if you mainly felt good or bad based on how close versus far you are to each goal, you would never feel like resuming work on a project whose fruition lies far ahead.

Conversely, self-regulation tends to go badly when self-awareness is impaired. When people are distracted or unwilling or unable to focus on themselves, their self-control breaks down. The harder it is to keep track of something, the more difficult it is to regulate. When I was a poor student trying to live on $2 per day, my grandmother gave me very good advice, which was to write down everything you spend money on. In her generation, in Europe, money meant cash, and so you could always monitor how much was left in your wallet. Credit cards have made that process much more complex and difficult, and there are many people with very good salaries who find themselves deeply in debt. It's much harder to monitor credit card than cash spending.

Alcohol provides a powerful example of the benefits of self-awareness. Even small amounts of alcohol reduce self-awareness (Hull, 1981)—and along with it, self-control goes downhill. Intoxicated people eat more, spend more, tip more, smoke more, and so on.

Self-regulation theory borrowed from the theories used by military scientists to help long-distance missiles reach their targets (Carver & Scheier, 1981, 1982). The simple framework for a control loop was test–operate–test–exit (TOTE). Missiles fired at far-off targets would often get blown off course by wind. Sometimes it was simply impossible to aim them precisely enough from an enormous distance, so they needed to correct their course during flight. The built-in computer would test whether its current trajectory was likely to hit the target. If not, then some minor correction would take place (the operate phase), such as nudging a bit to the left. Then another test, and perhaps another correction. When a test yielded the satisfactory result that the current flight was properly on target, the loop would be exited for the time being. According to Carver and Scheier, this is roughly how human self-awareness functions. One tests oneself against the standard (at least in terms of satisfactory progress), operates to make it satisfactory, tests again, and then exits the loop.

WILLPOWER AND EGO DEPLETION

Self-awareness contributes to self-regulation by providing tests against standards. What about the "operate" phase? This is what actually brings about the change. In this case, my own laboratory work has been centrally concerned with unraveling this puzzle, so I will provide a rough inside history.

At the time I began this work, psychology was dominated by information-processing theories. The brain was thought to be like a computer. The idea that the self would consist of energy, that self-control would depend on some kind of inner strength, was utterly foreign to that approach. But there were some early signs in the literature that prompted me to consider such a theory. One was that self-control seemed to break down when people had other demands on them, such as when they were under stress. Another was subjective reports: People experienced self-regulation failures as moments of weakness, temptations as strong, resistance as futile, and the like. Since then, of course, evidence has greatly expanded. For example, although many people seek to restrict both their eating and their smoking, restricting one seems to undermine efforts to restrict the other (Cheskin et al., 2005; Shmueli & Prochaska, 2009).

Mark Muraven, a graduate student, began conducting experiments to test a core prediction of the energy theory: that after exerting effort on one self-control task, the person would do worse on the next self-control task, even if it was different. This was the opposite of what the information-processing computer–brain theories would predict. They were based on loading the program (in computer-speak), or priming the concept, so if you are already in a self-controlling mode, you should do better at another self-control challenge. Muraven ran multiple studies and found results fitting the strength model. After doing a first self-control task, people did worse on a seemingly unrelated second self-control task—as if they had indeed expended some of their strength or willpower. Soon other graduate students also began to do studies on self-control as limited energy.

We needed a name for the effect. The only prior thinker we could find was Sigmund Freud, who had said that the *ego* (his term for self) was partly made of energy. In homage to Freud, we borrowed his term for self and dubbed the effect "ego depletion."

The basic pattern of ego depletion is that after exerting self-control, subsequent performance at self-control is worse, even on seemingly unrelated tasks (for reviews, see Baumeister & Tierney, 2011; Baumeister & Vohs, 2016; Baumeister, Vohs, & Tice, 2007). One study showed that after people tried to either suppress or amplify their emotional reaction to an upsetting film clip, they had poorer physical stamina on a handgrip squeezing task. (That was in comparison to people who watched the same film but did not try to control their feelings.) In another, after they tried to shut a forbidden thought (about a white bear, based on a famous anecdote from Tolstoy's life) out of their mind, they gave up faster on a frustrating word puzzle. These findings, and the hundreds of others that have been published since, show the limited nature of willpower. The first task uses up some of it, leaving less available for the second task.

Another point these studies make is that all types of self-control draw on the same energy; you have only one reservoir of willpower. Self-control is used in multiple domains, but they all draw energy from the same source.

A first revision to the theory was the recognition that ego depletion patterns reflect conservation, rather than a complete absence of willpower. Muraven found that offering people a compelling incentive to do well on the second test caused them to do well, sometimes remarkably well, despite having already exerted self-control on the first (Muraven & Slessareva, 2003). Thus, even when depleted, people can still self-regulate effectively. (However, they showed more severe depletion after this.) The brain had not run out of fuel! Further studies indicated that ego depletion effects are essentially a matter of conserving energy. If people are expecting further demands for self-control, they hold back more in the present (Muraven et al., 2006). All these patterns suggest that people are managing a limited energy supply.

The analogy to physical muscles was a useful guide in developing this theory (see also Evans et al., 2016). Ego depletion resembles how a muscle gets tired after exertion. It turns out that muscles can still exert maximum power when somewhat tired—the initial muscular fatigue is a signal to conserve energy, not a signal that the muscle is too worn out to function (though it can reach that point of exhaustion with continued strain). Just as distance runners pace themselves, people seem to respond to initial self-control exertion by curtailing other self-control exertions, and all the more so if they sense impending further demands.

With muscles, exercise produces fatigue in the short run, but regular exercise makes the muscle stronger. Might that work for self-control also? Multiple studies have had people perform various self-control exercises for a period of time (ranging from 2 weeks to 4 months; Baumeister, Gailliot, deWall, & Oaten, 2006). Recent meta-analyses have confirmed that these are often successful at boosting self-control, as measured by lab tasks that are carefully chosen to be quite different from the practice exercises (Friese, Frankenbach, Job, & Loschelder, 2017). It is always difficult to know how many failed studies exist. With regard to exercise improving self-control—akin to the Victorian notion of "building character"—success obviously depends on the research subjects actually doing the exercises, which is hard to verify. A further implication is that maybe it takes self-control to build self-control. People with low self-control might simply neglect to do the exercises and therefore fail to show any improvement.

Effects of Ego Depletion

Gradually, the evidence for ego depletion spread into multiple, diverse contexts. Depleted people were shown to eat more junk food, drink more alcohol, spend more money (especially on impulse purchases), have fewer sexual inhibitions, and respond more aggressively toward others who provoked them. They performed worse on intelligence tests (for reviews, see Baumeister & Tierney, 2011; Baumeister & Vohs, 2016).

The IQ test finding had some important qualifications (Schmeichel et al., 2003). Cognitive scientists sort mental processes into automatic and controlled ones. The automatic ones remained intact, indeed perfectly fine, among depleted people. They could still memorize and remember things. Many IQ tests include a vocabulary test, and depletion did not affect performance on those. But logical reasoning was impaired, often quite substantially. Thus, the higher forms of reasoning were the ones that suffered. Ego depletion and self-regulation are about the mind exerting effort for control—but the automatic mind works just fine. Indeed, excellent studies by Wilhelm Hofmann and colleagues (2007) showed that people might have different conscious and unconscious attitudes, and depletion enabled the unconscious attitudes to take over and guide action. Thus, people have sets of automatic responses that are set in motion when the right cue is encountered. Conscious self-control can override those responses, and indeed that is one of its prominent functions. But during ego depletion, the person ceases to exert conscious control as much as usual.

Habits

Habits are an important set of automatic response patterns. Habits take over all the more when one is depleted (Neal et al., 2013). Indeed, the fact that people so readily form habits is one sign that conscious control is costly. The mind is designed to conserve energy, and forming habits is an effective way to do this.

Habits turned out to be crucially relevant to trait self-control. Ego depletion focuses on capacity for self-control as a fluctuating state, but it seems rather obvious that some people are generally better than others at self-control. A questionnaire measure proved useful at telling those people apart (Tangney et al., 2004). After it had been in use for some years, a Dutch team compiled all the results they could (de Ridder et al., 2012). People who scored high on self-control generally did better than other people on a variety of measures, but some effects were larger than others. The strongest were on work and school performance; people scoring high on self-control did much better than others in those areas, whereas they were only slightly better at dieting and weight control.

The Dutch researchers tried coding all the different behaviors from the different studies as to whether they were automatic or controlled. The theoretical prediction was that self-control works on controlled behaviors, whereas automatic ones run on their own, without control. To their consternation, the results came out statistically significant in the opposite direction. People with high trait self-control mainly excelled on automatic behaviors, not the controlled ones. How could this be? The researchers went back to examine closely just what sorts of behaviors had been coded as automatic. Here, it emerged that these were mainly habits.

The link between self-control and habits changed our thinking about self-control. Many of us had assumed that people with good self-control somehow just had more willpower than other people. But apparently they do not—rather, they simply use it more effectively. In particular, they use their self-control to break bad habits and form good ones. People who perform well in work and school use their self-control to develop good work habits (unlike the procrastinators, who tend to score low on self-control). That way, they get things done without needing herculean last-minute struggles.

The notion that people with high self-control have more willpower received a blow from some other evidence. Many ego depletion experiments included a measure of trait self-control, to see who would be more affected by depletion. Would it be people with high self-control, as they had farther to fall? Or would it be those with low self-control because they were more prone to have self-control problems? Both theories were plausible and either would have been interesting, but most studies found no difference (see especially Vohs et al., 2021). People were equally affected by depletion, regardless of their level of trait self-control.

Yet in a recent study, we measured feeling depleted as people went about their daily lives, outside the laboratory. On this, people with low trait self-control reported feeling depleted much more frequently (Baumeister, Wright, & Carreon, 2019). Why might the laboratory findings be so different from everyday life?

Again, habits and planning likely account for the difference. In the laboratory, everyone performs the same task, and so everyone uses about the same amount of willpower—and everyone gets about the same amount of ego depletion. But in everyday life, people with high self-control are better organized, with better work habits and more planning. They also have fewer interpersonal clashes with friends, lovers, and coworkers, which turned out to be a big predictor of feeling depleted. So they felt less depleted outside the lab because their lives could run more smoothly, having fewer stresses and problems and crises to drain their willpower.

Willpower is a folk term and a metaphor. Does it correspond to anything specific in terms of brain activity or body processes? The 1990s were dubbed "The Decade of the Brain," and it became fashionable to look for the brain bases of many patterns and responses. Our foray into this realm started quite by accident.

One day Matt Gailliot, then a talented graduate student, came to me with a hypothesis: If resisting temptation makes you weaker, does indulging temptation make you stronger? I encouraged him to go ahead. He set up an experiment in which people were first depleted (or not, in the control condition), then later had their self-control performance measured, like many other studies. What set this one apart was that in between the two self-control tasks, some research subjects got to eat an ice cream milkshake. Ice cream is of course a delicious but fattening treat, and so eating it in the midst of a lab study constituted a nice self-indulgence, a yielding to temptation. There were two control conditions. In the first, people simply had to sit for a few minutes reading some boring, out-of-date technical magazines. The other consumed a nondelicious milkshake, made with unsweetened cream, essentially a yucky glob of tedious dairy product. The latter condition was included just to see whether there was something special about consuming food.

The experiment failed, but in an interesting way. The people who consumed ice cream after being depleted did actually perform well on the second test, so the ice cream did succeed in wiping out the ego depletion effect. Unfortunately, so did the nondelicious shake, even though people disliked it. The theory that indulging in one's impulses would lead to later improvements in self-control was not supported because people did not like the nontasty shake. But we reflected, if it was not the pleasure, might it be the calories? Both conditions that involved consuming food showed improvements in self-control.

Glucose Levels

Gailliot spent some weeks in the library and learned a great deal about glucose. Glucose is a chemical in the bloodstream, and it functions to carry energy throughout the body, to the muscles, brain, and other organs. Glucose is not just sugar but rather the energy extracted from any sort of food. Neurotransmitters, which enable the brain to function, are made from glucose, so it is fair to call it "brain fuel."

Our lab began to explore links between glucose and self-control. Several years' worth of experiments pointed to three conclusions, two of which have stood the test of time better than the third (Gailliot et al., 2007). First, after exerting effort on laboratory tests of self-control, people's blood glucose showed a drop. These initial findings seem to have been benefited by a control condition that was off from the usual baseline (which will sometimes happen). In subsequent work, we occasionally found this effect but often did not. Exerting self-control may consume glucose, but the process is much more complicated than we assumed, and so I do not have confidence in this first conclusion. But the other two are solid.

The second conclusion was that when blood glucose is low, self-control is poor. Our evidence on this was fairly consistent. It also emerged that there was already plenty of evidence for this, based on research by nutritionists (for a review, see Gailliot & Baumeister, 2007). They had not had a grand theory about how glucose affects self-control, but they had conducted many studies linking the effects of food deprivation or glucose deficiencies to various behavior patterns—most of them suggesting a loss of self-control. For example, in nicely controlled studies (e.g., Murphy et al., 1998; Wesnes et al., 2003), elementary school children would all skip breakfast before school, and by random assignment, some would be given something to eat at school while the others would not (and therefore would lack glucose). The children who had gotten a morning dose of glucose learned better and behaved better in the classroom. Around midmorning, everyone got a snack, and the differences disappeared. In other work, people who have chronic problems with glucose, such as diabetics, exhibit various kinds of problems with self-control.

The third key finding was that the ego depletion effect could be eliminated by giving people glucose. This is in a sense what we had done by accident in the ice cream study. Dianne Tice developed a better way to do this, which was to give people a glass of lemonade sweetened with either diet sweetener (which has no glucose) or sugar (lots of glucose) (Gailliot et al., 2007). People liked the lemonade about the same in either case, and the drinks could be prepared in advance so that neither the experimenter nor the research subject knew whether the drink had sugar or Splenda. We have used this procedure in many studies, and very reliably the depletion effect is eliminated among people who get the sugar drink, while those who get the diet lemonade show the usual depletion effect.

The idea that willpower can be translated as glucose is probably too simple. But given the weight of evidence, I am persuaded that glucose is an important part of the self-control process. Again, the matter is not as simple as the brain running out of fuel. In particular, a modern well-fed citizen of Western civilization has plenty of stored glucose (indeed obesity is far more common than malnutrition or starvation in the United States). Two British researchers published an important critique saying that self-control and ego depletion should be understood as changing allocation of glucose rather than running out of glucose (Beedie & Lane, 2012). I think they are mostly right. Still, selective allocation mainly happens when a precious and scarce resource is at stake. If you have lived in different parts of the world, you probably notice that water is sometimes freely available and casually consumed—but elsewhere is carefully measured and rationed. The rationing mainly occurs in deserts and other scarce-water places, whereas the casual and wasteful practices are found in places where water is abundant. If glucose is allocated selectively, that suggests it is a precious and depletable resource.

Modern life in Western civilization does not resemble the conditions under which the human psyche evolved. The ego depletion pattern may have evolved to help our prehistoric ancestors conserve vital energy in a way that is not necessary today. Those ancestors lived in a world in which food was uncertain, and it was always possible that one might not get to eat again for a few days. Protein, in particular, might often be absent from tomorrow's meager offerings. So conserving energy would be beneficial.

Another important difference between modern life and life before the mid-20th-century life involves medicine, including antibiotics. The immune system uses a great deal of glucose when it springs into action, though at other times it doesn't need much. For our ancestors, an infected cut on the foot could be lethal unless the immune system could fight it off because they had no recourse to modern medicine.

Ego depletion thus reflects an evolutionary adaptation—to conserve energy in the form of glucose, whenever possible, including by not exerting self-control. It continues to shape how the mind works. Nowadays, we could afford to expend more glucose on self-control, especially given how much better our lives run when self-control is operating effectively. But the brain evolved to husband its resources.

Trying to link self-control performance to physiology and glucose means trying to work on the classic mind–body problem that has dogged thinkers for centuries. We should not expect a quick, easy, or clear answer. The muscle analogy is helpful here because it seems that physical muscles also have some of these complexities (see Evans et al., 2016). Amid prolonged exertion, muscles do reach a point at which they can no longer function effectively. But they start to feel tired long before then. *The mind feels the muscle to be tired before the muscle is really unable to function.*

My best guess as to how these processes work is this. The brain does not have any way of knowing how much glucose the body has in storage; therefore, it tracks recent use. When it has been consuming extra glucose in some fashion, such as by exerting self-control, it is designed to notice this and cut back on further consumption. Given that glucose is used for so many different bodily functions, many of which are important for survival, it discourages excessive consumption in any one area. When physical muscular exertion is intense, the brain emits signals of tiredness so as to stop using those muscles. When it is investing resources in self-control, it likewise seeks to cut back after a while. This is a precaution based on circumstances of early evolution, and it is probably not all that helpful today but it takes a long time for physical evolution to adapt to new circumstances. Hence, ego depletion: The brain evolved to conserve energy after expending some.

Glucose enabled us to offer a new perspective on premenstrual syndrome (PMS) (Gailliot et al., 2010). During the luteal phase of the female cycle, the body's reproductive activities require more glucose than at other times. Women do tend to eat more during this phase—but not enough more to make up the difference. Hence, their bodies put them into a state akin to ego depletion, as in a shortage of glucose. PMS has the stereotype of women developing evil, wicked impulses at a certain time of the month, but the evidence does not support this. They do not seem to develop new impulses. Rather, the impulses that they normally have are not restrained as effectively during this phase because of the monthly glucose shortage.

Controversies

In the last couple of years, social psychologists have declared their field in crisis, and some outspoken critics have proposed that its entire knowledge base is riddled with fake findings and mistakes. I do not share their pessimism. Indeed, I would not be writing this book, which builds on the diligent work of hundreds of researchers, if I thought that their work was full of worthless nonsense. Nevertheless, let us acknowledge their viewpoints. Ego depletion has been a highly successful theory, with many diverse findings in many laboratories, and its very success makes it an appealing target for those wishing to claim the research literature is mostly garbage. If they could discredit ego depletion, they would have taken a substantial step toward discrediting the entire field.

The ego depletion theory has been subjected to two quite different kinds of attacks. One is the assertion that there is no such effect. This has been encouraged because some researchers have failed to find ego depletion effects. The other is to provide alternative theoretical accounts for its findings, dispensing with the notion of a limited energy resource.

It is important to realize that these two attacks contradict each other. No alternative theory can be true if there is no phenomenon—there cannot be a correct explanation of a nonexistent effect. Hence, one of the two challenges has to be completely wrong. Possibly both are wrong, but definitely at least one of them is.

My view is that it is wrong to assert there is no effect. I concede that ego depletion, as studied in laboratory experiments, does not always work, but it has worked hundreds of times, in multiple different laboratories operated by different researchers all over the world. If despite several hundred successful demonstrations of ego depletion, it is not really there, then I do not see how we can trust anything in social psychology or related fields.

Indeed, in a recent survey of the research literature on replications, I was pleasantly surprised to find that ego depletion has a fair claim to be the single best replicated finding in all of social psychology (Baumeister, Bushman, & Tice, 2021). There are well over 600 published findings supporting ego depletion and effectively none in the opposite direction. Pre-registered studies have supported it (Garrison, Finley, & Schmeichel, 2019). There are ample real-world findings, such as showing that health care workers neglect to wash their hands as they become depleted and parole judges make harsher-safer decisions as they become depleted (for a review, see Baumeister & Vohs, 2016; for a recent example, see Trinh, Hoover, & Sonnenberg, 2021). Last, there is at least one multisite replication providing an unqualified success (Dang et al., 2021) and two others providing mixed support. No other finding in social psychology can match that record.

The broader point is that psychology does not have laws, like gravity. It shows that causes produce effects, but none of those cause–effect pairings is universal. All psychology can show is that some patterns happen sometimes. Ego depletion is clearly one of these. Some people conduct experiments that fail to show it, but hundreds of studies have succeeded. The fact that it occurs sometimes, under some circumstances, is close to the best that psychology can expect for just about any psychological principle. My view is that social psychology's body of evidence is mostly sound, though of course things continue to change and evolve as more data become available. Effects that have been found only rarely may be questioned, but effects like ego depletion, with hundreds of successful demonstrations, clearly refer to something that is really happening.

The other form of challenge questions whether we have gotten the theory right. This is a normal part of science, and it is to be expected that as more studies are conducted and more findings shared, the early forms of any theory are likely to be supplanted by new, different, and usually more complex theories.

With a phenomenon as complex as ego depletion, the room for alternative theories can be large or small. A researcher might run an experiment that shows ego depletion in one condition and not in another, so he concludes that ego depletion is really all about whatever the difference between the two conditions was. The alternative theories typically focus on a small subset of the evidence, which they can explain very well. However, if they want to explain the full body of research findings, then formulating a new theory becomes difficult. Having reviewed these alternative theories, I concluded that some of them offer valuable insights that can improve the basic strength model, but none of them can really get rid of the core idea of limited resources and energy consumption.

The most compelling alternative account dispenses with limited energy and seeks to explain depletion in terms of motivation and attention (Inzlicht & Schmeichel, 2012). In this view, people perform the first self-control task, find it strenuous or mildly unpleasant, and so lose interest in pushing themselves to perform well on the second task. This alternative theory's core assumption, that an ego depletion manipulation would make people lose motivation to perform well on the second task, is not really a problem for the strength model because it is plausible that in order to conserve one's remaining energy, one would disengage from further demanding tasks. But abundant evidence now indicates that it is wrong. When this theory was published and gained acclaim, I asked my collaborators to start collecting data on how motivated people were to do well on the second task, and we found no change. Other researchers in other laboratories did and found the same. Lab depletion manipulations do not reduce people's motivation to perform well on the second task.

Hence, my take on the controversies is that they are simply a matter of business as usual, with a bit of extra hype and drama given the current atmosphere of an entire field in crisis. Is the version I have sketched here the all-time, final truth? Probably not. But it's largely on target, and future work will not demolish all this so much as improve on it. For now, this is the best educated guess as to how self-control works.

WILLPOWER, DECISION MAKING, AND PLANNING

If the limited willpower resource were only relevant to self-control, that would already be an important aspect of the self, given the importance of self-regulation to so many important aspects of how the self functions. But it is even more important than that. Indeed, ego depletion is an important key to the part of the self that does things.

The first major step was finding that ego depletion applied to making choices and decisions, apart from self-control (Vohs et al., 2008). We found that after making a series of choices, self-control was impaired. Conversely, when ego depletion was instilled by requiring people to exert self-control, their decision processes changed, and not for the better. This resulted in the new concept of *decision fatigue*. The next chapter takes a closer look at this.

If willpower is used for both making choices and self-regulating, it may well be involved in other processes that invoke the executive self. Often there is a difference between active and passive responding. Taking an active stance requires the self to exert self-control and seems to consume willpower. When people are depleted, they become passive. One of our (unpublished) studies involved having research subjects working alone on a computer that then abruptly stopped working, and we measured how long they just sat there before getting up to report the problem. Depleted people sat there twice as long as others. Initiative is apparently low during the depleted state.

Another study was needed to satisfy reviewers who complained, quite reasonably, that we could not assert passivity as a general effect of depletion, given that depleted people often actively indulged their impulses. We argued that depletion reduces top-down control, in which the conscious mind decides the right response, as opposed to letting automatic processes run the show. To satisfy the journal editors, we ran another study, borrowing a procedure from pioneering social psychologist Stanley Schachter. People were given questionnaires to fill out and, as a seeming gesture of friendly hospitality, they were offered some peanuts to eat. Did depleted people eat more, or less? It depended on whether the nuts were still in the shells. When the shells were gone and eating just meant grabbing a handful of nuts and tossing them into one's mouth, depleted people ate more than the nondepleted. But when the nuts were still in their shells so that eating them required a bit of active work—then depleted people ate significantly less than others (Vonasch et al., 2017).

One more important kind of executive activity is planning. Planning consumes willpower. When people are depleted, they avoid planning (Sjåstad & Baumeister, 2018). Having clear, simple plans enables them to perform well despite being depleted (Webb & Sheeran, 2003) because these plans enable the unconscious to do what is needed, without requiring the executive to expend more resources.

MISREGULATION

Thus far I have emphasized problems of self-regulation taking the form of underregulation, in the sense that the person fails to exert the requisite effort to live up to goals, ideals, and other standards. Although most failures of self-control probably fall into this category, there is another entire type. People sometimes bring themselves to grief, not because of failing to self-regulate, but by self-regulating based on false assumptions or in unsuitable ways.

Choking under pressure is misregulation because the person tries to impose conscious control on a skilled process that runs best automatically (Baumeister, 1984). Likewise, fruitless persistence, or throwing good money after bad, is also an exertion of self-control that executes just fine but produces a bad result because it was based on the false belief that such investment would bring success.

A particularly important form of misregulation involves giving priority to feeling better, at the expense of long-term goals and personal standards. Many modern uses of self-control involve stifling impulses and denying oneself pleasure, such as abstaining from food, sex, drugs, cigarettes, and alcohol. Often people recognize the problems these indulgences cause them and resolve to abstain but frequently they relapse and indulge again. Crucially, these self-regulation failures occur during times of stress and other demands. There are multiple possible reasons for failures and relapses to occur at these times, including ego depletion. After all, stressful times make extra demands on one's limited willpower, and so as the person devotes more resources to coping with the stress, there is less available for maintaining abstinence. One joke that ran through the comedy film *Airplane* was that as the stress got worse, the air traffic controller started saying, "Looks like I picked the wrong week to quit smoking," and then drinking, amphetamines, sniffing glue, and so on. The joke was based partly on audiences recognizing that it is more difficult to sustain abstinence at such times. Better to quit smoking when stress is low and you can focus your willpower on the project of resisting the urge to smoke.

Still, there are other ways that stress contributes to indulgence and relapse. Misregulation is relevant here. Stress makes you feel bad. Drinking alcohol, smoking tobacco (or indeed other drugs), and eating tasty albeit unhealthy foods make you feel good. Feeling bad can therefore make the person reach for the doughnut, the cigarette, the bottle.

The expression "If it feels good, do it!" was popular for a while around the turn of the century. A research article played on this in its subtitle, "If you feel bad, do it!" (Tice et al., 2001). Its studies manipulated some people into bad moods and showed that they abandoned self-regulation in favor of indulging in feel-good ways, such as eating unhealthy food, procrastinating on work while indulging in fun time-wasters, and taking immediate gratification rather than seeking better but delayed rewards. The procedures ruled out ego depletion and other explanations with a procedure that convinced some participants that their moods would not change regardless of what they did. *These people did not indulge, despite bad moods.* In other words, feeling bad makes people eat more cookies and junk food, but only if they expect that eating junk food will cure the bad feelings.

Thus, what looks like self-regulation failure, or what seems on the surface like underregulation, can in fact be misregulation. Self-regulation is often a matter of denying oneself pleasure here and now for the sake of better outcomes in the long run. Intense negative emotion shifts the priority to feeling better right now, even at the expense of the long run.

SELF-REGULATION AND THE UNITY PROJECT

Self-control is a vital part of how the self manages itself. The self is a process of constructing unity out of different pieces. Sure enough, self-regulation has important work to do as part of the unity project.

The self-control mechanism, operated by the brain, has to understand the present and mentally represent (i.e., think of) the various future outcomes. It has to link the future outcomes to present actions, select the best future outcome, and execute the present actions aimed at that outcome. Sometimes this has to be done in the teeth of some strong desire to do something else right now, eat that pie, gulp that beer.

To succeed, the self needs at least two types of processes. There is first a thinking part, the "supervisory loop" (to use Carver and Scheier's term). The mind must mentally project into the future, simulate the various possible outcomes associated with various actions possible in the present, compare these different outcomes to decide what is best—and then bring all that back into the present to act in the way that will bring the best results. But there's another part. The thinking part hands off to the executing part, the willpower part. (To be sure, some willpower was already expended in deciding and planning.) Willpower is what has to push this forward, despite opposition. Deciding that you'd better get started writing that report today in order to stay on schedule is an impressive mental feat, but it does not feel all that difficult. What makes it feel difficult is the temptation to join your friends at the beach or bar, when they are beckoning, and you have to resist that temptation in order to get to work.

Farming is an important example. Only humans are farmers, give or take a couple of borderline cases. That's because only the humans can really think of the present in relation to the distant future and act on that basis. What the farmer does at first is not natural or satisfying in any way: taking seeds or even edible food and burying it in the ground, leaving it, never to dig it up. Proper farming requires plenty of additional steps, such as weeding and watering. But then, months later, there is a harvest of food, and some of that can be stored to eat during the winter and spring. Farmers must project into the future, choose the best outcome, link that to what has to be done now (e.g., planting), and then execute those behaviors now despite feeling like there are many other things one would rather be doing, including nothing.

Indeed, one of the remarkable powers of the human mind is its ability to project into the future (prospection). Even so, it seems to me that the value and benefits of prospection depend on self-control. Otherwise, of what use is it to think out what present actions will bring the best future outcomes? This is reminiscent of Searle's (2001) argument about rational thought in general. Rational thought is likewise seen as one of the distinctive hallmarks and superior powers of the human mind. Rational thought enables you to use logic to decide what is the best thing to do in a given situation. But what good is that without at least enough free will to perform those actions? A rational thinker without sufficient free will would essentially be thinking, "I really ought to do X" but then would go ahead and do Y instead. He or she would often end up knowing "It would have been better if I had acted otherwise, but I didn't." Over and over.

Planning is not the same as self-control, but they both use the same willpower energy resource. Planning takes disciplined mental effort, so it is depleting. When people are depleted, they don't want to plan (Sjåstad & Baumeister, 2018). Planning is a kind of mental activity related to self-control, using the same resource, and also crucially helping to link the present with the future, thereby to manage the extended-time self.

Human self-control thus operates mostly for the extended-time self, helping to connect the present to the future. Often the right-now self is the enemy of self-control. It has strong desires (or maybe just feels lazy). These must be overcome in order to pursue the less satisfying course of action that will bring the best results in the long run, like having saved money, or not having an arrest record.

Indeed, self-control helps forge the unity of self across time. Instead of doing what it feels like at every moment, the human self connects the present to past and future, and chooses its actions accordingly. That's a main reason that human self-control is so much more advanced than ape self-control, and also why it is used much more frequently. Self-control pays off much better for an extended-time self than a mere right-now self.

KEY POINTS

- Three basic features of self-regulation are standards, monitoring, and capacity for change.
- Self-awareness is central to self-regulation.
- All types of self-control draw on the same limited reservoir of energy.
- After exerting self-control, there is less energy for further self-control. This is called "ego depletion."
- Ego depletion may be a function of the body conserving energy.
- Habits are automatic patterns that save energy or that take over when one is energy depleted.
- When blood glucose is low, self-control is poor. Ego depletion can be reversed by giving people glucose.
- Willpower resources can also be depleted by decision making, taking an active versus passive stance, and planning.

CHAPTER 19

Decision Making, Autonomy, and Free Will

Self-regulation is one key to understanding the human self. Making choices is a related key. Choosing is broader than self-regulation and also more fundamental. Simple animals with simple brains make simple choices, such as whether to move right or left, or whether to fight or flee. With human society and our more complex and powerful brains, incredibly complex choices can be made. If you've worked for a large organization recently, you may have faced bewildering sets of choices about health care plans and retirement investment options. Likewise, some young students arrive at university already knowing what their life's work will be, but for others, the assortment of options for a major field of study is dauntingly large and diverse.

Beyond psychology, there is a long intellectual tradition of asserting that choices define and thereby create the self. Existentialist philosophy may have been one of the foremost and radical versions of this view, though there are others. But at best that is only part of the story: The self *makes* choices, as much as (if not more than) choices make the self. One purpose of the self is to facilitate choices and guide them toward optimal outcomes for the animal body. A defective self will make choices that will bring problems on itself.

I do not embrace the view that the purpose of choice is to create the self. At most, some choices are seen as making a statement as to what sort of self the person is. For example, when Barack Obama ran against Hillary Clinton for the Democratic presidential nomination in 2008, the British magazine *The Economist* observed that many White middle-class voters felt more pressure to prove they were not racist (by voting for Obama) than to prove they were not sexist (by voting for Clinton). If that analysis is correct, then those particular choices were made more to express and establish something about the self than to select the best leader. In other spheres, people may choose their automobiles, hairstyles, outerwear, and vacation options based on identity claims rather than functional or hedonic payoff.

Decision making is one of the main jobs of the self. Decision making is not uniquely human, but humans decide differently from how other animals choose.

WHAT IS CHOICE, EXACTLY?

Choosing seems simple enough: pick A or B. But that is deceptive. Choice can be understood in multiple ways. Our goal is to understand the self's inner processes of choosing, and not all choices follow the same process. Choice may exist as an aspect of the objective situation, in the sense that it offers multiple options. Still, the person may not realize or appreciate all these options—while still being able to function effectively and get what he or she wants. When the coffee shop chain Starbucks advertised that it offered 19,000 beverage options, it was not intending to condemn every customer to make 19,000 decisions as a prerequisite for thirst-quenching. Most customers probably just order the same thing they had last time, without pondering the other 18,999 possibilities.

Let's recognize two widely different meanings of choice. One is an inner mental process of selecting among options. The other meaning is choice as an aspect of the situation, outside the person. The options were there, available, regardless of whether they were considered or even noticed, like those thousands of irrelevant beverage options.

It's a mistake to assume that the inner process of choosing is always basically the same, even if the person is cognizant of the various options. You may ponder and compare the various options at length, mentally simulating each possible course of action and carefully evaluating its potential consequences. Then again, you might make a quick, impulsive decision, or simply follow habit.

To put it simplistically, there are at least two main ways to choose. You can act on the first impulse, or you can think it through carefully and select the rationally best option. Both are possible for human beings. What decides whether a person follows impulse or makes a thoughtful, rational decision about what will be best in the long run? One function of the human self is to increase the odds of the latter.

Remember that humans are animals, underneath everything else. So the capacity for thinking it through and choosing in enlightened fashion is something evolution stuck on top of the older, simpler, animal-style mechanism for deciding. The first and dominant impulse is to do what you want most right now, which is usually what promises to yield immediate good feelings. Rational calculations can recommend an alternative action, but the self has to have a system to turn off the momentum of immediate desire, so as to follow the rational path.

CHOICE AND BEHAVIOR

Choice can be appreciated in the context of behavior, starting with simple animals. How does behavior happen? Simple animals learn how to react to a given situation by conditioning processes. In psychology's favored terms, they learn to associate a specific *response* as an effective way to deal with a particular *stimulus*. The stimulus is something out there in the environment, like a dangerous snake, or a cheeseburger, or a sexually attractive potential mate. The responses are actions. The links are stored in the brain: The brain is where stimulus meets response, and you can judge the quality of the brain's design based on how well it matches the stimulus with the right response. When you see a predator, run and hide; when you see good food, eat it. When choices are few and simple, the system does not require much. The job of the simple animal self is to coordinate the body parts so that they work together, so as to eat rather than be eaten.

Most behavior may not involve any choice, in terms of inner process. Does the squirrel really make a choice to run and hide? The stimulus (e.g., a big dog charging) sets off the response. Human deep thinkers can look down from on high and say, well, the animal could have acted differently, so it was sort of like a choice. But the animal did not ponder options. It just took off running when the dog approached.

When there is one clear response to the stimulus, no process of choosing is needed. In contrast, one does have to choose when there are multiple possible responses. The lab rat in the T-shaped maze gets to the choice point and can go either right or left. Compromises aren't possible, such as having two paws go left and the other two go right. Both responses are within the animal's power and have been used in the past, so some process must select one over the other.

The classic philosophical dilemma of Buridan's ass is instructive. The ass (donkey) is equally hungry and thirsty, and it stands between a pile of food and a bucket of water, equally distant. It is unable to decide whether to go right or left, and so it dies of hunger and thirst. In a variation, sometimes there are two buckets of food, equally full and equally distant, and the donkey starves, unable to find a reason to pick one over the other.

One crucial point, of course, is that *this doesn't ever really happen*. Out in the natural world, animals do not starve to death surrounded by food because they are unable to decide what to eat first. The arbitrary choice does get made. The animal may not even really do anything that qualifies as choice. It notices one stimulus, and if the response is activated, it acts on that unless another stimulus happens to intrude and generate an even stronger impulse to do something else. This is not full-blown choosing.

WHY CHOOSING IS DIFFICULT

Two main kinds of problems increase the difficulty of choosing and therefore require a big upgrade in inner mental processes. One is conflicting desires, or what researchers call "motivational conflict." A woman has two offers of marriage and can only accept one of them. She loves both men, but they are different, and choosing one means foregoing the fine qualities and advantages of the other. Even the simple choice of Buridan's ass, between eating and drinking, means that either hunger or thirst will continue for a bit longer while the other desire is quenched.

Uncertainty is the second kind of problem. Often one does not know what is best. The animal in the lab maze does not know whether the food is waiting to the right or the left. The woman does not know which of her suitors will grow kinder or more violent over the years, which one will earn a higher salary, which one will get fat and slovenly, which one will be tempted to run off and abandon her. She might make educated guesses, but she could be wrong. Thus, the inner processes of the self must find a way to decide without sufficient knowledge to make the best decision.

Advanced choosing mechanisms, as in the human self, must cope with these two problems.

SIMPLE CHOICES RIGHT NOW

Humans believe themselves to have something called "free will," and they further believe other animals generally do not have it. Free will is essentially the ability to do different things in the same situation. That requires the mental capacity to understand that different outcomes are possible.

A remarkable experiment by Redshaw and Suddendorf (2016) indicates that even the smartest animals cannot really grasp multiple possibilities. Their apparatus was a tube, into which the experimenter would drop a treat at the top. The treat would come out at the bottom, either caught by the research subject or dropping down into a hole and gone forever. Both human children and various other great ape adults easily learned to put the hand under the opening and catch the treat. Then, however, the experimenters changed the tube so that it had two openings at the bottom, thus shaped like an upside-down Y. The treat might come out of either opening. One approach is to guess left or right and thereby get the treat half the time.

But if one understands that both outcomes are possible, one can use both hands to cover both openings—enabling one to get the treat every time.

Most human children quickly figured out to use both hands. The youngest of them (2 years old) never quite got this, but from age 3 onward, nearly all of them quickly got it right and got the treat every time. In contrast, the adult apes never figured it out. Remarkably, a couple of apes accidentally happened to put out both hands and succeeded in catching the treat once—but then they went back to guessing with one hand, *not realizing that using both hands like they had just done would work every time.* These findings suggest that even our most intelligent animal relatives are still not smart enough to comprehend multiple different outcomes being possible. That means they do not really make choices, in the fullest sense, as humans do.

COMPLEX CHOICES BY THE ONGOING SELF

Now move from the simple animal, right-now self to the human self, which knows that it extends into past and future. The first thing to appreciate is that the choosing process that worked for the right-now self won't work for the self across time. The wisdom of the sages never boils down to "If it feels good, do it." Wisdom means doing what's best in the long run rather than in the heat of the moment.

In the history of psychology, this difference between how animals choose and how humans choose was a reason for the ultimate failure of behaviorism: All that knowledge that the researchers carefully assembled about animal choosing did not offer a valid basis for understanding human choosing. The ongoing self requires much more extensive inner processes than the right-now self, in order to make its choices. It must be able to envision future outcomes and circumstances, including sequences of events. ("If I say this, she'll say that, to which I can reply such-and-such, but she'll come back with something else, and then . . . ") Crucially, the present can be seen directly as it actually is, but the future branches off into multiple possibilities, so the extended-time human self must grasp and accept the reality of multiple possibilities.

Resolving motivational conflict is much more difficult for the ongoing self than the right-now self. The self has to be able to imagine a future version of itself, appreciate its perspectives, and sometimes use those preferences to override what it strongly wants right now. Essentially, it's "Don't just choose what will make you happiest right now—choose what you'll be glad to have chosen, next week, or even next year." That requires implementing the choice and hence blocking the standard tendency to do what you most strongly want to do. This will take some force. The stronger the impulse to eat another donut, yell at your boss, go to bed with the wrong person, then the stronger the self has to be to stifle that impulse and do the wise thing.

Human societies sometimes find ways to bolster the ability of individuals to resist the right-now impulses, to produce best results in the long run. A memorable example was provided in anthropologist Marvin Harris's (1974) explanation of why cows are sacred in some Indian religions. Poor farming families had one cow or ox, and they needed it to till the soil. During the hungry winter months, they might be tempted to kill and eat the cow—but then they would be unable to farm any more, and so all would starve. If everyone did this, the society would die out. How can you stop a man from killing the family cow to save his beloved children from starving? The power of religion helped him to make that hard choice to spare the sacred cow. And even if some children did starve to death, the family as a whole would continue. It's the best thing for society, but the father will be scarred for life by the memory of his little girl dying when he could have saved her by killing and cooking the family cow.

THE FULL CHOOSING PROCESS

I have said that there are degrees of choice. Let's consider the high end: the best, fullest process for choosing how to act. The mind has to be able to understand that there are multiple options that will lead to different outcomes in the long run. The person must be able to mentally simulate these various courses of events, up to and including their different outcomes. Human consciousness is essentially a powerful mechanism for mental simulations. The mind has to be able to think through what actions will lead to what outcomes, preferably in a pretty accurate manner. This occurs in narrative form. People think of themselves as a character in a story, mentally simulating how their possible decisions could lead to a happy or unhappy ending.

The person also has to be able to evaluate these various outcomes and compare them, so as to choose the best one. The happy ending is desired, but that might require doing something unpleasant in the short run.

Last, the person has to be able to execute the chosen option. That may require stifling the strongest impulse in the moment so as to do what will turn out to be wisest. No wonder self-control and decision making are linked.

Thus, we have a series of steps. First, simulate the options and outcomes. Second, evaluate each and compare them. Third, choose the best one. Fourth, perform the actions to produce that best outcome. All of this involves understanding one's own actions as events in stories (causal sequences of meaningful events). Goal pursuit unites a sequence of events, possibly interspersed with other, unrelated events, and leads to a happy or unhappy outcome.

WHAT SELF-KNOWLEDGE IS NEEDED?

Self-knowledge may at best be useful to help the right-now self avoid taking on overly difficult or dangerous tasks that exceed its capabilities. One might speculate that a young animal needs to know its fighting capabilities accurately, so as not to get into a fight that it will lose. But do animals really appraise themselves that way? The animal might just learn to appraise others as dangerous or not, without really having any sort of genuine knowledge about its own capabilities. It may have a few fights and learn what dangerous opponents look like, and what pushovers look like. The animal soon automatically sees other creatures either as ones you chase and kill or the ones who want to chase and kill you. Then it doesn't even have to fight every new rival it encounters. It merely sizes them up and acts accordingly. Stimulus and response, with a bit of internal processing to appraise the stimulus. But not choice.

Some fascinating studies with simple creatures are relevant. These simple creatures almost certainly do not have self-awareness or self-concepts. Researchers arranged for two of them to have an unfair fight: the claws for one were tied with string, thus neutralizing its best weapon. No surprise, the nonhandicapped one won the fight. Then the researcher took the winner and set it down next to another, who wasn't hampered. Time for brutal awakening and comeuppance, right? But no. The ones who had won the rigged fight strutted and blustered, and their new opponents backed off. Having won that first fight made them think they would win a similar one, so they regarded the new (but actually not handicapped) opponent as a pushover, and acted that way toward it. The other one knew the signs, looked at the confident and dominant behavior, and fell for it (e.g., Oyegbile & Marler, 2005; see also Robertson, 2013).

None of this shows that the birds or bugs appraise their own powers relative to others. Rather, they attend to how dangerous others look and to the outcomes of their bouts. They start to act more dominant after a victory (even a rigged one). The adjustments seem natural and adaptive, and so they can occur without self-concepts. The opponents operate on the principle that others who think they can thrash you usually can thrash you, so it's better to yield the field *before* taking a beating, rather than after.

Another key point is that researchers have usually studied self-knowledge as if it were a list of traits, but that's not the kind of self-knowledge one needs in order to make good decisions. To make an accurate forecast of its future circumstances, the self must have genuine knowledge about itself: what it will need and want, what it typically likes and dislikes, also its abilities. All those are useful for informing choices, too, like don't pick a fight with someone who will destroy you, or don't sign up for a course that requires math skills beyond yours. But even such choices require imagining a future in which you suffer because the situational demands exceed your capabilities.

An earlier chapter debated what the important and operative forms of self-knowledge are. The conclusion was that interests and abilities matter more than your own personality traits, as informational input into one's actions. That's what we are seeing again here.

EMOTION AND CHOICE

Psychology's theories about emotion have usually started by assuming that emotion exists to cause behavior. Fear makes you run away, and therefore helps you survive, according to the standard example. But the accumulation of evidence makes this view obsolete. Emotion is at best weakly and indirectly related to actual behavior, by and large (Baumeister, Vohs, deWall, & Zhang, 2007). And even when it does intrude, it makes people do maladaptive things. Emotion's reputation for provoking ill-advised, destructive behavior is well earned. One implication is that emotion probably didn't evolve to cause behavior, if it causes maladaptive behavior. Indeed, if emotion were mainly for the purpose of causing behavior, natural selection probably would have phased emotion out of the human psyche long ago.

What else, then? Emotion lets you evaluate future (possible) events: If such-and-such were to happen, you'd be sorry, or happy, or proud, or regretful. To appreciate this, imagine a mind that could accurately simulate future good and bad outcomes based on various possible actions, including having solid knowledge of self in terms of capabilities—but had no emotion, even the most basic feelings of liking and disliking. Such a mind could spin out many possible courses of action but would lack the ability to choose among them. Indeed, there is some evidence that this is precisely what happens. Damasio (1994) described patients with brain injuries that blocked their emotions. Some could elaborate every implication of every possible course of action. But they could not make up their minds which was best.

My best guess, though the evidence is far from conclusive, is that some aspects of human emotion evolved very much for this purpose: Emotion works with mentally simulating the future and gives thumbs-up or thumbs-down, which can then guide decisions in the present. Of course, emotional feelings are much older in evolution than prospection. But perhaps once humans began to think about the future, the emotion system was converted and modified so it could serve that crucial function.

In other words, maybe the evolved purpose of human emotion is to help the self decide about the future. Emotion is vitally helpful for behavior when it is focused on the future, but it is often unhelpful and counterproductive when dealing with the present.

Sometimes you actually feel sad, and other times you imagine what it would be like to be sad. The latter (imagining sadness) may actually be more important and adaptive for the human mind than the former (actually feeling sad at specific times). That's what human emotion evolved to do: You imagine performing a sequence of actions in response to your situation, and it yields an outcome—but you need emotion to evaluate whether this is a good or a bad outcome, and hence to decide whether you want to pursue this course or not. Imagine how you'd feel, and act accordingly so that you'll feel good, not bad.

Regret and guilt are obvious and important examples. These emotions are often derided as useless self-torture. After all, they involve feeling bad over something in the past, and by definition the past cannot be changed. Fair enough—but beside the point. People who can learn to anticipate correctly which actions will bring future regret or guilt can avoid those actions. The anticipatory guilt and regret thus enabled them to make decisions that are better in the long run. Someone who can do this effectively can minimize ever actually feeling guilty or regretful. *Imagining bad emotions can help prevent genuine bad emotions*—because the imagined emotions help you act so as to prevent the bad things from happening to you.

EGO DEPLETION AND DECISION FATIGUE

Making choices depletes willpower. As already explained, self-control uses a limited supply of energy so that after exertions of self-control, willpower is temporarily diminished. An important extension of that work shows that making decisions produces the same kind of effect. After making a series of decisions, self-control is impaired. Conversely, after people engage in acts of self-control, their decision making changes, typically for the worse. The term *decision fatigue* describes the state of ego depletion that comes from expending willpower in making choices.

Choice depletes willpower in proportion to the inner mental effort. Earlier I said that some choices are merely implicit aspects of the objective situation. The Starbucks customers are not depleted by the 19,000 beverage options if they always order the same drink. Indeed, that may be one of the crucial functions of habits (Neal et al., 2013). Habitual behavior does not require willpower. Habitual behavior is automatic. Crucially, this means the human mind can conserve its energy by forming habits so that it does the right thing automatically. *Habits are a low-effort way of dealing with situations that require choice* (Wood & Neal, 2007). Decision fatigue increases as one exerts more effort to ponder the alternatives. Some of the most depleting decisions are cases in which the person is acutely aware of what he or she is giving up.

Indeed, this research has resonated with decision makers, who sometimes seek to conserve their mental energy for important decisions by minimizing nonessential decisions. President Obama told an interviewer he always wore identical gray or blue suits, and likewise delegated his food choices, so that he did not waste any energy deciding what to eat or what to wear. Mark Zuckerberg, the founder of Facebook, also elected to wear the same-style clothes every day to avoid having to make those decisions in the morning. More broadly, most people have a standard morning routine, in which they do the same things in the same sequence, which probably appeals because it enables them to conserve their willpower for the day's choices and challenges. After all, in principle you could decide each morning whether your breakfast or shower should come first. But that would require expending willpower to decide. Doing them by habitual sequence conserves willpower. Indeed, that may be the functional purpose of habits.

Thus, ego depletion shifts the choosing process toward simpler, lower-effort processes. The human mind has involved magnificent powers of thought, but much of this goes out the window when people are depleted. Here are some of the patterns associated with decision fatigue (e.g., Pocheptsova et al., 2009; for reviews, see Baumeister & Tierney, 2011; Baumeister & Vohs, 2016):

- *Status quo bias.* People prefer to leave things as they are, rather than change. Assuming the status quo is tolerable, it's easiest to stick with it. Research shows depleted people prefer to stick with the status quo.

- *No compromise.* Decision researcher Itamar Simonson (1989) pointed that compromise is a difficult and strenuous way of deciding, though of course it offers many advantages. Compromise requires integrating multiple viewpoints and criteria, and then trading them off to find the optimal point. People with full mental powers appreciate the value of compromise and enjoy its benefits, which are worth the extra mental work. But depleted people avoid that exertion and hence do not compromise as readily. Even if the issue is a compromise between price and quality, the nondepleted decider may carefully study how price and quality rise, looking for the sweet spot where one can get the best increase in quality for the least increase in price. In contrast, the depleted decider thinks, "Just give me the cheapest" (or the best)—effectively just selecting one of the criteria and maximizing it, while ignoring the other.

• *Deciding not to decide.* Depleted decision makers prefer to postpone or avoid decisions if they can. This is one sign that deciding takes energy: when energy is down, people avoid deciding. This one also overlaps with the status quo bias: when depleted, do nothing.

• *Irrational bias.* Often choice points come with abundant information, some of which should be logically irrelevant. The effective decider must sort through and evaluate the relevance of various bits of information, so as to make the decision on the basis of what is most relevant and important. Depleted deciders sometimes fail to do this, and as a result, their decisions may succumb to irrational bias. They get swayed by facts or considerations that logically should have been irrelevant.

• *Impulsive, self-indulgent.* Depleted deciders may adopt a short-term, pleasure-oriented approach, doing what feels most appealing rather than what would be best in the long run. This indeed resembles what animals do, with their right-now selves: act on your strongest felt desire in the current moment.

All of these suggest a shift toward simpler, easier, lower-effort styles of deciding. When the self's executive energy has been depleted, people seek to conserve it. Putting a lot of hard thinking into making the best choice is precisely what they are inclined to avoid. So the depleted self conserves its energy by putting less thought into choosing. But of course that often means making poorer-quality decisions.

CHOICE EXPRESSES THE SELF

Making good choices is one of the self's core jobs. And the more complex the society, the harder it is to make good choices but also the more important it is to make them effectively. The contrary view, that choices create and define the self, misses the point that selves exist to make choices.

As always, however, there is a good point hidden amidst the overstatements. People's choices are seen by others and definitely do build one's reputation. The self must be mindful that what it chooses will be seen, interpreted, and judged by others as an expression of the inner self. Even if choices do not arise from a True Self and do not help the self achieve its true nature—they are a vital part of building that all-important public version of self.

Choices do indicate something about the inner contents of the self. Other people who see the choices you make will infer things about you and judge you. People may even make choices for the purpose of expressing something about themselves (as in the earlier example about voting in the Obama–Clinton primary election). There are plenty of other examples beyond voting, of course. People choose cars, wardrobes, homes, romantic partners, and more, in order to convey to other people the kind of person they want to be. My father was raised Catholic but switched to being Presbyterian when he worked for a company in which top brass were Presbyterian while low-wage workers were Catholic. The switch was not a matter of his revising his theological opinion on the fine points of doctrinal differences. He wanted to show the top brass he was their kind of guy.

The self has an inner drive to express itself, to communicate. This serves the vital reputation-building task. All else being equal, people prefer to talk about themselves rather than many other topics (Tamir & Mitchell, 2012). There is likely an innate push to send messages to others. Choices are a vital way in which that happens.

A startling implication is that if the drive to express yourself is temporarily sated, you may make different choices (Wicklund & Gollwitzer, 1982). This may be the essence of self-affirmation processes, which were covered in the chapter on self-knowledge. Essentially, self-affirmation procedures involve pausing to reflect on what is important to you, such as your values and relationships. Afterward, the self-affirmed person is less defensive, better able to accept criticism and tolerate alternative opinions and viewpoints, less insistent on proving him- or herself right (Sherman & Cohen, 2006). Conversely, hearing that you are not achieving the desired reputation may shift your behavioral choices so as to stake your claim to be who you want to be. In Wicklund and Gollwitzer's (1982) studies, people were led to feel that they were well on their way toward their desired identity—or weren't. In the latter case, they made choices that would help them stake the claim.

Moral Licensing

Moral licensing patterns show similar implications, though experts in this area acknowledge that the results go in both directions (Mullen & Monin, 2016). The basic idea in moral licensing is that if you perform one virtuous action, you become more willing to do something immoral or selfish in another context. In a sense, you have proven your good qualities by the first act, so, at least for the time being, you can relax and do what you feel like, even if it is a bit immoral. However, the contrary pattern is sometimes found, that is, the first moral act encourages greater virtue later, possibly because the person is thinking of self as morally virtuous and that carries over into the next choice. The implication is that people want to be good, and virtuous action can either prime one to keep showing oneself to be virtuous—or can satisfy that desire, freeing the self up for a bit of mischief.

AUTONOMY AND FREE WILL

Autonomy means self-government. Some degree of autonomy is essential to the self, in that it is not simply a part of a larger system, or a puppet whose actions are controlled by external forces. Selves become increasingly autonomous as people grow up.

A compelling case for autonomy is made in self-determination theory, the centerpiece of decades of work by Ed Deci, Richard Ryan, and many other researchers informed and inspired by their ideas (Ryan & Deci, 2017). They propose that autonomy is more than the simple matter of a child becoming an adult who can take care of self, provide for self, and not always have to be told what to do. Instead, they propose that autonomy is an innate need of the human psyche, alongside basic drives to connect with others and to be competent.

I have been skeptical, but they make a convincing case. My skepticism has to do with psychologists postulating innate needs, especially when these do not seem clearly linked to the basic requirements of life, namely survival and reproduction. Why would human beings have an innate drive to dictate their own actions, rather than going along with others?

The other two needs in self-determination theory, social connection and competence, seem well suited to the overarching view of the human psyche as evolved to participate in culture. The need to belong is well established and motivates people to affiliate with others, develop working relationships, cooperate, and more. And the drive to be competent fits well with the requirements of working in groups to produce more resources. But how do groups benefit from autonomous selves? Indeed, some groups, such as ant colonies, seem highly effective and powerful without autonomy.

Then again, human societies are very different from ant colonies. Ants seem to have a kind of robot-self, following simple built-in rules. It is plausible, though hardly proven, that autonomous selves are needed to create the kinds of dynamic societies humans have. If we evolved to have this sort of society, the human self may well have developed a drive, perhaps even a need, for autonomy. Not so as to totally do its own thing, independent from everyone and everything else, but so as to participate effectively in this kind of society.

In fact, maybe human societies do function best with autonomous individual members. Building a shared body of knowledge works best if the various information agents think for themselves, finding new information and questioning preliminary conclusions. An economic marketplace may work best with autonomous agents making their own decisions and pursuing individual self-interest. It is possible that the desire and capacity for autonomy evolved among humans so as to make these social systems viable.

Regardless, self-determination theory researchers have often found that people flourish when they can act on their own internal values and impulses. Conversely, people suffer and stagnate when they have to do someone else's bidding, when their own wishes are thwarted or subjugated to external forces. On various measures of well-being, mental health, and happiness, people do better when their need for autonomy is being satisfied. In fact, some of their work suggests autonomy is particularly important. Environments that support autonomy, such as by making people feel that they enjoy some control and can make their own decisions, contribute not only to satisfying the wish for autonomy but also desires for social connection and competence.

AUTONOMY AND THE UNITY PROJECT

Over the years, Ryan and Deci have developed their understanding of what autonomy is, and it is profoundly important. It does not mean that the self operates as an uncaused cause, as some theories about free will would have it. Rather, it means that actions are dictated by the whole self. The person considers the action and endorses it as something he or she does indeed want and choose to do.

Autonomy thus involves the unity project. What is the opposite of autonomy? The person performs an action based on external inputs, perhaps partly consenting but partly resisting and resenting having to do it. The person may respond to the stimulus without engaging the full self, such as by a quick and unthinking response. Or the person may do it reluctantly because some of the self's values and commitments oppose the action. Pondering and "owning" the action mean that the person first thinks about the action, which allows all parts of the self to generate thoughts as to why the action should not be performed, or why one should act otherwise. If none of those prevail, the person has essentially given it a full stamp of approval.

Remember, the self is the project of creating a coherent unity out of a welter of stimulus–response associations. It needs to understand the current situation from multiple perspectives (e.g., health, money, legality) before deciding to act. Most important, the self has to make the choice even among competing impulses, preferably on the basis of what will bring the self the best advantage in the long run. The difference underlies the legal distinction between a premeditated crime and an impulsive one. The premeditated crime deserves the greater punishment because the person committed it as a whole self.

Autonomy is a bit like when someone asks, "Are you sure?" That raises a question and causes a pause. All the different roles, values, commitments stashed in various parts of the brain and mind have the chance to raise their objections. If you go ahead and do the action anyway, then it is reasonable to say you as a whole self "own" the action. You had ample opportunity to change your mind, to override impulse, to act otherwise, and you went ahead anyway.

Autonomy is thus key to what the self is all about. The human mind has many different roles, many different values, goals, plans, intentions. Acting on one can impede progress toward other goals. Hence, the self requires a central executive, a psychological structure that can decide which goals take priority over which other goals, at least in the current situation. That process includes recognizing the demands, constraints, and opportunities that the cultural environment offers. Nevertheless, the autonomous self is a self-contained unit that acts as one: in the world but separable from it.

DOES THE SELF HAVE FREE WILL?

Somewhat by accident, my laboratory stumbled into one of the grand all-time philosophical debates, namely about free will. This occurred when ego depletion research expanded beyond self-control to encompass decision making, active responding, and planning (Vohs et al., 2008). Some people objected strenuously to me using the term, while others were quite sympathetic and supportive. I came to realize that the term *free will* is controversial because it means very different things to different people. I actually agree with both sides of the debate—because they do not really contradict each other.

For some thinkers, free will means exemption from causality, or having an immaterial and supernatural soul that causes actions. These scientists are usually skeptical of the idea of free will. I am happy to go along with them to dismiss such views. At best, they are not scientific theories, which work with causation in the natural (and cultural) world.

For other thinkers, however, free will means simply being able to act differently in the same situation. All that we have discussed in this chapter invokes that assumption. The very notion of full-blown choice invokes multiple options that are in fact genuinely possible.

Philosopher Alfred Mele has persuaded me that the real problem with *free will* is not the "free" part, which gets all the attention, but the "will" part. "Will" would seem to be a psychological process or system, yet no current theories of the psyche include something called "will." So the will in free will is to be understood as metaphor. The "free" part may be literal.

For present purposes, it is not necessary to take a strong stand on the grand question of free will. Both contexts can be used. Insofar as free will does not exist, these processes are what is mistaken for free will. Insofar as free will really exists, this is what it is. I regard it as implausible that humans have some genuine form of free will that does not encompass these processes of self-control and deliberate, rational choice, not to mention planning and initiative. The psychologist can map out how these processes work, and we can leave to the philosophers to judge whether these deserve to be called free will.

Regardless of the term, it is helpful to appreciate that some choices and acts are freer than others. People feel freer when their choices are easy and bring a good result, as compared to hard choices and negative outcomes (Lau et al., 2015). Thus, for ordinary people at least, free will is about getting what you want and need. The human self clearly evolved some capabilities for that, beyond what we see in other animals.

Indeed, ordinary people associate free will with much of what we have said about the executive self. Painstaking studies have mapped out how everyday people (as opposed to philosophers and other experts) understand free will (Monroe & Malle, 2010, 2014; Stillman et al., 2011). To them, free will means making deliberate choices and acting intentionally. It helps them get what they want. Free will typically involves conscious thinking and choosing. It is associated with long-term goals rather than short-term ones. Sometimes it means standing up to external pressures and resisting them. Often it means acting in accord with one's moral values. Those phenomena are real, and insofar as those constitute free will, people clearly have free will.

FREE WILL AS RESPONSIBLE AUTONOMY

What a book about the self offers to the grand debates over free will is the emphasis on acting as a unity. The brain or body might have competing impulses and uncertainties, but eventually it does one thing rather than another. Conscious reflection engages the whole self because any unconscious associations or concerns can be activated by their association to what the conscious mind is thinking. If you think about what to do before you do it, it expresses the full you. Free will, such as it is, works on that principle, so a premeditated action expresses you much more than an impulsive, spontaneous, or impromptu one.

What, then, should an individual self-system do in order to perform its duties as part of an effective social system? Elsewhere I have explained my tentative conclusion, which is that *responsible autonomy* is the essence of what human society needs from the individual (e.g., Baumeister & Monroe, 2014). In terms of what works in society, and what the human brain evolved to be capable of, free will boils down to a combination of responsibility and autonomy.

As already been discussed, autonomy is defined as self-government. Each individual self is capable of acting on its own. It makes choices and performs actions. It reacts to the environment but is somewhat independent of it.

More advanced versions of autonomy involve "owning" one's actions, and again, that is where the unity of self is most relevant (Ryan & Deci, 2017; Ryan & Ryan, 2019). The whole self forges a connection to the action. Ownership involves the whole self.

Responsibility means understanding and accepting the consequences of your actions. Children acquire autonomy pretty early on, but societies shield them because they lack responsibility. This requires the ability to think about future events and their consequences somewhat accurately (especially bad consequences because that's when society and the legal system start to care about responsibility). The self also needs to be able to make a choice, preferably a rational one, among those options. If the person chooses to act in illegal ways, he or she knowingly accepts the risk of prosecution. The responsible self understands the different levels of risk. Murder and speeding are both against the law, but the penalties for homicide far exceed those for minor traffic violations. A modern self recognizes the difference and adjusts behaviors accordingly.

Responsibility links the present self to the future self, often in fairly precise ways (even dollar amounts). Systems benefit enormously from individuals being responsible. Responsible individuals make their sacrifices and exertions as needed by society, so they perform their duties. They also avoid breaking the laws and misbehaving in other ways, so as to avoid punishment. When people follow the rules and do their jobs, the system can flourish. Ultimately, the system can provide more resources.

THE SELF AS ACTIVE AGENT

The evolution of self was not so much to create a brand-new way for complicated thought processes to initiate behavior. Instead, it was to create a new structure that could intervene constructively in what was already happening. Put another way, the brain was already producing a constant stream of behavior, and the advanced human self was merely a new input into this causal process.

The human self alters the course of action in diverse ways. It imagines multiple future outcomes, and it uses those to guide current actions. It understands its present actions as part of a story extending into past and future. Moreover, it self-regulates extensively, altering its own responses based on ideas (standards) from diverse sources—including its own inner processes.

Regardless of whether you favor the term *free will*, it is clear the human self controls actions in ways that are quite different from the rest of nature. All this, presumably because the self evolved so as to be able to have societies with culture. Cultural societies make effective use of selves with responsible autonomy (my formula for the operative form of free will). It is thus not just a property of the single brain but rather part of how that brain relates to society and culture. Free will in this sense would hardly exist apart from culture.

KEY POINTS

- There are two meanings of choice: the inner mental process of selecting among options, and choice as an aspect of the situation, outside the person.
- Two processes involved in choice are: following the initial impulse or rationally evaluating options and consequences.
- Two problems increase the difficulty of choosing: conflicting desires and uncertainty.
- The full choosing process has four steps: (1) simulate options and outcomes, (2) evaluate and compare, (3) choose the best one, (4) execute the choice.
- The evolved purpose of human emotion is to help the self decide about the future.
- Self-knowledge is needed for decision making.
- Decision fatigue describes the state of ego depletion that comes from expending willpower in making choices.
- Autonomy means self-government, and some degree of it is essential to the self.
- Free will, to the extent it exists, means being able to act differently in the same situation.
- Responsibility means understanding and accepting the consequences of your actions. Responsible autonomy is the essence of what human society needs from the individual.

PART FIVE

THE SELF IN RELATION TO OTHERS

CHAPTER 20

The Interpersonal Self

The self is not found in solitude. Without other people, there is not much need of self. For example, Neil Ansell (2011a, 2011b) lived alone in a remote section of Wales for 5 years. Without other people around, he found that he ceased to look inside or care much about his inner self. As he wrote, "Alone, there was no need for identity, for self-definition." He thought being away from other people would intensify his inner focus, but he experienced the opposite, "My focus shifted almost entirely outwards." What he learned about himself was how much one's sense of self comes from interacting with other people. This chapter looks at the self in terms of relating to others.

The solitary brain ceases to bother with selfhood. We mainly need selves to help us interact with other people. We evolved to live in groups, and selves improved group life. Selves by themselves are only minimally useful, and mainly for basic tasks like coordinating the legs for walking. Complex, intricate selves are mainly useful for negotiating complex, intricate social groups. In particular, the central importance of reputation has been a theme of this book. Obviously, reputation involves not just the self but other people. Without social interaction, there is no such thing as reputation. Apparently, that removes a major reason for thinking about the self.

NEEDING TO BELONG

No one disputes that humans are highly social animals. When Mark Leary and I set out to review the literature on people's need to belong, we were stunned by the vast amount, diversity, and consistency of the evidence

271

(Baumeister & Leary, 1995). People form relationships readily, and they resist letting them end (even after they have served their purpose, as in a temporary training group). Belongingness shapes how people think and feel in countless ways. Both mental and physical health are strongly tied to belongingness. While most objective facts of life, such as money and health, have only small effects on happiness, social connection stands out as having a large effect. People who lack friends and companions are generally quite unhappy.

The drive to connect is so strong that many people use artificial substitutes such as becoming attached to fictional characters on television shows as if they were in a relationship with that person (Gabriel et al., 2016). Possibly the human brain does not make a strong distinction between real and nonexistent people, and so as it watches a television show week after week, it comes to feel that it knows the fictional social world and is part of it, including having relationships to its various (technically fictional) characters. In parallel, some people follow news about their favorite celebrity and come to feel as if they have a relationship with that individual, even though they have never met in person and the celebrity does not even know they exist. Various odd phenomena such as "comfort foods" indicate the importance of belongingness. Comfort foods typically remind people of a warm, supportive relationship, such as with their mothers.

The self works to satisfy the need to belong, such as by forming relationships and gaining membership in groups. Indeed, the belongingness literature led us to distinguish two different social spheres, a large and a small one (Baumeister & Sommer, 1997). The small sphere involves one-to-one relationships, which typically include the most important, powerful, and satisfying human connections. The larger sphere involves groups and organizations, and the larger number of interpersonal connections generally means that these are mostly shallow relationships. The two have somewhat different rules and processes, so the self can be more attuned to one or the other. For example, women typically focus more on the small sphere of close relationships, while men are more involved in the larger network of more shallow relationships (Gabriel & Gardner, 1999).

THE FIRST SELF: YOURS OR THEIRS?

Does the self start with one's own self, or with other people's selves?

One year I was invited to a panel discussion on the self at the New York Academy of Sciences (see Paulson et al., 2011). We were a diverse group—myself, a philosopher with neuroscience background, and a child psychology expert, as well as a noted science writer who posed the questions. At one point the moderator asked us a seemingly simple question: Do we first know our own self, or the selves of others? We were all stumped.

When experts do not know how to answer a question, often it is because the question is being posed in a way that prevents the truth from emerging. That's what I gently suggested. I said neither own self nor other came first. The big step, I said, was the discovery that there is a difference between self and other. In a sense, one's own self and other selves are discovered (or perhaps invented) at the same moment. It's not that I first learn about me and then about you, or vice versa. The big step involves recognizing that you and I are different, that we have different feelings and thoughts, different goals, different perspectives. This fits Ansell's impression from his hermit years. *The self by itself alone is hardly a self at all.* Selves mainly matter when there are two or more of them.

We need to move past the habit of thinking of the self as a thing, and so one discovers one thing and then another, my self and your self. The breakthrough is that you and I have different selves, with different interior lives, different goals, different perspectives, different inner decision processes. We relate to each other on the basis of being different selves cooperating.

US VERSUS THEM

One of the most inspiring ideas of 20th-century psychology was Gordon Allport's (1954) analysis of prejudice as ignorance. He said, when people do not know members of other groups, they fill the blanks in their knowledge with negative views. He proposed that reducing ignorance would put an end to prejudice and intergroup hostility. The so-called contact hypothesis held that simply promoting more interaction (more contact) between groups would spell the end of prejudice. If White people could get to know Black people, or whatever two groups, they would recognize their common humanity and get along better, with prejudice melting away.

Researchers tested the contact hypothesis and were soon discouraged. If anything, the evidence went in the opposite direction: increasing the contact between two groups led to more hostility, not less. As a vivid example, a colleague of mine happened to be in Paris when the soccer world championship was in its final stages, and the semifinal match pitted their next-door neighbors (Germany) against a team from the other side of the world (South Korea). Obviously, the French had had plenty of contact with Germans but not much with Koreans. Yet, my colleague observed that the crowd wanted South Korea to win. Centuries of contact had apparently fueled animosity, not eliminated it.

Recent work has scaled back the contact hypothesis to positive, mutually satisfying interactions (which may be more what Allport meant in the first place; see Dixon, Durrheim, & Tredoux, 2005). When people from different groups have pleasant, positive contact, their prejudices do indeed diminish (Pettigrew & Tropp, 2006). But frequent intergroup contact can fuel both negative and positive attitudes, and any conflict or negativity in the contact sharply escalates the negative ones (Paolini, Harwood, & Rubin, 2010).

Is this natural? Consider research on ants (Moffett, 2019). Presumably, ants lack self-awareness and self-concepts. They have a brain, to be sure, but it is not well endowed. There is no evidence that an ant can recognize a specific other ant, even if it is a recently important companion or a sibling. Ants can however tell the difference between an ant from their colony and an ant from another colony, especially if the other is a competitor.

Hostility between groups does not depend on advanced mental capabilities for categorizing us against them, and on interpreting one's own self as a member of this group threatened by a different group. Ants have small brains, but they know that ingroup members are fine while outgroup members must be killed at once.

People have a need to belong to groups, but this need has strong roots in group conflict. Moffett's (2019) impressive survey of societies, from ants to modern humans, concludes there is generally no "us" without "them." Indeed, humans and insect societies are the only ones who have managed to construct societies bigger than several dozen members based on being able to recognize every member of one's group. Insects do not even recognize each other individually. They rely on cues such as smell to tell their own group apart from enemies. Humans rely on group identity markers to know whether strangers are part of their group or not.

The Comanches were the last great indigenous empire in the Western hemisphere (Gwynne, 2010). They lived in small groups in which everyone knew everyone. Periodically, they would encounter another small group which they did not know. Yet, they could tell right away whether these were fellow Comanches or enemy Apaches. If the other group were Comanches, they would spend time together, trade information and goods, perhaps arrange some marriages. If the others were Apaches, it was immediate, ruthless warfare aimed at killing or enslaving them.

Yet, even these historical enemies could join forces if an external threat materialized. In the First Battle of Adobe Walls (1864), for example, Comanches joined with Kiowas and even Apaches to fight against the U.S. Army troops led by Kit Carson. The combined Indian forces forced the White soldiers to retreat, possibly the last time that Native Americans drove U.S. troops from a battlefield.

The modern United States is unusual in not having nearby enemies. Older citizens remember the Soviet Union as the enemy, but the Soviets were far away. When the Soviet empire collapsed in 1991, America stood alone as the only super-power, and soon internal divisions emerged, as indicated by an escalation in racial conflict, gender conflict, and, most strikingly, increased political polarization between Democrats and Republicans. Moderate centrists lost elections and lost hope. I do suspect that if a serious external threat were to emerge, Americans might go back to finding more common ground with each other.

Thus, the self has a strong drive to belong to a group, and part of that drive comes from knowing there are other, different groups out there. The self cares most about its group when there is an opposing group.

DOES PART OF YOUR SELF RESIDE IN OTHER PEOPLE'S BRAINS?

You have a concept of yourself. Other people also have a concept of you. Different people may have slightly different concepts, though your identity is the same and the differences are mainly about personality traits. If one of them mentions you to another, they refer to exactly the same person, even if one quite likes you and the other doesn't. The differences are important, but so is the sameness.

Much of what people do is aimed at constructing, maintaining, and sometimes repairing this public image of self. There are many other people who may have impressions of you, and in various small ways you seek to make slightly different impressions on them—but again, the similarities outweigh the differences. Making and maintaining radically different impressions of yourself on different people are difficult and risky. Even keeping track of which audience knows which version of you is mentally taxing. Hence, across one's social environment, the unity project is central to the self. One mostly seeks to create a common, consistent view of oneself in other people's minds.

Meanwhile, the influence of other people's impressions of you on your inner self is much more extensive than you might think. Early but striking evidence of this came from the Korean war. The Chinese captured some American soldiers and decided to convert them to Communism. The Chinese did not have a general theory about how to brainwash captives but set about experimenting, using methods that had worked with their own people. At first their efforts were unsuccessful, but then they realized one key flaw: the Americans would listen to the Communist indoctrination all day but then return to the prison barracks and rejoin the other Americans, who reset and reaffirmed their American identity. The Chinese tried keeping the Americans separate from each other, and then their brainwashing methods were much more successful (Group for Advancement of Psychiatry, 1957). The implication is that the stable sense of self, including political values, is held together by the public self. When you stop interacting regularly with people who know you, your self becomes much more malleable. This is akin to Neil Ansell's insight: The self exists mainly to relate to other people.

Remember, people think of other people in terms of stable traits. They seek to find patterns in each other's behavior, so they can predict. Knowing your patterns of thinking, feeling, and acting enables other people to pre-pare to interact with you. If you change, that makes it harder for them. People therefore expect you to be consistent, and they may put pressure on you to be consistent. Informally, many people report that they change most when they move to a new social environment, such as a new home or new school (Harter, 1993, 2012).

Experimental research on self-concept change has likewise confirmed the importance of the public self. Early work had found that people's rat-ings of their traits and attitudes could be changed by asking them leading questions (Fazio et al., 1981). For example, "What are some of the things you dislike about loud parties?" prompts people to scan their memories for more introverted sentiments, and afterward they rate themselves as more introverted than people who were asked, "What kinds of things would you do to liven up a dull party?" Researchers thought that the effect came from scanning one's memory in biased fashion, and no doubt that helped. But some researchers noticed that these situations had a strong interpersonal dimension: the essence of the procedure involved people telling someone else about themselves.

To tease apart the inner and interpersonal processes, Tice (1992) administered these same loaded questions in two different ways. Some people answered them in face-to-face conversations, while others recorded their answers on an audiotape, anonymously, while alone. The questions were the same and presumably the memory-scanning exercise was also the same in both conditions. But only the face-to-face interactions produced any change in self-ratings. Put another way, your self-concept changes when other people come to see you differently, and not simply because you scan your memory for one or another sort of information.

Psychology has long assumed that the human mind seeks consistency (e.g., Festinger, 1957). But it is only when the self's executive agent starts to be concerned with its reputation, and to adjust its actions accordingly, that consistency across time starts to become a social and moral obligation.

Ceremonies achieve the crucial goal of updating the shared under-standing of the group. It is not what you privately think that matters but what everyone (more or less) knows and accepts. When you graduate or marry, the ceremony enables the group to agree on the change in your sta-tus. As noted earlier, historians say that in ancient history, land sales had to be publicly witnessed, probably for that same reason (Bernstein, 2004). It was important that everyone in the group know that the ownership had changed.

That people realize this importance of collective acknowledgment is also attested in experimental work. Robert Wicklund and Peter Gollwitzer (1982) conducted an impressive series of studies on what they called "sym-bolic self-completion." They understood that selves have aspirations of who and what they want to be—and that selves need public validation of this.

In a study typical of their others, they recruited aspiring guitarists and gave them a personality test. By random assignment, half were told that their personality profile very closely matched the typical profile of a successful guitarist, while the others were told they did not resemble successful guitarists. Then, in a seemingly unrelated development, they were offered the chance to teach guitar lessons to beginners. Those who had been told they already resembled successful guitarists did not want to bother giving lessons, but the ones who had gotten the more threatening information (i.e., they were not the typical sort of person who becomes a successful guitarist) signed up to give lessons. Teaching guitar is one way of claiming for oneself the public recognition that one is a guitarist. Just satisfying yourself is not enough; you need other people to validate your claim to that identity.

In modern life, many identities require validation by the group, sometimes including earning a license. You cannot call yourself a cosmetologist unless you have a license. Thus, the state determines whether you are entitled to claim that identity. Note, though, that claiming the identity is not the point. Rather, earning money by doing people's hair and nails is the point, and getting a license is a step along the way to that. When you earn your cosmetology license, you have successfully claimed that identity, but that does not mean the self's job is done. That is not the endpoint. The goal is to perform that job day after day so as to earn money to pay the rent and buy groceries.

Keeping records has made things more precise. Someone may earn a cosmetologist's license, which takes effect on a particular day, so that the person can be paid for beauty work after that date but not before. In the past, record keeping was less precise, and indeed our hunter-gatherer ancestors did not have written records. For them, the way that an event entered the doxa was to be recognized by the full group. After a wedding ceremony, everyone knew the couple belonged to each other. Also, crucially, everyone knew that everyone else knew it, too.

MORALITY AND SELF-INTEREST

Morality typically restrains selfish, self-interested behavior so as to promote behaviors that benefit the group. The moral dilemmas people encounter and struggle with often involve choices between doing something to benefit themselves and doing something that would produce a good group outcome. For example, consider not stealing the property of others. Selfishly, one benefits by taking something that belongs to someone else. But if people respect each other's property in general, then society flourishes: property rights are one of the foundations for the "birth of plenty," that is, society moving into an era of abundant resources (Bernstein, 2004; also Fukuyama, 2011; de Soto, 2000). Most big animals will just take what they want from smaller, weaker members of the group. To refrain from doing so improves the group's cultural system, especially its ability to make resources abundant.

Being unselfish fits one's enlightened self-interest. Individuals only survive and reproduce to the extent their group is successful, by and large. (There can be occasional exceptions.) By obeying the moral rules along with everyone else, individuals help the group to succeed, and their own prospects for survival and reproduction improve along with those of the group. Every human has some investment in the success of his or her group. Nevertheless, sometimes there is a chance to benefit oneself at the expense of the group, especially if this is a minor thing that does not damage the fortunes of the group as a whole. For example, a country's economic fortunes are unaffected by whether any particular single taxpayer cheats on his or her taxes. Thus, the cheater can enrich him- or herself at expense of the group, without noticeably damaging the group.

People adopt morality because it improves relations with others. The self comes into being as the brain learns to manage a role in the social system. That includes getting along with others. In the evolutionary past, it meant cooperating with others, and to induce other people to cooperate with you, the best strategy was to behave so that others see you as morally good. Then they can trust you, rely on you, cooperate with you. That's how early humans survived. That's still how it is done.

The crucial point is this: Whether other people regard you as morally good matters a lot. It comes down to reputation.

That leaves open a window for selfishness. One can act morally when others are watching because only those actions contribute to the reputation. What you do when nobody is looking is irrelevant to reputation as long as it's certain that no one will ever know. Moreover, because people gossip, if one person knows you did something bad, there's a pretty good chance others will know it, too. It therefore becomes essential to keep up what Batson (2008) called the "moral masquerade." In the article "Moral Actor, Selfish Agent," Frimer and colleagues (2014) wrote: "When people feel watched—on stage—they take on the role of the moral actor. Yet, when the curtain falls and the stage lights dim, the selfish agent takes over" (p. 790).

Nature taught animals to want what is good for them. Morality requires sometimes resisting those wants. Self-regulation emerged as the brain's capacity to resist them, despite a brain and psychological architecture that are aimed at getting the self what it wants (which is what will make it survive and reproduce). Self-regulation has to help enlightened (long-term) self-interest at the expense of immediate self-interest. Stealing something might have short-term appeal, but becoming known as a thief will be costly down the road.

Morality thus combines three of this book's main themes. First, the self is interpersonal, and its job is to connect the individual to the group. Second, and related, reputation is important, so people must choose their actions with an eye toward how their reputations will be affected. And third, the human self extends across time, mainly because that's what human social systems demand.

KEY POINTS

- Selves mainly matter when there are two or more of them.
- People have a need to belong.
- The need to belong has strong roots in group conflict.
- Others' impressions of you influence your self.
- Ceremonies update the shared understanding of the group.
- Whether you are morally good matters a little, but whether others regard you as morally good matters a lot.

CHAPTER 21

The Self as Group Member

Let's now consider the self as a member of groups and categories. The modern self is partly defined by these categories: woman, wife, mother, Episcopalian, Walmart cashier, gun owner, Libertarian Party member, Weight Watcher. Some of these overlap (many but not all Libertarians are women); some are subsets of others (all mothers are women, but not all women are mothers). The ancient self was strongly rooted in belonging to a particular band or tribe and a larger society, and as far as I know, all societies have defined identities partly by gender.

These collective identities are in some ways the opposite of the idea that each person is a thoroughly unique and special person, as in radical individualism. Indeed, according to some theories, people begin to think of themselves as largely interchangeable with other members of their group.

SOCIAL IDENTITY THEORY

A forceful and highly influential theory about identity deriving from groups and categories is known as "social identity theory" (Hornsey, 2008; Tajfel, 1978; Tajfel & Turner, 1979). It emphasizes how each individual self is built from memberships in groups and categories. Social identity theory is less appreciated in the United States than elsewhere, such as Europe and Asia, perhaps because Americans encounter deadly enemies less often and can maintain the comforting myth that humans are "all one tribe." Europe, in particular, has a long and bloody history of conflict between groups, and so it is no surprise that social identity theory based on different and competing group memberships originated in Europe and flourishes there.

The theory starts with the idea that how people think of themselves can slide along a continuum from radical individualism to total identification with a group (Hornsey, 2008). At any given moment, the more you are aware of yourself as a unique individual, the less you embrace group identities, and vice versa. The excesses of mob violence and riots occur, not just because people lose their individual self-awareness, but also because they identify more and more with the group. They act on the basis of the current, violent group norms rather than respecting their inner values and conscience. Put another way, a mob is not really a collection of autonomous individuals who deliberately make decisions to commit specific acts of violence. Instead, they join in the group and help carry out its project using the violent means that are its norm at the moment.

Likewise, two people can interact as two unique individuals, as representatives of their respective groups or somewhere along the continuum between the two. For example, when the presidents of two different countries meet, they can relate to each other as individuals would, such as talking about their families. But they presumably must also remain aware of themselves and each other as representing their respective countries.

Recent work has applied social identity theory to a variety of aspects of social life and its problems. Leadership is one key domain, and indeed modern leadership has to get people from diverse backgrounds and different groups to work together for the common good (Haslam et al., 2010). The implications of social identity for health are also important, given that belongingness has immense benefits for both physical and mental health (Haslam et al., 2018).

Social identity theory got started in an effort to understand some surprising findings. Henri Tajfel had an excellent idea for a research program aimed at identifying the key factors that made people identify with groups. He'd start with random, meaningless groups (called the "minimal group"), such as assigning research subjects into one group or another based on how much they liked abstract paintings by Klee or Kandinsky, and similarly trivial dimensions. Then he would add in other factors, such as shared goals, interdependence, acquaintance, and more, in order to see at what point people would begin to show signs of loyalty to the group.

But *he never found the starting line*—indeed, it was always already past. People favored their own group even in the minimal group situation. If you preferred Klee over Kandinsky, you favored other people with the same preference. The lab studies were never able to create a situation in which people treated outgroup members as favorably as ingroup members.

Tajfel concluded that people categorized themselves based on belonging to a group, and this act of thinking "I am one of these" was enough to produce biased behavior, such as assigning a bigger share of rewards to fellow group members than to outgroup members. Tajfel and his colleagues reasoned that the most powerful and basic factor is the desire for a positive view of self, which people seek by trying to elevate their group over other groups (see Hornsey, 2008, for an overview).

To me, this is maybe on the right track, but ultimately backward. The ultimate goal of group interaction is not a comforting sense of collective superiority, let alone a boost to individual self-esteem based on belonging to a superior group. Going back to evolutionary history, survival and reproduction depended on one's group, and so competition among groups was a basic fact of life. Put another way, the antagonism between French and Germans, or between Israelis and Palestinians, has less to do with people's desire to feel superior and more to do with their evolved inclination to recognize members of outgroups as deadly threats. When the food isn't enough for everybody, it either goes to your kids or their kids. One group might remain pacifist or individualistic, while the other works together to obtain and protect resources and to kill enemies so that their own children get fed. Guess which group we're descended from. It is normal and natural to align with one's own kind against other groups, and this is probably rooted in deep, evolutionary pressures. The human mind's advanced powers of classifying, categorizing, identifying, and evaluating people as belonging to us or them, as well as the mental tricks that boost collective self-esteem, are fancy new forms of this old impulse toward group antagonism. The us-versus-them mentality was prevalent in plenty of other animals, long before human culture emerged (Moffett, 2019).

A key insight of social identity theory is that self-awareness moves toward the group identity end of the continuum when social interactions involve people from different groups. Much of life is lived with members of one's own group. In that case, individual identity becomes more salient and important. Within the group, people act as individuals, but when confronting another group, they focus on solidarity with their fellow members.

People tend to think their own groups are fairly diverse, whereas members of other groups are similar to each other (e.g., Linville & Jones, 1980). "They look alike, they act alike, they think alike—we don't," to quote the title of an early paper on this pattern (Quattrone, 1976). This has been interpreted as reflecting prejudice, ignorance, and other factors, but it may be a result of the social identity shift. People encounter members of their own group when outgroups are absent, which is much of the time, and so they may be quite aware of how different their ingroup members are from each other. In contrast, situations that involve multiple groups cause people to focus on what they have in common with their own group. In those group-to-group situations, the members of each group do probably shift toward thinking and acting alike. And since they only see other groups in these intergroup situations that pull for group solidarity, they might easily conclude that the others are all fairly similar to each other. They don't realize that the similarity is the result of being in a group-versus-group situation.

In other words, you mainly see your own group members when no other group is around, and under those circumstances you focus on how the individuals in your group are different. Meanwhile, you mainly see other groups in intergroup situations, when within-group similarity dominates, so then the focus is on similarities. Your own group becomes more similar in those situations, too. You just don't realize it.

When it is group against group, one of the self's key jobs is to advance its group. People are naturally sensitive to the status of their group. They may seek social change, such as by trying to get more status and resources from other groups. High-status groups have collectively worked to create a social system that works for them (though many individuals in their group are basically free riders, inheriting their privileged status from others). They may seek to preserve the status quo. For low-status groups, the issue is more complicated. They want to gain prestige and resources, but there are two routes to doing this: fight to raise up one's group at the expense of the others, or transfer individually into the better group. Individuals have to appraise these two strategies that depend partly on opportunities

Social identity theory has made much of whether it is possible to change groups or not. If your group is outranked by other groups, you can boost your own personal self-esteem by changing groups, and so you focus your efforts on getting into the elite group. This puts the emphasis on individual identity. In contrast, if it is not possible to change groups, then group-versus-group conflict becomes the focus because the only pathway to higher self-esteem is raising the relative status of your group. That can occur either by bolstering the prestige of your group or tearing down the others.

To illustrate, America long embraced social mobility, epitomized in popular rags-to-riches stories. This ostensible openness kept poor people from identifying too strongly with their poverty, and from forming into groups with other poor people. This was unlike Europe, where socioeconomic differences had a much longer history of rigid class structures. The first President Roosevelt remarked that American society had no place for hyphenated Americans—a view that seems quaint today when hyphenated identities permeate social and political life. The change in American politics arose partly because of groups that did not permit change, such as race and gender. As social identity theorists emphasize, group conflict with impermeable group boundaries leads to collective action.

Blending into the group and focusing on group identity can create problems in a society committed to inclusion and diversity. Group-to-group interactions tend to be nastier, more competitive, more antagonistic than person-to-person interactions (for a review, see Wildschut et al., 2003). A thought experiment is helpful: Imagine two individuals from different groups negotiating to solve a problem. Then imagine half a dozen individuals from each group negotiating the same problem. Two individuals from different groups might be able to focus on common grounds and work out a compromise, but if the interaction has half a dozen members of each group, the prospects for amicable resolution dwindle.

MIXING GROUPS:
HARD AND SOFT GROUP BOUNDARIES

Scientists treasure observations, but sometimes the most interesting thing to notice is what isn't happening. While writing his book on societies, Mark Moffett (2019) visited a Starbucks and recorded various impressions. Afterward, he was struck by the most amazing part, which was something that didn't happen. In that coffee shop, dozens of strangers took turns, ordered beverages, consuming them, or taking them away for later consumption. In general people respected each other's privacy and left each other alone. Moffett reflected that if you put a couple dozen nonacquainted chimpanzees into a small space like that, utter chaos would break out: sniffing, screeching, fighting, and more. Chimps are humankind's closest biological relatives, but they aren't capable of being near each other, especially as strangers, without bothering each other.

The human mastery of respectful, polite tolerance of strangers is all the more remarkable because it was not part of our evolutionary past. Hunter-gatherers rarely encountered strangers and certainly did not politely ignore them when they turned up. Even more impressive, perhaps, is the modern movement to be not just tolerant but positively welcoming to members of other groups. Modern Western society embraces diversity of peoples, encouraging the belief that there are large net advantages to working and living with people different from oneself.

Regardless, diversity is here to stay. That means working with different kinds of people, as well as unequal groups. In today's United States, identity politics have become an increasingly tense as some politicians try to play groups off against each other (Fukuyama, 2018). Europe is not far behind. Presumably, the same problems will come to Asia and Africa in time, and some of these trends are already evident.

The boundaries between groups can be hard or soft, which brings us back to the question of whether there are opportunities for changing groups. When the group boundaries are not rigid so that people can move from one group into another, then low-status people focus on their own individual traits and strive to move from the loser group into the winner group. When group boundaries are strict, then belonging to a low-status group presents a problem for which there is no clear solution. The lower-status group may shift its values and enforce criteria by which their group looks better. For example, if status is linked to money in society, and the prospects for moving from poor to rich are not good, then people in the poorer group might seek group pride based on something other than money (Crocker & Major, 1989). Perhaps they are creative, or happy, or talented in some domains that do not involve money. Another strategy would be to identify with one's group as unfairly oppressed, and to campaign for radical social change so as to reduce or even overturn the status differences between groups.

The emphasis on perceived possibility of change has often been used to explain why left-wing political movements (Communism and socialism) fared better in Europe than in the United States. Much of European history is marked by strict boundaries between social classes. The idea that a poor man could become a rich man was absurd. In contrast, the United States maintained the popular belief that a poor man could indeed become rich. (How much the reality corresponded to this ideal has been debated.) American poor folks often thought that their continued poverty reflected their own personal failure, not a basic unfairness built into the social system. The United States did have a strong labor movement, but except during the Great Depression of the 1930s, it did not fuel socialist or Communist attempts to take over the system. In plainer terms, the poor folks were not out to destroy the rich folks because the poor folks hoped that they or their children might eventually themselves become rich folks.

TOKENISM

In larger groups, one solution to unequal groups is called "tokenism." The high-status group takes in individual members (tokens) from the low-status group. That may not have much of an overall impact, but it fosters the perception that group boundaries are soft and that it is possible to move from one to another. As a result, the low-status people focus on improving their individual attainments in the hope that they, too, can move into the high-status group.

What does this mean for the selves of tokens? First off, they have heightened awareness of their differentness (McGuire et al., 1978, 1979). A boy in a group of boys is not necessarily aware of himself as a boy, but a boy in a group of girls will be highly aware of his gender. The same goes for other sorts of differences such as well-meaning efforts to integrate races. What makes you different from others stands out, especially to you.

Standing out can be good, but it brings costs. A classic study (Lord & Saenz, 1985) had a student engage in an ostensible group conversation. In reality, the other group members were on videotape, so there was no possibility that they treated the research subject any differently. Half the participants thought they were sharing views with other members of their gender, while the rest thought they were the sole member of their gender in the group (i.e., they were a token). The tokens found it harder to remember the conversation than the non-tokens, even though the content was the same. They even had trouble remembering what they themselves had said. Observers, meanwhile, remembered what the tokens said better than the non-tokens. Thus, if you're the only woman in a group of men, you will have more trouble processing and remembering what is said at the meeting compared to being a woman among other women, but what you said will stand out more to others. For men among the men, who said what was also somewhat blurry.

BEING YOURSELF IN THE GROUP

Each self is both a unique individual and a member of assorted groups and categories. Both of these run through how you think of yourself, as well as how others view you.

These days, in many American universities, it has become the norm to introduce one's comments with "Speaking as an XXX" in which one recites one's category memberships, which confer varying degrees of prestige and status upon what one is about to say. So, the meaning and value of an individual's comments will rise or fall depending on what category the individual person falls into. One may regard such self-introductions as a humble way of noting that one's membership in a group would be a source of bias, so one's comments should be taken with a grain of salt. More likely, however, people use their memberships to claim special insight or authority.

One of the great thinkers in psychology's history was Abraham Maslow (1968), who contributed many major ideas to the field. For one of his lesser-known ideas he coined the term "resistance to rubricization." People don't like to be categorized, pigeonholed, stereotyped. Maslow thought people want to be recognized as unique individuals. Yet clearly, people identify, often proudly, with their groups and categories.

The tension between individuality and group membership reveals once again the self's function of relating the individual to society. Each person is a unique combination of genes, experiences, and meanings. Yet, each person's life involves fitting into groups. Before others can know you well enough to appreciate your unique individuality, they know what categories you belong to. Categories are based on something that is the same among all members. Groups likewise have an element of sameness, not just that everyone belongs to the group, but also that everyone shares some common assumptions, beliefs, values. Roles such as nurse, accountant, police officer are in some ways the same for everyone—but each person may perform that role slightly differently. This is what the self is all about. An individual brain learns to be part of the group.

How the Group Views You Is at Stake

Some of the problems of tokenism may be due to the disruptive effects of self-awareness. As I have already briefly covered, heightened self-awareness contributes to choking under pressure. Choking means performing badly when one is trying to perform well. Pressure means that the situation is important. Unfortunately, the mind responds to importance by paying extra attention—and that can disrupt the automatic processes that normally enable a person to perform skillfully (Baumeister, 1984). When you believe, even falsely, that everyone is looking at you, it is harder than usual to maintain normal skills. Even when the audience is supposedly on your side, the attention can be disruptive. People choke more when they have friends and family in the audience, which is why some performers specifically ask their parents and other loved ones not to attend. Some people think it will be helpful to have their loved ones present because normally having them close is a good barrier against anxiety—but they heighten self-consciousness and impair performance (Butler & Baumeister, 1998). People actually perform better in front of strangers than in front of family and friends.

As a classic example, most people are very skilled at talking, which they do frequently—but speaking in public, when the entire group is all looking at you, inspires widespread anxiety and causes people to stumble over simple phrases and forget what they meant to say. Expressing love and commitment to one's beloved should be easy, but standing in church to make wedding vows in front of a host of family and friends, people forget what they meant to say. This is presumably why presiding ministers typically tell the bride and groom simply to "repeat after me" and then spoon-feed them their vows in short phrases.

The broader point is that speaking in public is oddly terrifying to large segments of the population. Why? A likely explanation is that it taps into the deeply rooted fear of reputation damage. You might make a fool of yourself. This resembles the "Facebook anxiety" that some teenagers suffer these days; what they post is immediately out there for many to see, and a misstep could do lasting harm to how one is seen by the group.

All of this brings us to the topic of the next chapter: how the individual manages the way he or she is perceived by other people.

KEY POINTS

- In social identity theory, each individual self is built from memberships in groups and categories along a continuum from radical individualism to total identification with a group.
- When social interactions involve people from different groups, self-awareness moves toward the group identity end of the continuum.

- When it is group against group, one of the self's jobs is to advance its group.
- When group boundaries are strict, belonging to a low-status group presents a problem that can lead to collective action.
- Tokenism is one solution to strict boundaries in which the high-status group takes in a few individuals from the low-status group.
- Being a token heightens self-awareness of difference.

CHAPTER 22

Self-Presentation

This chapter addresses one of the core themes of this book, that reputation is of crucial importance. Much of what people do is designed to construct, repair, and maintain a reputation (Goffman, 1959). Self-presentation is a matter of shaping how others perceive you. This may be useful for direct pragmatic reasons, as in job interviews, when your future occupation depends on making the right impression. Still, the human concern with self-presentation seems to run deeper than simple pragmatic strategy. The human mind seems designed to want to be well thought of by others. This does not go back that far in evolution, and indeed it is unlikely that other animals can even understand that impressions of them exist in their fellows' minds. But for most human beings, being well regarded by their fellows is an ongoing concern and motivates strategic action.

Experimental studies by Vonasch and colleagues (2018) have recently shown that modern college students and, more generally, modern American citizens say they would often accept jail time, amputation, and even death rather than have a bad moral reputation. For example, half of the sample said they would rather die now, thereby forfeiting most of their entire life, rather than live a full life but be known as a child molester after death. Obviously, these were only hypothetical choices, but the fact that a third said they would prefer death over posthumous dishonor shows how deeply rooted is the human concern with a positive reputation. Indeed, further experiments showed that many White students actually did undergo a highly unpleasant, disgusting experience (submerging their hand into a jar full of gross super-worms), rather than let the researchers make public the results of a reaction-time test that purported to reveal them as racially prejudiced.

Outside the lab, there is fairly dramatic evidence of the importance people place on self-presentation. In particular, the quest to make a good impression leads people to do various unhealthy and even dangerous things. The urge to sustain life is one of the most fundamental drives in all of life, and the human instinct for self-preservation is strong. Yet sometimes, self-presentation trumps self-preservation.

One day at a conference by North Carolina's coast, a self-presentation researcher, Mark Leary, met a colleague he had known during graduate school, who was now herself a professor. The talks were finished for the day, and she was heading out to the beach for sunbathing. They exchanged small talk, and she happened to mention that she had recently had a minor operation for skin cancer. Mark was incredulous: you had skin cancer, and you're going back out to sunbathe? "But I look so good with a tan," she explained.

Leary was intrigued. Eventually, he and some coauthors compiled a review of evidence about the things people do that are bad for their health but serve their goals of self-presentation (Leary, Tchividjian, & Kraxberger, 1994). Sunbathing, including in the aftermath of skin cancer, is one of many:

- People ride motorcycles and play sports without wearing helmets. This enables them to be seen, complete with hair. It also conveys an image of insouciant bravery.

- People engage in risky casual sex without using a condom. In addition to increasing the pleasurable sensations, this enables them to avoid raising the issue of having sexually transmitted diseases, against which protection might be needed. They can also avoid possibly offending partners by suspecting them of being diseased.

- The quest for a fashionably slender body causes people to do all sorts of unhealthy things, including abusing laxatives and inducing vomiting after eating, dieting to excessive and harmful degrees, and falling into some patterns of eating disorders. Fashionable thinness is one reason people give for smoking cigarettes; nicotine suppresses the appetite for food. When the Surgeon General convinced millions of Americans to quit smoking in the 1970s, obesity rates rose sharply and have stayed high ever since.

- Most young people who start consuming alcohol, cigarettes, or drugs do so with other people whom they seek to impress by doing these things. Concern over looking good is what gets you started.

- Some people skip healthy exercising because they fear embarrassment. Sometimes overweight women want to have exercise classes filled exclusively with other overweight women, so they will not have to feel bad about how men or thin women look at them. Without such safe spaces, these women simply don't exercise.

• While some young women fall into anorexia in their quest to be attractively slim, some young men start using steroids to make their bodies appear more attractively muscular. Some though not all of these men also seek to increase their success at sports, which again is often sought for self-presentational reasons.

Subsequent work has confirmed the accuracy and wisdom of Leary's conclusion. Men, in particular, perform risky stunts to impress women. A field experiment involved observing skateboarders attempting risky jumps (Ronay & von Hippel, 2010). They were observed either by a nondescript man or an attractive woman. When it was a woman, the young adult male skateboarders attempted more ambitious stunts. The skateboarders had the option of aborting the trick if the start was not auspicious. But in front of the lovely woman they were less likely to bail out in this way and so they crashed more frequently. Better a bruising hard fall than to let her think you are chicken.

The point of all this is that people are strongly and deeply motivated to be regarded favorably by others. People will make serious sacrifices for its sake. This willingness is hard to square with the assumption that people are basically rational in seeking to make their lives long and comfortable. In my view, this desire shows the importance of the public dimension of the self and the building of a good reputation.

THE LONG REACH OF SELF-PRESENTATION

The concept of "self-presentation" was introduced to the social science community in a 1959 book by renegade sociologist Erving Goffman, who analyzed social interactions as theatrical performances with roles, back-stage etiquette, and the like. By the 1970s, experimental studies on self-presentation were under way, though some researchers favored the term "impression management." I shall explain a bit later why this term was unfortunate.

The basic method for establishing self-presentation was to compare public and private situations: Do people act differently when others are watching? They do.

Early controversy and resistance arose when researchers began to tackle cognitive dissonance, a pattern of attitude change that was one of the most widely studied phenomena in all of social psychology at that time. Many studies had found that getting people to express an opinion contrary to their own initial view led them to revise their initial view to be more consistent with what they had expressed. In the original classic study, subjects endured two long boring tasks and then were recruited to tell the next subject that the procedure had been interesting and fun, after which many of them did claim it had been kind of interesting after all. Seeking to explain such findings, researchers put forward theories that emphasized inner mental processes in service of the mind's quest for consistency. An inner mental urge to be consistent would of course be the same regardless of whether others are watching.

Against that view, the self-presentation researchers doubted that the mind innately cares about consistency. Instead of wanting to *be* consistent, they said, people wanted to *appear* consistent to others (Tedeschi et al., 1971). There are social pressures to be consistent, so what matters is consistency in your reputation, your public self.

Studies showed that dissonance effects worked much better when people were publicly identified than when they expressed the same views privately or anonymously (for reviews, see Baumeister, 1982; Schlenker, 1980, 1982). If the inner quest for consistency were all that mattered, then signing one's name should not matter that much. But people seemed much more diligently consistent when they signed their names. Likewise, they conformed more to what they had said in a brief videotaped speech, thus identified with name and face, than when they had made a similar speech on an anonymous audiotape. Some thinkers said the mind does not have any inner drive for consistency and merely wants to seem consistent because other people expect it. At the extreme, some suggested that the research subjects did not really change their attitudes at all in dissonance studies—they merely changed what they said, so as not to appear inconsistent, hypocritical, or wishy-washy.

Naturally, this really annoyed the attitude researchers who had built their careers on studying this form of attitude change. And they had a right to be annoyed because it was an overreach to suggest that people were just making phony statements so as to give the impression of consistency. Later work came around to agree that attitudes really changed via dissonance, while recognizing that these changes occurred much more in public than private settings (Baumeister & Tice, 1984; Cooper & Fazio, 1984). Thus, the private attitude depended on the public impression.

Plenty of other behaviors changed as a function of whether they were performed in secret or in the presence of others. Evidence for this unfolded gradually, as here and there various groups of researchers would try out the public versus private research design on one phenomenon after the other. Here are some of the differences (reviewed by Baumeister, 1982; Schlenker, 1980):

- People are more generous and helpful when others are watching than in private.
- Public settings make people a bit reluctant to accept help, unless they can reciprocate or in some other way save face.
- People conform more in public and yield more to influence, as compared to private situations—unless overdoing it will make them look

spineless, in which case they assert their independence more in public than private. People assert and defend their freedom of choice more vigorously in public than private settings.

- People are more affected by and concerned about public evaluations than private ones, and they resort to tactics like self-handicapping (creating obstacles that can be blamed for failure) more in public.
- People are often more aggressive in public, especially when pride is at stake and to back down would make them look weak—but if their aggression is illicit, they do it more in secret. Being humiliated in front of others is a particularly strong impetus to aggression.
- People work harder on tasks when others are watching. (School-teachers, military officers, and work supervisors will not be surprised by this!)

Self-presentation was not a replacement for cognitive dissonance theory. It was an added motivational element. This tells us something about human nature. We evolved multiple inner processes to help us create and sustain a good reputation. That's one of the main tasks of the self. Throughout human history a good reputation has been very helpful for both survival and reproduction. Conversely, a bad reputation has often been an obstacle to surviving and reproducing.

One of the basic laws of psychology is that bad is generally stronger than good (Baumeister, Bratslavsky, Finkenauer, & Vohs, 2001). A bad reputation is to be avoided at all costs. To be sure, "bad" has different forms and meanings. In some contexts, being seen as overly aggressive would be bad, such as in church groups, or women's friendship networks. In others, such as male youth gangs, being overly aggressive might be a fine reputation, whereas being seen as delicate and sensitive would be bad. Indeed, one researcher who spent a decade living with gangs and observing their daily life noted that some guys had reputations as highly dangerous, aggressive, nasty fighters—yet he never saw or heard about any of them actually fighting (Jankowski, 1991). A reputation as a wimp invites others to beat on you. A reputation as aggressive saves you from having to fight.

Nevertheless, your social success, and to some extent even your prospects for surviving and reproducing, depend on having a good reputation. And perhaps especially on avoiding a bad one.

ULTIMATE GOALS OF SELF-PRESENTATION

As a first-year professor, long ago, I spent plenty of time in the library getting material for my lectures on one area of social psychology after another. I kept noticing that for each area, there were some experiments showing that people act differently in public than in private (as listed above). After the semester, I wrote a review article to pull all these diverse findings together.

I sent it off to one of the top journals thinking I had made a strong case that self-presentation was a major feature of human social behavior. The reviewers raised a serious criticism, however. They said, if self-presentation was simply a matter of looking good to the audience, why did people sometimes present themselves in antagonistic ways? For example, why might a Democrat assert his political views in conversation with Republicans?

Stumped, I went back and read through the findings again. They brought me to the conclusion that self-presentations are guided by two different motives (Baumeister, 1982). Sometimes you just want to live up to other people's expectations, to make a favorable impression on the audience based on what the audience favors. This motive can be called "pleasing the audience." But other times, you want to assert your core values and beliefs, in order to get social validation for them. Even if other people disapprove, as in the political party example, the public assertion still helps you claim that identity. Indeed, some people give you extra credit for asserting views in the face of immediate disapproval. The Republicans might not like the assertive Democrat, but other Democrats will give you credit for having stood up for what you believe in despite disapproval. This is part of the process of constructing and claiming the identity you desire.

The idea of constructing the self through self-presentation lent a new aura of dignity and respectability to self-presentation. Psychology's thinking about self-presentation had gotten off to a disreputable start. Many researchers thought it meant simply pretending to be something you were not. Pleasing the audience encompassed some of this disreputable aspect. But claiming identity, or constructing the self, is more respectable.

The basis for self-presentation in the more ambitious, identity-claiming form is something like this: You have in your mind the person you want to be, an ideal self. You could try to become that person, which is one of the main goals of the self. But you need other people to validate your identity. For example, you might aspire to be a great artist. You might paint some pictures or compose some tunes and persuade yourself that they are great, and so voilà, mission accomplished! But that's not really enough, for at least two reasons. One, you might be kidding yourself. (Indeed, if you think you're a great artist but nobody else does, you probably *are* kidding yourself!) Two, part of being a great artist is being recognized as such, at least by some people. For both of those reasons, it is essential to persuade others to see you as a great artist.

TWO MISTAKES WE MADE BACK THEN

Research on self-presentation flourished during the 1980s, as the findings spread from one area to another, in the main journals, symposia at conferences multiplied, and the importance was widely recognized. This passed, however, and self-presentation is not widely studied or discussed today. Partly, the basic points were made, and although the conclusions are still respected today, nobody could much think of further studies to do. Careers in science require young researchers to find something new and interesting.

Perhaps, however, there were some flaws in the research approach that made the work seem slightly off, so the field shook its head and moved away. Looking back at what was all around me during this early stage of my career, I can see two serious mistakes in how we all approached self-presentation.

The first mistake was epitomized in the alternate term "impression management." Social psychology in the 1970s tested their theories with lab experiments, and so it focused on what could be done in that context. That meant most interactions involved people meeting each other for the first time. Self-presentation research followed this pattern, studying how people sought to make a good first impression on a stranger. But most of life is not about first impressions. Rather, it is spent with people you know, who already have an impression of you, and with whom further interactions are expected. Self-presentation occurs in that context of ongoing interactions. In a word, what matters is reputation, and indeed "reputation management" captures the essence of what the self does much better than "impression management." On this, to be sure, the field was not completely wrong back then. Impressions do matter, and making a good first impression is an important step toward building a reputation. Still, the emphasis needs to be on the reputation, not the first impression.

The second mistake was thinking that self-presentation ultimately serves the private, inner goal of constructing your ideal self. What is the guiding purpose behind asserting a self that will meet with immediate disapproval? The answer back then was that people held private notions of their "ideal self" and that self-presentation was a means of validating that self. A Democrat surrounded by Republicans would assert liberal opinions despite the listeners' disapproval—presumably because the Democrat held private ideals of selfhood that included liberal political views. It was a way to claim that identity and establish "that's who I am!" But the public self matters more than the private. The person's ultimate goal is not some private, inner mental state of becoming a particular kind of person. Rather, reputation is the overriding goal.

This second mistake is parallel to my objection to social identity theory (see the previous chapter): It gave undue priority to the private concern with self, as if what matters ultimately is how people think of themselves. Back then we thought the public self was a means to cultivate and fulfill the private self. But slowly I became convinced it's the other way around. The public self, the reputation, is what matters, in terms of how you fare in life. Your private thoughts about yourself are mainly there to support the public one.

The next sections elaborate these mistakes and the revised, modern thinking that seeks to correct them.

MANAGING REPUTATIONS RATHER THAN MERE IMPRESSIONS

A crucial difference between first impressions and reputations lies in the time dimension. Impressions are here and now. Reputations endure across time. Hence, the human concern with reputation management is part of the unity project, that is, of moving from the right-now self to the ongoing (extended-time) self (Vonasch & Sjåstad, 2020).

Let's start with a remarkable experiment that was run with both 5-year-old (human) children and adult chimpanzees (Engelmann et al., 2012). The procedures were complicated but the gist was offering some of them a chance to help someone else, while others were offered a chance to steal from someone else. So, they had a chance to make a moral choice, good or bad (or neutral). Crucially, some of the subjects made their decisions while alone, whereas others made them in the presence of another subject. Children did it in the presence of another child, chimps in the presence of another adult chimp. Human children helped more and cheated less when someone else was watching than when alone. Chimps were completely indifferent to an observer's presence: they cheated and helped at the same rate. The report's title articulated the conclusion: "Five-year-olds, but not chimpanzees, attempt to manage their reputations." Human morality is tied to our understanding that others form lasting impressions of us.

Now, one could ask, does the finding really prove that concern is with reputation rather than fleeting impressions? Perhaps not. But the fleeting impression was of no value to either child or ape. Perhaps the humans care about fleeting impressions while apes don't. Or perhaps, human children know that others will form a fleeting impression based on morally proper behavior, whereas apes don't care about that. Still, apes do form stable impressions of each other, as do humans. Apparently, the apes do not sense that they are better off if others hold positive views of their moral traits, and so the apes do not try to cultivate moral reputations. Humans do, starting from early childhood.

The main point: Even humankind's closest animal relatives seem to lack any concern with moral reputation. Meanwhile, people recognize its importance and adjust their behavior accordingly, already by age 5. The ability to see oneself from other people's perspectives increases in fits and starts, from childhood to adulthood. This ability to see oneself from others' perspectives takes a particular leap at adolescence, often accompanied by a drop in self-esteem; it is a downer to realize that others don't share your view of how wonderful you are!

Two particular mental powers separate humans from other apes and make the reputational concerns possible. One is what researchers call "theory of mind": knowing that other minds see the world differently and being able to simulate other perspectives. The other is the extension of self across time.

Clearly, animals do things that impress each other—though it's far from clear (indeed far from likely) that they knowingly try to make a particular impression. We have already talked about the "winner effect," in which an animal who wins a fight will strut and bluster when encountering another potential rival (Robertson, 2013). And of course the peacock spreads his fabulous feathers as a way of impressing potential mates. Still, there is no sign that any of these animals realize that they are engaging in self-presentation or can understand how their actions are perceived by others. Natural selection has merely rewarded ancestors who acted that way, without their having a full understanding of how others would interpret it. In contrast, people are often highly aware of adjusting their behavior based on how they expect others to view it, with an eye on the reputation they are building.

IDEAL SELF OR DESIRED REPUTATION?

The second mistake from the heyday of self-presentation research was elevating the private notion of the ideal self to the ultimate goal. This puts self-presentation essentially in service of inner processes. Instead, it is more often correct to assume that inner thoughts and other mental processes serve interpersonal goals. We should drop the idea that each human self comes equipped with an inner ideal toward which it strives.

What you think of yourself privately in your mind has mostly minor and indirect effects on what happens to you. In contrast, what matters for your health, happiness, and very survival is what other people think of you. This point has come up repeatedly in this book.

The human child does not start off with some built-in notion of what she wants to become. Rather, she learns what roles are available in society, and she learns about her own talents and preferences. She then selects a role in society that she strives to achieve based on how she wants to be included and treated by other people. The operative part is the desired reputation.

The role of other people is not just to stamp your ticket, validating your identity claims. Rather, the recognition by others is the key point, the main goal. The person settles on the desire to become a great artist, not purely out of some inner drive or compulsion, but because that is a respected role in society and one that the person feels some aptitude for and interest in acquiring. What matters, ultimately and pragmatically, is whether the group recognizes you as a great artist. Whether you privately think of yourself as a great artist and are internally satisfied with your artistic achievements, independent of what the rest of the world thinks, is not so important.

In other words, it was probably a mistake to think of the ideal self that is under construction as being something emerging from inside, independent of the social world. Reputation is what matters. The so-called ideal self is some kind of ostensible inner representation based on what you want your reputation to be. The mistake resembles the mythology of the True Self. It is the desired reputation that the person wants to make into reality, not a private inner opinion about oneself.

ONE REPUTATION, OR MANY?

A much-quoted line by William James (1892/1948) proposed that a man has as many social selves as there are people who know him. James quickly adjusted that claim downward, saying the tally should correspond to groups of people, not individuals, who know him. The different people who know you may have somewhat different impressions of you. Still, these seem more like minor variations on a common image than truly different public selves (cf. Chen, 2019). Sometimes people wish to be regarded differently by different groups, but this is difficult to maintain (Tesser & Moore, 1986). Gossip, in the broad sense of people sharing information about other people (not just in the narrow sense of blackening someone's reputation), means that if two groups know you, at some point information about you is likely to transfer from one group to the other. All the people who know you at work have roughly the same impression of you, which may differ in a few respects from how your family thinks of you, but at some point the colleague and relatives may come into contact. If they realize they have seriously different impressions of you, they will talk about and resolve the inconsistency. The fact that they feel the need to resolve this shows that the fundamental assumption is there is one real you, but their differences show that you are not fully consistent. As always, the unity project is fundamental to the self, but every case remains incomplete.

Hence, I think it is more appropriate to think in terms of a single reputation or public self, rather than a cluster of them. Admittedly, different people will have slightly different impressions of a given person. But the similarities outweigh the differences, and over time, as people share information, the different impressions are likely to converge. This was especially true in our evolutionary past, in which people mainly lived in small groups. As society grew larger and more complex, it became possible to maintain somewhat different reputations with different groups. In the current age of social media, we may be back to converging on a single public self. This was noted already in 2010 by Mark Zuckerberg, founder and CEO of Facebook: "The days of you having a different image for your work friends or co-workers and for the other people you know are probably coming to an end pretty quickly."[1] Self-presentation thus again invokes the unity project (i.e., stitching together various responses and experiences into a coherent whole, across time). When interacting with one person, you have to be mindful that others may find out. Thus, you are not merely presenting yourself to the other person who happens to be there at the time, but to the community at large. Hence, the human child has to learn rather early to anticipate how his or her actions will be perceived by others and to project into the future.

HOW SELF-PRESENTATION IS ACHIEVED

Self-presentation affects many diverse actions. In the lab, researchers typically ask people to present by rating themselves on various traits, but in daily life that hardly ever happens. Nevertheless, consider the things people do in service of conveying some image of themselves, or some information about themselves, to other people. They tell stories that make them look good. Occasionally, they tell stories that make them look bad, often with self-deprecating humor, to burnish their reputations for humility and sense of humor. They act nicely, friendly, funny, and in other valued ways. They clean up their home before guests arrive. They carefully choose what to wear. They comb their hair. They go on diets to lose weight. As already seen, they do plenty of dangerous things, too, from sunbathing to omitting helmets to trying drugs. Some will pick fights, or at least take part in fighting. They smile when they don't feel like smiling. They buy fancy cars or otherwise engage in conspicuous consumption.

People seem more inclined to present themselves favorably than honestly (Schlenker, 1975). Some self-presentations are simply a matter of letting people know something true and good about you, such as your volunteer work or your piano skills. Others are quite false. As an example, one year a small psychology conference was held in the same hotel as a corporate sales conference, and the two crowds mingled. Two young psychology professors were talking, and one briefly excused himself. When he returned, his friend was chatting up a pair of pretty young women from the other conference. When the friend introduced him, the women eagerly asked, "Oh, are you an astronaut, too?" As for how widespread self-presentational dishonesty is, a 2015 *USA Today* poll found that one-third of Americans admitted that

---

[1]This assertion has been widely quoted online, including *www.michaelzimmer. org/2010/05/14/facebooks-zuckerberg-having-two-identities-for-yourself-is-an-example-of-a-lack-of-integrity*.

they had served a store-bought pie at Thanksgiving dinner but pretended they had baked it themselves.

How people strategically adjust their actions for self-presentation reveals the importance of reputation. First off, people seek to present themselves positively. Researchers spotted that right away, led by the pioneers of lab experiments on self-presentation, Barry Schlenker and Jim Tedeschi. People don't just make all manner of extravagantly positive claims, though. They respect objective evidence and adjust their actions based on what the other person knows. Schlenker (1975) summarized this by saying people present themselves as favorably as they can get away with. They rate their competence lower if they have taken a test and the other person will know how they performed, as compared to if they took the test but its results are confidential. Creatures who live in the present might just opt for the best possible self-presentation at each moment, but human adults who know the self extends across time know that others will combine information from multiple sources and that inconsistency will look bad.

What happens when other people already know something bad about the self-presenter? If someone thinks you're a liar, a coward, or a backstabber, you naturally wish to contradict that, but you probably need some proof in action rather than just claiming, "No, I'm not." But in some situations, talking is the only option. In those, self-presenters know that they will lose credibility if they deny the bad traits that others already know about.

Instead, the common response in that situation is to bolster your self-descriptions on other, unrelated dimensions (Baumeister & Jones, 1978). You might present yourself as extra-intelligent, or skilled at cooking, or athletic. The fact that people do this indicates that they have some notion of their whole, integrated public image. Even if you cannot credibly erase any bad areas, at least not right away, you can salvage the total image by increasing the positive aspects.

Further strategic twists reflect the complexity. Bragging is disliked, and despite variations in culture and circumstances, that appears to be fairly true almost everywhere. Recent studies suggest that some of the dislike of bragging is that it implies a negative judgment about everyone else, including the listener. To say you are great is implicitly to belittle others—or at least that is how many listeners interpret it. It makes a negative impression and sometimes elicits aggression (Van Damme, Deschrijver, Van Geert, & Hoorens, 2017; Van Damme, Hoorens, & Sedikides, 2016).

Perhaps most broadly, self-presentation seems to backfire when it is too obvious. An early form of this was the so-called ingratiator's dilemma (Jones, 1964; Jones & Wortman, 1973). The dilemma was this: You want to be liked and therefore do various things in order to get others to like you, but if it becomes clear that you are doing those things mainly in order to be liked, they will be less effective.

All of this probably reflects the constraints on the social system. If you could simply claim any reputation you wanted for yourself, and everyone else could do likewise, then people would simply claim to be loaded with good traits and free from faults. Reputations would become essentially useless. People seek to discern patterns in each other's behavior, so they know who can be counted on, who is capable, whose promises are kept, who will help in dire straits, and so on. People then invest their own limited time and energy being good to those who can be expected to return the favor. But fakers can game the system by simply creating the appearance that they will be reliably good partners, collect the good things you do for them, and then walk away without repaying, leaving you in the lurch. Indeed, people with high-quality reputations may get an extra share of benefits because everyone wants to be their friend. That makes it all the more important to earn the good reputation, not just assert it. Talk is cheap.

When meeting for the first time, however, the strategy shifts toward being more favorable. After all, if you don't tell them how great you are, they might never find out. A bit of judicious positivity is therefore helpful. When my PhD dissertation found some evidence of people self-presenting modestly, my advisor was surprised and pointed out that modesty is largely absent in lab studies. That turned out to be because lab studies mostly involve people meeting for the first time, so the usual norms of modesty can be self-defeating. In my dissertation, modesty was found when participants were meeting someone who had already gotten independent information depicting them in a highly favorable manner (Baumeister & Jones, 1978). If others already think well of you, it is less urgent to make a positive impression. We return to this in the chapter on close relationships.

SOCIAL MEDIA: REVOLUTIONIZING SELF-PRESENTATION

Social life among young people has changed radically in a few short decades. Not long ago, social interaction was mainly accomplished face-to-face in the same room, augmented with occasional phone calls. Today, much interaction occurs by electronic media, including computer social media websites such as Facebook and Instagram. Young people have changed some, too; today's youth have higher self-esteem but also higher anxiety, more narcissism, and more entitlement than previous generations. Some experts, such as Jean Twenge (2017), think these various trends are interrelated.

On the positive side, social media hold out the promise of a revolutionary advance in self-presentation. Instead of relying on multiple interactions and the whispered gossip about you as people compare notes, you can create your own public self as you wish it to be. You can't control what people think, of course, but you can create a highly visible public image that corresponds pretty closely to your desired reputation, complete to even subtle details. And it's there for the whole online community to see. This is vastly different from the past, when you needed to establish your reputation with each person, or else you risked losing control.

Social media are thus the self-presenter's dream. You construct self at a safe distance from other people, so you don't have to worry about building reputation one person at a time via conversations that could always produce awkward or unintended outcomes. The narcissistic personality (Lasch, 1978) especially likes this because he or she seeks admiration and can therefore send each viewer a carefully crafted, dazzlingly admirable image of self.

I suspect that the addictive nature of social media resides in its appeal as a seemingly perfect solution to an ancient problem. Human selves everywhere are fundamentally concerned with how others regard them. Managing a reputation is a tough job, given how little control you have and how many different people form impressions of you. But with social media, you can supposedly fashion precisely the reputation you want and present it to everyone in the world who might be interested.

Yet, social media can also be stressful and nerve-wracking (hence the anxiety). Yes, creating a profile is an efficient way to reach many people with exactly the image you want —but is it really perfect? Given how many people will see it, any flaws will have a wide impact. No wonder people keep making changes, fretting that they could do better. I've long been baffled by the craze for taking "selfie" photographs (after all, who wants to look at a picture of themself?). But some of the appeal of selfies may be driven by the ongoing anxiety about whether one could improve one's online profile with some new and better pictures.

Another factor that may contribute to the stressful aspects of social media is that it is always "on," and so you may be evaluated any moment, day or night. One lesson from stress research is that the effects of threat are cumulative, so the lack of any break compounds the negative impact. This has been shown everywhere from lab rats to soldiers in combat: having regular periods of safety greatly reduces stress (Weiss, 1971a, 1971b, 1971c). There is no safe period from online exposure, however.

Online self-presentation via social media is thus likely to be engrossing, even consuming, based on being a combination of temptation (a great way to tell others how we want to be known) and anxiety (fear that we have not done it right). We may become vulnerable to that sort of online mob trashing that has been on the rise. Some writers have talked about Internet use as an addiction. The analogy captures some important insights. Like addictive drugs, online self-presentation appeals to basic motives and offers satisfaction but may skimp on some of the healthy, adaptive parts that are the reason for the motive. That is, nature shaped us to feel intense pleasure when we do something helpful for survival and reproduction, such as having great sex with a wonderful partner, or achieving some great success with food or status. Drugs find a way to release similar feelings of intense pleasure, only without the success. Drugs are thus a much easier route to bliss, but in terms of how evolution designed the mind, the bliss was not the point; rather, success was the point. In a similar way, laboring over one's online profile may appeal to the natural inclination to want to make a good impression on others and achieve one's desired reputation, but fussing with the details of one's online profile is not the same as building relationships with actual people.

Hence, the paradoxical patterns of social networking correlates. Spending a large amount of time on social media sites goes with narcissism (seeking admiration) but also loneliness (it is the illusion of interpersonal connection). Relatively few genuine close relationships form among people who meet online (perhaps apart from dating sites). Instead, online contacts seem very good at forming networks of shallow relationships and, occasionally, of strengthening the connection to someone whom one has met in reality.

KEY POINTS

- The self's success or failure at social acceptance depends on how it is viewed by others: one's reputation. Self-presentation is directly concerned with building a reputation.

- A good reputation is a key to sharing in society's resources and rewards. It pays to work carefully to build a good reputation.

- The general reputation you are building is mostly the same across different social settings. What changes is not the positive attributes themselves but the emphasis.

- Modesty is better for relationships: narcissistic entitlement, the opposite of modesty, makes for endless friction.

- With new acquaintances, it is important to let them know your good points. Once the bond is formed, however, mutual modesty produces the best results.

- The purpose of self-presentation is integrating into the group; its strategies aim at sustainable positivity, and it strives toward unity across time.

CHAPTER 23

Self as Close
Relationship Partner

The human need to belong is rooted in close relationships. The baby's self starts with learning about itself in the context of one or two close relationships. Close relationships remain a central and important part of life. The self adapts to them and operates in them.

There is an immense research literature on close relationships. This chapter focuses on a few central themes.

SELF-BELIEFS

A theme asserted by many thinkers, including pioneering psychiatrist Harry Stack Sullivan (1955), is that the child's early understanding of self is deeply intertwined with the mother (or other caregiver). This certainly seems quite plausible, for the very young brain learns about the world from the perspective of self with mother. To be sure, there is some separation early, as the child communicates with mother. The human pattern of shared attention often starts with mother and child calling each other's attention to the same things and thus seeing them together.

The overlap of self and mother diminishes as the child grows and becomes separate, but it may never entirely disappear. Even grown college students show some overlap between their beliefs about themselves and their mother, and the same sort of overlap shows up in other close relationships.

The most assertive theory about overlapping self-concepts was put forward by Art Aron and his colleagues, under the rubric "including others in the self." They grounded their theory by postulating that people are driven to expand the self, which they define as the motive "to acquire resources, perspectives, and identities that enhance one's ability to accomplish goals" (Aron et al., 2004, p. 103). To them it is based on a desire for self-efficacy and the rather vague wish to accomplish goals. This desire leads to confusing one's own traits and memories with someone else's, especially a partner in a close relationship, such as a parent or lover. The grand aspect of their theory I find unconvincing: How do you build self-efficacy by confusing your memories with your mother's? Moreover, their theory appears to start with the self and its motivations at least in vague terms of achieving unnamed goals. In this book I have sought to explain the properties of the self in terms of more fundamental motives.

Nevertheless, they have provided some fascinating evidence, in which one's own perspective, resources, and identity are occasionally confused with those of a close other, such as a best friend. The resource evidence boils down to the finding that lab research subjects will assign cash rewards to a best friend as similar to themselves. Friendly acquaintances, strangers, and (especially) disliked others get considerably less. People seek to take good care of those close to them. This does not require any serious revision of our theory of self.

The perspective findings are more promising. Aron and his group use the example of attending the ballet with a spouse, thereby experiencing the ballet not just from one's own perspective but also through the spouse's eyes. Indeed, if you are alone in a room watching a funny movie, you laugh more if you think a close friend or lover is watching the same movie at exactly the same time in another room (Fridlund, 1991). Another finding from Aron's group was that people make excuses for their best friends in the same way they do for themselves, while they resist doing this for less close people.

On various other lab tasks, people process information about their close relationship partner similarly to how they process information about themselves and differently from how they process information about others. For example, when asked to rate trait words as to whether they themselves have the trait, people remember those words better than other words asked without an association to the self (the self-reference effect). When they consider whether those words apply to their best friend, they show a similar bias, unlike for other people.

All in all, I find these studies to be impressive, charming evidence that the mental tricks, patterns, and flattering biases associated with self-beliefs are often extended to close relationship partners. The notion that the other is included in the self is too grandiose for me. Certainly, people know the difference between self and partner. I suspect that even in the most intimate of marriages, people still know which spouse was the one who ate the last banana, who works as an engineer for a particular company, who has diabetes, who was born in Seattle, and so forth. There may be occasional cases in which one was not sure who first had a particular idea that you both like. But I suspect the mental boundaries remain largely intact.

Another limited challenge to privileged self-knowledge is found among children. It takes some years to accept the idea that one knows one's mind better than anyone else can know it. One researcher asked children who knows best what they are really like, "deep down inside." Adults generally say that they themselves know themselves best, but up until about age 11, many children say their mother knows them best (Rosenberg, 1979). This suggests that the overlap between self and mother lingers for many years, perhaps especially because children are not aware of keeping some of their thoughts and feelings private so that their mother does not know them.

MODESTY IN RELATIONSHIPS

As discussed in the previous chapter, modesty is rare among laboratory research subjects. My dissertation advisor, the great Edward E. Jones, noticed that people were modest when their positive reputation was already established. The definitive studies were done several decades later. These showed that self-presentation is quite different in close relationships as opposed to first-time interactions with a stranger. Dianne Tice and her colleagues (1995) recruited pairs of friends for a laboratory study. Each session had two pairs of friends, and by random assignment each person was assigned to interact either with the friend he or she had come with, or with a stranger (from the other pair). This enabled the researchers to compare how people describe themselves to friends as opposed to strangers.

Modesty was the big difference. When dealing with strangers, people put their best foot forward and presented themselves very positively. When dealing with their friends, people shifted heavily toward a modest, self-deprecating style. Why? One reason follows the principle that people present themselves as favorably as they can plausibly pull off (as we saw in the chapter on self-presentation). You can tell a stranger you're a whiz at chess or violin, even if you're just barely passable, but your friends will know the truth.

Yet, there may be something else at work. Egotism causes problems in long-term relationships. When meeting someone new for the first time, it may be useful, even necessary, to be positive about yourself. Good first impressions matter. In contrast, a long-term relationship requires sharing and accommodating each other. It is normal for both persons to think they are contributing or investing more because your own efforts and contributions are more easily noticed (by you) than the other person's. Indeed, Tice herself once surveyed five student suitemates on how often each of them emptied the trash in the main common living area. One said he did not do it very often (maybe 10–20%), one said he did it half the time, and the other three each claimed to do it 90% of the time! Adding these up furnished the statistically impossible conclusion that the trash was emptied over 300% of the time. Even so, sometimes it still sat there overflowing.

Humility is a boon to relationships. If each person is willing to accept a bit less than he or she deserves, there will be plenty to go around. In contrast, if each person claims more than he or she deserves, there won't be enough. If you have ever lived or worked closely with someone who has a big, narcissistic ego, you probably are familiar with the problem. The conventional wisdom of my parents' generation was that in order to make a successful marriage, both spouses had to go more than halfway. That helps counteract the tendency to overestimate what you yourself did (as in the emptying trash example). But narcissists and other egomaniacs are unlikely to accept having to do more than half.

A colleague told a story about visiting an elderly couple in their family home, which was rather empty now that the children had grown and moved away. He happened to use the husband's private bathroom, where he found a note taped to the mirror, apparently from long ago. The note read, "You're no bargain either!" Apparently, the husband had found it helpful to remind himself that he had faults and drawbacks, to help balance out any dissatisfaction with his wife.

IDEALIZING YOUR PARTNER

The absence of narcissism and related patterns of egotism doesn't mean low self-esteem. It simply means not trying to maintain an inflated view of how great you are. Two humble people can get along well for much longer than a pair of narcissists can.

Although idealizing yourself may be counterproductive, idealizing your partner can be good. When people fall in love, they often have an idealized image of their partner. This is not entirely accidental. Early in courtship, people are often on their best behavior. This helps the partner to see them at their best.

There is a popular contrary opinion, which says idealizing one's partner is bad and that the best foundation for a strong relationship is to understand each other accurately and honestly. Indeed, one of the motives behind the quest for self-knowledge is to confirm what one already believes about oneself (self-verification), and this can be extended to assuming people want their partners to know them accurately. If your partner idealizes you, there is the ongoing risk that the partner might someday discover what you are really like and then cease to love you. If he or she loves you despite knowing your worst faults, you can be confident the love will last.

These competing theories were tested on a sample of 121 young dating couples in Canada that had established relationships (about a year and a half, on average). They were followed up for another full year (Murray & Holmes, 1997). By comparing how the individuals rated themselves with how their partners rated them, the researchers could assess which ones were idealizing each other and which ones were seeing each other fairly accurately. Idealization won the contest. The more the couples idealized each other, the happier they were with the relationship and the less likely they were to break up. Their doubts about the relationship and conflicts with each other diminished. Impressively, people's self-views changed for the better when their partners idealized them, as if they came to accept and believe the positive image their partner held of them (see also Murray, Holmes, & Griffin, 1996a, 1996b).

The seeming triumph of idealization over self-verification led to some thoughtful reconsideration of the consistency motive. Surely, it must offer some advantage to have your spouse know you accurately. One resolution pointed out that the idealization in this study was global, whereas self-verification is most useful at a highly specific level. For example, if you are terrible at cooking, or playing guitar, or remembering errands, would you really want a spouse to think you are good at those things? You want your spouse to think you are a wonderful person overall, but dealing with the demands of daily life may go better if your partner does know your specific limitations, and vice versa.

LOVING SELF, LOVING OTHERS

One of the grand clichés from recent decades is that you must love yourself in order to love others. But is this true? Do self-love and other-love really go together? Taking a hard look at this idea as a rigorous scientific hypothesis raises immediate doubts. For example, women have slightly lower self-esteem than men on average, but does that mean women are less able than men to love their families?

Narcissists are worth a close look. Narcissism is a personality trait based on self-love. It is named after the character from Greek mythology who fell in love with his own reflection in the water. If self-love empowers loving others, then narcissists should be among the best lovers.

The leading authority on this issue is W. Keith Campbell. His 2005 book *When You Love a Man Who Loves Himself* offered a dispiriting picture of (male) narcissists as husbands and boyfriends. To be sure, they are great lovers at first, and so many of them are highly successful at attracting sexual and romantic partners. Charming, self-confident, exciting, good-looking, and well-dressed, exuding an aura of power and success, these men seem like dreamboats.

But in the long run the relationship does not go well. Narcissists love themselves first, and that interferes with loving others. A narcissistic man regards his partner as a status symbol. He likes to show off his conquests, but making sacrifices for her does not appeal to him. He may become controlling and aloof. His commitment is shallow, and if a better partner comes along, he will readily ditch the old in favor of the new. Ultimately, narcissists use other people for the narcissists' advantage and ends. After a while, many narcissists become bullying and manipulative, intent on dominating the relationship. Male narcissists have more sex partners but fewer long-term romantic relationships than other men. Probably the same is true for narcissistic women. Self-absorbed people have difficulties with commitment and mutual respect, and thus with good long-lasting relationships. As Campbell puts it in a more recent book, "Narcissists want to be loved, but they're not as interested in loving back or reciprocal emotional support" (Campbell & Crist, 2020, p. 117).

One common pattern is that the narcissist initially seeks admiration from the romantic conquest, and so the early stages glow with positive feeling. Once the conquest is complete and the relationship has stabilized, the narcissist no longer gets much satisfaction from it and may instead compete with the partner or even seek satisfaction by putting down the partner in order to make him- or herself feel superior.

What narcissists seem to want most of all is to be admired. Narcissism is not simply having a high opinion of oneself, but rather it is the desire to have a highly favorable image of self in both one's own and other people's minds (Morf & Rhodewalt, 2001). Narcissism seems to have its roots in parental overvaluation (Brummelman et al., 2015). That is, parents who frequently praise their children and treat them as superior to others end up with narcissistic offspring. Children need their parents' love, and when that love is linked to your being superior to everyone else, you come to think that being superior is both an essential part of who you are (fortunately) and an essential requirement for being loved and accepted in the future. As adults, narcissists are no different from anyone else in terms of wanting to be liked and loved—but they far exceed others in wishing to be admired.

Well, then, does that mean we should go to the opposite extreme? Will people with low self-esteem make the best partners? People with low self-esteem bring their own baggage and problems to relationships. A compelling research program by Sandra Murray and John Holmes has elucidated these. The core of the problem is that people with low self-esteem can't have faith in their partner's love and commitment. After all, if you think you are a low-quality person, why would someone as good as your partner want to stay with you? Your partner could easily find someone better.

Most people desire closeness but fear rejection (Murray, Holmes, & Collins, 2006). This poses a problem. If you plunge ahead into love in order to achieve this closeness, you make yourself vulnerable to rejection.

As covered in the chapter on self-esteem, people who think highly of themselves are more willing to take risks because they think things will work out fine. In a romantic context, this means not being afraid to love. (This may have been the basis for the cliché that loving yourself is a prerequisite for loving others.) In contrast, people with low self-esteem focus more on protecting themselves against risks and losses. The risks of giving in to love are what stand out to them.

In the thinking of Murray and colleagues, the tension between seeking closeness and avoiding rejection doesn't end once the relationship is established, even with marriage—rather, it continues, influencing the course of day-to-day interactions. If you feel there is some danger that your partner is not fully committed to you, you pull back your own emotional investment. This can be destructive, especially if your partner's signals were merely the result of his or her being preoccupied with work, or the baby, or some other issue. People with low self-esteem are extra-sensitive to any possible sign that a partner may be pulling away, which makes them pull away for real.

This process was demonstrated with an ingenious laboratory procedure (Murray et al., 2002). Couples came to the laboratory and were told the goal was to understand couples' thoughts and feelings. They were seated near each other but at separate tables and instructed not to speak to each other while filling out the questionnaire.

They were led to believe they were each filling out the same questionnaire, but in fact their questionnaires were different. One person's questionnaire asked for a list of the other partner's main faults and said it was fine to stop at one if that's all that came to mind. The other partner's questionnaire asked for a list of items in their apartment or dormitory room, with a minimum of 25. Thus, the first partner made a quick response about some fault of his or her beloved—and then sat and listened to the other partner writing and writing, seemingly making a very long list of the first partner's faults. This would likely be deeply disturbing.

Participants with both high and low self-esteem felt threatened by the thought that their partner had a long list of their faults to report. But they reacted differently. People with high self-esteem were a bit shaken, but they expressed high regard for their partner and for the relationship. In contrast, people with low self-esteem pulled back emotionally from the relationship. They reported more negative views of their partner (as well as of themselves) and rated the relationship less favorably, and as less close.

The bigger picture is that the self in a close relationship has two goals, which sometimes pull in opposite directions (Murray et al., 2006). One is to have a strong connection to the partner, which makes you dependent on him or her. The other goal is to protect the self. In a happy marriage, these goals go together. Feeling close to your partner and getting support from the partner protect the self against the stresses and problems of daily life. However, if the partner is critical or rejecting or bullying, then the two goals are in conflict. Do you try to cling more closely to the relationship, invest more of your love and energy and self into it? That increases your dependence and hence the risk of being hurt. It is hardly surprising that many people react by withdrawing emotionally from the relationship. Withdrawal reduces your dependence, and with it, your vulnerability to being hurt.

This is where low self-esteem is a problem. As the chapter on self-esteem shows, high self-esteem is a kind of resource that enables people to take risks and weather storms. Low-self-esteem people lack that resource. The threat of a rejecting or hostile partner is too much for them, and so they quickly shift into protecting themselves. They withdraw.

Low self-esteem is often a kind of basic insecurity. People with low self-esteem doubt themselves and fear that their partners will abandon them when their bad traits are found out. Any slight threat can set off this reaction, and often people with low self-esteem cope with it badly. Withdrawing emotionally, thinking bad things about the partner, and downgrading the relationship are not healthy strategies. Your low self-esteem also makes it harder for a partner to sustain an idealized view of you—and so your relationship lacks those mutually idealized views that normally strengthen and prolong a relationship.

Withdrawing isn't the only response people with low self-esteem have. Another is to seek reassurance. Now and then, this can be fine: If your partner seems critical or distant, you ask whether anything is wrong, and the partner assures you that you are still loved and appreciated. But doing it often quickly becomes tiresome. Indeed, other research has found that reassurance-seeking is one of the most annoying habits of depressed (and low-self-esteem) people, and a major reason why others avoid them (Joiner et al., 1999).

What's the bottom line? Perhaps the best partners are people with moderately favorable views of self, not narcissistic, not insecure. In a sense the crucial test is whose relationships last the longest. On this, I have not seen any convincing data. People with high self-esteem tend to rate their relationships as better, but then they rate most things about their lives as better, and objective data rarely confirm their positive self-appraisals.

BRINGING OUT THE BEST IN EACH OTHER

Let's return now to one point I mentioned briefly in covering the work by Murray and colleagues (1996a, 1996b). Being in a relationship with someone who sees the best in you apparently helps you start to take a more positive view of yourself.

Even better, the right partner might make you become a better person. There have long been suspicions of this in the popular culture, mostly flowing from female support to male improvement. The theme of a troubled man being redeemed and elevated by the love of a good woman has run through countless novels over the centuries. Far less often have novels suggested that a troubled heroine benefits from the love of a good man.

The Michelangelo Phenomenon

Recent research has supported the idea that spouses and lovers can make each other better. This has come to be known as the "Michelangelo phenomenon," based on the sculptor Michelangelo's comment that the sculptor does not so much create something new but release the potential that is already inside the stone (Finkel, 2009; Rusbult, Finkel, & Kumashiro, 2009). The ideal is that spouses help each other to fulfill the best potentialities that lie inside each other.

What is new and important about the Michelangelo phenomenon is the contrast with seeing goal pursuit as mainly something individuals do on their own. The traditional view is no doubt rooted in psychology's habit of thinking in terms of the individual mind. Individuals have goals, pursue them, succeed and fail. But actual life is heavily interpersonal, and the self is not a solitary enterprise so much as an adaptation for social life. Yes, you have your goals and ideals. Your romantic partner may be indifferent to these. Or indeed, the partner may oppose your goals, blocking you from reaching them. But if you have chosen well or are lucky, your partner will be an ally who will actually and substantially help you along your way toward those goals.

Just having your partner see you as similar to your ideals, or as moving toward them, is helpful. The most helpful partners not only hold these views but also actively do things to help you move toward them. Your partner might encourage you in taking up your exercise program and getting fit. Your partner might listen to your presentation and offer suggestions for improvement. If you need to change your diet for health reasons, your partner might change along with you.

The Michelangelo phenomenon offers a useful bridge between the competing theories of whether it is best for partners to see each other accurately (at least, as they see themselves) or in positive, idealized fashion. Both have a place. You must have some realistic understanding of what your partner is like and what is possible, but you must also see and appreciate the potential. If you understand both, you can be most helpful.

The Michelangelo researchers maintained an important distinction between their effect and the so-called Pygmalion phenomenon, named after a play by George Bernard Shaw. In both the Michelangelo and the Pygmalion phenomena, someone tries to mold the partner into someone better. The difference is who decides what is "better." In the Pygmalion phenomenon, Mary seeks to mold John according to what Mary thinks he could and should become. In the Michelangelo phenomenon, Mary seeks to mold John according to what John himself wishes to become. There are certainly plenty of cases of each, especially when people think they know what is best for their partner.

The difference matters, however. Pygmalion-type couples suffer assorted problems, indeed both at the level of the individual and at the level of the couple (the relationship). The process may do more harm than good. Trying to mold your partner into the person you think he or she should be is not generally a promising or positive approach, hard as it may be to refrain from pointing out specific areas where you think improvement is needed. (Your partner calls this "nagging.") In contrast, Michelangelo-type couples benefit, again both individually and as a couple. Mold your partner into the person your partner wants to become.

Avoiding the Negative

Consider for a moment the flip side of that crucial job of bringing out the best in each other (e.g., Finkel, 2019). What brings out the worst between intimate partners, and how can that be avoided? What should the executive self do to improve relationship outcomes? There are many things you can do to improve your relationship. But perhaps such advice misses the mark. The first and foremost duty of the executive self is to avoid the negative (Tierney & Baumeister, 2019). To strengthen the relationship, reducing bad things will help more than increasing the good things.

Long-married couples will often tell interviewers and adult children that their relationship has improved year by year. This is probably the result of self-flattering illusions and selective memory. Researchers who actually track couples year by year find almost none who actually show that pattern (e.g., Sprecher, 1999; VanLaningham et al., 2001). Some couples stay about the same. Others go downhill. The key to long-term relationship success is therefore to stay among the happy few whose marital satisfaction remains about the same, as opposed to the group that goes downhill. In other words, a successful marriage avoids the negative factors that ruin satisfaction.

In marriage, as in life, bad is stronger than good. A good marriage needs plenty of good things, but the top priority is to minimize the bad ones. This is where the executive function comes in. If you can avoid saying nasty or hurtful things, or doing other negative things, your relationship has a much better chance to be one of the happy ones. Inevitably, sometimes you will feel angry, upset, frustrated, but this is where good self-control helps stop you from saying anything damaging, or from doing something abusive or destructive. Indeed, research suggests that destructive responses to destructive actions are statistically powerful causes of marital deterioration. In plainer terms, things go downhill fast when one person responds negatively to negative acts by the other as in a nasty argument or fight. Everyone is negative now and then, but you need to stop being negative and dumping on your partner before your partner starts reciprocating. And if it's your partner who is being the negative one, and you are loyally enduring it, you need to say something to the effect of, "I know you're having a hard time, but I've nearly run out of sympathy and patience, so I'll need you to stop soon." Ideally, you and your partner have already discussed this pattern, and so your partner can take this to heart and stop the negativity before serious damage is done.

Winning an argument (or just getting your way) at the cost of damage to the relationship fits the formula we saw for self-destructive behavior: short-term gain with long-term cost. It may be tempting to think you can make it up to your partner another time, and things will go back to the lovely way they were. The data suggest they won't. Self-control has much value for close relationships, but one of its biggest contributions is to avoid the hurtful words and destructive actions in the first place.

To put this more positively: The way to have the best possible relationship is to avoid the negative. Remember, the best thing is for your partner to see you in an idealized way, as the best you can be. The executive self should choose behaviors that live up to your partner's best image of you. If both partners do that, the relationship has a much improved chance to be long, strong, and mutually satisfying.

KEY POINTS

- When dealing with friends, people tend to have a more modest, self-deprecating style, unlike when dealing with strangers.
- Humility is a boon to relationships.
- Idealizing your partner can be good.
- Narcissists and those with low self-esteem have problems in relationships.
- The self in a close relationship has two goals: (1) to have a strong connection and (2) to protect the self from harm.
- The Michelangelo phenomenon is when partners help each other fulfill their own best potentialities.
- To have the best possible relationship, avoid the negative.

PART SIX

PROBLEMS OF SELF

CHAPTER 24

Problems of the Modern Self

There are multiple problems with the modern self. Some of them concern difficulty in knowing the self, while others hamper the operation of the self. Let's consider them in turn.

PROCESSES UNDERMINING SENSE OF SELF

The brain creates the self to enable the body to survive and flourish in a complex social system that is based on roles and identities. Over the centuries, as society has become more complex, the process of creating and sustaining a self has become more difficult (Baumeister, 1986, 1987).

The things that once provided a solid definition of who a person is have ceased to do so, through two processes. First, they have ceased to matter (i.e., they became trivial). Second, even if they still matter, they have become changeable, so they aren't as effective at stitching together a coherent self across time. Consider a few of the key changes across the last dozen centuries:

- *Gender.* Through most of history, whether you were male or female (there were very few other options) made a huge difference in your life path. Modern societies have tried to create the same sets of opportunities for both genders, so whether you are male or female matters much less than in the past. Despite the outpouring of rhetoric about gender wars, modern society has trivialized gender, as compared to the past. Similar efforts are under way in many modern societies to

317

reduce the defining importance of race and ethnicity so that, again, all life paths and opportunities are available to everyone.

• *Social rank and class.* Traditional, rigid societies kept people in their place, but social mobility has enabled people to change in either direction. There have also been many efforts to offer more opportunities to people in lower classes. Indeed, IQ tests were developed in order to increase the educational and work opportunities for smart low-class people. Thus, social class has been destabilized and somewhat trivialized.

• *Marriage.* Marriage has often been a lifetime commitment, but in the modern world divorce is widely available, and many people churn through multiple marriages, with spates of single life in between. Although marriage is still a stabilizing influence on identity, it is not nearly as stable as it once was.

• *Religion.* Religious affiliation continues to be an important aspect of identity for many people, but both destabilization and trivialization have reduced its import from what it was in the Middle Ages. Discrimination based on religion has largely been outlawed, so people with different faiths have the same career options. Contrast this with medieval Europe, in which Jews were barred from many professions, while Christians were often unable to participate in banking (as money lenders). Having no religion is also accepted. People can and do change their religions rather freely. Thus, religion has also been destabilized and trivialized.

None of this is to say that religion, gender, and the like have become irrelevant to identity or self-concept. But their importance for channeling a person into a given pathway in life (and keeping that person from changing to another path!) has been greatly reduced. The long-term trend has been increased tolerance for allowing individuals to change. Religion, gender, class, and marriage do not guarantee lifelong unity of self as well as they once did. Even if you stay in the same religion or marriage, you know you could have changed.

These changes made self-knowledge more difficult because the previously simple and clear things that people knew about themselves became changeable and lost importance for making life decisions. They also affected the operation of the individual self, which needed new kinds of information on which to base its choices and actions.

Medieval people knew who they were, and all their friends and neighbors knew it, too. Identity was solidly based on objective, unchanging facts, many of which were there at birth. But over the centuries, the defining features of identity that established once and for all who you were gradually became slippery, uncertain, and subject to change.

UNCONSCIOUS, HIDDEN ASPECTS OF SELF

It's bad enough to think that self-knowledge requires discovering facts and features that are hidden. But the difficulty of self-knowledge also increased over time. At the end of the Middle Ages, society began to believe increasingly that important parts of the self were hidden from view—hidden from others and then, increasingly, hidden even from oneself (Weintraub, 1978).

What were these hidden aspects of self? Abilities, talents, potentialities, even as-yet-unrealized creative ideas were among them. The 19th century's widespread interest in writers and artists was partly based on a sense that these individuals had fascinating depths of inner selfhood (Altick, 1965). In the 20th century, the idea was that creative inspirations originated deep in the unconscious mind. That is, the unconscious self of the artist presumably contained the seeds of his or her future creative works. Instead of an external source (the muse), the inner self now became the source of creative inspiration.

The hidden self might also contain personality traits, especially ones contrary to one's actions. In the Freudian era, the unconscious was seen as containing desires, impulses, feelings, and even thoughts, especially ones that the person was reluctant to acknowledge. Thus, it contained not just buried treasure (as with the artists) but purposefully concealed material. Full self-knowledge, if such a thing were even possible, would require the person to recognize things that he or she was highly motivated to avoid knowing. The most famous of these from the Freudian canon was the ostensible desire to have sex with one's mother or father. Countless people bowed to therapeutic wisdom and accepted that they had such desires even though they had never felt any such desire, let alone acted on it.

The separation of self from one's social roles was a big step in complicating the search for self. Once we separated the self from its public display, and from the sum of its roles in society, there was no way even to assess how thorough self-knowledge was. How much more buried treasure (or repressed nastiness) might remain?

SELF AS VALUE BASE

Thus far we have covered how the self has become more complicated and elusive and hence ever more difficult to know. Those developments have compounded the problems of knowing oneself. There is however another entire class of problems; we are expecting more from the self than our ancestors did.

This may seem like a double whammy, and in a sense it is. The self is both more important to know and harder to know. But probably the two are related. As the self takes on additional duties, it is expected to contain more and more buried treasures (Baumeister, 1986; see also Finkel, 2017).

For centuries, Western civilization was heavily infused with Christian religion. Ultimate questions about the meaning of life and the highest levels of human potential were answered in that context. Values were firmly grounded in God's plans and messages. The purpose of life was to get to heaven.

Christian faith has remained strong in many places, but society ceased to operate based on the assumption that we're pretty much all Christians and thus all children of the same god. Even for many believers, daily life and work lost some of the connection to religion. Meanwhile, religious faith became weaker for many, and some stopped believing altogether.

All this created something of a crisis as to the meaning and purpose of life, including what basic values should be consulted. The rise of individual selfhood during this time may have been pure coincidence, though I suspect not. In either case it was pressed into service to fill the gap in meaning. Knowing, cultivating, and fulfilling the self came to be understood as an important, valuable goal in life, at least in some of the leading and influential segments of society. Fulfilling the self stepped into the vacuum created by the retreat of religiosity.

The heavy increase in concern with self as a central value has had some consequences. In the 1970s (called the "me decade"), there was talk among serious scholars that Western civilization was becoming a "culture of narcissism" (Lasch, 1978). Since then, personality researchers have recorded a steady rise in scores in narcissism and self-esteem in major parts of the population (Twenge & Campbell, 2009; Twenge & Foster, 2010). But anxiety has gone up, too. On the face of it, the combination is paradoxical. A large survey of research found that anxiety and self-esteem are negatively correlated, rather substantially (−.5; Leary & Kowalski, 1995). Such a strong a relationship suggests that as one goes up, the other goes down. How can both go up at the same time, across a large society?

The anxiety may reflect the tenuousness of putting individual selfhood at the center of one's purpose in life. (To be sure, I suspect there are multiple causes behind the rise in anxiety.) People mostly draw meaning from things that go beyond the self, and especially things that will long outlast the self. Religion makes a good source of meaning in life because religion brings your life into the context of eternal things. Political causes and patriotism (country, ethnicity) likewise extend into the future beyond one's own life. Parenthood may combine self-love with a future beyond one's own life. But if your purpose in life is cultivation of your self, then your death mostly erases whatever meaning or value your life had.

One might predict that making the self the ultimate basis for value in life would simplify things by encouraging people to do whatever they felt like and to be selfish. Perhaps this has happened to some extent. Again, though, meaning and value are drawn from larger contexts, and the individual self as an end in itself lacks enduring value, given that the individual self will cease to exist upon death.

THE RISE AND FALL OF THE IDENTITY CRISIS

As briefly mentioned in Chapter 3, the term *identity crisis* did not exist until Erik Erikson began using it in the late 1940s. The term resonated with something people felt throughout society because it caught on and began to be used in all sorts of contexts. Erikson (1968) noted that Harvard's divinity school students advertised that they were going to hold a collective identity crisis one afternoon. The mass media embraced the term. When I began researching the self for my first book, early in the 1980s, identity crisis was a major research theme, and I spent a great deal of time mastering the research findings and even published an article trying to sort out the messy, complicated literature and impose some coherent structure on what was known (Baumeister, Shapiro, & Tice, 1985). My first book was titled *Identity*, and it did rather well because back then plenty of people (both researchers and ordinary citizens) wanted to know more about identity.

The whole notion of identity crisis got a boost in the 1970s with the notion of midlife crisis. Struggling to redefine oneself is not just an adolescent concern, though Erikson's observation that many teenagers have that struggle was legitimate. Around the age of 40, many people, perhaps especially men, also struggle. In the modern world, careers mean climbing the corporate ladder. Around age 40, a man either reaches the promised land, at least with a job that has a clear path to the top, or else he is shunted aside and can tell that he will not make it to the top (Levinson, 1978).

Ironically, both outcomes bring letdowns. For many years, life has been oriented toward a particular goal, and a sort of identity crisis emerges either way. If one reaches the goal, then one no longer has that goal. (Moreover, one has to recognize that reaching the goal will not bring happiness ever after. The roof still leaks, the spouse is annoying in the same old or maybe new ways, the kids have troubles and continue to disappoint. . . .) Meanwhile, the shunted aside men realize they will never reach the goal—and so they, too, lose their goal. (And the roof leaks for them as well.)

Attempting to make sense of a chaos of research findings, mostly stemming from well-intentioned but simple and weak research methods, we concluded it was necessary to distinguish two different kinds of identity crisis (Baumeister et al., 1985). Boiled down to the bare essentials, they are: too much versus not enough identity. The two kinds probably feel quite different.

Identity Deficit

"Not enough" identity is typically the plight of the adolescent identity seeker, the sort Erikson made prominent and famous. Choices have to be made, but there is not enough of a coherent understanding of self and world to make them. The male midlife crisis sufferer may also be in a not-enough situation because the goals that guided him for the past decade or two no longer apply. Either he reached them, or he learned that he won't—but in both cases, he needs a new vision of his purpose in life.

Identity deficit often involves exploring new things, including ideas and activities and kinds of relationship. There may be feelings of rebellion as well as indecisiveness. The person knows "I don't want that" but is slower to grasp what he or she does want. (This echoes the argument that there are false selves but no True Self.) Feelings of self-awareness, preoccupation with grand questions, confusion and discouragement alternating with passionate fascinations, and other such emotional roller-coaster patterns are common. The person may recognize the wish to make some identity commitments, while also being reluctant to give up some options and potentialities, which is precisely what commitment often requires.

Identity Conflict

Too much identity means inner conflict: the person has multiple roles, and they make conflicting demands. Identity conflict arises when people feel pulled in different directions. Someone who marries into a different religious faith may struggle to reconcile the old and new religions. Likewise, immigrants may seek to maintain the connection to their country of origin while embracing their new society. Even the adolescent identity crisis may take on more conflict than deficit, especially for girls. A possible reason is that girls do not reject their parents as strongly as boys do, and so the newly forming adult identity may clash with the filial identity. Meanwhile, during adulthood many women likewise have identity conflicts as they seek to have a full life with a rewarding career, an intimate marriage, and well-raised children.

Identity conflict can feel like being in an impossible situation, unable to meet the incompatible demands of the two identities. Exploration holds no appeal. The person wants to hide, not go out and try new things. Self-awareness brings guilt. There may be a pervasive sense of impending doom, and the person wishes to avoid action that will betray either side of the inner conflict.

Resolving Identity Crises

What resolves them? A full-on identity deficit crisis requires two major steps. First, one has to settle on which values one will use to guide one's life.

Second, one has to find the specific roles and commitments that will enable one to live by those values. If the identity crisis does not lead to serious questioning of basic values, the focus might be on the second one. A classic historical example of this was how young Christian men went through adolescence in America during colonial times (Greven, 1977). There was often a phase of adolescent rebellion, marked by various misbehaviors, including some sexual misdeeds (at least masturbation), drunkenness, and other "sins of youth" such as fighting. This was experienced as departing from the young fellow's Christian faith, and there may well have been some anti-religious behavior, such as taking the Lord's name in vain (swearing) and skipping church. In many cases this period ended with a powerful personal reawakening of religious faith, such as a conversion experience that brought the youth back into the fold. The Christian values were never really repudiated but just seemed impractical for the adolescent trying to control an adult's urges with a child's powers of self-control.

Identity conflicts are probably harder than identity deficits to resolve, and more upsetting. The solution does not require finding something new to incorporate into the self, but rather cutting out a part of the self. One has to accept the loss and move on. Sometimes there are possibilities for limited compromise. Sometimes the solution is enforced by the situation, but other times the person must find a way to make the choice. I would not like to bet on which of those is reliably more painful.

The Retreat of Interest in Identity Crisis

Today, one rarely hears anyone mention identity crises. A few intrepid souls have continued to collect and publish data based on the research methods that were popular decades ago. But most researchers have lost interest. The term *identity* does not dominate symposium titles at major conferences, as it did in the 1970s and 1980s.

That is a rough summary of what psychologists learned about identity crises. As to why the phrase has largely disappeared from public discourse, one can only speculate. Several factors strike me as potentially relevant.

First, the rebellion aspect is less necessary than it was. Parents have become far less authoritative than they once were. Observing families in public today, I see fathers kissing their sons and sometimes even apologizing to them. These actions would have been unthinkable in my youth. Young men no longer have to defy their fathers to become men themselves. Indeed, more and more young men grow up without fathers.

Second, indefinite postponement is much more possible than in the past. Half a century ago, one's adult roles were largely selected by one's early 20s. People married early and soon had children, and the man at least had to have a steady job to support the family. It was common to work for decades for the same company. Now, people put off marrying till much later. Job changes have become common, even expected, and even sweeping changes in career direction happen frequently. College takes longer than 4 years, and many a college graduate moves back into the parental home. Finalizing one's adult identity can be postponed into one's 30s, so the whole process is less urgent and less compelling. The multiple career paths, plus the vast expansion in women's careers, have probably blurred the timing of what used to be called midlife crises also. These, too, can be allowed to drag on for longer.

Third, the idea that answers lie buried inside the self is no longer the occasion for inner search. Today's young people live in a world characterized by online activity (Twenge, 2017), which puts much more emphasis on the outer, public image of self than on inner processes. Social media allow people to fashion their image however they wish, though others may criticize. Perhaps today's adolescents may be preoccupied with how they present to the world, rather than what can be found buried deep inside their minds. As to which of these pursuits (obsessing over a social media profile vs. navel-gazing) is more usefully constructive in the long run as opposed to which is the bigger waste of time and energy, well, it is hard to choose.

A more intriguing theory has been put forward by a trailblazing scholar of generational change, Jean Twenge (2006). To paraphrase her view, people have become increasingly fascinated with themselves over the decades. In the middle of the 20th century, they began to grasp the problems that came with that (hence all the talk of identity crises). Those who came along at the end of the century did not go backward so much as farther forward. They were not baffled by the newly discovered difficulty and importance of being themselves. They took that for granted. In the 21st century, the pervasive concern with online social interactions did not lessen identity crises so much as shift the focus outward. One doesn't have time or energy to worry about finding out what lies buried deep inside one's True Self. Rather, one has to worry about what dozens of peers and hundreds of strangers will think based on seeing one's social media profile or blog.

A last possibility is that identity crises are still happening but have changed their names. The term *identity* has gradually been taken over by other usages. Today, it is used to refer more to group identification than individual self-understanding. The terminology for finding oneself got caught up in issues of gender identity, referring to people who are reluctant to accept the roles associated with their birth gender. Racial and ethnic identities took on new importance in self-definition because many people rely on their group identification to campaign for more respect and resources to be given to their group. So-called identity politics have become a feature of the national conversation. As the term *identity* finds frequent usage in that context, it perhaps lost its suitability to describe the struggle for self-definition among young people.

The self seeks acceptance in society, and that includes respect. How much respect is automatically owed each person, and how much depends on the person's actions to earn respect, is an ongoing problem in society, and there may be no one objectively correct answer. But the quest for respect is deeply rooted in the self.

KEY POINTS

- Things that once provided a solid definition of who you were have ceased to do so. First, they have ceased to matter. Second even if they matter, they have become changeable.

- The importance of gender, social rank and class, marriage, and religion has become greatly reduced for defining one's self.

- Self-knowledge came to mean discovering increasingly hidden aspects of self.

- Erikson's observation that many teenagers struggle to define themselves (identity crisis) was legitimate. Around age 40 many, perhaps especially men, also struggle (midlife crisis).

- Not enough identity (an identity deficit) is typically the plight of the adolescent identity seeker.

- Too much identity means inner conflict. The person has multiple roles, and they make conflicting demands.

CHAPTER 25

The Stress of Self, and Some Escape Routes

This chapter continues the inquiry into the problems of selfhood by suggesting there may be something stressful at the self's core. Some people find ways of reducing the stress through methods that help them forget themselves.

The idea that selves can be stressful dawned on me slowly. My first clue was the result of an accidental detour. I was doing research for a book on life's meaning, so I was looking for research on different kinds of meanings, which I hoped to find by learning about people with quite unusual lives. I thought perhaps people who enjoy being tied up and spanked must have very interesting lives. Within the first couple of hours in the library (before the Internet), I realized that sadomasochistic sexuality is not rich with deep existential meanings.

Meanwhile, I realized that the data on sexual masochism posed a serious challenge to our theories about the self (Baumeister, 1988, 1989a). Most theories assumed that the self is for avoiding pain and seeking pleasure—but masochists seemed to seek out pain. Most theories assumed that the self is motivated to gain control over events, but masochists seek to lose control, which indeed is the essential appeal of being tied up. Most theories emphasize that the self seeks positive esteem, but masochists desire to be embarrassed and humiliated, reduced in sexually symbolic ways to extremely low status. I came to see that these are not merely misleading appearances. Instead, they were the essence of what masochism is all about, namely obliterating the normal self from awareness. One forcibly replaces the everyday self with one that is totally incompatible, such as meekly accepting spankings and other humiliations. Pain destroys meaning, as explained in a philosophy book, *The Body in Pain,* by Elaine Scarry (1985). The self is rich with meaning and operates by meaning, so destroying meaning helps block out the self.

Popular conversation mistakenly confuses masochism with self-destructive behavior. We joke that someone is a masochist based on volunteering for some unpleasant duty, which in fact is usually motivated by trying to contribute to the group. But masochism is not about harm to self, and in fact S&M groups are extremely careful about not causing any injury while making use of limited pain to generate sexual excitement. Instead, it is about erasing the self. As far as I could make out, participating in masochistic sex does no long-term harm, nor does it bring any long-term benefit. It is neutral with respect to anything lasting. That's one reason it was irrelevant to life's meaning, which is about stitching individual daily events into long-term narratives.

One sign that masochism is an escape from a burdensome self is that it is more common among elite, successful, thriving members of society than among its downtrodden. The point was made in an intriguing way by a team of researchers who hit upon the clever idea of writing a juicy book about the call girls in Washington, D.C. They managed to meet and interview an assortment of them. Disappointingly, these call girls were not much different from sex workers anywhere else. But as luck would have it, the researchers found out plenty about their clients, who comprised some of the most powerful men in the world's most powerful society, including U.S. senators, congressmen, and federal judges. The researchers shifted their focus from the prostitutes to their clients (Janus, Bess, & Saltus, 1977).

One of the most striking findings was how much the clients wanted to be dominated. Some people like spanking as part of sex, and the prostitutes catered to these wishes. But requests to be spanked outnumbered requests to deliver a spanking, by about 8 to 1. Thus, some of the world's most powerful, prestigious, and influential men found sexual excitement in being spanked like naughty schoolboys of centuries past.

Indeed, humiliation was at least as appealing to these men as the pain of spanking. (Presenting one's bare bottom for a call girl to chastise is a posture of submissive defeat.) Why would a rich, powerful, successful man allow himself to be treated in such a degrading manner?

The stress of self is high for such men. Politicians must present themselves as impeccable human beings: virtuous, caring, intelligent, competent, responsive. They win elections by having a public self that is superior to that of an opponent, who is also trying to come across as an admirable leader. And here's the catch: Their effort to construct this shining reputation for themselves goes right into the teeth of forces that are eagerly seeking to tear them down, from the media who love to expose scandals and sordid misdeeds among politicians, to their opponents whose path to success involves shredding the other politician's good name and character.

Meanwhile, prostitutes who cater to lower-class clients are not often asked for such services. Being put down, humiliated, and deprived of control is hardly an escape for people who lack power and status in everyday life. But the people who struggle to maintain a super-self periodically want to lose themselves. This is an important clue: Maintaining the modern self, especially an exceptionally positive version, is stressful.

A powerful man cannot be himself when he is kneeling on the floor and licking the toes of a call girl. These actions are so contrary to his everyday identity that to perform them releases him from his normal self. For a brief time, he ceases to carry the burden of maintaining a larger-than-life self. The situation enables him to let go of self.

Before delving deeper into the stress of self, let's consider some of the other escapes.

WHY *NOT* BE A SELF?: PATTERNS OF ESCAPE

Each human being puts plenty of mental and physical energy into maintaining an identity. Each person is highly self-aware as a means of adjusting various features of self to meet external demands (and inner goals, which are often selected from external offerings). Yet sometimes, people seek to escape self-awareness, or to transform themselves so thoroughly that their ordinary self-awareness becomes temporarily impossible (as in masochism).

Obviously, the brain must do a great deal of work to operate a self, and this must be kept up hour after hour, year after year. If the body produces the self to comply with external demands, then that must sometimes be stressful. It may pay off in the long run, but there are still costs and struggles along the way.

Probably the definitive treatment of problems of selfhood is Leary's *The Curse of the Self* (2004a). He records many problems that come from excessive egotism, self-reflection, and preoccupation with self. As he says, many spiritual regimens undertake to get rid of self as a step toward happiness and enlightenment. How far these disciplines really get rid of selfhood is debatable, as discussed in Chapter 4. Moreover, it is doubtful that a society could function without selves. My take, then, is that the self is not a wholesale curse, but rather a mostly beneficial adaptation that does have some costs and excesses.

WAYS OF ESCAPING SELF-AWARENESS

People do many things to escape from self-awareness (Baumeister, 1991a). They are not uniformly harmful, by any means, though some are. Here are some examples.

Suicide

At the destructive extreme is suicide. I spent several years reading a vast research literature, trying to understand why people kill themselves. There are many pathways and reasons, and no one theory will capture them all, but still there are dominant patterns. Typically, something bad has happened, and the person blames him- or herself. This makes self-awareness acutely unpleasant because one is intensely aware that the self is far worse than the standard prescribes. One feels oneself to be a failure, a disappointment to others, poor at one's job, undesirable as a romantic partner, or in some other way bad. The presuicidal state is often marked by efforts to avoid thinking about the self, such as by trying to focus narrowly on simple, basic, concrete events like making a sandwich or doing the laundry. But the mind fails at shutting out these negative thoughts about the self. The suicide is not usually some grand effort to punish oneself for having failed or misbehaved. Rather, it is an attempt to *make it all stop*, put an end to the misery of self-awareness colored as bad. The suicide attempt is an escalation of the efforts to avoid being aware of oneself as bad. Oblivion is what is sought (Baumeister, 1990, 1991a).

Suicidal people are not simply losers or incompetent persons. On the contrary, they are often people who have been successful and expect a great deal from themselves. Poor people do not kill themselves at higher rates than rich people—but rich people who abruptly become poor do kill themselves at higher rates. In other words, it is not a matter of being poor all your life that causes suicide, but becoming poor after you have been rich. In parallel, suicidal college students have been found to actually have higher than average grade point averages in college—except for the most recent semester, when their grades dropped below average. They were doing well and can't accept suddenly doing badly, especially letting everyone down.

Alcohol

Alcohol was already discussed in connection with addiction (Hull, 1981). Part (not all) of the appeal of alcohol is undoubtedly due to its effectiveness at blotting out self-awareness. When people stop comparing themselves to standards, they become less inhibited, less worried about the consequences of their actions, for good and ill. There are two main types of reasons for drinking: one is to enhance a positive feeling, such as in celebration, and the other is to shut down or minimize bad feelings. Alcohol is abundantly used for both purposes. People drink when celebrating and socializing. And they drink when trying to cope with bad feelings, such as from a humiliating failure or rejection. Crucially, Sher concluded, alcohol use is generally more of a problem for people who use it to escape and minimize than for those who use it to enhance. Alcohol can be quite harmful, though plenty of people manage to avoid most of the harm by using alcohol in small doses and only occasionally.

Meditation

If suicide is a highly destructive way of escaping from self-awareness, meditation is a largely beneficial one. Meditation trains the mind to focus on the here and now, with low levels of meaning. In that respect it achieves similar changes to what masochism and alcohol intoxication do. Writings about meditation often emphasize loss of self, dissolving the ego, and similar points.

Meditation probably does not appeal to those who wish to forget themselves because of some recent personal disaster. Setting the mind without anything to focus on leaves room for intrusive, unbidden thoughts precisely about the disaster.

But for people who wish to strengthen their mind while getting rid of the stress of self, meditation is a powerful tool. The beginner's exercise in Zen meditation involves focusing attention on breathing. You breathe normally and count breaths up to 10 and then start over. Breathing is one of the simplest, most basic human activities. It happens constantly, and it evokes no meaning or emotion (unless for some reason your ability to breathe is temporarily blocked!). Focusing your conscious mind on breathing thus strips away meaning, identity, past and future, emotion, worries, and much else.

Binge Eating

Many individuals find solace in eating, and for some troubled ones, this develops into what has become recognized as an eating disorder. These people have binges in which they consume large amounts of food in a brief period of time. Some also then induce vomiting (bulimia). Binge eating conforms to the same psychological processes of getting rid of self-awareness as we saw in suicide, masochism, and alcohol (Heatherton & Baumeister, 1991). Attention becomes narrowly focused on the here and now in a relatively meaningless activity, involving simple bodily processes (in this case biting, tasting, chewing, and swallowing). Immersing oneself in this simple, attention-grabbing activity blots out the more meaningful aspects of self, which are the ones that bring concern and anxiety. Studies suggest that the people most prone to binge eating are ambitious, high-achieving, self-critical young women. They have high standards and worry they are not living up to them. Eating everything in the fridge blots out those worries and anxieties for a while.

Materialism

Some people escape from self-awareness by immersing themselves in buying things. The term *materialism* has multiple meanings, and the one meant here is the belief that buying and acquiring valuable things is an important goal in life that can increase happiness, as well as indicate success in life that others will recognize and appreciate. In practice, people who hold that attitude tend to be dissatisfied with their lives, and their endless quest to buy more things does not bring lasting happiness. Still, the project of shopping and buying provides temporary escape from troublesome or negative views of self (Donnelly et al., 2016).

Alien Abduction

Probably the weirdest phenomena on which I have published in my long, strange career involve being abducted by alien scientists onto flying saucers. I had the good fortune of working with Leonard Newman, at the time a postdoctoral fellow. He had compiled vast amounts of published information about people who claimed to have had such experiences. We assumed that all these reports were false, as neither of us believed in flying saucers. But the people who furnished these reports mostly believed sincerely in them. So, the question became, why would people come to have the false belief that this had happened to them?

The abduction reports had powerful resemblances to the other escapes from self (Newman & Baumeister, 1996). They interrupted the person's normal life. Many had masochistic overtones, such as being subjected to painful medical tests and humiliating sexual experiences.

COMMON THEMES AMONG ESCAPES FROM SELF

Across these diverse ways of forgetting the self, there are some common general patterns. Not every escape fits all of them, of course. The process can be summarized in six steps (Baumeister, 1990, 1991a).

- *High standards, falling short.* Typically, people seeking escape have high ambitions and expectations, sometimes shading into perfectionism. They may judge themselves harshly or feel others do. As a result, they often have the sense that they are not doing as well as they would like. In some cases, such as suicide, the episode is often sparked by a major problem or disappointment.

- *Self-blame.* If one falls short of standards or experiences a problem, but blames this on external circumstances, then there is no need to escape self-awareness. Escape is motivated by feeling that oneself is responsible for the problems.

- *High (and unpleasant) self-awareness.* From being responsible for the recent problems, the person develops a heightened awareness of self as bad. It's no fun to go through your days with an ongoing, pervasive sense of being a terrible person.

- *Feeling bad.* Frequently being aware of yourself as somehow bad or inadequate can give rise to unpleasant emotions.

- *Mental shifting.* The person responds to feeling badly about him- or herself by shifting to a kind of low-level thinking. It focuses on concrete things that are largely devoid of meaning and emotion. It emphasizes the here and now rather than future and past. All this tends to avoid reminders of problems and worries, and in that way the emotional distress is kept at bay. Open-minded, creative thinking is kept to a minimum.

- *Consequences and side effects.* This narrow, here-and-now focus has assorted effects beyond shutting out emotion and meaningful thought. Careful, rational analysis and consideration of long-term consequences diminish. The person may lose sensible concerns and inhibitions, thereby become willing to engage in strange, unusual activities (weird sexual activities, even self-harm). Yet, there is often a kind of passivity, even fatalism, linked to not caring about the long run. Failing to question odd ideas can make the person vulnerable to irrational, even bizarre beliefs. (Remember the space aliens.) Sometimes the mind starts to wander back to important, meaningful topics, which brings back the emotional distress, followed by redoubled efforts to maintain the escape.

THREE REASONS TO ESCAPE FROM SELF

The brain works hard to operate, create, and sustain an identity in the social system. Why does it sometimes relish an interruption from this activity? I have three answers.

- *Coping with a damaged identity.* Coping with a spoiled or damaged identity is one reason to escape the self, correct as far as it goes. Suicides often follow from some personal disaster that reflects badly on the self. Eating and drinking binges also seem more likely to occur after some major setback or personal failure. None of this is terribly surprising: People want to forget themselves when the self is loaded with unpleasant thoughts and feelings.

● *Having a good time.* A second reason for escaping self-awareness is more positive than the other two. Sometimes people wish to shed their inhibitions in order to have a good time. Indeed, it is arguable that loss of self-awareness is inherently pleasant. Meditators supposedly achieve states of intense mental bliss from transcending their own ego. The very term *ecstasy* derives from Greek roots meaning "to stand outside oneself," and many supreme moments of spiritual achievement are linked to losing concern and even awareness of one's separate, individualized, everyday self. Nevertheless, the idea that losing self-awareness directly produces bliss goes beyond the data.

● *Getting a break from stress.* The most provocative and interesting answer is that maintaining the self is stressful. Stress research established long ago that having an occasional break from stress substantially reduced its negative effects (e.g., Weiss, 1971a, 1971b, 1971c). This has been shown with stresses that have little to do with problems of selfhood. The combat stress that caused men to break down puzzled military leaders in the two world wars, who called it "shell shock" (World War I) and "combat stress" (World War II). (*Posttraumatic stress disorder* [PTSD] is the currently favored term, though that typically refers to a specific trauma rather than the accumulation of stress.) There was no specific event that caused it but rather the accumulation of being exposed to bombardment and other dangers day after day, with no letup. Gradually, the generals discovered that giving soldiers an occasional break, back behind the lines where they were safe, greatly reduced the frequency of these nervous breakdowns. Later on, psychologists found similar effects with laboratory rats and monkeys (Brady, 1958; Weiss, 1971a, 1971b, 1971c). Constant stress produced ulcers, but with occasional safe periods, the ulcers did not develop even if the total amount of stress was the same.

The same logic may apply to the stress of self as to other kinds of stresses. As I said, the brain has to work hard to maintain a self, and so a periodic break from it reduces the stressful effects.[/bpl]

THE STRESS OF SELF

The stress of self is important to keep in mind. Not everyone suffers from it, but some people will struggle and suffer considerably. There is reason to think it has gotten worse in recent centuries and even in recent decades. Sexual masochism, for example, is essentially a modern, Western phenomenon (though also found in Japan). One scholar who wrote a history of sex noted that almost all the sexual practices known today were found in ancient Chinese sex manuals—with the lone exception of sexual masochism (Tannahill, 1980).

Indeed, recent work by Jean Twenge (2017) has concluded that today's young people are under more stress than previous generations, all tied to how much time they spend online. There can be various explanations to why spending time online is stressful and causes psychological problems, but the stress of self is prominent. Adolescents everywhere worry about fitting in, but maintaining an online presence has no breaks. By way of contrast, when I was in high school, I certainly worried about how others viewed me, but when I went home, there was no need to deal with peer interactions until the next morning at school. In contrast, today's young people have Facebook profiles and other online activities that can go on around the clock, so at any time one could be working on one's public presentation of self (and others might be evaluating you at any time of day or night). Like the shell-shocked soldiers of World War I, they never get a respite.

The self may be a burden. This is especially true for the modern self, now that modern life expects so much more of the self. People need to maintain a positive image and avoid looking bad. The Internet with its social media has compounded the problem, for adults as well as adolescents. A single moment of saying the wrong thing can ruin a person's image or reputation.

Internet anxiety aside, the conclusion is that the brain's efforts to create and maintain a self involve work, sometimes difficult and unpleasant work. It is the high-maintenance selves, often the most successful ones, that are often in need of escapes.

KEY POINTS

- The stress of self can be high, and sometimes people seek to escape self-awareness.

- Ways of escaping self-awareness include suicide, sexual masochism, meditation, alcohol, binge eating and bulimia, and materialism.

- Common patterns in seeking escape from self-awareness are: falling short of high standards, self-blame, unpleasant self-awareness, feeling bad, mental shifting, and vulnerability to irrational beliefs.

- Reasons to escape from self include coping with a damaged identity, having a good time, getting a break from stress.

- There is reason to think the stress of self has gotten worse in recent decades. Young people may be under more stress than previous generations, all tied to being online.

CHAPTER 26

Selves and Mental Illness

Just as brain researchers today learn how the brain functions normally by studying cases in which it fails to do so, we can garner insights about the normal self by studying abnormal ones. The research literature is vast and complicated. I will therefore just dip into it for a few useful insights.

Let's be clear: There is no intent here to explain mental illness. Rather, the limited goal is to learn something about how the self goes wrong and what that tells us more broadly about the self.

One intuitive theory about mental illness is that the self has some missing, damaged, or defective parts. Leading candidates for this might be delusions, that is, seriously mistaken views about the self. Indeed, public fascination with mental illness often centers on major delusions. But such cases of mistaken self-identity are quite rare and have relatively little to teach us.

Overall, mistaken views of self do not seem to be a major factor in mental illness. It is quite plausible that mistaken self-views are more symptoms than causes of affliction, or even, in the case of gender identity, may be normal and fine (especially if the person is happy). The mistakes mainly involve negatively biased views of self, which contrast to the favorably biased views of self enjoyed by mentally healthy and normal people (Taylor & Brown, 1988). Perhaps they are exaggerations of the virtues of modesty and humility, which are widely extolled and appreciated in society. This would fit Seligman's (1995) general comment that many forms of mental illness are simply exaggerations of what is healthy and desirable.

In any case, we do not learn much about the self from the link between some mental illnesses and holding a low opinion of oneself. Taylor and Brown made this point in their influential 1988 review: Normal, healthy minds tend toward moderately overestimating the quality of the self, and the lack of this self-flattering distortion is a cause or symptom of various afflictions. An earlier chapter documented the favorable distortions of self-views. This should not be seen as a major problem, but rather as part of how the mind functions effectively under normal circumstances.

THE POORLY ORGANIZED SELF

When researching this book, I came across an excellent compilation of writings by various authors on how the self is implicated in mental illness (Kyrios et al., 2016). The different chapters were written by different authors, with widely different theoretical backgrounds and different approaches to therapy. Yet, they converged on the conclusion that in mental illness, the problem often lies in how the self is organized. In plain terms, it's not a defective piece, but rather a defect in how the pieces are working together.

Indeed, the term *disorder* has become increasingly common as the psychiatric professional community continues to rename various mental illnesses. The literal meaning of *disorder* is a "failure of organization": something is not in the proper order.

Here are some of the key ways that the self suffers from failure of proper organization in various mental illnesses.

Bipolar Disorder

Formerly known as manic–depressive syndrome, bipolar disorder is an obvious first example of a divided self (Leitan, 2016). During difficult periods, the person compartmentalizes self-knowledge into good and bad versions of self. These are subjectively good and bad. Bipolar persons feel manic when the good self is prominent, although the manic self is often far from good in terms of how other people see it. The person feels depressed when the bad one takes over. Behavior changes accordingly. The theme here is that the person is unable to bridge the two different versions of self. For example, a minor event might activate some thought about a positive aspect of the self, which snowballs into a powerful sense of the self as possessing fabulous virtues and powers, and the person acts with supreme overconfidence. People in this state may resist therapy because they like their all-positive view of self and fail to see why they need help or adjustment. The positive one gets carried away, makes foolishly risky and costly decisions based on unjustified confidence and optimism. The all-good self or all-positive self is not an effective one.

The depressed self also may resist therapy because what's the point, it's all hopeless. Confidence is gone, energy is gone; the self loathes both itself and the rest of the world. Plus, it gets stuck dealing with the disasters stemming from the manic phase. It might seem nice to split oneself into the good and bad parts so that at least sometimes one could inhabit the all-good one. But that's often a road to disaster.

To be sure, people with bipolar disorder are not always in one or the other extreme state. They have periods when they feel more integrated, and these seem to go better. That underscores the point that the compartmentalization is the problem. It does however complicate the theory of self. The self is not always categorically split, just sometimes. Still, the pathology does invoke the divided self.

Posttraumatic Stress Disorder

Posttraumatic stress disorder (PTSD) is set off by a trauma. To be sure, most people who suffer traumas do not get PTSD. By some counts, post-traumatic growth is far more common that PTSD (see Calhoun & Tedeschi, 2013). The difference suggests some people are more vulnerable than others because the same sort of external crisis provokes different reactions in different people (Horowitz & Sicilia, 2016).

Vulnerability to PTSD is increased by weakness or deficiency in how the self is organized. People whose selves are not as coherently integrated are more likely than others to develop PTSD if a trauma happens.

A theme in many cases of PTSD is that the person has a new, damaged sense of self but wishes to restore or recover the version of self prior to the trauma. Dissociation, which again means splitting into parts, occurs in some cases, as does "depersonalization," which again indicates a loss of coherent sense of who one is. The traumatized self reorganizes its understanding of itself, along with how it functions, and the new organization does not work as well as the old. That is presumably because the new organization is aimed at protecting the self from recurring pain, rather than carrying out the normal functions of the self.

Obsessive–Compulsive Disorder

Obsessive–compulsive disorder (OCD) often revolves around a tension between the surface self and a hidden self that the person fears is bad (or at least might do bad things, such as harming others). Intrusive thoughts and worries are interpreted as revealing some of these important but hidden aspects of the self. Any negative aspect is a distressing sign that this hidden self is a terrible person. That produces anxiety, anger, pathological doubt, disgust, or other negative emotions. Hence, the obsessions or compulsions to make sure that the person did not make a mistake. Washing hands over and over, or checking repeatedly whether the lights are all turned off and the door is locked, are part of the struggle to keep the bad inner self from taking over. The person with OCD may even recognize that these reactions are irrational, but they help deal with the disturbing thoughts, which otherwise are overwhelming.

People suffering from OCD do not have a coherent sense of who they are, and they flounder among contradictory self-beliefs and a general uncertainty about whether they are good or bad. Perfectionism seems the only safe solution because if they do everything perfectly, then they are not bad after all. The perfectionism often takes on a moral aspect, too: the person is ever-vigilant against doing anything less than virtuous, and generally overcompensates for feared inner wickedness. Naturally, the quest for perfection is unrealistic, and the inevitable experiences of falling short of perfection fuel worries about the bad self (Ahern & Kyrios, 2016).

Depression

Depression often involves experiences that threaten the self's coherence and continuity (Luyten & Fonagy, 2016). The guilt and shame, self-loathing, despair, hopelessness, and other feelings undermine the chances for the depressed person to feel like a normal self, as a reasonably competent, good person would presumably feel. It is perhaps not the thoughts and cognitions themselves, but the process of thinking, that is where the basic problems lie—and those processes are what constitute the self. Like OCD sufferers, depressed people may adopt perfectionistic standards as a way of battling their own perceived faults and failings. Of course, the perfectionism leads to more failing because perfection is impossible to sustain. Depressed people may also come to understand themselves socially as dependent on other people, which undermines any sense of autonomy. Self-knowledge comes to be organized around two themes: dependency on others and self-criticism. These make a sad pair.

Dementia

In dementia, the right-now self continues to function reasonably well, but it loses its connection to time (Luyten & Fonagy, 2016). One's own past gradually disappears, as does the future, leaving one in the eternal present. Indeed, the person may mistake the present for a previous point in time. My father, when an old man living in Florida, would often think he was in Germany, the country where he was born, and would try to go to the *Bahnhof* (train station), though his Florida town did not even have one. His sister, my aunt, also got dementia. I later found out she would get in her car and drive to do an errand, but on the homebound freeway her mind would wander and she'd miss her exit and then drive another hundred miles before realizing her mistake. The right-now self enabled her to drive safely, and she had no accidents or tickets. But her awareness of the present as part of an ongoing story (driving home) was defective. The connections were lacking.

Social Anxiety Disorder

As the name implies, social anxiety disorder is mostly a problem with interpersonal relations, but even it has aspects of poor self-organization. One review observed that "all current cognitive conceptualizations of the disorder are based on the premise that individuals with social anxiety have maladaptive cognitive scheme[s] that activate negative beliefs" (Gregory, Peters, & Rapee, 2016, p. 96). That is, their troublesome ideas about themselves and about their social world are linked to unhappy, disturbing thoughts. As a result, many seemingly innocuous social interactions set off these miserable thoughts and feelings. The problem was not so much the existence of these thoughts in the mind but how they were connected so that ordinary events or interactions would evoke them.

Hoarding

Multiple disorders show an unfortunate pattern of organizing the self in which the value of the whole self is overly tied to one aspect or part of the self (Moulding et al., 2016). In hoarding disorder, for example, people compulsively collect and save items, to an excessive and irrational extent. The underlying dynamic seems to be that people endow these items with great power and value as vital parts of the self. It is not so much the items themselves that the person values, but the self to which they are symbolically linked. Hoarders, like others (and especially OCD sufferers, whose affliction is similar), lean toward perfectionism. The items they store up can represent possible future versions of self, which obviously discourages throwing them away.

Body Dysmorphic Disorder

A related pattern, body dysmorphic disorder, comprises wide-ranging dissatisfaction with one's physical body (Moulding et al., 2016). Here, too, the person equates the self with one particular aspect, in this case the body or even just a part of it. The person with this problem resorts to perfectionism to try to compensate for the feared inadequacy of the actual body.

Trichotillomania

A final version of the same problem, namely linking the whole self with one specific item or kind of thing, may underlie trichotillomania, which is a pattern of pathological hair-pulling. This time it is the hair that is equated with the shameful version of self. Pulling the hair somehow comes to help the person cope with feelings of shame, as if he or she is punishing or removing the bad version of self (Moulding et al., 2016).

Overinvesting one part or piece of the self is a clear flaw in how the self is organized. Most people can keep their hair in its place. When it comes to be a substitute for the whole self, or the bad parts of the self, and is punished for that, there is a problem. It is the flawed organization of self-understanding that is the problem.

Borderline Personality Disorder

Borderline personality disorder owes its name to the idea that these people were on the borderline of psychosis, and psychosis roughly means hallucinations and other disturbances in thinking. Failure of the unity project is evident in multiple aspects of borderline personality disorder, including chaotic and turbulent relationships with other people (Liotti & Farina, 2016). After all, other people want a reasonably stable relationship with a reliable, consistent person. They cannot relate effectively to someone who is highly unstable.

Views of self are not well integrated among borderline sufferers and may include some contradictory self-beliefs. Dissociation, which means detaching the self from its personal and emotional experiences, is a common feature, and indeed two scholars entitled their treatise on this disorder and the role of self in it as "painful incoherence" (Liotti & Farina, 2016). The person's understanding of self does not get properly integrated with daily experiences (nor with ongoing relationships). Compartmentalization is a familiar problem: Self-beliefs are not all forged into a common unity but kept in separate groupings.

Autism

In autism spectrum disorder, as with borderline personality disorder, we again find a mixture of two types of disorganization, one interpersonal, the other a failure to integrate beliefs about the self with experiences (Molnar-Szakacs & Uddin, 2016). Deficits in self-understanding show up in early and basic forms. Autistic children are slower than other children to recognize their own face in the mirror, though most get there eventually. Researchers have found that the standard self-reference effect is absent, or at least greatly reduced, among autistic adults. The self-reference effect means that people have better memory for things processed in relation to the self than other things, events, or stimuli, indicating that the self functions in part as a powerful memory "hook" (Rogers et al., 1977). Apparently, that hook does not work well in autism. Over time, this cuts them off from their own memories, so they lack a sense of their own past and the continuity of self across time. They also have trouble updating their self-beliefs based on recent experiences.

Autistic individuals are able to control their behavior and carry out activities, but they have some problems in connecting intentions to outcomes. The brain and mental processes associated with intention are complex, but they seem to have something to do with intention-shaping actions while giving rise to predictions about the results of one's actions. For example, to turn on the light, you reach for the switch and flick it, while your mind automatically generates the prediction that the lights will start to shine. If they don't, your error-monitoring system will leap into action and prompt you to search for what went wrong, such as you are turning the wrong switch, or perhaps the lightbulb has burned out, or the power may be off. In autism, this prediction system linking one's actions to intended outcomes does not work properly.

Schizophrenia

Perhaps the best-known form of disordered selfhood is schizophrenia. Many researchers and therapists believe that "a disturbance of the basic sense of self is at the clinical core of the schizophrenia spectrum" (Nelson et al., 2016, p. 158). Most people take for granted that the contents of their minds belong to them: my thoughts, my feelings. For people with schizophrenia, that level of "mine-ness" in mental organization doesn't work properly. That may be why some of them think their thoughts were planted by other people or mysterious forces. They generate inner speech, like other people do, but they fail to integrate it as "mine," and so it seems alien to them. Bodily experience is likewise not fully integrated into the self (Nelson et al., 2016).

All in all, the boundary between self and world, and in particular the boundary between oneself and other people, is not a clear firm boundary for the schizophrenic individual as it is for most other people. That boundary is one of the key foundations of even the basic, right-now self, and so selfhood is an ongoing problem for people with schizophrenia. Without a clear system for "owning" their thoughts, that is, for knowing that the thoughts in their minds belong to them, they are prone to confusing themselves with other people. One team of researchers (van der Weiden et al., 2015) illustrated this problem with the simple exercise of passing the salt at the dinner table. A successful passing requires both people to predict their own muscle movements and outcomes, so the hands can be coordinated and the saltshaker can pass smoothly from one person's hand to another. For someone afflicted with schizophrenia, the demands of passing the salt can be difficult and confusing because the mind fails to keep straight who is making what movements and what exactly the intended outcome is. They suffer so-called goal contagion, that is, mistaking someone else's intentions for their own. The salt is supposed to be passed, but whose hand is supposed to end up holding it?

Another seemingly mundane illustration of the problem involves tickling. Many people are susceptible to being tickled by others, but hardly anyone can tickle him- or herself. People who have schizophrenia can tickle themselves, however. The reason most people cannot is that when you make muscle movements, your mind automatically creates an idea of how the outcome is supposed to feel, and when these match, the experience is not very intense. (Studies show that most people can tickle themselves if this expectation process is thwarted by inserting a brief delay, such as when you turn a crank that moves a feather on your skin a few seconds later; Blakemore et al., 1999, 2000; see also Weiskrantz et al., 1971). In schizophrenia, the process of linking one's bodily movements to expected outcomes is impaired because one does not so readily link one's movements and intentions to oneself, so the sensation is not reduced when it turns out as expected.

Social life presents multiple difficulties for the person suffering from schizophrenia. Some of these arise from the inadequate mental organization of the self. If you mistakenly sometimes think that what you did was actually done by someone else, and vice versa to boot, it is hard to assign moral responsibility or coordinate group action.

In conclusion, many mental illnesses involve disorganization, literally dis-orders of the self. The whole is overly linked to a part, the self is divided into separate, incompatible parts, or one strives virtuously to keep bad aspects of self subdued. The normal unity across time is deficient, and lack of connection to one's past or future creates problems in daily life. Lack of clear understanding of self leads to a sense of incoherence. In more extreme cases (like schizophrenia and autism), the various pieces and parts are not experienced as hanging together in the essential unity of self.

SELF-CONTROL IN MENTAL ILLNESS

Given how important self-control is for successful functioning in human social life, it is hardly surprising that many mental illnesses involve some breakdown in such control. Failure or misuse of self-control is often a factor. The two main kinds of self-control problems are called "underregulation" and "misregulation" (Carver & Scheier, 1981). Underregulation means not exerting self-control, or not enough. Misregulation means doing it wrong.

Underregulation

Poor self-regulation is central to various addictions, from drugs to gambling. Good self-control holds the present in check for the sake of the future. As we have already seen, addicts focus inordinately on the present, discounting or ignoring the future—which is why their lives have the pattern of intense, fleeting pleasures, but end up full of regrets. The manic phase of bipolar disorder often involves clear loss of self-control, as the person may get carried away into spending huge amounts of money, taking risks, getting into fights, engaging in impulsive sex, and the like.

Fear of losing self-control contributes to some problems (Kyrios et al., 2016). That is, the person may be capable of effective self-control but fears being bad at self-control, which prompts various responses that cause problems. PTSD is often marked by fear of losing control. People who suffer from OCD likewise often fear that they are losing control, and the obsessions and compulsive behavior patterns, like washing their hands hundreds of times every day, are part of a struggle to maintain control. Women with eating disorders often report feeling that life in general is out of control, and their intake of food is one of the few things that they can control. In binge eating disorder, the binge can be seen as a breakdown of control: The woman normally maintains tight control over what she eats, but during the episode this is gone. Attention-deficit/hyperactivity disorder is defined as the inability to maintain attentional focus, and at least some major analyses of it feature deficient self-control as the central problem (Barkley, 1997).

Problems with setting goals have been linked to various pathologies. The hoarding disorder is saturated with this problem. The hoarders collect items in the mistaken and poorly articulated sense that some valuable purpose will be served by accumulating them. Meanwhile, they fail to follow through on ordinary goals of discarding items that are no longer needed. People with social anxiety disorder have trouble setting attainable social goals, instead thinking they need to make a perfect impression on others and becoming painfully self-conscious of every detail or potential imperfection as a result. Compulsive gamblers may set goals, such as when to quit, but they often fail to keep to these, leading to losses and debts far beyond what they had initially had in mind. Bipolar disorder sufferers, in the manic phase, likewise either set goals badly or fail to stick to their goal pursuits.

More broadly, perfectionism is a kind of self-regulation problem based on unrealistic goals, and quite a few mental illnesses have some element of this. Perfectionism is obviously central to some of them, such as bulimic and anorexic individuals' pursuit of a hopeless ideal of thinness. It is less obvious but still widely noted in some others, such as chronic fatigue syndrome, social anxiety disorder, and OCD.

Misregulation

What about too much self-control? Some lines of thinking depict high levels of self-control as bad, such as in anorexia, or obsessive–compulsive personality disorder. Typically, these people inhibit themselves to a high extent. In anorexia, for example, the person may hardly eat anything. For most people, refraining from eating is one goal of self-control, so it is natural to think that someone who almost never eats must have superlative powers of self-control, and that any problems stemming from this reflect the over-abundance of self-control. However, the seeming restraint in anorexia may not even involve much self-control, if the person has managed to cultivate a disgust reaction to food in general.

In my view, it is a mistake to interpret such problems as due to excessive self-control. It is not as if a person who merely improves his or her self-discipline will end up suffering from anorexia or a similar mental illness. When June Tangney and I validated our trait measure of self-control, we searched hard for any sign that high levels were associated with bad outcomes, but we could not find any (much as we would have liked to). One hears many people complain that they wish they had more self-control but not that they wish they had less. People with anorexia probably have high self-control, but that is not the source of the problem. (If they had lower self-control, they would probably develop a different affliction.) They use their self-control in service of a destructive goal, namely seeking to be super-thin and avoiding almost all eating. Thus, these are examples of misregulation, not overregulation.

In short, problems in self-control show both kinds of patterns, namely not doing it enough (underregulation) and doing it wrong or in service of a bad goal (misregulation). Self-control is how the self manages itself, including setting and pursuing goals, ensuring a positive future, obeying society's rules, and performing one's roles in society. Failing to exert control effectively prevents the self from doing those things, and self-regulating inappropriately (such as to wrongheaded goals) is likewise unhelpful. Many people with these problems have at least some inkling that they are failing at self-control, which is why fear of losing control is such a common report. It also may explain why people sometimes resort to perfectionism or other extreme measures in the hope of counteracting the deficits they see in themselves.

All in all, there is a vast amount of evidence that self-control is beneficial, and almost no evidence that it is destructive or pathological. It is a tool, and just like a hammer or screwdriver can be used to injure someone, self-control can be used for destructive ends. But the fact that hammers can be used to kill is not proof that hammers are bad.

The pathology findings indicate that the developmental task of acquiring self-control has two main aspects. First, one needs to develop powers of self-control, such as by strengthening willpower (building character) and learning how to break bad habits while forming good ones. Second, one needs to acquire wisdom and maturity for how to use self-control effectively. Self-discipline increases one's ability to achieve things, large and small, good and bad, and so one needs to learn how to employ it toward achieving the important good outcomes.

DOES SELF-AWARENESS CONTRIBUTE TO MENTAL ILLNESS?

Self-awareness also deserves mention. Back in 1990, Rick Ingram reported that high levels of self-focused attention had been "linked to depression, various anxiety disorders, alcoholism, fear, paranoid ideation, schizophrenia, psychopathy, mania, psychosis, binge eating, obsessive disorders, and disorders of impulse control" (1991, p. 544). His article triggered some debate as to whether high self-awareness was a pattern common to *all* mental illness or just certain ones (Pyszczynski et al., 1991). In general, social scientists run into trouble when they claim their theories apply universally, and Ingram did not make that claim. He did, however, suggest that self-awareness was so broadly relevant to diverse mental illnesses that it might be misguided to develop theories about it that were specific to any one of them. It is therefore not surprising that theorists who developed such illness-specific theories took exception.

Self-awareness has indeed been found to be high among multiple and assorted clinical (psychological) disorders. It is therefore quite reasonable to look for common patterns, rather than develop a different theory for each case. On the other hand, the fact that self-awareness is high in different mental illnesses does not mean it contributes to these illnesses in the same way. Self-awareness is a very basic part of the self, and it would be surprising if assorted mental illnesses bypassed self-awareness completely. After all, simply knowing that you have some sort of problem might trigger self-awareness: *What's wrong with me?* Only the few mentally ill people who fail to realize anything is wrong with them might be impervious.

Indeed, causation might even go in the other direction. Possibly people with high self-awareness are quicker to recognize that something is wrong with them. After all, a diagnosis of mental illness depends on going to a professional and acknowledging one's symptoms and problems. It is at least plausible that other people have the same problems and symptoms but, lacking self-awareness, never regard themselves as someone who might need professional help. Hence, the people who have been diagnosed will be mainly the ones with high self-awareness.

One disorder for which high self-awareness may be especially problematic is paranoid thinking. Fenigstein (1984) found that many normal college students had a tendency to think of themselves as a target, thereby suggesting that paranoia is a pathologically extreme version of what might be a normal pattern. In one of his experiments, he would go into class on the day that he was to return exams or term papers and make a brief talk about how one particular paper was much worse than all the rest. Students then rated the odds that the paper he was discussing was theirs. In a class of 50 students, each had only a 2% chance of being the one, but many students were pretty sure, or at least seriously worried, that he was talking about them specifically. (The average guess was over 20%.) Students who scored high in public self-consciousness—being highly sensitive to how they were viewed by others—were most likely to assume that external events were referring to them, and especially bad events.

Ingram made the further case that self-awareness in mental illness is "excessive, rigid across situations, and prolonged" (1990, p. 172). Excessive and prolonged simply mean too much self-awareness, and so those assertions are quite compatible with the idea that self-awareness can play different roles in different problems. As to rigidity, being inflexible is also a generic sort of problem that could take many forms in practice.

A further question has to do with whether self-awareness is itself a problem. People with problems have high self-awareness. Does that mean high self-awareness leads to problems? After all, self-awareness could rise as a result of mental illness, as one dwells on one's own woes and symptoms and tries to make sense of them.

The link between high self-awareness and pathology has to be set against the positive value of high self-awareness. As already explained, self-awareness evolved further in humans than other apes, presumably to help reputation management and self-regulation. With low self-awareness, it is difficult to exercise self-control, given that monitoring oneself is a key part of the process. It is hard to argue that a lack of self-awareness is a key to mental health. After all, we just saw that poor self-control was also implicated in assorted mental problems.

Hence, I am reluctant to conclude that high self-awareness is itself bad, or conducive to mental illness. Self-awareness may increase in the normal course of events when self-regulation is needed, and mental illness is typically accompanied by some sense that things are not working properly and so self-regulation would be good.

A recent review (Moore et al., 2017) took an approach similar to Ingram's, essentially distinguishing between too much and too little self. These authors confirmed the conclusion that too much self is implicated in many psychological problems. By "too much self" they appear to have meant excessive self-awareness. More provocatively, they conclude that too little self is hardly ever a problem. This may be true for self-awareness, but certainly it is not true for self-control, as the previous section showed. When the executive self is not effective, especially in misregulation, many problems ensue. In that sense, at the very least, too little self is indeed a cause of problems.

PROBLEMS WITH THE INTERPERSONAL SELF

While Freud saw mental illness as an inner problem, others shifted the emphasis to interpersonal relations. Harry Stack Sullivan was an early pioneer of this approach and deserves credit for treating the human self as an inner system designed to relate to others, such as outlined in his *Interpersonal Theory of Psychiatry* (1955), which was published after his death in 1949. In his view, mental illness arose when one adopted ineffective ways of relating to others, mostly as a result of anxiety stemming from interpersonal interactions. As one sign, I recall being told that people do not typically show up at mental hospitals of their own accord. Rather, they are brought there by family members or other relationship partners who cannot deal with them.

Untangling the intertwined roots of inner vulnerabilities and relationship problems is a job for another book, indeed probably a task for a legion of researchers. For now, the crucial point is that people learn ways of dealing with interpersonal problems that protect them from pain and anxiety but that cause further problems.

KEY POINTS

- Psychological disorders often include some problems of the self. Some patterns common to multiple disorders were poor self-control, low self-esteem, and high self-awareness. Of those, poor self-control seems the most obviously linked to causing multiple problems.

- A great many disorders involve some problem or failure in how the self is organized.

- I do not see high self-awareness as inherently bad, and it may be a result of knowing that you've got problems.

CHAPTER 27

The Deep Puzzle
of Self-Defeating Behavior

It is soberingly useful to delve into the self's systematic failures. If the self is a system, then self-defeating behavior is an important example of systematic failure.

DO PEOPLE EVER WISH TO FAIL OR SUFFER?

Multiple theories have tried to explain self-defeating tendencies, and some have been at least briefly fashionable. Freud's eventual conclusion was that the striving for death and failure is there inside everyone's individual mind, constantly competing with the opposite striving for life, joy, and success.

An alternative, more plausible version is that some people have self-destructive tendencies as part of their personality. Thus, some people are like that and others aren't. I have not seen any researchers find success at developing a measure of self-destructive motivation that will discriminate who does and who does not have this tendency, especially one that has valid indicators of intentional self-harm.

Another idea, also rooted in Freud's theories, is that guilt makes people desire punishment. This could potentially offer the explanation for why some people desire self-defeat or destruction and others don't. People who have taken on a burden of guilt would be the ones seeking harm to self as a just, fitting punishment for their bad actions. The burden of guilt would presumably be a mixture of having done bad things and vulnerability to feeling guilty about things, and some people might have far more of one than the other, but a little bit of each would presumably be necessary. Psychopaths do truly horrible things but seem immune to guilt, so they would not seek punishment.

Still, I do not find convincing evidence that guilt makes people seek harm or failure as punishment. *Au contraire*, the evidence looks to me like even genuinely guilty people typically do all they can to avoid punishment, even if they do apologize and try to make amends voluntarily. That is, even people who feel guilty and know they did something wrong do not become self-defeating, though they may accept costs to self in order to make up for what they did.

Two additional phenomena make perhaps the best case for intentionally self-destructive behavior. One is suicide, and the other is its lesser known cousin, self-injurious behavior (such as cutting one's own skin or pulling out one's hair). On closer inspection, even these are not fully convincing. The suicidal person seeks escape from a hellish life situation. The goal is not to inflict punishment or harm on a bad self, but rather to obtain release from misery—essentially to achieve the hedonic improvement of moving from feeling awful to feeling nothing: moving up from negative to zero. (In particular, it is an escape from oneself because the self has become unbearable, painful; see Baumeister, 1990, 1991a, and Chapter 25, this volume, on escape from self.) It is perhaps revealing that although the suicidal person is both killer and victim, the person tends to identify overwhelmingly as victim rather than killer. If suicide were experienced as a righteous execution of a bad person, you would expect the suicidal person to self-identify more as the killer. The self wants the virtuous reputation. *People should respect and admire me because I killed a bad person (i.e., myself).* But no.

As for the people who engage in lesser forms of self-abuse, such as cutting their skin, I know less about them, but several experts have told me that they, too, fit the pattern of escaping the self. The physical pain is an intense focus that takes the mind away from the broader problems. The pain is not sought for its own sake but more as a kind of narcotic, to blot out the bad feelings. It thus fits the tradeoff pattern (see the next section).

In sum, the data do not support the idea that people are ever engaged in deliberate attempts to bring suffering, harm, or failure upon themselves, per se, at least not in reliable or systematic ways. To be sure, it may happen occasionally, here and there, and perhaps especially among people suffering from some forms of mental illness. And people may harm or kill themselves to escape when their own self and life have become intolerable. But as a systematic pattern, no. Self-defeating behavior must be explained without postulating a desire for self-defeat or self-destruction.

TRADEOFFS

People do engage in self-defeating and even self-destructive behavior. How and why might that happen? (For detailed reviews of the literature, see Baumeister, 1997; Baumeister & Scher, 1988; Berglas & Baumeister, 1993.)

Consider some ways that people actually accomplish self-destruction. Cigarette smoking is a fine example. But people don't smoke cigarettes because they want to ruin their health and die young. They smoke for the pleasures and benefits of smoking. The data (reviewed by Baumeister, 2017) show that smoking produces improved mental performance; even nonsmokers having their first cigarette will score higher than otherwise on an intelligence test. (A small improvement, to be sure.) It is a mild stimulant, and this is accompanied by a brief sensation of overall well-being, a mini-euphoria. Also, nicotine suppresses appetite for food, and some people use it to help their diets. So, smoking makes you smarter, happier, and thinner, plus gives you energy. No wonder so many people like it.

Today, all smokers must know that smoking has serious risks to health. Most packs of cigarettes explain these risks, so it is hard to miss them. Still, the risks are merely possibilities in the distant future, whereas the pleasures are immediate and definite.

Self-defeating behavior thus also takes the form of tradeoffs, in which good and bad outcomes are linked. To be sure, the combination of good and bad does not always mean self-destruction. Often sacrifice is necessary to produce important benefits, such as in strenuous physical exercise. Exercise is not (usually) self-defeating because the long-run outcome contains far more good than bad. Smoking is the opposite, however. All those small pleasures of smoking thousands of cigarettes seem not worth it when the person gets emphysema and lung cancer. Tradeoffs only qualify as self-defeating if the cost outweighs the benefit, in the final analysis.

Tradeoffs offer one solution to the problem of how to explain self-defeating behavior without a death drive. The person is not trying to create a bad outcome or experience for the self. Rather, the person is going after something good. The problem arises because the good the person wants is tied to something bad. The person takes the bad with the good. The net result only counts as self-defeating if the bad outweighs the good, in the end.

Why would anyone choose a benefit tied to a greater cost? The answer reveals much about the executive self. Many self-defeating behaviors fit a powerful formula of short-term gain, long-term cost (Baumeister, 1997; Baumeister & Scher, 1988). Another pattern is definite gain and merely possible cost.

In an important sense, self-defeating tradeoffs pit the right-now self against the extended, narrative self. The right-now self gets the good part, and the cost is paid by the future self. Fully rational and wise human beings build the future into their current decisions, so they do not engage in self-defeat. But remember that underneath the human parts we are also animals, and so it is not surprising that sometimes the immediate and definite are given precedence over the distant, uncertain future.

Let's have a quick review of some of these self-defeating tradeoffs (from Berglas & Baumeister, 1993; see also Baumeister & Scher, 1988).

Self-Handicapping

One of the most creative ideas to emerge from 1970s psychology is that some people actually create barriers in the way of their own performance, so they can have an excuse in case things go bad. This was first put forward by Edward E. Jones and Steven Berglas (1978) as a theory of why successful people develop alcohol addictions. Remarkable early success gives the young person a reputation as a rising star or genius—but creates a heavy burden of expectations. The person faces doubts as to whether the next performance will match the breakthrough brilliance of the first. By developing an alcohol or drug problem, the person can preserve the brilliant reputation even while failing to live up to the hype. Many people would rather be regarded as a troubled genius than exposed as a mediocrity after all. Part of the beauty of the self-handicapping strategy is that if the next performance is brilliant anyway, the person gets extra credit for having done well despite the addiction.

The researchers showed that a random sample of normal people would take "stupid-making" drugs to give themselves an excuse for failure under those circumstances (Berglas & Jones, 1978). Subjects in their experiment were told that the research involved final testing of two drugs almost ready for market and was designed to verify preliminary findings indicating temporary effects on thinking. One of these drugs supposedly made you smarter, and the other stupider, for an hour or two. To get baseline data, every subject first took a contrived intelligence test and was told he had scored extremely highly, which the experimenters remarked on and congratulated the subject for. The difference was that for some people, the questions were carefully chosen so that the subject really did get them right. For others, however, many (multiple-choice) questions had no right answer, and the subject had to guess—but kept getting told that his answers were correct. These young men developed a worry that they would not be able to repeat this level of success. After all, they did not really know the answers. They were just guessing.

The situation resembles the popular concept of the "impostor phenomenon." The man had achieved a high score and was congratulated on his ostensible brilliance, but deep down he knew, or at least suspected, that he had just made some lucky guesses. Genuine brilliance can replicate its work, but lucky success cannot, so he felt like an impostor when being congratulated for his outstanding performance. The upcoming second test would probably reveal him to be not as smart as the experimenters were saying.

When invited to pick between the two drugs, most subjects in the control condition naturally favored the one that supposedly would make them smarter. Wouldn't you love to know what it would feel like to be a bit smarter? In sharp contrast, however, the ones who had gotten the high score while guessing (the impostors) chose the one that would make them less smart. Why? That way, if their score on the upcoming second test were to be well below their stellar baseline, their reputation for brilliance would be intact. The poor score would just be taken as evidence that the drug did indeed have those detrimental effects.

The idea of self-handicapping was soon extended beyond alcohol to a variety of other actions. Procrastination means one has to scramble to meet the deadline and cannot live up to one's potential; so, doing work at the last minute offers a fine self-handicapping excuse. Some illnesses and injuries could be sought, or even faked, to provide an excuse. Not studying (or even getting drunk) on the night before a major exam provides a lovely excuse for not getting a top grade.

The self-handicapper benefits regardless of whether the outcome is success or failure. Failure is attributed to the handicap, while success brings extra credit because the person seemingly overcame the handicap. What makes it self-defeating is that the handicap does actually increase the odds of failure. Drunk people and procrastinators really do perform worse than other people. It is a sacrifice of substance for style, lowering the quality of actual performance in exchange for a boost in the interpretation of that performance.

Underachievement is another puzzle self-handicapping can solve. Underachievement might reflect withholding effort so that the performance is not a proper measure of one's ability. People know at some level that performance depends on two things, effort and ability. If they can get an initial reputation for high ability, they can preserve it by withholding effort. If you didn't try your best, then failure doesn't really disconfirm the reputation for ability. In contrast, putting forth maximum effort is risky: If you do your best and flop, well, your best is apparently not good enough. There goes plausible deniability!

Self-handicapping is indeed like plausible deniability. Both operate on the principle that the goal is to set things up so that if things go bad, the meaning will be ambiguous, and nothing bad can be proved about oneself.

Procrastination

The previous section noted that procrastination is sometimes a form of self-handicapping, a strategic ploy to give oneself an excuse. More often, however, procrastination occurs because people prefer to do something nice in the present and postpone unpleasant chores into the vague future. It is thus a pure and obvious case of the basic formula for tradeoffs: short-term gain but long-term cost.

Is the cost real? Remember, if the benefits outweigh the costs, it is not self-defeating. Many procrastinators assert that the last-minute pressure brings out their best work, which contradicts the idea that procrastination is self-destructive (Ferrari et al., 1995). Then again, that might be an excuse or rationalization.

The question of whether procrastination is really self-defeating was settled in two semester-long studies of university students (Tice & Baumeister, 1997). Students taking health psychology consented to contribute their class data. A questionnaire identified some as procrastinators and others as not. Exams and term papers were graded by an expert who did not know which students were procrastinators. The procrastinators got lower grades every time, that is, both exams and the term paper, in both semesters. That made six comparisons, and every one was statistically significant. So yes, putting things off is bad for performance (on all six measures), not neutral and certainly not good.

The health data had a surprise, though, right in the first semester study. For the health psychology course, the students kept diaries of their own health, each day recording things like whether they had a headache or sneezed or felt dizzy, or went to the clinic. It turned out that the procrastinators were healthier. That made the tradeoff seem a much better deal, and indeed one could argue that it would be better to go through life slightly healthier even if it means that your work is consistently a bit worse. Procrastination is at least somewhat good for you. At least it seemed that way.

The health data were collected for 4 weeks during the middle of the first semester. That raised another question, however: Were the procrastinators really healthier overall? The data came from the middle of the semester, while they were procrastinating. During those weeks, the non-procrastinators were chugging along, pushing themselves to get things done, while the procrastinators were perhaps relaxing with a beer or two, watching television, having a fun after-dinner chat with friends. Is that a healthier lifestyle? At that point the deadlines are still far off. What happens to health at crunch time, when things are due?

There was no way to find out, so we reran the entire study, including the early-term health data but also collecting health data onward right through final exams. As before, the procrastinators had fewer sicknesses and symptoms early in the semester. But at the end of the semester they had more—far more. In fact, when you added them all together, not only was the early-term advantage of procrastinators wiped out, it was significantly reversed. The procrastinators were sicker overall.

Thus, procrastination looks extremely self-destructive. First, it seems to make your work poorer in quality. Second, it's self-defeating just in terms of health. Procrastination trades increased future sickness for better health today.

Still, it is clear why people do it. There are short-term gains, which attract people despite the eventual problems. In the present, while deadlines are far off, procrastinators can enjoy more leisure and better health. That's the classic formula for self-defeating tradeoffs: short-term gain coupled with long-term cost.

Other Tradeoffs

A few other self-destructive tradeoffs are worth mentioning (reviewed by Baumeister & Scher, 1988; Berglas & Baumeister, 1993). Modern Western societies spend enormous amounts of money on health care, and highly trained physicians prescribe medicines and treatments for assorted diseases—yet many patients fail to follow through (e.g., Dunbar & Stunkard, 1979; Sackett & Snow, 1979). They don't take their medicine, they don't show up for follow-up appointments, and they don't follow the instructions and restrictions that their doctor has specified. Clearly, people would be healthier if they followed expert advice. What's the point of getting expert medical advice if one isn't going to follow it? Various estimates of how well people follow their doctor's orders range from 80% at best down to a dismal 20%.

What makes a tradeoff in medical treatment? People are most likely to quit their treatments when these are uncomfortable, difficult, painful, or embarrassing. Thus, they sacrifice their health for the sake of comfort, ease, pride, and the like. Even mere inconvenience plays a role: People are more likely to quit treatments that interfere with their daily routine, as opposed to others that are compatible with it.

Shyness is a widespread problem with multiple aspects and roots (see Jones et al., 1986; Zimbardo, 1977), but part of it is a self-defeating tradeoff. Shy people want to have friends and sometimes suffer intensely from loneliness. But they fear rejection, so they fail to reach out to others. People meet others and make friends at parties, but the shy person will turn down an invitation to a party—or perhaps attend but stay back in the corner, failing to engage with others, and then leave, lonely and depressed, with an acute feeling of failure. If they do get into conversation, they fail to open up and share information about themselves, remaining content with nodding and smiling and saying a few things.

Shyness is not always self-defeating, but many patterns are. Interacting with others raises the possibility of rejection, and that brings anxiety. By hanging back and avoiding parties, they gain freedom from this anxiety, as well as minimizing the danger of being rejected. Thus, they do gain some emotional peace in the short run. But in the long run, probably many of them regret that they didn't push themselves to go out and meet people and take more social chances. The strategy of preventing anxiety and rejection by not approaching others leads in the long run to loneliness.

Violence and revenge also deserve mention. Like shyness, these are complicated patterns with many, complex causes. Still, experimental studies have confirmed that people will seek revenge even when it is costly to themselves (Brown, 1968). More broadly, violence is inherently risky. Sometimes the outcomes will be bad. Many murders, in particular, start off as mere arguments among acquaintances, which then escalate until someone resorts to violence. The killer is typically much worse off for having killed, not least because the police will find him or her and prosecution leads to spending years in prison. Whatever the argument was about, and whatever was gained in the context of the argument by killing the other person, pale in comparison with being sent to prison.

For many people, self-defeating behavior comes via binges, in which they indulge in pleasures to destructive excess. Dieters relax their diets and then go on an eating binge; eating the first cookie does not hurt your diet, but going ahead to finish the pack of them does. Drinking and drug binges put health and relationships at risk. Gambling binges empty one's bank account and leave heavy debts. In all these the initial steps bring pleasure and satisfaction, and the short-term pleasure brings sometimes ruinous long-term costs.

Summing Up Self-Defeating Tradeoffs

Clearly, people bring failure, suffering, and other misfortunes on themselves, not by design or death wish, but by pursuing good outcomes that have bad ones attached. The executive agent has good intentions but sometimes executes in a flawed manner.

The primary formula for a self-defeating tradeoff is short-term gain linked to long-term, delayed cost. Because the harm or loss is delayed, it does not influence the decision in proportion to its importance.

A related pattern combines a definite gain with a merely possible harm. Some people smoke cigarettes for decades without getting any illness from doing so. (Less than 10% of long-term heavy smokers get lung cancer.) It is difficult to say where irrational and self-defeating begin when one is dealing with possibilities. The smoker who gets lung cancer might well regret having smoked all those years. For the lucky ones who don't suffer consequences, was their behavior self-defeating because of the risk, even if there was no cost?

The marvelous rationality of the human mind enables us to incorporate thinking about futures and probabilities into our decisions—but perhaps it should not be surprising that that doesn't always work properly.

BACKFIRES

Not all patterns of self-defeating behavior are tradeoffs. There is another large category, backfires, though it is something of a hodge-podge. That is, it lacks the common theme of the tradeoff.

The essence of a *backfire* is that the person is trying to accomplish something good but goes about it in a way that produces the opposite. The person makes some mistake based on a false understanding of either self or world. Or the self just goes about doing something based on standard procedure, which unfortunately does not work properly in this case. A few examples will suffice.

Throwing Good Money after Bad

Perseverance is widely admired, and sometimes it enables someone to reach success despite initial setbacks. Sometimes, however, the endeavor is doomed, and persevering merely increases the cost of failure. Such self-defeating persistence has been linked to egotistical motivations (e.g., Fox & Staw, 1979; Staw, 1976). It is more common among people with high than low self-esteem, and it is especially likely if the person has staked pride or reputation on a particular course of action—so that giving up involves admitting one was wrong, and losing face. The core of this pattern is the false assumption (or misguided hope) that continuing to try will bring eventual success.

Choking under Pressure

Pressure is high when it is important to do well, and so people want to perform at their best. But sometimes it is precisely those situations that cause people to perform badly (Baumeister, 1984). The main reason is that people focus consciously on their inner processes in the hope of ensuring a good outcome—but this self-focused attention disrupts the smooth automatic execution of skills. Pianists or typists may seek to avoid mistakes by attending to their finger movements, golfers or tennis players may attend to their handgrip or arm movements, and the like. This extra attention ends up spoiling the performance.

Others

Various other patterns indicate self-defeating backfires. Setting overly high goals can indicate ambition and confidence, but soon the person is discouraged because the hopelessness of reaching the lofty goal becomes apparent. Many performances require trading off speed and accuracy, and people negotiate these poorly. For example, high anxiety might prompt people to be so worried about making mistakes that they slow down too much, resulting in failing to get much done—or, alternatively, causes them to speed up excessively, resulting in more mistakes. Learned helplessness can also qualify as a self-defeating behavior pattern, given that people mistakenly conclude that all their efforts are doomed and so give up when progress or solutions would have been possible.

THE ROLE OF EMOTION
IN SELF-DEFEATING BEHAVIORS

The executive branch of the self seeks to guide action so as to benefit the self. Cognition and emotion (thinking and feeling) are there essentially to help it do this. Feelings start with knowing what is good and bad. Emotion is not invariably helpful, though.

Emotional distress and emotional vulnerability often increase the tendency to do self-defeating things (see a review by Baumeister, 1997). Self-handicapping is often motivated by the fear of looking bad, as is choking under pressure. Shyness is linked to social anxiety and fear of rejection. Medical noncompliance is sometimes linked to embarrassment and other negative feelings. Procrastination has many roots, but one contributing cause is that people have anxiety about their work and therefore can dodge those feelings by not working. (Teach children to deal with performance anxiety by starting earlier and working harder, not by avoiding the task!) Addicts who quit smoking or drinking often report relapsing when they feel stressed out by work or family issues. Revenge seeking and indeed violent actions are often shaped by anger, indignation, and similar feelings. Binges are often set off by anxiety or distress or other bad feelings.

How the self's agent uses emotion will be complex. Sometimes emotion clearly helps, and people without good emotional reactions are dysfunctional, as we shall see. But strong emotions, especially perhaps negative emotions, mess up the executive and prompt it to do stupid, self-destructive things.

Another theme running through many of these patterns is what I call "threatened egotism." Threat is the possibility (not guaranteed) that something bad might happen, reflecting badly on the self. Egotism is the tendency to embrace overly positive views of self. As we have seen, people are willing and indeed eager to believe positive things about themselves. They are especially desirous of having these positive views of self accepted by other people. When that process of building a good reputation goes awry, people lose some of their rationality and start to succumb to self-defeating patterns.

Threatened egotism lurked in much of the evidence for self-defeating behavior. It is central to self-handicapping: People create obstacles for themselves to create excuses for possible failure so that the failure will not reflect so badly on them. Choking under pressure is likewise driven by a desire to succeed and to be acclaimed as successful. Revenge is sought much more intensely for blows to pride and reputation than for merely material losses. More broadly, threatened egotism is one of the main roots of violence, and violence is usually risky and often costly. Throwing good money after bad, or time and other resources, is more common when their ego is invested in the project so that abandoning the course would entail a loss of face. Medical regimens that are embarrassing or require admission of personal fault (e.g., treatment for sexually transmitted diseases) likewise are more prone to be abandoned out of a costly egotistical impulse.

Many binges are triggered by blows to one's pride or reputation. Indeed, some research suggests that gamblers rationalize their continued gambling by reinterpreting some of their losses in self-serving ways (Gilovich, 1983); specifically, sports bettors focus on cases in which their team lost due to bad luck or a questionable referee call, and the bettors interpret those as "near wins," thereby sustaining their view of themselves as wise and competent bettors: "My bet would have won except for that fumble/ bad call/unlucky bounce near the end." Of course, luck is part of sports, and a ruthlessly honest bettor would use the same logic to devalue some successful bets: "The team I bet on would have lost except for that lucky bounce," but people scrutinize their successes much less carefully than their defeats (Gilovich, 1983). The gambler thinks, a win is a win, period, but some losses are near wins so that I should get credit for having made the wise bet even though I lost. Such processes help explain the paradox that gamblers continue to think gambling will bring them more money despite the accumulating evidence that their gambling is reducing their net worth.

LESSONS FROM SELF-DEFEATING BEHAVIORS

We have two patterns of response by the self that cause problems for the self. The self's control of action breaks down first because of high negative emotion (or even just the possibility of it) and, second, because of threatened egotism, that is, the tendency to do irrational and present-focused (future-disregarding) actions when one's positive view of self, or perhaps especially one's reputation, is in jeopardy of changing downward.

Remember, there seems to be a broad general tendency, the self-enhancement motive, to seek and cultivate and embrace ever more positive views about oneself. When that gets thwarted, the self is not operating to satisfaction, so you'd think there would be humility and constructive self-criticism and plans for change, but instead there is often resentment, or resistance, frequently extending into irrational and even self-defeating, self-destructive courses of action. Clearly, the goal is good: Creating and maintaining a superb reputation for oneself is a major and advantageous achievement. The self that can successfully pull that off can look forward to a comfortable happy life, and so it can regard itself as a success. But when progress toward that goal is frustrated, many a person turns nasty.

A final lesson to extract from the litany of self-defeating patterns is the importance of self-regulation. Two different kinds of self-regulation failure were implicated. Underregulation means not regulating enough. The tradeoffs that take short-term gain at long-term cost are prominent examples of underregulation. Normally, self-regulation helps resist momentary temptations for the sake of long-term benefits; such acts of self-control help one resist impulses to eat unhealthy foods, consume excessive amounts of alcohol or drugs, lash out aggressively, have sex with the wrong person, and the like.

In contrast, misregulation involves successful acts of self-control that fail to produce the desired results because they are guided by a defective plan, such as a poorly specified goal or a mistaken view about what will work. Misregulation is evident in choking under pressure (paying attention where it doesn't help), in costly perseverance (thinking further efforts or resources will bring the elusive success), in dysfunctional speed–accuracy tradeoffs, and in misguided goal setting.

Broadly, then, the tradeoff patterns of self-defeat are brought on by underregulation, while the backfiring patterns involve misregulation.

KEY POINTS

- The executive self generally seeks a good outcome even though it sometimes produces bad ones. It does not cultivate its own misery as an end in itself.

- Self-defeating behaviors often take the form of tradeoffs, which is short-term gain linked to long-term, delayed cost. Examples of tradeoffs include self-handicapping and procrastination,

- Another form of self-defeating behavior is a backfire. The person is trying to accomplish something good but the procedure doesn't work, or the person goes about it in a way that produces the opposite. Examples include throwing good money after bad and choking under pressure.

- Emotional distress and emotional vulnerability often increase the tendency to do self-defeating things. Fear of looking bad can motivate self-handicapping; anxiety can motivate shyness.

- Threatened egotism can also lead to self-defeating behaviors. It is central to self-handicapping. Choking under pressure is often driven by a desire to be acclaimed as successful.

- Two patterns of response by the self cause problems: the self's control breaks down because of high emotion and threatened egotism can lead to irrational actions.

CHAPTER 28

Ways the Mind Can Organize Self-Beliefs

No two selves are exactly alike. Yet, this book has sought to explain the common features of selfhood. This chapter looks at one dimension along which selves can vary—their organization. As we saw in Chapter 26, this can sometimes cause problems.

Self-knowledge is composed of many specific bits of information. Most researchers have focused on specific beliefs, but an ambitious few have asked how all this information is organized in the mind. What is linked to what? The basic unit of thought is an association, which links one concept to another. The mind's store of information in memory consists of many specific concepts and ideas, linked together one-to-one in clusters of information. Selves rely on that memory store of information for making behavioral choices. Not everyone organizes self-knowledge in the same way, hence the differences. Even selves with roughly the same parts may be put together in very different ways.

INFORMATION IN MEMORY: FROM SEPARATED TO LINKED

Repressors are typically defined as people who claim their lives are going great. Thus, they report unusually low rates of anxiety and other unhappy feelings. They hardly ever feel bad, or so they say. To be sure, truly happy people say the same thing. But repressors are set apart by another questionnaire, one that looks for signs of defensive boasting, like saying "true" that I always fully check the safety features of my vehicle before going on a car trip (Crowne & Marlowe, 1964; Weinberger et al., 1979). Nobody really does that. (Maybe a few highly anxious control freaks do.) But people desperate to make a good impression would rather say true than false. They distort the facts to look good. The inference is that their claims about never feeling bad are likewise distorted by their wanting to look good.

At first, researchers thought that somehow these people managed to bury away their unhappy experiences so thoroughly that they would not remember any. The very concept of repression suggests a mental erasing of bad experiences.

More advanced work disputed that view, however (Hansen & Hansen, 1988). Repressors have just as many bad memories as other people. The difference is that these bad experiences are not linked by mental associations to other thoughts and memories. This resembles the defense mechanism that Freud dubbed "isolation": The thought continues to be there in the mind's memory, but it does not come into contact with other thoughts. Not being linked to the networks of associations, it hardly ever pops into the active part of the mind. As the mind wanders along pathways of associations, it does not stumble on these bad memories because they are off the path. Yes, the person can remember the bad experience if need be, but in practice it rarely comes up. Not much reminds the repressor of the bad experience.

By way of contrast, research on depressed people suggests that their minds are wired quite the opposite (Wenzlaff et al., 1988). (No wonder they're depressed.) They may not have more bad experiences than other people—but the bad experiences are linked together by associations in a long chain of doom. One bad thought reminds them of other bad thoughts and unhappy memories, which in turn activate more of the same. Thus, if you take a repressor and a depressed person and make them each think of something bad, both of them can remember it and know that it was bad. For the repressor that goes nowhere, and the next thought will be on something unrelated and probably cheerful. Meanwhile, the depressed person is off on a long winding road leading from one miserable thought to another to another.

SELF-COMPLEXITY

Building on such approaches, Patricia Linville (1985, 1987) introduced the notion of self-complexity as a dimension along which self-concepts differ. A complex self has many dimensions and different aspects, with information about the self nicely sorted and distributed. It is as if there are barriers to keep different clusters of information about the self separate from each other. In contrast, the simple self puts all its eggs in one basket. Everything is linked to everything else: store manager, father, husband, taxpayer, voter, Saints fan, bowling team captain. Are these separate sets of information about the self, or are all interlinked? As usual, it's a matter of degree, along a continuum.

To be sure, writers of fiction have long been intrigued by people who build mental walls between different sets of information about themselves. Charles Dickens's classic novel *Great Expectations* contained a memorable minor character, Wemmick, who keeps his home and work selves quite distinct. In the office, he is all business. But then he invites Pip, the novel's main character, to his home at Walworth, where Wemmick is revealed as a creative, playful man, cheerfully caring for his handicapped father, and styling his modest home as a castle. Asked at home about his boss, Wemmick demurs: "[T]he office is one thing, and private life is another. When I go into the office, I leave the Castle behind me, and when I come into the Castle, I leave the office behind me." The next morning, as they walk to the office, Pip observes the gradual transformation of Wemmick: "By degrees, Wemmick got dryer and harder as we went along, and his mouth tightened. . . . "

Some of the initial excitement about Linville's theory came from the idea that a complex self would provide protection against stress and bad feelings. A setback in one domain of life (e.g., divorce, or occupational defeat) would not be as upsetting to someone with a complex as compared to a simple self—because it would only have impact on one aspect of the self. A divorce might be upsetting to your self-concept as a good loving partner, but your self-concept with regard to your job would be unaffected.

Linville's method for assessing self-complexity started with a stack of cards, each containing one possible attribute. The person was instructed to sort these into piles, "where each group of traits describes an aspect of you or your life" (Linville, 1987, p. 666). Complexity was calculated using an obscure statistical formula that took into account the number of piles and the number of cards in each pile. Critics have however suggested that the formula is misleading and does not measure the complexity of the self-concept (see a review in Rafaeli-Mor & Steinberg, 2002). I'm not expert enough to judge, though my mathematical intuition leans toward skepticism, too.

Regardless, the research findings have not been strong or consistent. A review of several decades of research concluded that the hoped-for benefits of a complex self-concept had not materialized (Rafaeli-Mor & Steinberg, 2002), including the notion that it would buffer against stress. Overall, the dismal conclusion was that self-complexity was associated with lower overall well-being, so the net effect was negative, not positive. Even that effect was quite weak and variable.

The self-complexity saga is relevant to our question of how the self is organized. The focus was on a self highly compartmentalized, with many separate domains. It was hoped such a self would confer exciting advantages. Instead, that kind of self was overall a bit worse. Clearly, this brings up the unity project. The more the self is all put together into one whole, the better off it is.

The idea that a complicated, multifaceted self-concept would confer advantages was given new life by Carolin Showers (1992). She adapted Linville's approach to focus on compartmentalizing good versus bad aspects of the self separately. This also solved the mathematical problems with Linville's measure. Her metaphor was "keeping bad apples out of the barrel," based on the once-crucial knowledge that brown spots (rot) would spread from one apple to another. Her point was that maintaining a separation between good and bad aspects of self would allow people to enjoy the good without the detrimental effects of negative thoughts. You might enjoy your promotion, your new car, your tennis victory, or your birthday without being haunted by nagging thoughts about that overdue bill or a romantic rejection.

Once again, as the data accumulated, the hoped-for advantages of the complex, compartmentalized self faded away. For a lucky few, there did seem to be some boost to self-esteem that emerged from keeping the bad aspects of the self stored separately in memory, especially when they were focused on the good things. (Remember, this was the strategy repressors use!) Mostly, though, the people who maintained a strong separation between good and bad aspects of self were worse off. Indeed, in some of Showers's later work, she found that the compartmentalized selves were more prone to engage in unethical actions, such as cheating (Showers et al., 2017; Thomas, Showers, & Leister, 2018). Indeed, compartmentalizing self-beliefs into separate good and bad baskets has come to be associated with some mental illnesses such as bipolar disorder.

Is a Compartmentalized Self Useful?

An alternative, more nuanced theory is that compartmentalizing is mainly useful under stressful situations. The issue is whether a setback in one area affects the entire self or only one segment of it. Keeping distress compartmentalized might reduce its total negative impact. A scientist or artist whose latest project is a total failure will feel bad—but may still feel fine when at home with family, as long as the self is compartmentalized. In contrast, someone with a non-compartmentalized self would be upset at home, too. Conversely, though, when things go well, the non-compartmentalized self can rejoice totally, whereas the compartmentalized self only feels good in that one area. Thus, the scientist whose project is a big success would not feel any benefit at home with family, if the self is compartmentalized. This pattern could account for the general finding that split selves have more problems and pathologies than integrated selves, if we assume that most people's lives are good most of the time.

Bad is stronger than good (Baumeister et al., 2001). But good is more frequent than bad, often by a wide margin, which is why life is mostly good despite the power of bad. That means, most of the time, people with non-compartmentalized selves will benefit from the spread of positive feelings rather than suffer from the spread of bad ones.

Lab studies on people who had to keep secret a key part of who they were (Sedlovskaya et al., 2013) showed they had successfully split apart their identities. This was true for gays who lived or worked in intolerant settings and so could not come out. It was also true for devoutly religious students attending a secular university who had to keep their faith secret. Clearly, these people suffered ample stress in their lives, and maintaining carefully separate versions of self was a vital coping strategy. Yet even there, the finding was that more differentiation was linked to more distress. It may still be that splitting self-knowledge into separate compartments is useful and adaptive under some circumstances, and maybe people do it to cope with difficult life circumstances, so it would be helpful—but it is a costly way of coping. At present, the most likely conclusion seems to be that integrated self-knowledge is healthy, while compartmentalized or otherwise divided self-knowledge is linked to unhappiness and problems: at best a response to troubles, at worst a cause of them.

Another approach to disorganized self-knowledge is to treat it as a lack of full clarity in self-understanding. Essentially, the difference is between having a firm, clear, and stable sense of who you are, as opposed to an uncertain and fluctuating sense. Self-concept clarity is a feature of high rather than low self-esteem (Campbell, 1990). Low self-concept clarity, as measured, takes several forms, including these: contradictory self-ratings (multiple answers that contradict each other); saying you do not know or are uncertain as to whether you have a particular trait; rating yourself one way today and differently next week. Thus, with low self-concept clarity, the person's self-knowledge is chaotic, disorganized, full of gaps and contradictions. Again, the people with unclear self-concepts came off worse than others. In particular, they suffer from more mood swings (emotional volatility), seeming to overreact to events. They also ended up with lower self-esteem, and indeed we shall soon revisit this as a profound contribution to the psychology of self-esteem.

The implication is that complex, compartmentalized knowledge about the self produces more bad than good effects. This fits the view that these people have been less successful than others at the unity project. All of this invokes one of this book's themes. It has emphasized that each self engages in a unity project, seeking to reconcile the welter of divergent feelings, impulses, thoughts, and actions into a coherent and continuous whole. Compartmentalization produces disunity. The compartmentalized self can cheat a bit on the unity project because, for example, it doesn't link the moral aspects of self to the present situation. It can comfortably view its actions as merely pragmatic or normative ("what everyone else would do"), while simply not dwelling on the violation of moral principle. But as we see over and over, maintaining multiple and separate or inconsistent versions of self is a problem. It detracts from effective functioning of the self.

SELF-CONCEPT DIFFERENTIATION

A crackerjack team of some of the top personality researchers led by Eileen Donahue (1993) performed an ambitious study of what they called "self-concept differentiation." As they introduced the notion, "one woman might see herself as fun-loving and easygoing with her friends but as serious and responsible with her parents" (p. 834) in contrast to another woman who would regard herself as fun-loving and easygoing with both friends and parents. Who is better off? College students resembling the first woman, with the more distinct versions of herself suited to different relationships and situations, tended to be more depressed and more neurotic, and had lower self-esteem, than students who resembled the second. The ones with multiple tailor-made selves had higher anxiety and poorer self-control. They were less well adjusted, less well socialized, and had various other problems. They did not get along as well with other people. They were less happy in general.

The researchers recognized the appealing theory that having different versions of self, each suited to a different role or relationship, might be adaptive, but their data argued against that view. They followed up their first study by delving into one of the great long-running studies, in which a group of a hundred women were followed from 1959 for many decades. Self-concept differentiation was introduced only in the 1990s, when the women were in their early 50s—thus quite different from the student population. These late-middle-aged women had presumably had much more life experience than the teenage college students, including marriage, children, chronic illness, divorce, and all the rest. But once again, fragmenting the self was maladaptive. The more the women held different self-concepts for different relationships and roles, the higher they scored on neuroticism and anxiety, and the lower on self-realization and well-being. They scored worse on self-control, which is a powerful predictor of all manner of success in life.

Some of Donahue and company's findings reveal how things develop. Women who went through more life changes, such as marriage and divorce and frequent job changes, had more differentiated self-concepts than women whose lives had involved fewer role swaps. The accumulation of these diverse experiences did not apparently lead to a healthier, happier self, however—apparently the opposite.

None of this proves that differentiated or compartmentalized self-knowledge is itself bad for you. These are correlational findings. My best guess is that compartmentalization is indeed harmful, but it is a reaction to problematic experiences. It is possible that the bad outcomes cause compartmentalization. That is, the unhealthy and unhappy woman is moved to develop views of herself as different in different roles. It is also possible that some third variable produced the two effects independently, that is, something (perhaps a rogue genetic combination?) pushed the woman both into these difficult life experiences and into forming a differentiated, compartmentalized self-concept.

Nevertheless, researchers have largely struck out at showing the benefits of compartmentalizing self-beliefs. And not for lack of trying.

WHAT CAN WE LEARN?

Self-knowledge is more than a list of traits and attributes, or a jumble of stories. You know a whole lot of specific things about yourself. You could make a long list. But in your mind, they aren't just a list. The information is organized in some ways, so some self-beliefs are more closely connected than others. Moreover, crucially, not all people organize their self-beliefs in the same way. These differences among people have been studied with several creative methods.

Most of what is known thus far pertains to the difference between linking all self-beliefs together and sorting them into separate compartments. As this chapter found repeatedly, researchers typically start off on this topic by assuming that the sorted compartments would confer advantages—but few have ended with that faith intact. Two main lessons emerge from these theories.

First, there is clearly a wide and resurgent appeal in the idea that it is good for self-beliefs to be kept apart. Such a compartmentalized view of self does seem like a better way to organize that information than simply relating it all to one big self. The ideal was perhaps to have several distinct sets of self-beliefs, only distantly or loosely connected to each other but each well organized in itself. The extreme form of this approach is the view that each person has multiple selves.

Yet over and over, the evidence has failed to validate the seductive appeal of compartmentalized self-knowledge. Perhaps there will eventually be found some adaptive advantages of splitting self-beliefs into separate compartments. Mostly, though, it is a sign of trouble, and possibly a source of difficulties.

In general—such as in large organizations, societies, other structures—organizational complexity with separate parts gains in flexibility, but it also costs in terms of central management. This may apply to self-knowledge as well. Merely keeping track of which version of me is appropriate for which situation takes extra mental work. And the more different these various versions are, the more mental work in keeping track of where and when to use each version.

Hence, compartmentalized self-knowledge creates a burden. The possible advantages would have to offset that, at least. I have to think that there must be at least some advantages somewhere—or else why would some people compartmentalize? Perhaps it is a less bad way of dealing with bad situations, and the general negativity comes from the bad situations. Nevertheless, from multiple selves to self-complexity and self-compartmentalization, there was precious little evidence of benefit.

The second main lesson from this work is thus an affirmation of the unity project. The self emerges as the animal brain seeks to integrate all the different thoughts, feelings, and experiences into a unity, in order to fit in well with society. The unity project remains incomplete in everyone—but far more incomplete in some than others. Compartmentalizing self-beliefs into different, separate structures can be considered a failure to integrate. This failure may arise from internal personality problems or in response to external threats and demands, but in either case, it is nevertheless a failure. In general, the better integrated self-knowledge is, the better off the person is.

KEY POINTS

- Not everyone organizes self-knowledge the same way.
- In repressed people, bad memories are not linked to a network of associations. In depressed people, bad memories are linked together in a long chain of associations.
- Complex, compartmentalized knowledge about the self produces more bad than good effects.
- The better integrated self-knowledge is, the better off the person is.

The Self

A Summary

T his epilogue revisits many key themes of the book. 'The goal is to put all the pieces together. Let's start with evolution.

EVOLUTIONARY ROOTS

The human self is a cultural solution to natural problems: how to survive and reproduce. Humankind has succeeded very well at both of those criteria by means of a highly unusual strategy: culture.

The self is a vital tool by which each human animal participates in culture. You can't get the full benefits of culture without a self. That in turn requires a brain that can understand and perform its roles in the social system—in other words, a brain that can create a self. That's what enables humans to create culture and reap its benefits, including better survival and reproduction.

The self is a tool for making cultural society possible because a society creates more resources, so survival and reproduction improve. Apes have societies, as do plenty of simpler animals, but human society is qualitatively different because of so much more culture. Human societies have advanced organizational systems. They also have an extensive body of shared information and understandings, built up over many generations. They can interact with each other on the basis of that shared vision of reality.

In human sports contests, the contestants share understanding of rules and accept the decisions by referees. It is hard to imagine any animal competition having a referee. The referee represents the culture, with its

369

agreements about rules and fairness. What matters most is not either player's belief, but rather that they both know that they both accept the rules and obey the referee. The sharedness is crucial. The human self is designed for sharedness, for "I know that you know I know, and that we agree."

SELVES ARE SHAPED TO SUCCEED IN GROUPS

The forms and features of the human self are shaped by the requirements of successful groups. The self is the way it is *based on what would make for the best groups*. Individual humans succeed by helping their group succeed. This is not invoking the controversial idea of group selection because it emphasizes individual selection, though mediated by groups. Being a highly talented and successful individual would be of no avail if your group was conquered by another and you were all massacred or enslaved. We are descended from successful members of successful groups. The individual's traits had to be suitable to help the group flourish. Thus, the human self comes into being as the brain learns to perform a role in society. Selves are not solitary things. Rather, they work within a social system—among and with other selves—to produce more resources and share them. The group benefits that way. Most of the members are better off because of this cooperation within systems and shared understandings. By doing this, individual human bodies survive and reproduce better. The population thrives.

THE ROLES OF THE SELF IN GROUPS

People strive to belong to groups. How successfully they survive and reproduce, depends both on their individual performance and on the group. Both similarities and differences among group members are important. Similarity is part of the essence of the group. It means not just resembling others in some superficial way, but also sharing common understandings, knowledge, and systems. As the studies on overimitation show, human children learn from others not just about how the world works but *how we do things* in our group. The human self is for integrating the body into the group. That requires more than garnering acceptance and approval. Each self must play its part to help the group to succeed.

Groups flourish by capitalizing on the talents and inclinations of individuals, and differences among them are important. We have seen that people identify most strongly with their unusual traits and abilities. Those are precisely what society needs people to do so as to find their way into positions in the social system that will enable the system to succeed. In short, the human self evolved to be able to take on a role in society, either by choice or by being assigned to it, and it performs that role knowingly and with some degree of autonomy. Selves are quite capable of leaving one role and taking on another. Essentially, evolution produced a human self to be good at performing roles in an advanced social system.

COMMUNICATION IN HUMAN GROUPS

Communication is the original and essential human trait, as I have argued at length elsewhere (e.g., Baumeister & Masicampo, 2010). This view clashes with the species name *homo sapiens*, which extols intelligence as the essence of humankind. I think advanced communication is what makes us human.

Big brains are biologically expensive: They require plenty of energy (e.g., Dunbar, 1998, 2009). Brains only pay off when there is plenty of information to process. And preferably that's information that leads, directly or indirectly, to getting more food. Life requires calories.

That's where communication becomes important. Communication brings more information. *Every* known human society has language. It is an absolute universal even by the most stringent criteria (see Norenzayan & Heine, 2005). Language is thus one of the crucial defining traits of humankind. Communication enables one creature's experience or observation to become information in others' brains. Communication led to the formation of shared knowledge. The self not only has to work in the context of shared understanding but also to maintain its own place (its social identity and reputation) in the collectively shared stock of information.

COOPERATION

Communication helps cooperation (massively). It's when all the individuals in a group suddenly can share information about the environment that they start to get more food, enabling their population to increase and spread.

Reputation and Self-Presentation

Reputation is vital to social success and hence an ongoing concern of the self. One of the great lessons of self-presentation research is that most people care much more about how they are regarded by others than about their own private self-regard. Self-presentation is the vital task of creating and maintaining a good reputation, and it is a much stronger driver of human behavior than is self-esteem. Reputations are negotiated with language, both between you and your audience, and among them (when they discuss their impressions of you, and gossip).

A vital purpose of a good reputation is cooperation. Only with a good reputation will others cooperate with you for mutual benefit. In the words of eminent thinker Jonathan Haidt (2012), human beings are the world champions at cooperation, compared to all other species. People cooperate with people they don't even know. A large corporation, for example, is essentially a cooperative resource-producing enterprise that gets thousands of people, many of whom never meet or even set eyes on each other, to work together for their common good. Moreover, the corporation only succeeds if it benefits society as well as itself, mainly by providing goods and services that consumers wish to enjoy (and are therefore willing to pay for).

The Extended-Time Self

Cooperation depends on the extended-time self, very much including appreciating reputation and on advanced mental processes: You must project into the future and see yourself from others' point of view, and on that basis you alter your present behavior. The bigger human could consume the fruits of the joint hunt, but he (or she) would soon lack for cooperative partners for future joint hunting. The human realizes this and therefore shares the fruits of the joint action. This is an important step in building the self. Sharing is essentially human, and it requires self-regulating present behavior.

The human self is tailored to help communication and cooperation. Understanding others, caring about reputation, trafficking in information, and regulating one's own actions are some of these essential abilities.

SELF CONSISTS PARTLY OF ENERGY

All brain activity consumes energy, and the brain makes the self. Moreover, making the self by performing actions according to an organizing system takes energy, probably more than simpler ways of responding. This is especially true when it has to override some strong natural impulse, so as to do what society approves. The hundreds of findings on ego depletion, and plenty of others, fit the view that the self consists partly of energy.

The body's energy is channeled into brain activities that produce the self. These include overcoming strong impulses for quick pleasures so as to do what will be best in the long run. An effective self avoids regrets. Regret is a signal of having made a bad choice. Bad in this case means detrimental to long-term *self*-interest. An effective self minimizes those choices. Regret pushes the brain (in the present) to analyze what the self did wrong in the past and to not repeat the misstep in future situations.

There is lively scientific debate as to whether the brain's activities are really seriously impaired by lack of energy after some has been expended on hard work. There is plenty of evidence of impairment, but is lack of energy the fundamental cause of the problems? Nevertheless, the brain clearly acts *as if* energy is limited.

Self-regulation is a major part of the process of being a human self. This is true regardless of what one thinks of ego depletion theory. The human self is constantly adjusting itself and its responses. It uses energy to do this. And the body's energy is ample but nevertheless limited.

CREATING UNITY BY IMPOSING A SYSTEM

If the self is systems, the unity project aims to bring all actions of the body into the same system. Acting on an immoral impulse at one single moment can bring misery and social stigma for many years ahead. That goes to an essential core function of the self, which is the creation of unity. Unity is part of the meaning of self. It starts with the boundary between self (inside) and world (outside). Human brains strive to satisfy the requirements of unity: consistency, responsibility, ownership, reputation, and their ilk.

Learning is a matter of knowing how to act in a given situation so as to get a good result. In psychology, learning means forming a mental association between stimulus and response, based on which responses produce good outcomes. The brain is where the stimulus is matched to the response. In learning, the nervous system does both its jobs. First, it brings information to the brain about the situation (stimulus). Then it chooses and executes what to do (response). It uses the senses again to send the brain information about whether that response turned out well or badly, and the self carries that lesson forward for future reference in similar situations. It is from these stimulus–response pairs that the psychological self is constructed. It is the self as a unity, the right-now self, that executes the response based on what it knows and feels about the stimulus. That's the purpose of having a center to the central nervous system.

Speech is an additional form of unity. Humans are information agents. They spend much of each day exchanging information, mostly by talking. And a person has only one mouth, so you can only say one thing at a time. Talking is acting as a whole person. (And people do a lot of talking.) Indeed, some utterances are more than just giving information and are important social behaviors themselves, as in promising, commanding, warning, offering. In all these, the self is acting as a whole, a unity. To accomplish that, the brain uses systems to impose organization, and that creates the self.

Unity of Self across Time

The human self is linked in vital ways to past and future. The unity project builds the self by integrating across time. The self as it exists right now is connected to, informed by, responsible for, and (mostly) consistent with past and future versions of self. There is an underlying continuity of self as everyone understands. For example, a person might change jobs or residence, but the person remains the same person in crucial respects.

The right-now self can use simple decision rules to decide what to do. Those rules will not work as well when the self extends across time. You can't simply act on what you most strongly feel like doing at the present moment. The extended-time self needs a more elaborate supervisory structure than the right-now self. This inner part of the executive self must be able to sort through competing impulses, based on both immediate and delayed effects, to choose the best one, and then to implement it. All of this takes a more extensive organizing system than the animal self. The brain creates that. That's a big part of the self.

All three of the main aspects of the self are transformed by the extension across time:

1. Self-knowledge (Part Three, Chapters 11–16) is greatly expanded by time. Narrative self-understanding becomes fundamental so that people think of their present self and its circumstances in the context of the past and future. The present is thus part of an ongoing story, and the present self is understood to be a character in that story. You are constrained by the past (that's what got you to where you are), and you decide how to act so as to shape the future.

2. The workings of the executive self (Part Four, Chapters 17–19) become much more complicated as a result of extending across time. (On the plus side, it can accomplish much more.) Much human self-control involves sacrificing something in the present for the sake of the future. Outside the sun is shining and you are tempted to go out to play or relax but you forego that pleasure to stay indoors and work because that will be better in the long run. The self-controlling self mentally simulates future possibilities, then uses the result of those calculations to alter behavior in the present. Planning is a pervasive human activity that functions in the present to link together future actions so as to produce good outcomes. The executive self is also a moral and economic agent, and continuity across time is vital to both.

3. The interpersonal self (Part Five, Chapters 20–23) also gains depth and complexity from extending across time. I have emphasized cooperation as a major advance in human evolution, regarding the way that humans readily cooperate even with non-kin to work for mutual advantage. Commitments and promises, debts and obligations, and other features of human social life extend across time and improve relationships.

Moral Rules

The moral foundations of the self are relevant here also. Individuals learn and embrace morality because it is a strategy that helps attract cooperative partners. Moral rules are largely the same in most societies because they promote the same kinds of behavior that help the society to thrive.

Individuals are motivated to learn and follow them because that is how they get others to accept them and cooperate with them to produce rewards.

Morally virtuous behavior is motivated mostly by concern with reputation. Moral reputations are built over months and years, and the fear of reputational damage encourages people to treat each other morally—which helps the system function better at delivering resources for a longer and better life. Moral guidelines help the executive know how best to act and choose, so as to enable the individual to maintain good interpersonal relationships. Systems of economic trade require selves that endure across time. Financial knowledge enables the self's executive to know how best to plan, decide, and act, so as to flourish in society. Extending the self across time is the supreme achievement of the unity project.

Last Words

We are who we are because of culture. And by that I mean much more than the truism that some traits and attitudes are influenced by society. We are who we are because nature selected brains that could perform ongoing roles in complex, productive social systems. Culture has made the good life possible, for countless people. Human culture has functioned very well, increasing quantity and quality of life. But a high-functioning culture needs high-functioning selves, to make it work.

The human self is not a physical thing, but rather a combination of performance, organized system, and shared concepts. Human brains capitalize on advanced social systems, and these systems need individual selves that extend across time, follow rules, make responsible choices, cooperate, and communicate. To create the self, the brain uses organizing systems that strive toward unity. The creation of unity in the present starts with the coordination of body parts so as to move the whole body. Establishing continuity across time requires the human self to be much more complex, but the payoffs are huge. The unity project is largely successful but not completely so. The quest for unity, like other features of the human self, is shaped by what enables cultural systems to flourish, so they can produce more resources and support the growing human population. Each human self attends to how it is different and what it can offer to society. It carefully tracks how others view it and adjusts its own actions and patterns so as to maintain the best possible reputation, within constraints that include other goals.

The self is a social reality. Indeed, it is one of the most fundamental of social realities, without which many others (marriage, citizenship, laws and morals, ownership and marketplaces) could hardly exist.

References

Abbott, R. (2018). Meaning, autonomy, symbolic causality, and free will. *Review of General Psychology, 22,* 85–94.

Acemoglu, R., & Robinson, J. (2012). *Why nations fail.* New York: Crown.

Ahern, C., & Kyrios, M. (2016). Self processes in obsessive-compulsive disorder. In M. Kyrios, R. Moulding, G. Doron, S. S. Bhar, M. Nedeljkovic, & M. Mikulincer (Eds), *The self in understanding and treating psychological disorders* (pp. 112–122). Cambridge, UK: Cambridge University Press.

Ainslie, G. (2001). *Breakdown of will.* New York: Cambridge University Press.

Alloy, L. B., & Abramson, L. Y. (1979). Judgment of contingency in depressed and nondepressed students: Sadder but wiser? *Journal of Experimental Psychology: General, 108,* 441–485.

Allport, G. A. (1954). *The nature of prejudice.* Reading, MA: Addison-Wesley.

Allport, G. A. (1958). The functional autonomy of motives. In C. Stacey & M DeMartino (Eds.), *Understanding human motivation* (pp. 69–81). New York: Howard Allen Publishers.

Altick, R. (1965). *Lives and letters: A history of literary biography in England and America.* New York: Knopf.

Aman, M. (2020, September 24). Dolly Parton once entered a Dolly look-alike contest and lost—to a man. *Woman's World.* www.womansworld.com/posts/entertainment/dolly-parton-lookalike-164680

Amsterdam, B. (1972). Mirror self-image reactions before age two. *Developmental Psychobiology, 5,* 297–205.

Andersen, S. M. (1984). Self-knowledge and social inference: The diagnosticity of cognitive/affective and behavioral data. *Journal of Personality and Social Psychology, 46,* 294–307.

Andersen, S. M., & Ross, L. (1984). Self-knowledge and social inference: The impact of cognitive/affective and behavioral data. *Journal of Personality and Social Psychology, 46,* 280–293.

Andersen, S. M., & Williams, M. (1985). Cognitive/affective reactions in the improvement of self-esteem: When thoughts and feelings make a difference. *Journal of Personality and Social Psychology, 49*, 1086–1097.

Ansell, N. (2011a). *Deep country*. London: Hamish Hamilton.

Ansell, N. (2011b, March 27). My life as a hermit. *The Guardian*. www.theguardian.com/environment/2011/mar/27/neil-ansell-my-life-as-hermit

Aries, P. (1962). *Centuries of childhood: A social history of family life* (R. Baldick, Trans.). New York: Random House.

Aries, P. (1981). *The hour of our death* (H. Weaver, Trans.). New York: Knopf.

Aron, A., McLaughlin-Vope, T., Mashek, D., Lewandowski, G., Wright, S. C., & Aron, E. N. (2004). Including others in the self. *European Review of Social Psychology, 15*, 101–132.

Aronson, E., & Mettee, D. (1968). Dishonest behavior as a function of differential levels of induced self-esteem. *Journal of Personality and Social Psychology, 9*, 121–127.

Arrow, K. J. (1974) *The limits of organization*. New York: Norton.

Asch, S. E. (1955, November). Opinions and social pressure. *Scientific American*, 31–35.

Asch, S. E. (1956). Studies of independence and conformity: A minority of one against a unanimous majority. *Psychological Monographs, 70*(No. 417).

Baars, B. J. (1997). *In the theater of consciousness: The workspace of the mind*. New York: Oxford University Press.

Bachman, J. G., & O'Malley, P. M. (1977). Self-esteem in young men: A longitudinal analysis of the impact of educational and occupational attainment. *Journal of Personality and Social Psychology, 35*, 365–380.

Bachman, J. G., & O'Malley, P. M. (1986). Self-concepts, self-esteem, and educational experiences: The frog pond revisited (again). *Journal of Personality and Social Psychology, 50*, 35–46.

Bard, K. A., Todd, B. K., Bernier, C., Lover, J., & Leavens, D. A. (2006). Self-awareness in human and chimpanzee infants: What is measured and what is meant by the mark and mirror test. *Infancy, 9*, 191–219.

Barkley, R. A. (1997). *ADHD and the nature of self-control*. New York: Guilford Press.

Batson, D. (2008). Moral masquerades: Experimental exploration of the nature of moral motivations. *Phenomenology and the Cognitive Sciences, 7*, 51–66.

Baumeister, R. F. (1982). A self-presentational view of social phenomena. *Psychological Bulletin, 91*, 3–26.

Baumeister, R. F. (1984). Choking under pressure: Self-consciousness and paradoxical effects of incentives on skillful performance. *Journal of Personality and Social Psychology, 46*, 610–620.

Baumeister, R. F. (1986). *Identity: Cultural change and the struggle for self*. New York: Oxford University Press.

Baumeister, R. F. (1987). How the self became a problem: A psychological review of historical research. *Journal of Personality and Social Psychology, 52*, 163–176.

Baumeister, R. F. (1988). Masochism as escape from self. *Journal of Sex Research, 25*, 28–59.

Baumeister, R. F. (1989a). *Masochism and the self*. Hillsdale, NJ: Erlbaum.

Baumeister, R. F. (1989b). The optimal margin of illusion. *Journal of Social and Clinical Psychology, 8,* 176–189.

Baumeister, R. F. (1990). Suicide as escape from self. *Psychological Review, 97,* 90–113.

Baumeister, R. F. (1991a). *Escaping the self: Alcoholism, spirituality, masochism, and other flights from the burden of selfhood.* New York: Basic Books.

Baumeister, R. F. (1991b). *Meanings of life.* New York: Guilford Press.

Baumeister, R. F. (Ed.). (1993). *Self-esteem: The puzzle of low self-regard.* New York: Plenum.

Baumeister, R. F. (1996). *Evil: Inside human cruelty and violence.* New York: Freeman/Times Books/Henry Holt.

Baumeister, R. F. (1997). Esteem threat, self-regulatory breakdown, and emotional distress as factors in self-defeating behavior. *Review of General Psychology, 1,* 145–174.

Baumeister, R. F. (1998). The self. In D. T. Gilbert, S. T. Fiske, & G. Lindzey (Eds.), *Handbook of social psychology* (4th ed., pp. 680–740). New York: McGraw-Hill.

Baumeister, R. F. (2005). *The cultural animal: Human nature, meaning, and social life.* New York: Oxford University Press.

Baumeister, R. F. (2017). Addiction, cigarette smoking, and voluntary control of action: Do cigarette smokers lose their free will? *Addictive Behaviors Reports, 5,* 67–84.

Baumeister, R. F. (2019). Stalking the true self through the jungles of authenticity: Problems, contradictions, inconsistencies, disturbing findings—and a possible way forward. *Review of General Psychology, 23,* 143–154.

Baumeister, R. F., Ainsworth, S. E., & Vohs, K. D. (2016). Are groups more or less than the sum of their members?: The moderating role of individual identification. *Behavioral and Brain Sciences, 39,* e137.

Baumeister, R. F., Bratslavsky, E., Finkenauer, C., & Vohs, K. D. (2001). Bad is stronger than good. *Review of General Psychology, 5,* 323–370.

Baumeister, R. F., Bushman, B. J., & Campbell, W. K. (2000). Self-esteem, narcissism, and aggression: Does violence result from low self-esteem or from threatened egotism? *Current Directions in Psychological Science, 9,* 26–29.

Baumeister, R. F., Bushman, B. J., & Tice, D. M. (2021). *A narrative review of multi-site replication studies in social psychology: Methodological utopia or social psychology's self-destruct mechanism?* Manuscript in preparation.

Baumeister, R. F., & Cairns, K. J. (1992). Repression and self-presentation: When audiences interfere with self-deceptive strategies. *Journal of Personality and Social Psychology, 62,* 851–862.

Baumeister, R. F., Campbell, J. D., Krueger, J. I., & Vohs, K. D. (2003). Does high self-esteem cause better performance interpersonal success, happiness, or healthier lifestyles? *Psychological Science in the Public Interest, 4,* 1–44.

Baumeister, R. F., Campbell, J. D., Krueger, J. I., & Vohs, K. D. (2005, January). Exploding the self-esteem myth. *Scientific American, 292,* 84–91.

Baumeister, R. F., Dale, K., & Sommer, K. L. (1998). Freudian defense mechanisms and empirical findings in modern social psychology: Reaction formation, projection, displacement, undoing, isolation, sublimation, and denial. *Journal of Personality, 66,* 181–1124.

Baumeister, R. F., Gailliot, M., deWall, C. N., & Oaten, M. (2006). Self-regulation and personality: How interventions increase regulatory success, and how depletion moderates the effects of traits on behavior. *Journal of Personality, 74*, 1773–1801.

Baumeister, R. F., & Jones, E. E. (1978). When self-presentation is constrained by the target's knowledge: Consistency and compensation. *Journal of Personality and Social Psychology, 36*, 608–618.

Baumeister, R. F., & Leary, M. R. (1995). The need to belong: Desire for interpersonal attachments as a fundamental human motivation. *Psychological Bulletin, 117*, 497–529.

Baumeister, R. F., Maranges, H. M., & Vohs, K. D. (2018). Human self as information agent: Functioning in a social environment based on shared meanings. *Review of General Psychology, 22*, 36–47.

Baumeister, R. F., & Masicampo, E. J. (2010). Conscious thought is for facilitating social and cultural interactions: How mental simulations serve the animal–culture interface. *Psychological Review, 117*, 945–971.

Baumeister, R. F., Masicampo, E. J., & Vohs, K. D. (2011). Do conscious thoughts cause behavior? *Annual Review of Psychology, 62*, 331–361.

Baumeister, R. F., & Monroe, A. E. (2014). Recent research on free will: Conceptualizations, beliefs, and processes. *Advances in Experimental Social Psychology, 50*, 1–52.

Baumeister, R. F., & Newman, L. S. (1994). Self-regulation of cognitive inference and decision processes. *Personality and Social Psychology Bulletin, 20*, 3–19.

Baumeister, R. F., & Scher, S. J. (1988). Self-defeating behavior patterns among normal individuals: Review and analysis of common self-destructive tendencies. *Psychological Bulletin, 104*, 3–22.

Baumeister, R. F., & Senders, P. S. (1989). Identity development and the role structure of children's games. *Journal of Genetic Psychology: Research and Theory on Human Development, 150*, 19–37.

Baumeister, R. F., Shapiro, J. P., & Tice, D. M. (1985). Two kinds of identity crisis. *Journal of Personality, 53*, 407–424.

Baumeister, R. F., Smart, L., & Boden, J. M. (1996). Relation of threatened egotism to violence and aggression: The dark side of high self-esteem. *Psychological Review, 103*, 5–33.

Baumeister, R. F., & Sommer, K. L. (1997). What do men want?: Gender differences and two spheres of belongingness: Comment on Cross and Madson (1997). *Psychological Bulletin, 122*, 38–44.

Baumeister, R. F., Stillwell, A., & Wotman, S. R. (1990). Victim and perpetrator accounts of interpersonal conflict: Autobiographical narratives about anger. *Journal of Personality and Social Psychology, 59*, 994–1005.

Baumeister, R. F., & Tice, D. M. (1984). Role of self-presentation and choice in cognitive dissonance under forced compliance: Necessary or sufficient causes? *Journal of Personality and Social Psychology, 46*, 5–13.

Baumeister, R. F., Tice, D. M., & Hutton, D. G. (1989). Self-presentational motivations and personality differences in self-esteem. *Journal of Personality, 57*, 547–579.

Baumeister, R. F., & Tierney, J. (2011). *Willpower: Rediscovering the greatest human strength*. New York: Penguin Press.

Baumeister, R. F., & Vohs, K. D. (2016). Strength model of self-regulation as limited resource: Assessment, controversies, update. *Advances in Experimental Social Psychology, 54*, 67–127.

Baumeister, R. F., Vohs, K. D., deWall, C. N., & Zhang, L. (2007). How emotion shapes behavior: Feedback, anticipation, and reflection, rather than direct causation. *Personality and Social Psychology Review, 11*, 167–203

Baumeister, R. F., Vohs, K. D., & Funder, D. C. (2007). Psychology as the science of self-reports and finger movements: Whatever happened to actual behavior? *Perspectives on Psychological Science, 2*, 396–403.

Baumeister, R. F., Vohs, K. D., & Oettingen, G. (2016). Pragmatic prospection: How and why people think about the future. *Review of General Psychology, 20*, 3–16.

Baumeister, R. F., Vohs, K. D., & Tice, D. M. (2007). The strength model of self-control. *Current Directions in Psychological Science, 16*, 351–355.

Baumeister, R. F., Wright, B. R. E., & Carreon, D. (2019). Self-control "in the wild": Experience sampling study of trait and state self-regulation. *Self & Identity, 18*, 494–528.

Beaman, A. L., Klentz, B., Diener, E., & Svanum, S. (1979). Self-awareness and transgression in children: Two field studies. *Journal of Personality and Social Psychology, 37*, 1835–1846.

Becker, E. (1973). *The denial of death.* New York: Academic Press.

Beckley, M. (2010). Economic development and military effectiveness. *Journal of Strategic Studies, 33*, 43–79.

Beedie, C. J., & Lane, A. M. (2012). The role of glucose in self-control: Another look at the evidence and an alternative conceptualization. *Personality and Social Psychology Review, 16*, 143–153.

Beggan, J. K. (1992). On the social nature of nonsocial perception: The mere ownership effect. *Journal of Personality and Social Psychology, 62*, 229–237.

Belk, R. W. (1988). Possessions and the extended self. *Journal of Consumer Research, 15*, 139–168.

Bem, D. J. (1965). An experimental analysis of self-persuasion. *Journal of Experimental Social Psychology, 1*, 199–218.

Bem, D. J. (1972). Self-perception theory. In L Berkowitz (Ed.), *Advances in experimental social psychology* (Vol. 6, pp. 1–62). New York: Academic Press.

Berglas, S., & Jones, E. E. (1978). Drug choice as a self-handicapping strategy in response to non-contingent success. *Journal of Personality and Social Psychology, 36*, 405–417.

Berglas, S. C., & Baumeister, R. F. (1993). *Your own worst enemy: Understanding the paradox of self-defeating behavior.* New York: Basic Books.

Bernstein, W. J. (2004). *The birth of plenty: How the prosperity of the modern world was created.* Camden, ME: International Marine.

Blakemore, S.-J., Frith, C. D., & Wolpert, D. M. (1999). Spatio-temporal prediction modulates the perception of self-produced stimuli. *Journal of Cognitive Neuroscience, 11*, 551–559.

Blakemore, S.-J., Smith, J., Steel, R., Johnstone, E. C., & Frith, C. D. (2000). The perception of self-produced sensory stimuli in patients with auditory hallucinations and passivity experiences: Evidence for a breakdown in self-monitoring. *Psychological Medicine, 30*, 1131–1139.

Blasi, A. (1980). Bridging moral cognition and moral action: A critical review of the literature. *Psychological Bulletin, 88,* 1–45.

Bloom, P. (2008). First person plural. *The Atlantic Online.* www.theallantic.com/doc/print/200811/multiple-personalities

Bosson, J., Swann, W. B., & Pennebaker, J. W. (2000). Stalking the perfect measure of implicit self-esteem: The blind men and the elephant revisited? *Journal of Personality and Social Psychology, 79,* 631–643.

Brady, J. V. (1958). Ulcers in "executive" monkeys. *Scientific American, 199,* 95–100.

Branden, N. (1969). *The psychology of self-esteem.* New York and San Francisco: Nash/Jossey-Bass/Wiley.

Brockner, J., Davy, J., & Carter, C. (1985). Low self-esteem and survivor guilt: Motivational, affective, and attitudinal consequences. *Organizational Behavior and Human Decision Processes, 36,* 229–244.

Brown, B. R. (1968). The effects of need to maintain face on interpersonal bargaining. *Journal of Experimental Social Psychology, 4,* 107–122.

Brummelman, E., Thomaes, S., Nelemans, S. A., Orobio de Castro, B., Overbeek, G., & Bushman, B. J. (2015). Origins of narcissism in children. *Proceedings of the National Aacademy of Sciences of the USA, 112,* 3659–3662.

Buehler, R., Griffin, D., & Peetz, J. (2010). The planning fallacy: Cognitive, motivational, and social origins. In M. Zanna & J. Olson (Eds.), *Advances in experimental social psychology* (Vol. 43, pp. 1–62). San Diego, CA: Academic Press.

Buehler, R., Griffin, D., & Ross, M. (1994). Exploring the "planning fallacy": Why people underestimate their task completion times. *Journal of Personality and Social Psychology, 67,* 366–381.

Buhrmester, D., Furman, W., Wittenberg, M. T., & Reis, H. T. (1988). Five domains of interpersonal competence in peer relationships. *Journal of Personality and Social Psychology, 55,* 991–1008.

Bushman, B. J., & Baumeister, R. F. (1998). Threatened egotism, narcissism, self-esteem, and direct and displaced aggression: Does self-love or self-hate lead to violence? *Journal of Personality and Social Psychology, 75,* 219–229.

Bushman, B. J., & Baumeister, R. F. (2002). Does self-love or self-hate lead to violence? *Journal of Research in Personality, 36,* 543–545.

Bushman, B. J., Baumeister, R. F., Thomaes, S., Ryu, E., Begeer, S., & West, S. G. (2009). Looking again, and harder, for a link between low self-esteem and aggression. *Journal of Personality, 77,* 427–446.

Butler, J. L., & Baumeister, R. F. (1998). The trouble with friendly faces: Skilled performance with a supportive audience. *Journal of Personality and Social Psychology, 75,* 1213–1230.

Buunk, B. P., Kuyper, H., & van der Zee, Y. G. (2005). Affective responses to social comparison in the classroom. *Basic and Applied Social Psychology, 27,* 229–237.

Calhoun, L. G., & Tedeschi, R. G. (2013). *Posttraumatic growth in clinical practice.* New York: Routledge.

California Task Force to Promote Self-Esteem and Personal and Social Responsibility. (1990). *Toward a state of self-esteem.* Sacramento: California State Department of Education.

Cameron, J. J., & Granger, S. (2019). Does self-esteem have an interpersonal imprint beyond self-reports?: A meta-analysis of self-esteem and objective interpersonal indicators. *Personality and Social Psychology Review, 23,* 73–102.

Campbell, A. (1981). *A sense of well-being in America.* New York: McGraw-Hill.

Campbell, J. D. (1990). Self-esteem and clarity of the self-concept. *Journal of Personality and Social Psychology, 59,* 538–549.

Campbell, W. K. (2005). *When you love a man who loves himself.* Naperville, IL: Sourcebooks.

Campbell, W. K., & Crist, C. (2020). *The new science of narcissism.* Boulder, CO: Sounds True.

Caruso, E. M. (2010). When the future feels worse than the past: A temporal inconsistency in moral judgment. *Journal of Experimental Psychology: General, 139,* 610–624.

Carver, C. S., & Scheier, M. F. (1990). Origins and functions of positive and negative affect: A control-process view. *Psychological Review, 97,* 19–35.

Carver, C. S., & Scheier, M. F. (1981). *Attention and self-regulation: A control theory approach to human behavior.* New York: Springer-Verlag.

Carver, C. S., & Scheier, M. F. (1982). Control theory: A useful conceptual framework for personality-social, clinical and health psychology. *Psychological Bulletin, 92,* 111–135.

Carver, C. S., & Scheier, M. F. (1998). *On the self-regulation of behavior.* New York: Cambridge University Press.

Chen, S. (2019). Authenticity in context: Being true to working selves. *Review of General Psychology, 23,* 60–72.

Cheskin, L. J., Hess, J. M., Henningfield, J., & Gorelick, D. A. (2005). Calorie restriction increases cigarette use in adult smokers. *Psychopharmacology, 179*(2), 430–436.

Cheung, W., Wildschut, T., Sedikides, C., & Pinter, B. (2014). Uncovering the multifaceted self in the domain of negative traits: On the muted expression of negative self-knowledge. *Personality and Social Psychology Bulletin, 40,* 513–525.

Chiu, C., Tollenaar, M. S., Yang, C., Elzinga, B. M., Zhang, T., & Ho, H. L. (2019). The loss of self in memory: Self-referential memory, childhood relational trauma, and dissociation. *Clinical Psychological Science, 7,* 265–282.

Church, A. T., Katigbak, M. S., Arias, R. M., Rincon, B. C., Vargas-Flores, J., Ibanez-Reyes, J., . . . Ortiz, F. A. (2014). A four-culture study of self-enhancement and adjustment using the social relations model: Do alternative conceptualizations and indices make a difference? *Journal of Personality and Social Psychology, 106,* 997–1014.

Cohen, G. L., & Sherman, D. K. (2014). The psychology of change: Self-affirmation and social psychological intervention. *Annual Review of Psychology, 65,* 333–371.

College Board. (1976–1977). *Student descriptive questionnaire.* Princeton, NJ: Educational Testing Service.

Cooley, C. H. (1902). *Human nature and the social order.* New York: Scribner's.

Cooper, J., & Fazio, R. H. (1984). A new look at dissonance theory. In L. Berkowitz (Ed.), *Advances in experimental social psychology* (Vol. 17, pp. 229–266). New York: Academic Press.

Coué, E. (1922). *Self-mastery through conscious autosuggestion* (A. Orden, Trans.). New York: Malkan.

Crocker, J., & Major, B. (1989). Social stigma and self-esteem: The self-protective properties of stigma. *Psychological Review, 96*, 608–630.

Crocker, J., & Park, L. E. (2004). The costly pursuit of self-esteem. *Psychological Bulletin, 130*, 392–414.

Crocker, J., Voelkl, K., Testa, M., & Major, B. (1991). Social stigma: The affective consequences of attributional ambiguity. *Journal of Personality and Social Psychology, 60*, 218–228.

Cross, P. (1977, Spring). Not can but will college teaching be improved? *New Directions for Higher Education*, No. 17, 1–15. Reported in D. G. Myers (1990), *Social psychology* (3rd ed.), New York: McGraw-Hill.

Cross, S. E., & Madson, L. (1997). Models of the self: Self-construals and gender. *Psychological Bulletin, 122*, 5–37.

Crowne, D. P., & Marlowe, D. (1964). *The approval motive.* New York: Wiley.

Cunningham, S. J., Turk, D. J., Macdonald, L. M., & Macrae, C. N. (2008). Yours or mine?: Ownership and memory. *Consciousness and Cognition, 17*, 312–318.

Curry, O. S. (2016). Morality as cooperation: A problem-centred approach. In T. Shackelford & R. D. Hansen (Eds.), *The evolution of morality* (pp. 27–51). Cham, Switzerland: Springer.

Curry, O. S., Mullins, D. A., & Whitehouse, H. (2019). Is it good to cooperate: Testing the theory of morality-as-cooperation in 60 societies. *Current Anthropology, 60*, 47–69.

Daly, M., Delaney, L., Egan, M., & Baumeister, R. F. (2015). Childhood self-control and unemployment throughout the lifespan: Evidence from two British cohort studies. *Psychological Science, 26*, 709–723.

Daly, M., Egan, M., Quigley, J., Delaney, L., & Baumeister, R. F. (2016). Childhood self- control predicts smoking throughout life: Evidence from 21,000 cohort study participants. *Health Psychology, 35*, 1254–1263.

Damasio, A. (1994). *Descartes' error: Emotion, reason, and the human brain.* New York: Grosset/Putnam.

Damon, W., & Hart, D. (1982). The development of self-understanding from infancy through adolescence. *Child Development, 53*, 841–864.

Damon, W., & Hart, D. (1988). *Self-understanding in childhood and adolescence.* Cambridge, UK: Cambridge University Press.

Dang, J., Barker, P., Baumert, A., Bentvelzen, M., Berkman, E., Buchholz, N., . . . Zinkernagel, A. (2021). A multilab replication of the ego depletion effect. *Social Psychological and Personality Science, 12*, 14–24.

de Ridder, D., Lensvelt-Mulders, G., Finkenauer, C., Stok, F. M., & Baumeister, R. F. (2012). Taking stock of self-control: A meta-analysis of how trait self-control relates to a wide range of behaviors. *Personality and Social Psychology Review, 16*, 76–99.

de Soto, H. (2000). *The mystery of capital.* New York: Civitas Books.

de Waal, F. (2001). *The ape and the sushi master: Cultural reflections of a primatologist.* New York: Basic Books.

DePaulo, B. M., & Kashy, D. A. (1998). Everyday lies in close and casual relationships. *Journal of Personality and Social Psychology, 74*, 63–79.

Devine, P. G. (1989). Stereotypes and prejudice: Their automatic and controlled components. *Journal of Personality and Social Psychology, 56,* 5–18.

Diener, E., Fraser, S. C., Beaman, A. L., & Kelem, R. T. (1976). Effects of deindividuation variables on stealing among Halloween trick-or-treaters. *Journal of Personality and Social Psychology, 33,* 178–183.

Diener, E., Wolsic, B., & Fujita, F. (1995). Physical attractiveness and subjective well-being. *Journal of Personality and Social Psychology, 69,* 120–129.

Ditto, P. H., & Lopez, D. F. (1992). Motivated skepticism: Use of differential decision criteria for preferred and nonpreferred conclusions. *Journal of Personality and Social Psychology, 63,* 568–584.

Dixon, J. A., Durrheim, K., & Tredoux, C. (2005). Beyond the optimal contact strategy: A reality check for the contact hypothesis. *American Psychologist, 60,* 697–711.

Donahue, E. M., Robins, R. W., Roberts, B. W., & John, O. P. (1993). The divided self: Concurrent and longitudinal effects of psychological adjustment and social roles on self-concept differentiation. *Journal of Personality and Social Psychology, 64,* 834–846.

Donnellan, M. B., Trzesniwski, K. H., Robins, R. W., Moffitt, T. E., & Caspi, A. (2005). Low-self-esteem is related to aggression, antisocial behavior, and delinquency. *Psychological Science, 16,* 328–335.

Donnelly, G. E., Ksendzova, M., Howell, R. T., Vohs, K. D., & Baumeister, R. F. (2016). Buying to blunt negative feelings: Materialistic escape from the self. *Review of General Psychology, 20,* 272–316.

Druckman, D. E., & Swets J. A. (1988). *Enhancing human performance: Issues, theories, and techniques.* Washington, DC: National Academy Press.

Dufner, M., Gebauer, J. E., Sedikides, C., & Denissen, J. J. A. (2019). Self-enhancement and psychological adjustment: A meta-analytic review. *Personality and Social Psychology Review, 23,* 48–72.

Dunbar, J. M., & Stunkard, A. J. (1979). Adherence to diet and drug regimen. In R. Levy, B. Rifkind, B. Dennis, & N. Ernst (Eds.), *Nutrition, lipids, and coronary heart disease* (pp. 391–423). New York: Raven Press.

Dunbar, R. I. M. (1998). The social brain hypothesis. *Evolutionary Anthropology, 6,* 178–190.

Dunbar, R. I. M. (2009). The social brain hypothesis and its implications for social evolution. *Annals of Human Biology, 36,* 562–572.

Dunning, D., Meyerowitz, J. A., & Holzberg, A. D. (1989). Ambiguity and self-evaluation: The role of idiosyncratic trait definitions in self-serving assessments of ability. *Journal of Personality and Social Psychology, 57,* 1082–1090.

Duval, S., & Wicklund, R. A. (1972). *A theory of objective self-awareness.* New York: Academic Press.

Engelmann, J. M., Herrmann, E., & Tomasello, M. (2012). Five-year-olds, but not chimpanzees, attempt to manage their reputations. *PLOS One, 7,* e48433 (1–7).

Epstein, S. (1998). Cognitive-experiential self-theory. In D. Barone, M. Hersen, & V. Van Hasselt (Eds.), *Advanced personality* (pp. 211–238). New York: Springer.

Erikson, E. H. (1950). *Childhood and society.* New York: Norton.

Erikson, E. H. (1968). *Identity: Youth and crisis.* New York: Norton.

Evans, D., Boggero, I., & Segerstrom, S. (2016). The nature of self-regulatory fatigue and "ego depletion": Lessons from physical fatigue. *Personality and Social Psychology Review, 20,* 143–153.

Farrelly, D., Clemson, P., & Guthrie, M. (2016). Are women's mate preferences for altruism also influenced by physical attractiveness? *Evolutionary Psychology, 14*(1), 1–6.

Fazio, R. H., Effrein, E. A., & Falender, V. J. (1981). Self-perceptions following social interactions. *Journal of Personality and Social Psychology, 41,* 232–242.

Felson, R. B. (1981). Self and reflected appraisal among football players: A test of the Meadian hypothesis. *Social Psychology Quarterly, 44,* 116–126.

Felson, R. B. (1989). Parents and the reflected appraisal process: A longitudinal analysis. *Journal of Personality and Social Psychology, 56,* 965–971.

Fenigstein, A. (1984). Self-consciousness and the overperception of self as a target. *Journal of Personality and Social Psychology, 47,* 860–870.

Ferrari, J. R., Johnson, J. L., & McCown, W. G. (1995). *Procrastination and task avoidance: Theory, research, and treatment.* New York: Plenum.

Festinger, L. (1957). *A theory of cognitive dissonance.* Stanford, CA: Stanford University Press.

Festinger, L., & Carlsmith, J. M. (1959). Cognitive consequences of forced compliance. *Journal of Abnormal and Social Psychology, 58,* 203–210.

Fincher, C. L., Thornhill, R., Murray, D. B., & Schaller, M. (2008). Pathogen prevalence predicts human cross-cultural variability in individualism/collectivism. *Proceedings of the Royal Society B, 275,* 1279–1285.

Finkel, E. J. (2017). *The all-or-nothing marriage: How the best marriages work.* New York: Penguin/Random House.

Finkel, E. J. (2019). Complementing the sculpting metaphor: Reflections on how relationship partners elicit the best or the worst in each other. *Review of General Psychology, 23,* 127–132.

Finkel, E. J., Slotter, E. B., Luchies, L. B., Walton, G. M., & Gross, J. J. (2013). A brief intervention to promote conflict-reappraisal preserves marital quality over time. *Psychological Science, 24,* 1595–1601.

Fleeson, W., & Wilt, J. (2010). The relevance of Big Five trait content in behavior to subjective authenticity: Do high levels of within person behavioral variability undermine or enable authenticity achievement? *Journal of Personality, 78,* 1353–1387.

Forsyth, D. R., Kerr, N. A., Burnette, J. L., & Baumeister, R. F. (2007). Attempting to improve the academic performance of struggling college students by bolstering their self-esteem: An intervention that backfired. *Journal of Social and Clinical Psychology, 26,* 447–459.

Fox, F. V., & Staw, B. M. (1979). The trapped administrator: Effects of insecurity and policy resistance upon commitment to a course of action. *Administrative Sciences Quarterly, 24,* 449–471.

Frankfurt, H. G. (1971). Freedom of the will and the concept of a person. *Journal of Philosophy, 68*(1), 127–144.

Fridlund, A. J. (1991). The sociality of solitary smiles: Effects of an implicit audience. *Journal of Personality and Social Psychology, 60,* 229–240.

Friese, M., Frankenbach, J., Job, V., & Loschelder, D. D. (2017). Does self-control training improve self-control?: A meta-analysis. *Perspectives on Psychological Science, 12,* 1077–1099.

Frimer, J. A., Schaefer, N. K., & Oakes, H. (2014). Moral actor, selfish agent. *Journal of Personality and Social Psychology, 106,* 790–802.

Fukuyama, F. (1995). *Trust: The social virtues & the creation of prosperity.* New York: Free Press.

Fukuyama, F. (2011). *The origins of political order: From prehuman times to the French Revolution.* New York: Farrar, Straus & Giroux.

Fukuyama, F. (2018). *Identity: The demand for dignity and the politics of resentment.* New York: Farrar, Straus & Giroux.

Gabriel, M. T., Critelli, J. W., & Ee, J. S. (1994). Narcissistic illusions in self-evaluations of intelligence and attractiveness. *Journal of Personality, 62,* 143–155.

Gabriel, S., & Gardner, W. L. (1999). Are there "his" and "her" types of interdependence?: The implications of gender differences in collective and relational interdependence for affect, behavior, and cognition. *Journal of Personality and Social Psychology, 75,* 642–655.

Gabriel, S., Valenti, J., & Young, A. F. (2016). Social surrogates, social motivations, and everyday activities: The case for a strong, subtle, and sneaky social self. *Advances in Experimental Social Psychology, 53,* 189–243.

Gadamer, H.-G. (1975). *Truth and method* (J. Weinsheimer & G. Marshall, Trans.). New York: Continuum.

Gailliot, M. T., & Baumeister, R. F. (2007). The physiology of willpower: Linking blood glucose to self-control. *Personality and Social Psychology Review, 11,* 303–327.

Gailliot, M. T., Baumeister, R. F., deWall, C. N., Maner, J. K., Plant, E. A., Tice, D. M., . . . Schmeichel, B. J. (2007). Self-control relies on glucose as a limited energy source: Willpower is more than a metaphor. *Journal of Personality and Social Psychology, 92,* 325–336.

Gailliot, M. T., Hildebrandt, B., Eckel, L. A., & Baumeister, R. F. (2010). A theory of limited metabolic energy and premenstrual syndrome symptoms: Increased metabolic demands during the luteal phase divert metabolic resources from and impair self-control. *Review of General Psychology, 14,* 269–282.

Gallagher, S. (2000). Philosophical conceptions of the self: Implications for cognitive science. *Trends in Cognitive Sciences, 4,* 14–21.

Gallup, G. G. (1970). Chimpanzees: Self recognition. *Science, 167,* 86–87.

Gallup, G. G. (1982). Self-awareness and the emergence of mind in primates. *American Journal of Primatology, 2*(3), 237–248.

Garrison, K. E., Finley, A. J., & Schmeichel, B. J. (2019). Ego depletion reduces attention control: Evidence from two high-powered preregistered experiments. *Personality and Social Psychology Bulletin, 45,* 728–739.

Gebauer, J. E., Nehrlich, A. D., Stahlberg, D., Sedikides, C., Hackenschmidt, A., Schick, D., . . . Mander, J. (2018). Mind–body practices and the self: Yoga and meditation do not quiet the ego but instead boost self-enhancement. *Psychological Science, 29,* 1299–1308.

Gilovich, T. (1983). Biased evaluation and persistence in gambling. *Journal of Personality and Social Psychology, 44,* 1110–1126.

Gilovich, T. (1991). *How we know what isn't so.* New York: Free Press.

Gino, F., Sharek, Z., & Moore, D. A. (2011). Keeping the illusion of control under control: Ceilings, floors, and imperfect calibration. *Organizational Behavior and Human Decision Processes, 114*, 104–114.

Glass, D. C., Singer, J. E., & Friedman, L. N. (1969). Psychic cost of adaptation to an environmental stressor. *Journal of Personality and Social Psychology, 12*, 200–210.

Goffman, E. (1959). *The presentation of self in everyday life.* New York: Anchor Books.

Golubickis, M., Falben, J. K., Cunningham, W. A., & Macrae, C. N. (2018). Exploring the self-ownership effect: Separating stimulus and response biases. *Journal of Experimental Psychology: Learning, Memory, and Cognition, 44*, 295–306.

Goodwin, G. P., Piazza, J., & Rozin, P. (2014). Moral character predominates in person perception and evaluation. *Journal of Personality and Social Psychology, 106*(1), 148–168.

Gottfredson, M. R., & Hirschi, T. (1990). *A general theory of crime.* Stanford, CA: Stanford University Press.

Green, J. D., Sedikides, C., Pinter, B., & Van Tongeren, D. R. (2009). Two sides to self-protection: Self-improvement strivings and feedback from close relationships eliminate mnemic neglect. *Self and Identity, 8*, 233–250.

Greenberg, J., Solomon, S., Pyszczynski, T., Rosenblatt, A., Burling, J., Lyon, D., . . . Pinel, E. (1992). Why do people need self-esteem?: Converging evidence that self-esteem serves an anxiety-buffering function. *Journal of Personality and Social Psychology, 63*, 913–922.

Greenwald, A. G. (1980). The totalitarian ego: Fabrication and revision of personal history. *American Psychologist, 35*, 603–618.

Greenwald, A. G., & Banaji, M. R. (1989). The self as a memory system: Powerful, but ordinary. *Journal of Personality and Social Psychology, 57*, 41–54.

Greenwald, A. G., & Banaji, M. R. (1995). Implicit social cognition: Attitudes, self-esteem, and stereotypes. *Psychological Review, 102*, 4–27.

Greenwald, A. G., McGhee, D. E., & Schwartz, J. K. L. (1998). Measuring individual differences in implicit cognition: The Implicit Association Test. *Journal of Personality and Social Psychology, 74*, 1464–1480.

Gregory, B., Peters, L., & Rapee, R. M. (2016). The self in social anxiety. In M. Kyrios, R. Moulding, G. Doron, S. S. Bhar, M. Nedeljkovic, & M. Mikulincer (Eds), *The self in understanding and treating psychological disorders* (pp. 91–101). Cambridge, UK: Cambridge University Press.

Greven, P. (1977). *The Protestant temperament.* New York: Knopf.

Group for Advancement of Psychiatry. (1957). *Methods of forceful indoctrination: Observations and interviews.* New York: Author.

Gur, R. C., & Sackeim, H. A. (1979). Self-deception: A concept in search of a phenomenon. *Journal of Personality and Social Psychology, 37*, 147–169.

Gwynne, S. C. (2010). *Empire of the summer moon: Quanah Parker and the rise and fall of the Comanches, the most powerful Indian tribe in American history.* New York: Scribner.

Haidt, J. (2012). *The righteous mind: Why good people are divided by politics and religion.* New York: Pantheon.

Hansen, R. D., & Hansen, C. H. (1988). Repression of emotionally tagged memories: The architecture of less complex emotions. *Journal of Personality and Social Psychology, 55*, 811–818.

Hardin, G. (1968). The tragedy of the commons. *Science, 162*, 1243–1248.

Hardy, C. L., & van Vugt, M. (2006). Nice guys finish first: The competitive altruism hypothesis. *Personality and Social Psychology Bulletin, 32*, 1402–1413.

Hardy, S. A., & Carlo, G. (2011). Moral identity: What is it, how does it develop, and is it linked to moral action? *Child Development Perspectives, 5*, 212–218.

Harris, M. (1974). *Cows, pigs, wars, and witches: The riddles of culture.* New York: Random House.

Harris, M. (1997). *Culture, people, nature.* Boston: Addison-Wesley.

Harris, M. A., & Orth, U. (2020). The link between self-esteem and social relationships: A meta-analysis of longitudinal studies. *Journal of Personality and Social Psychology, 119*, 1459–1477.

Harter, S. (1993). Causes and consequences of low self-esteem in children and adolescents. In R. F. Baumeister (Ed.), *Self-esteem: The puzzle of low self-regard* (pp. 87–116). New York: Plenum Press.

Harter, S. (2012). *The construction of the self: Developmental and sociocultural foundations.* (2nd ed.). New York: Guilford Press.

Haslam, C., Jetten, J., Cruwys, T., Dingle, G., & Haslam, S. A. (Eds.). (2018). *The new psychology of health: Unlocking the social cure.* London: Routledge.

Haslam, S. A., Reicher, S. D., & Platow, M. J. (2010). *The new psychology of leadership: Identity, influence, and power.* London: Psychology Press.

Heatherton, T. F., & Baumeister, R. F. (1991). Binge eating as escape from self-awareness. *Psychological Bulletin, 110*, 86–108.

Heidegger, M. (1927). *Sein und Zeit* [Being and time]. Tubingen, Germany: Max Niemeyer Verlag.

Heine, S. J., Lehman, D. R., Markus, H. R., & Kitayama, S. (1999). Is there a universal need for positive self-regard? *Psychological Review, 106*, 766–794.

Henrich, J. (2018). *The secret of our success.* Princeton, NJ: Princeton University Press.

Henrich, J. (2020). *The WEIRDest people in the world.* New York: Farrar, Straus & Giroux.

Higgins, E. T. (2019). *Shared reality: What makes us strong and tears us apart.* New York: Oxford University Press.

Higgins, E. T., & Rholes, W. S. (1978). "Saying is believing": Effects of message modification on memory and liking for the person described. *Journal of Experimental Social Psychology, 14*, 363–378.

Hofmann, W., Luhmann, M., Fisher, R. R., Vohs, K. D., & Baumeister, R. F. (2014). Yes, but are they happy?: Effects of trait self-control on affective well-being and life satisfaction. *Journal of Personality, 82*, 265–277.

Hofmann, W., Rauch, W., & Gawronski, B. (2007). And deplete us not into temptation: Automatic attitudes, dietary restraint, and self-regulatory resources as determinants of eating behavior. *Journal of Experimental Social Psychology, 43*, 497–504.

Hogan, R. (1973). Moral conduct and moral character: A psychological perspective. *Psychological Bulletin, 79*, 217–232.

Hood, B. (2012). *The self illusion: How the brain creates the self.* Edinburgh, UK: Constable.

Horan, R. D., Bulte, E., & Shogren, J. F (2005). How trade saved humanity from biological exclusion: An economic theory of Neanderthal extinction. *Journal of Economic Behavior and Organization, 58,* 1–29.

Hornsey, M. J. (2008). Social identity theory and self-categorization theory: A historical overview. *Social and Personality Psychology Compass, 2,* 204–222.

Horowitz, M. J., & Sicilia, M. A. (2016). The self in posttraumatic stress disorder. In M. Kyrios, R. Moulding, G. Doron, S. S. Bhar, M. Nedeljkovic, & M. Mikulincer (Eds.), *The self in understanding and treating psychological disorders* (pp. 102–111). Cambridge, UK: Cambridge University Press.

Hull, J. G. (1981). A self-awareness model of the causes and effects of alcohol consumption. *Journal of Abnormal Psychology, 90,* 586–600.

Hume, D. (1739). *A treatise of human nature.* Project Gutenberg. www.gutenberg.org/files/4705/4705-h/4705-h.htm

Humphrey, N. (1986). *The inner eye.* London: Faber & Faber.

Ingram, R. E. (1990). Self-focused attention in clinical disorders: Review and a conceptual model. *Psychological Bulletin, 107,* 156–176.

Ingram, R. E. (1991). Tilting at windmills: A response to Psyzczynski, Greenberg, Hamilton, and Nix. *Psychological Bulletin, 110,* 544–550.

Inzlicht, M., & Schmeichel, B. J. (2012). What is ego depletion?: Toward a mechanistic revision of the resource model of self-control. *Perspectives on Psychological Science, 7,* 450–463.

James, W. (1892/1948). *Psychology: Briefer course.* Cleveland, OH: World.

Janis, I. L. (1972). *Victims of groupthink.* New York: Houghton Mifflin.

Jankowski, M. S. (1991). *Islands in the street: Gangs and American urban society.* Berkeley: University of California Press.

Janoff-Bulman, R. (1989). Assumptive worlds and the stress of traumatic events: Applications of the schema construct. *Social Cognition, 7,* 113–136.

Janoff-Bulman, R. (1992). *Shattered assumptions.* New York: Free Press.

Janus, S., Bess, B., & Saltus, C. (1977) *A sexual profile of men in power.* Englewood Cliffs, NJ: Prentice-Hall.

Jecker, N. S., & Ko, A. L. (2017) Is that the same person?: Case studies in neurosurgery. *American Journal of Bioethics—Neuroscience, 8,* 160–170.

Joiner, T. E., Metalsky, G. I., Katz, J., & Beach, S. R. (1999). Depression and excessive reassurance-seeking. *Psychological Inquiry, 10,* 269–278.

Jones, E. E. (1964). *Ingratiation: A social-psychological analysis.* New York: Appleton-Century-Crofts

Jones, E. E., & Berglas, S. (1978). Control of attributions about the self through self-handicapping strategies: The appeal of alcohol and underachievement. *Personality and Social Psychology Bulletin, 4,* 200–206.

Jones, E. E., & Nisbett, R. E. (1971). *The actor and the observer: Divergent perceptions of the causes of behavior.* Morristown, NJ: General Learning Press.

Jones, E. E., & Wortman, C. (1973). *Ingratiation: An attributional approach.* Morristown, NJ: General Learning Press.

Jones, W. H., Cheek, J. M., & Briggs, S. R. (Eds.). (1986). *Shyness: Perspectives on research and treatment.* New York: Plenum Press.

Jongman-Sereno, K. P., & Leary, M. R. (2019). The enigma of being yourself: A critical examination of the concept of authenticity. *Review of General Psychology, 23*, 133–142.

Kagan, J. (1981). *The second year: The emergence of self-awareness.* Cambridge, MA: Harvard University Press.

Kahneman, D. (2011). *Thinking, fast and slow.* New York: Farrar, Straus & Giroux.

Kahneman, D., Knetsch, J. L., & Thaler, R. H. (1990). Experimental tests of the endowment effect and the Coase theorem. *Journal of Political Economy, 98,* 1325–1348.

Kalm, L. M., & Semba, R. D. (2005). They starved so that others be better fed: Remembering Ancel Keys and the Minnesota experiment. *Journal of Nutrition, 135,* 1347–1352.

Kant, I. (1797/1967) *Kritik der praktischen Vernunft* [Critique of practical reason]. Hamburg, Germany: Felix Meiner Verlag.

Karau, S. J., & Williams, K. D. (1995). Social loafing: Research findings, implications, and future directions. *Current Directions in Psychological Science, 4,* 134–140.

Karlsson, N., Loewenstein, G., & Seppi, D. (2009). The ostrich effect: Selective attention to information. *Journal of Risk and Uncertainty, 38,* 96–115.

Keltner, D., Capps, L., Kring, A. M., Young, R. C., & Heerey, E. A. (2001). Just teasing: A conceptual analysis and empirical review. *Psychological Bulletin, 127,* 229–248.

Kim, Y., & Cohen D. (2010). Information, perspective, and judgments about the self in face and dignity cultures. *Personality and Social Psychology Bulletin, 36,* 537–550.

Kling, K. C., Hyde, J. S., Showers, C. J., & Buswell, B. N. (1999). Gender differences in self-esteem: A meta-analysis. *Psychological Bulletin, 125,* 420–500.

Koltko-Rivera, M. E. (2006). Rediscovering the later version of Maslow's hierarchy of needs: Self-transcendence and opportunities for theory, research, and unification. *Review of General Psychology, 10,* 302–317.

Kross, E. (2009). When the self becomes other: Toward an integrative understanding of the processes distinguishing adaptive self-reflection from rumination. *Values, Empathy and Fairness Across Social Barriers, 1167,* 35–40.

Kross, E., & Ayduk, O. (2011). Making meaning out of negative experiences by self-distancing. *Current Directions in Psychological Science, 20,* 187–191.

Kuhn, M. H., & McPartland, T. (1954). An empirical investigation of self-attitudes. *American Sociological Review, 19,* 68–76.

Kyrios, M., Moulding, R., Doron, G., Bhar, S. S., Nedeljkovic, M., & Mikulincer, M. (Eds.). (2016). *The self in understanding and treating psychological disorders.* Cambridge, UK: Cambridge University Press.

Langer, E. J. (1975). The illusion of control. *Journal of Personality and Social Psychology, 32,* 311–328.

Lasch, C. (1978). *The culture of narcissism: American life in an age of diminishing expectations.* New York: Norton.

Latané, B., Williams, K., & Harkins, S. (1979). Many hands make light the work: The causes and consequences of social loafing. *Journal of Personality and Social Psychology, 37,* 822–832.

Lau, S., Hiemisch, A., & Baumeister, R. F. (2015). The experience of freedom in decisions—Questioning philosophical belief in favor of psychological determinants. *Consciousness and Cognition, 33,* 30–46.

Leary, M. R. (2002). The interpersonal basis of self-esteem. Death, devaluation, or deference? In J. Forgas & K. Williams (Eds.), *The social self* (pp. 143–159). New York: Psychology Press.

Leary, M. R. (2004a). *The curse of the self.* New York: Oxford University Press.

Leary, M. R. (2004b). The function of self-esteem in terror management theory and sociometer theory: Comment on Pyszczynski et al. (2004). *Psychological Bulletin, 130,* 478–482.

Leary, M. R. (2004c). Sociometer theory and the pursuit of relational value: Getting to the root of self-esteem. *European Review of Social Psychology, 16,* 75–111.

Leary, M. R. (2012). *Sociometer theory.* In P. A. M. Van Lange, A. W. Kruglanski, & E. T. Higgins (Eds.), *Handbook of theories of social psychology* (pp. 151–159). London: SAGE.

Leary, M. R., & Kowalski, R. (1995). *Social anxiety.* New York: Guilford Press.

Leary, M. R., Tambor, E. S., Terdal, S. K., & Downs, D. L. (1995). Self-esteem as an interpersonal monitor: The sociometer hypothesis. *Journal of Personality and Social Psychology, 68,* 518–530.

Leary, M. R., Tchividjian, L. R., & Kraxberger, B. E. (1994). Self-presentation can be hazardous to your health: Impression management and health risk. *Health Psychology, 13,* 461–470.

Leimgruber, K. L., Shaw, A., Santos, L. R., & Olson, K. R. (2012). Young children are more generous when others are aware of their actions. *PLoS ONE, 7,* 1–8.

Leitan, N. D. (2016). The self in bipolar disorder. In M. Kyrios, R. Moulding, G. Doron, S. S. Bhar, M. Nedeljkovic, & M. Mikulincer (Eds), *The self in understanding and treating psychological disorders* (pp. 82–90). Cambridge, UK: Cambridge University Press.

Lerner, J. S., & Tetlock, P. E. (1999). Accounting for the effects of accountability. *Psychological Bulletin, 125,* 255–275.

Lerner, J. S., & Tetlock, P. E. (2003) Bridging individual, interpersonal, and institutional approaches to judgment and decision making: The impact of accountability on cognitive bias. In J. Lerner & P. Tetlock (Eds.), *Emerging perspectives on judgment and decision research* (pp. 431–457). New York: Cambridge University Press.

Lester, D. (2015). *On multiple selves.* Rutgers, NJ: Transaction.

Levine, J. M., & Moreland, R. L. (1990) Progress in small group research. *Annual Review of Psychology, 41,* 585–634.

Levinson, D. J. (1978). *The seasons of a man's life.* New York: Ballantine.

Lifton, R. J. (1967). *Death in life.* New York: Simon & Schuster.

Linder, D. E., Cooper, J., & Jones, E. E. (1967). Decision freedom as a determinant of the role of incentive magnitude in attitude change. *Journal of Personality and Social Psychology, 6,* 245–254.

Linville, P. W. (1985). Self-complexity and affective extremity: Don't put all your eggs in one cognitive basket. *Social Cognition, 3,* 94–120.

Linville, P. W. (1987). Self-complexity as a cognitive buffer against stress-related illness and depression. *Journal of Personality and Social Psychology, 52,* 663–676.

Linville, P. W., & Jones, E. E. (1980). Polarized appraisals of out-group members. *Journal of Personality and Social Psychology, 38,* 689–703.

Liotti, G., & Farina, B. (2016). Painful incoherence: The self in borderline personality disorder. In M. Kyrios, R. Moulding, G. Doron, S. S. Bhar, M. Nedeljkovic, & M. Mikulincer (Eds.), *The self in understanding and treating psychological disorders* (pp.169–178). Cambridge, UK: Cambridge University Press.

"Look out, Vegas." (2000, July 15). *The Economist,* pp. 30–31.

Lord, C. G., & Saenz, D. S. (1985). Memory deficits and memory surfeits: Differential cognitive consequences of tokenism for tokens and observers. *Journal of Personality and Social Psychology, 49,* 918–926.

Luyten, P., & Fonagy, P. (2016). The self in depression. In M. Kyrios, R. Moulding, G. Doron, S. S. Bhar, M. Nedeljkovic, & M. Mikulincer (Eds.), *The self in understanding and treating psychological disorders* (pp. 71–81). Cambridge, UK: Cambridge University Press.

MacIntyre, A. (1981). *After virtue.* Notre Dame, IN: University of Notre Dame Press.

Mahadevan, N., Gregg, A. P., & Sedikides, C. (2019). Is self-regard a sociometer or a hierometer?: Self-esteem tracks status and inclusion, narcissism tracks status. *Journal of Personality and Social Psychology, 116,* 444–466.

Malle, B. F. (2006). The actor–observer asymmetry in attribution: A (surprising) meta-analysis. *Psychological Bulletin, 132,* 895–919.

Malouf, E. T., Schaefer, K. E., Witt, E. A., Moore, K. E., Stuewig, J., & Tangney, J. P. (2014). The Brief Self-Control Scale predicts jail inmates' recidivism, substance dependence, and post-release adjustment. *Personality and Social Psychology Bulletin, 40,* 334–347.

Marcus-Newhall, A., Pedersen, W. C., Carlson, M., & Miller, N. (2000). Displaced aggression is alive and well: A meta-analytic review. *Journal of Personality and Social Psychology, 78,* 670–689.

Markus, H. R. (1977). Self-schemata and processing information about the self. *Journal of Personality and Social Psychology, 35,* 63–78.

Markus, H. R., & Kitayama, S. (1991). Culture and the self: Implications for cognition, emotion, and motivation. *Psychological Review, 98,* 224–253.

Marsh, H. W. (2006). *Self-concept theory, measurement and research into practice: The role of self-concept in educational psychology.* Leicester, UK: British Psychological Society.

Marsh, H. W. (2016) Cross-cultural generalizability of year in school effects: Negative effects of acceleration and positive effects of retention on academic self-concept. *Journal of Educational Psychology, 108,* 256–273.

Marsh, H. W., & Craven, R. G. (2006). Reciprocal effects of self-concept and performance from a multidimensional perspective: Beyond seductive pleasure and unidimensional perspectives. *Perspeectives on Psychological Science, 1,* 133–163.

Marsh, H. W., Pekrun, R., Parker, P. D., Murayama, K., Guo, J., Dicke, T., & Lichtenfeld, S. (2017). Long-term positive effects of repeating a year in school: Six-year longitudinal study of self-beliefs, anxiety, social relations, school grades, and test scores. *Journal of Educational Psychology, 109,* 425–438.

Marsh, H. W., Trautwein, U., Lüdtke, O., Köller, O., & Baumert, J. (2006).

Integration of multidimensional self-concept and core personality constructs: Construct validation and relations to well-being and achievement. *Journal of Personality, 74,* 403–455.

Martin, A. S., Sinacuer, M., Madi, A., Tompson, S., Maddux, W. M., & Kitayama, S. (2018). Self-assertive interdependence in Arab culture. *Nature Human Behavior, 2,* 830–837.

Maslow, A. H. (1968). *Toward a psychology of being.* New York: Wiley.

Mazar, N., Amir, O., & Ariely, D. (2008). The dishonesty of honest people: A theory of self-concept maintenance. *Journal of Marketing Research, 45,* 633–644.

McAdams, D. P. (2001). The psychology of life stories. *Review of General Psychology, 5,* 100–122.

McAdams, D. P. (2013). The psychological self as actor, agent, and author. *Perspectives on Psychological Science, 8,* 272–295.

McAdams, D. P. (2019). "First we invented stories, then they changed us": The evolution of narrative identity. *Evolutionary Studies in Imaginative Culture, 3,* 1–18.

McArdle, M. (2011, August 9). British looters are still "queuing up" as they wait their turn to rob abandoned stores. *Business Insider.* www.businessinsider.com/british-looters-are-still-queuing-up-as-they-wait-their-turn-to-rob-abandoned-stores-2011-8

McGuigan, N., Whiten, A., Flynn, E., & Horner, V. (2007) Imitation of causally opaque versus causally transparent tool use by 3- and 5-year-old children. *Cognitive Development, 22,* 353–364.

McGuire, W. J., McGuire, C. V., Child, P., & Fujioka, T. (1978). Salience of ethnicity in the spontaneous self-concept as a function of one's ethnic distinctiveness in the social environment. *Journal of Personality and Social Psychology, 36,* 511–520.

McGuire, W. J., McGuire, C. V., & Winton, W. (1979). Effects of household sex composition on the salience of one's gender in the spontaneous self-concept. *Journal of Experimental Social Psychology, 15,* 77–90.

McNulty, J. K. (2011). The dark side of forgiveness: The tendency to forgive predicts continued psychological and physical aggression in marriage. *Personality and Social Psychology Bulletin, 37,* 770–783.

Mead, G. H. (1934). *Mind, self, and society.* Chicago: University of Chicago Press.

Meehl, P. E. (1956). Wanted—a good cookbook. *American Psychologist, 11,* 263–272.

Mezulis, A. H., Abramson, L. Y., Hyde, J. S., & Hanking, B. L. (2004). Is there a universal positivity bias in attributions?: A meta-analytic review of individual, developmental, and cultural differences in the self-serving attributional bias. *Psychological Bulletin, 130,* 711–747.

Miller, D. T., Turnbull, W., & McFarland, C. (1988). Particularistic and universalistic evaluation in the social comparison process. *Journal of Personality and Social Psychology, 55,* 908–917.

Mintz, S. (2004). *Huck's raft: A history of American childhood.* Cambridge, MA: Harvard University Press.

Mischel, W. (1968/1996). *Personality and assessment.* Hillsdale, NJ: Erlbaum.

Mischel, W., Shoda, Y., & Peake, P. K. (1988). The nature of adolescent competencies predicted by preschool delay of gratification. *Journal of Personality and Social Psychology, 54,* 687–696.

Moffett, M. W. (2019). *The human swarm: How our societies arise, thrive, and fall.* New York: Basic Books.

Moffitt, T. E., Arseneault, L., Belsky, D., Dickson, N., Hancox, R. J., Harrington, H., . . . Caspi, A. (2011). A gradient of childhood self-control predicts health, wealth, and public safety. *Proceedings of the National Academy of Sciences USA, 108,* 2693–2698.

Molnar-Szakacs, I., & Uddin, L. Q. (2016). The self in autism. In M. Kyrios, R. Moulding, G. Doron, S. S. Bhar, M. Nedeljkovic, & M. Mikulincer (Eds.), *The self in understanding and treating psychological disorders* (pp. 144–157). Cambridge, UK: Cambridge University Press.

Monroe, A. E., & Malle, B. F. (2010). From uncaused will to conscious choice: The need to study, not speculate about people's folk concept of free will. *Review of Philosophy and Psychology, 1,* 211–224.

Monroe, A. E., & Malle, B. F. (2014). Free will without metaphysics. In A. Mele (Ed.), *Surrounding free will: Philosophy, psychology, neuroscience* (pp. 25–48). New York: Oxford University Press.

Monson, T., Tanke, E., & Lund, J. (1980). Determinants of social perception in a naturalistic setting. *Journal of Research in Personality, 14,* 104–120.

Moore, B. (1984) *Privacy: Studies in social and cultural history.* New York: Routledge.

Moore, K. E., Christian, M. A., Boren, E. A., & Tangney, J. P. (2017). A clinical psychological perspective on hyper- and hypo-egoicism: Symptoms, treatment, and therapist characteristics. In K. W. Brown & M. Leary (Eds.), *Oxford handbook of hypo-egoic phenomena* (pp. 95–105). New York: Oxford University Press.

Morf, C. C., & Rhodewalt, F. (2001). Unraveling the paradoxes of narcissism: A dynamic self-regulatory processing model. *Psychological Inquiry, 12,* 177–196.

Morling, B., & Epstein, S. (1997). Compromises produced by the dialectic between self-verification and self-enhancement. *Journal of Personality and Social Psychology, 73,* 1268–1283.

Moss, S. (2016). *Self-affirmation theory.* SICO Tests. www.sicotests.com/psyarticle.asp?id=51

Moulding, R., Mancuso, S. G., Rehm, I., & Nedeljkovic, M. (2016). The self in the obsessive-compulsive-related disorders: Hoarding disorder, body dysmorphic disorder, and trichotillomania. In M. Kyrios, R. Moulding, G. Doron, S. S. Bhar, M. Nedeljkovic, & M. Mikulincer (Eds.), *The self in understanding and treating psychological disorders* (pp. 123–133). Cambridge, UK: Cambridge University Press.

Mullen, B., Johnson, C., & Salas, E. (1991). Productivity loss in brainstorming groups: A meta-analytic integration. *Basic and Applied Social Psychology, 12,* 3–23.

Mullen, E., & Monin, B. (2016). Consistency versus licensing effects of past moral behavior. *Annual Review of Psychology, 67,* 363–385.

Muraven, M., Shmueli, D., & Burkley, E. (2006). Conserving self-control strength. *Journal of Personality and Social Psychology, 91,* 524–537.

References

Muraven, M., & Slessareva, E. (2003). Mechanism of self-control failure: Motivation and limited resources. *Personality and Social Psychology Bulletin, 29,* 894–906.

Murphy, J. M., Wehler, C. A., Pagano, M. E., Little, M., Kleinman, R. F., & Jellinek, M. S. (1998). Relationship between hunger and psychosocial functioning in low-income American children. *Journal of the American Academy of Child & Adolescent Psychiatry, 37,* 163–170.

Murray, S. L., Derrick, J. L., Leder, S., & Holmes, J. G. (2008). Balancing connectedness and self-protection goals in close relationships: A levels-of-processing perspective on risk regulation. *Journal of Personality and Social Psychology, 94,* 429–459.

Murray, S. L., & Holmes, J. G. (1997). A leap of faith?: Positive illusions in romantic relationships. *Personality and Social Psychology Bulletin, 23,* 586–604.

Murray, S. L., Holmes, J. G., & Collins, N. L. (2006). Optimizing assurance: The risk regulation system in relationships. *Psychological Bulletin, 132,* 641–666.

Murray, S. L., Holmes, J. G., & Griffin, D. W. (1996a). The benefits of positive illusions: Idealization and the construction of satisfaction in close relationships. *Journal of Personality and Social Psychology, 70,* 79–98.

Murray, S. L., Holmes, J. G., & Griffin, D. W. (1996b). The self-fulfilling nature of positive illusions in romantic relationships: Love is not blind, but prescient. *Journal of Personality and Social Psychology, 71,* 1155–1180.

Murray, S. L., Rose, P., Bellavia, G. M., Holmes, J. G., & Kusche, A. G. (2002). When rejection stings: How self-esteem constrains relationship, enhancement processes. *Journal of Personality and Social Psychology, 83,* 556–573.

Nagell, K., Olguin, R. S., & Tomasello, M. (1993). Processes of social learning in the tool use of chimpanzees *(Pan troglodytes)* and human children *(Homo sapiens). Journal of Comparative Psychology, 107,* 174–186.

Neal, D. T., Wood, W., & Drolet, A. (2013). How do people adhere to goals when willpower is low?: The profits (and pitfalls) of strong habits. *Journal of Personality and Social Psychology, 104,* 959–975.

Nelson, B., Sass, L. A., & Parnas, J. (2016). Basic self disturbances in the schizophrenia spectrum: A review and future directions. In M. Kyrios, R. Moulding, G. Doron, S. S. Bhar, M. Nedeljkovic, & M. Mikulincer (Eds.), *The self in understanding and treating psychological disorders* (pp. 158–168). Cambridge, UK: Cambridge University Press.

Newman, L. S., & Baumeister, R. F. (1996). Toward an explanation of the UFO abduction phenomenon: Hypnotic elaboration, extraterrestrial sadomasochism, and spurious memories. *Psychological Inquiry, 7,* 99–126.

Newman, L. S., Duff, K. J., & Baumeister, R. F. (1997). A new look at defensive projection: Thought suppression, accessibility, and biased person perception. *Journal of Personality and Social Psychology, 72,* 980–1001.

Nichols, S., Strohminger, N., Rai, A., & Garfield, J. (2018). Death and the self. *Cognitive Science, 42,* 1–19.

Nielsen, M., Mushin, I., Tomaselli, K., & Whiten, A. (2014). Where culture takes hold: "Overimitation" and its flexible deployment in Western, Aboriginal, and Bushmen children. *Child Development, 85,* 2169–2184.

Nielsen, M., & Tomaselli, K. (2010). Overimitation in Kalahari Bushman children and the origins of human cultural cognition. *Psychological Science, 21,* 729–736.

Nisbet, R. (1973). *The social philosophers: Community and conflict in Western thought.* New York: Crowell.

Nisbett, R. E., & Wilson, T. D. (1977). Telling more than we can know: Verbal reports on mental processes. *Psychological Review, 84,* 231–259.

Norenzayan, A. (2013). *Big gods: How religion transformed cooperation and conflict.* Princeton, NJ: Princeton University Press.

Norenzayan, A., & Heine, S. J. (2005). Psychological universals: What are they and how can we know? *Psychological Bulletin, 131,* 763–784.

Norenzayan, A., Shariff, A. F., Gervais, W. M., Willard, A. K., McNamara, R. A., Slingerland, E., & Henrich, J. (2016). The cultural evolution of prosocial religions. *Behavioral and Brain Sciences, 39,* e1.

Olson, M. A., Fazio, R. H., & Hermann, A. D. (2007). Reporting tendencies underlie discrepancies between implicit and explicit measures of self-esteem. *Psychological Science, 18,* 287–291.

Olweus, D. (1994). Bullying at school: Long-term outcomes for the victims and an effective school-based intervention program. In L. R. Huesmann (Ed.), *Aggressive behavior: Current perspectives* (pp. 97–130). New York: Plenum Press.

O'Mara, E. M., Gaertner, L., Sedikides, C., Zhou, X., & Liu, Y. (2012). A longitudinal- experimental test of the panculturality of self-enhancement: Self-enhancement promotes psychological well-being both in the West and the East. *Journal of Research in Personality, 46,* 157–163.

Orth, U., Robins, R. W., & Widaman, K. F. (2012). Life-span development of self-esteem and its effects on important life outcomes. *Journal of Personality and Social Psychology, 102,* 1271–1288.

Oyegbile, T. O., & Marler, C. A. (2005). Winning fights elevates testosterone levels in California mice and enhances future ability to win fights. *Hormones and Behavior, 48,* 259–267.

Paolini, S., Harwood, J., & Rubin, M. (2010). Negative intergroup contact makes group memberships salient: Explaining why intergroup conflict endures. *Personality and Social Psychology Bulletin, 36,* 1723–1738.

Park, J. H., & Schaller, M. (2009). Parasites, minds and cultures. *The Psychologist, 22,* 942–945.

Paulhus, D. L. (1998). Interpersonal and intrapsychic adaptiveness of trait self-enhancement: A mixed blessing? *Journal of Personality and Social Psychology, 74,* 1197–1208.

Paulson, S., Flanagan, O., Bloom, P., & Baumeister, R. F. (2011). Quid pro quo: The ecology of the self. *Annals of the New York Academy of Sciences, 1234,* 29–43.

Peale, N. V. (1952). *The power of positive thinking.* New York Prentice-Hall.

Pettigrew, T. F., & Tropp, L. R. (2006). A meta-analytic test of intergroup contact theory. *Journal of Personality and Social Psychology, 90,* 751–783.

Phillips, J., & Cushman, F. (2017). Morality constrains the default representation of what is possible. *Proceedings of the National Academy of Sciences, 114,* 4649–4654.

Pinker, S. (1997). *How the mind works.* New York: Norton.

Pipher, M. (1994). *Reviving Ophelia: Saving the selves of adolescent girls.* New York: Riverhead.

Pocheptsova, A., Amir, O., Dhar, R., & Baumeister, R. (2009). Deciding without resources: Resource depletion and choice in context. *Journal of Marketing Research, 46,* 344–355.

Povinelli, D. J., & Cant, J. G. H. (1995). Arboreal clambering and the evolution of self-conception. *Quarterly Review of Biology, 70,* 393–421.

Pratt, T. C., & Cullen, F. T. (2000). The empirical status of Gottfredson and Hirschi's general theory of crime: A meta-analysis. *Criminology, 38,* 931–964.

Pryor, J. B., Gibbons, F. X., Wicklund, R. A., Fazio, R. H., & Hood, R. (1977). Self-focused attention and self-report validity. *Journal of Personality, 45,* 514–527.

Pyszczynski, T., Greenberg, J., Hamilton, J., & Nix, G. (1991). On the relationship between self-focused attention and psychological disorder: A critical reappraisal. *Psychological Bulletin, 110,* 538–543.

Pyszczynski, T., Greenberg, J., & Solomon, S. (1997). Why do we need what we need?: A terror management perspective on the roots of human social motivation. *Psychological Inquiry, 8,* 1–20.

Quattrone, G. (1976). *They look alike, they act alike, they think alike—we don't.* Unpublished master's thesis, Duke University.

Rafaeli-Mor, E., & Steinberg, J. (2002). Self-complexity and well-being: A review and research synthesis. *Personality and Social Psychology Review, 6,* 31–58.

Redshaw, J., & Suddendorf, T. (2016). Children's and apes' preparatory responses to two mutually exclusive possibilities. *Current Biology, 26,* 1758–1762.

Ridley, M. (2020) *How innovation works.* New York: HarperCollins.

Righetti, F., & Finkenauer, C. (2011). If you are able to control yourself, I will trust you: The role of perceived self-control in interpersonal trust. *Journal of Personality and Social Psychology, 100,* 874–886.

Ritter, M. (1995, August 27). Psychology: Small study of college students finds a paucity of veracity: And they lie even more to strangers than to friends and family. *Los Angeles Times.* www.latimes.com/archives/la-xpm-1995-08-27-mn-39318-story.html

Rivera, G. N., Christy, A. G., Kim, J., Vess, M., Hicks, J. A., & Schlegel, R. J. (2019). Understanding the relationship between perceived authenticity and well-being. *Review of General Psychology, 23,* 113–126.

Robertson, I. (2013). *The winner effect: How power affects your brain.* New York: Bloomsbury.

Robins, R., & Trzesniewski, K. (2005). Self-esteem development across the lifespan. *Current Directions in Psychological Science, 14,* 158–162.

Robson, D. A., Allen, M. S., & Howard, S. J. (2020). Self-regulation in childhood as predictor of future outcomes: A meta-analytic review. *Psychological Bulletin, 146,* 324–354.

Rogers, T. B., Kuiper, N. A., & Kirker, W. S. (1977). Self-reference and the encoding of personal information. *Journal of Personality and Social Psychology, 35,* 677–688.

Ronay, R., & von Hippel, W. (2010). The presence of an attractive woman elevates testosterone and physical risk taking in young men. *Social Psychological and Personality Science, 1,* 57–64.

Röseler, L., Ebert, J., Schütz, A., & Baumeister, R. F. (2021). The upsides and downsides of high self-control: Evidence for effects of similarity and situation dependency. *Europe's Journal of Psychology, 17,* 1–15.

Rosenberg, M. (1979). *Conceiving the self.* New York: Basic Books.

Rothbaum, F., Weisz, J. R., & Snyder, S. S. (1982). Changing the world and changing the self: A two-process model of perceived control. *Journal of Personality and Social Psychology, 42,* 5–37.

Rounds, J., & Su, R. (2014). The nature and power of interests. *Current Directions in Psychological Science, 23,* 98–103.

Rusbult, C. E., Finkel, E. J., & Kumashiro, M. (2009). The Michelangelo phenomenon. *Current Directions in Psychological Science, 18,* 305–308.

Ryan, R. M., & Deci, E. L. (2017). *Self-determination theory.* New York: Guilford Press.

Ryan, W. S., & Ryan, R. M. (2019). Toward a social psychology of authenticity: Exploring within-person variation in autonomy, congruence, and genuineness using self-determination theory. *Review of General Psychology, 23,* 99–112.

Sackeim, H. A., & Gur, R. C. (1979). Self-deception, other-deception, and self-reported psychopathology. *Journal of Consulting and Clinical Psychology, 47,* 213–215.

Sackett, D. L., & Snow, J. C. (1979). The magnitude of compliance and noncompliance. In R. Haynes, D. Taylor, & D. Sackett (Eds.), *Compliance in health care* (pp. 11–22). Baltimore: Johns Hopkins University Press.

Sande, G. N., Goethals, G. R., & Radloff, C. E. (1988). Perceiving one's own traits and others': The multifaceted self. *Journal of Personality and Social Psychology, 54,* 13–20.

Santos, H. C., Varnum, M. E. W., & Grossman, I. (2017). Global increases in individualism. *Psychological Science, 28,* 1228–1239.

Sartre, J.-P. (1953). *The existential psychoanalysis* (H. E. Barnes, Trans.). New York: Philosophical Library.

Sartre, J.-P. (1974). *Being and nothingness.* Secaucus, NJ: Citadel. (Original work published 1943)

Scarry, E. (1985). *The body in pain: The making and unmaking of the world.* New York: Oxford University Press.

Schäfer, M., Haun, D. B., & Tomasello, M. (2015). Fair is not fair everywhere. *Psychological Science, 26,* 1252–1260.

Scheirer, M. A., & Kraut, R. E. (1979). Increased educational achievement via self-concept change. *Review of Educational Research, 49,* 131–150.

Schlegel, R. J., Hicks, J. A., Davis, W. E., Hirsch, K. A., & Smith, C. M. (2013). The dynamic interplay between perceived true self-knowledge and decision satisfaction. *Journal of Personality and Social Psychology, 104,* 542–558.

Schlenker, B. R. (1975). Self-presentation: Managing the impression of consistency when reality interferes with self-enhancement. *Journal of Personality and Social Psychology, 32,* 1030–1037.

Schlenker, B. R. (1980). *Impression management: The self-concept, social identity, and interpersonal relations.* Monterey, CA: Brooks/Cole.

Schlenker, B. R. (1982). Translating actions into attitudes: An identity-analytic approach to the explanation of social conduct. *Advances in Experimental Social Psychology, 15,* 193–247.

Schmeichel, B. J., Garrison, K. E., Baldwin, C., & Baumeister, R. F. (in press). Making memorable choices: The self-choice effect in memory and the role of executive control. *Self and Identity.*

Schmeichel, B. J., Vohs, K. D., & Baumeister, R. F. (2003). Intellectual perfor-mance and ego depletion: Role of the self in logical reasoning and other infor-mation processing. *Journal of Personality and Social Psychology, 85*, 33–46.

Scully, D. (1990). *Understanding sexual violence.* London: HarperCollins Academic.

Searle, J. R. (2001). *Rationality in action.* Cambridge, MA: MIT Press.

Sedikides, C. (1993). Assessment, enhancement, and verification determinants of the self-evaluation process. *Journal of Personality and Social Psychology, 65*, 317–338.

Sedikides, C., Gaertner, L., & Toguchi, Y. (2003). Pancultural self-enhancement. *Journal of Personality and Social Psychology, 84*(1), 60–70.

Sedikides, C., Gaertner, L., & Vevea, J. L. (2005). Pancultural self-enhancement reloaded: A meta-analytic reply to Heine (2005). *Journal of Personality and Social Psychology, 89*(4), 539–551.

Sedikides, C., & Gregg, A. P. (2008). Self-enhancement: Food for thought. *Perspectives on Psychologcal Science, 3*, 102–116.

Sedikides, C., Lenton, A. P., Slabu, L., & Thomaes, S. (2019). Sketching the con-tours of state authenticity. *Review of General Psychology, 23*, 73–88.

Sedikides, C., Meek, R., Alicke, M. D., & Taylor, S. (2014). Behind bars but above the bar: Prisoners consider themselves more prosocial than non-prisoners. *British Journal of Social Psychology, 53*, 396–403.

Sedlovskaya, A., Purdie-Vaughns, V., Eibach, R. P., LaFrance M., Romero-Canyas, R., & Camp, N. P. (2013). Internalizing the closet: Concealment heightens the cognitive distinction between public and private selves. *Journal of Personality and Social Psychology, 104*, 695–715.

Seligman, M. E. P. (1995). *What you can change . . . and what you can't.* New York: Knopf.

Sennett, R. (1974). *The fall of public man.* New York: Random House.

Shapiro, J. P., Baumeister, R. F., & Kessler, J. W. (1991). A three-component model of children's teasing: Aggression, humor, and ambiguity. *Journal of Social and Clinical Psychology, 10*, 459–472.

Shaw, A., DeScioli, P., & Olson, K. R. (2012). Fairness versus favoritism in chil-dren. *Evolution and Human Behavior, 33*, 736–745.

Shaw, A., Montinari, N., Piovesan, M., Olson, K. R., Gino, F., & Norton, M. I. (2014). Children develop a veil of fairness. *Journal of Experimental Psychol-ogy: General, 143*, 363–375.

Sherman, D. K. (2013). Self-affirmation: Understanding the effects. *Social and Per-sonality Psychology Compass, 7*, 834–845.

Sherman, D. K., & Cohen, G. L. (2006). The psychology of self-defense: Self-affirmation theory. *Advances in Experimental Social Psychology, 38*, 183–242.

Shmueli, D., & Prochaska, J. J. (2009). Resisting tempting food and smoking behavior: Implications from a self-control theory perspective. *Health Psychol-ogy, 28*, 300–306.

Shoda, Y., Mischel, W., & Peake, P. K. (1990). Predicting adolescent cognitive and self-regulatory competencies from preschool delay of gratification: Identify-ing diagnostic conditions. *Developmental Psychology, 26*, 978–986.

Showers, C. J. (1992). Compartmentalization of positive and negative self-knowledge: Keeping bad apples out of the bunch. *Journal of Personality and Social Psychology, 62*, 1036–1049.

Showers, C. J., Thomas, J. S., & Grundy, C. S. (2017). Defensive self-structure predicts unethical behavior. Unpublished manuscript, University of Oklahoma.

Shrauger, J. S. (1975). Responses to evaluation as a function of initial self-perceptions. *Psychological Bulletin, 82*, 581–596.

Shrauger, J. S., & Schoeneman, T. J. (1979). Symbolic interactionist view of self-concept: Through the looking glass darkly. *Psychological Bulletin, 86*, 549–573.

Shteynberg, G. (2015). Shared attention. *Perspectives on Psychological Science, 10*, 579–590.

Sicherman, N., Loewenstein, G., Seppi, D. J., & Utkus, S. P. (2015). Financial attention. *Review of Financial Studies, 29*, 863–897.

Simonson, I. (1989). Choice based on reasons: The case of attraction and compromise effects. *Journal of Consumer Research, 16*, 158–174.

Sjåstad, H., & Baumeister, R. F. (2018). The future and the will: Planning requires self-control, and ego depletion leads to planning aversion. *Journal of Experimental Social Psychology, 76*, 127–141.

Sjåstad, H., & Baumeister, R. F. (2019). Moral self-judgment is stronger for future than past actions. *Motivation and Emotion, 43*, 662–680.

Smith, A. (1776/1991). *The wealth of nations*. New York: Knopf.

Snyder, C. R., & Fromkin, H. L. (1977). Abnormality as a positive characteristic: The development and validation of a scale measuring need for uniqueness. *Journal of Abnormal Psychology, 86*, 518–527.

Sparks, S., Cunningham, S. J., & Kritikos, A. (2016). Culture modulates implicit ownership-induced self-bias in memory. *Cognition, 153*, 89–98.

Sprecher, S. (1999). "I love you more today than yesterday": Romantic partners' perceptions of changes in love and related affect over time. *Journal of Personality and Social Psychology, 76*, 46–53.

Staras, S. A. S., Livingston, M. D., & Wagenaar, A. C. (2016). Maryland alcohol sales tax and sexually transmitted diseases. *American Journal of Preventive Medicine, 50*, E73–E80.

Stasser, G. (1999). The uncertain role of unshared information in collective choice. In J. M. Levine, L. L. Thompson, & D. M. Messick (Eds.), *Shared cognition in organizations: The management of knowledge* (pp. 49–69). Mahwah, NJ: Erlbaum.

Stasser, G., & Titus, W. (1985). Pooling of unshared information in group decision making: Biased information sampling during discussion. *Journal of Personality and Social Psychology, 48*, 1467–1478.

Staw, B. M. (1976). Knee-deep in the big muddy: A study of escalating commitment to a chosen course of action. *Organizational Behavior and Human Performance, 16*, 27–44.

Steele, C. M. (1988). The psychology of self-affirmation: Sustaining the integrity of the self. In L. Berkowitz (Ed.), *Advances in experimental social psychology* (Vol. 21, pp. 261–302). New York: Academic Press.

Stillman, T. F., Baumeister, R. F., & Mele, A. R. (2011). Free will in everyday life: Autobiographical accounts of free and unfree actions. *Philosophical Psychology, 24*, 381–394.

Stinson, D. A., Logel, C., Zanna, M. P., Holmes, J. G., Cameron, J. J., Wood, J. V., & Spencer, S. J. (2008). The cost of lower self-esteem: Testing a self- and social-bonds model of health. *Journal of Personality and Social Psychology,* *94,* 412–428.

Stipek, D., Recchia, S., McClintic, S., & Lewis, M. (1992). Self-evaluation in young children. *Monographs of the Society for Research in Child Development, 57*(1), 1–95.

Strohminger, N., & Nichols, S. (2014). The essential moral self. *Cognition, 131,* 159–171.

Strohminger, N., & Nichols, S. (2015). Neurodegeneration and identity. *Psychological Science, 26,* 1469–1479.

Su, R., Rounds, J., & Armstrong, P. I. (2009). Men and things, women and people: A meta-analysis of sex differences in interests. *Psychological Bulletin, 135,* 859–884.

Suddendorf, T. (2013). *The gap: What separates us from other animals.* New York: Basic Books.

Suddendorf, T., & Collier-Baker, E. (2009). The evolution of primate visual self-recognition: evidence of absence in lesser apes. *Proceedings of the Royal Society, 276,* 1671–1677.

Sugiyama, L. S. (2004). Illness, injury, and disability among Shiwiar forager-horticulturalists: Implications of health-risk buffering for the evolution of human life history. *American Journal of Physical Anthropology, 123,* 371–389.

Sullivan, H. S. (1955). *The interpersonal theory of psychiatry.* New York: Tavistock.

Surowiecki, J. (2004). *The wisdom of crowds.* New York: Anchor.

Svenson, O. (1981). Are we all less risky and more skillful than our fellow drivers? *Acta Psychologica, 47,* 143–148.

Swann, W. B. (1985). The self as architect of social reality. In B. R. Schlenker (Ed.), *The self and social life* (pp. 100–125). New York: McGraw-Hill.

Swann, W. B. (1987). Identity negotiation: Where two roads meet. *Journal of Personality and Social Psychology, 53,* 1038–1051.

Swann, W. B., Griffin, J. J., Predmore, S. C., & Gaines, B. (1987). The cognitive-affective crossfire: When self-consistency confronts self-enhancement. *Journal of Personality and Social Psychology, 52,* 881–889.

Swann, W. B., Hixon, J. G., Stein-Seroussi, A., & Gilbert, D. T. (1990). The fleeting gleam of praise: Cognitive processes underlying behavioral reactions to self-relevant feedback. *Journal of Personality and Social Psychology, 59,* 17–26.

Swartz, K. B., Sara, D., & Evans, S. (1999). Comparative aspects of mirror self-recognition in great apes. In S. T. Parker, R. W. Mitchell, & M. L. Boccia (Eds.), *The mentalities of gorillas and orangutans* (pp. 283–294). Cambridge, UK: Cambridge University Press.

Sweeny, K., & Krizan, Z. (2013). Sobering up: A quantitative review of temporal declines in expectations. *Psychological Bulletin, 139,* 702–724.

Tajfel, H. (Ed.). (1978). *Differentiation between social groups: Studies in the social psychology of intergroup relations.* London: Academic Press.

Tajfel, H., & Turner, J. C. (1979). An integrative theory of intergroup conflict. In W. G. Austin & S. Worchel (Eds.), *The social psychology of intergroup relations* (pp. 33–47). Monterey, CA: Brooks/Cole.

Tamir, D. I., & Mitchell, J. P. (2012). Disclosing information about the self is intrinsically rewarding. *PNAS, 109,* 8038–8043.

Tangney, J. P., Baumeister, R. F., & Boone, A. L. (2004). High self-control predicts good adjustment, less pathology, better grades, and interpersonal success. *Journal of Personality, 72,* 271–322.

Tannahill, R. (1980). *Sex in history.* New York: Stein and Day/Scarborough.

Taylor, K. M., & Shepperd, J. A. (1998). Bracing for the worst: Severity, testing, and feedback timing as moderators of optimistic bias. *Personality and Social Psychology Bulletin, 24,* 915–926.

Taylor, S. E. (1983). Adjustment to threatening events: A theory of cognitive adaptation. *American Psychologist, 38,* 1161–1173.

Taylor, S. E., & Brown, J. D. (1988). Illusion and well-being: A social psychological perspective on mental health. *Psychological Bulletin, 103,* 193–210.

Taylor, S. E., Neter, E., & Wayment, H. A. (1995). Self-evaluation processes. *Personality and Social Psychology Bulletin, 21,* 1278–1287.

Tedeschi, J. T., Schlenker, B. R., & Bonoma, T. V. (1971). Cognitive dissonance: Private ratiocination or public spectacle? *American Psychologist, 26,* 685–695.

Tenney, E. R., Logg, J. M., & Moore, D. A. (2015). (Too) optimistic about optimism: The belief that optimism improves performance. *Journal of Personality and Social Psychology, 108,* 377–399.

Tesser, A., & Moore, J. (1986). On the convergence of public and private aspects of self. In R. Baumeister (Ed.), *Public self and private self* (pp. 99–116). New York: Springer-Verlag.

Thunstrom, L., Norström, J., Shogren, J. F., Ehmke, M., & van't Veld K. (2016). Strategic self-ignorance. *Journal of Risk and Uncertainty, 52,* 117–136.

Thurston, A. F. (1987). *Enemies of the people: The ordeal of the intellectuals in China's Great Cultural Revolution.* New York: Knopf.

Tice, D. M. (1992). Self-presentation and self-concept change: The looking glass self as magnifying glass. *Journal of Personality and Social Psychology, 63,* 435–451.

Tice, D. M., & Baumeister, R. F. (1997). Longitudinal study of procrastination, performance, stress, and health: The costs and benefits of dawdling. *Psychological Science, 8,* 454–458.

Tice, D. M., Bratslavsky, E., & Baumeister, R. F. (2001). Emotional distress regulation takes precedence over impulse control: If you feel bad, do it! *Journal of Personality and Social Psychology, 80,* 53–67.

Tice, D. M., Butler, J. L., Muraven, M. B., & Stillwell, A. M. (1995). When modesty prevails: Differential favorability of self-presentation to friends and strangers. *Journal of Personality and Social Psychology, 69,* 1120–1138.

Tierney, J., & Baumeister, R. F. (2019). *The power of bad.* New York: Penguin/Random House.

Tomasello, M. (2014). *A natural history of human thinking.* Cambridge, MA: Harvard University Press.

Tomasello, M. (2016). *A natural history of human morality.* Cambridge, MA: Harvard University Press.

Tomasello, M. (2018). *Becoming human: A theory of ontogeny.* Cambridge, MA: Harvard University Press.

Tomasello, M., Melis, A. P., Tennie, C., Wyman, E., & Herrmann, E. (2012). Two key steps in the evolution of human cooperation: The interdependence hypothesis. *Current Anthropology, 53,* 673–692.

Trilling, L. (1971). *Sincerity and authenticity.* Cambridge, MA: Harvard University Press.

Trinh, P., Hoover, D. R., & Sonnenberg, F. A. (2021). Time-of-day changes in physician clinical decision making: A retrospective study. *PLOS One, 16*(9), e0257500.

Turner, R. H. (1976). The real self: From institution to impulse. *American Journal of Sociology, 81,* 989–1016.

Twenge, J. M. (2006). *Generation me.* New York: Free Press.

Twenge, J. M. (2017). *iGen: Why today's super-connected kids are growing up less rebellious, more tolerant, less happy—and completely unprepared for adulthood.* New York: Atria Books.

Twenge, J. M., & Campbell, W. K. (2009). *The narcissism epidemic: Living in the age of entitlement.* New York: Simon & Schuster.

Twenge, J. M., & Foster, J. D. (2010). Birth cohort increases in narcissistic personality traits among American college students, 1982–2009. *Social Psychological and Personality Science, 1,* 99–106.

Uhlmann, E. L., Pizarro, D. A., & Diermeier, D. (2015). A person-centered approach to moral judgment. *Perspectives on Psychological Science, 10,* 72–81.

Van Damme, C., Deschrijver, E., Van Geert, E., & Hoorens, V. (2017). When praising yourself insults others: Self-superiority claims provoke aggression. *Personality and Social Psychology Bulletin, 43,* 1008–1019.

Van Damme, C., Hoorens, V., & Sedikides, C. (2016). Why self-enhancement provokes dislike: The hubris hypothesis and the aversiveness of explicit self-superiority claims. *Self and Identity, 15*(2), 173–190.

van der Weiden, A., Prikken, M., & van Haren, N. E. M. (2015). Self-other integration and distinction in schizophrenia: A theoretical analysis and a review of the evidence. *Neuroscience and Biobehavioral Reviews, 57,* 220–237.

VanLaningham, J., Johnson, D. R., & Amato, P. (2001). Marital happiness, marital duration, and the U-shaped curve: Evidence from a five-wave panel study. *Social Forces, 79,* 1313–1341.

Vohs, K. D., Baumeister, R. F., Schmeichel, B. J., Twenge, J. M., Nelson, N. M., & Tice, D. M. (2008). Making choices impairs subsequent self-control: A limited-resource account of decision making, self-regulation, and active initiative. *Journal of Personality and Social Psychology, 94,* 883–898.

Vohs, K. D., Finkenauer, C., & Baumeister, R. F. (2011). The sum of friends' and lovers' self-control scores predicts relationship quality. *Social Psychological and Personality Science, 2,* 138–145.

Vohs, K. D., Schmeichel, B. J., Lohmann, S., Gronau, Q., Finley, A. J., Wagenmakers, E. J., . . . Albarracín, D. (2021). A multi-site preregistered paradigmatic test of the ego depletion effect. *Psychological Science.* https://journals.sagepub.com/doi/abs/10.1177/0956797621989733

Volkow, N. (2015, June 12). *Addiction is a disease of free will* [Web blog post]. National Institute on Drug Abuse. www.drugabuse.gov/about-nida/norasblog/2015/06/addiction-disease-free-will

von Hippel, W. (2018). *The social leap.* New York: HarperCollins.

von Hippel, W., Hawkins, C., & Schooler, J. W. (2001). Stereotype distinctiveness: How counterstereotypic behavior shapes the self-concept. *Journal of Personality and Social Psychology, 81,* 193–205.

von Hippel, W., & Trivers, R. (2011). The evolution and psychology of self-deception. *Behavioral and Brain Sciences, 34,* 1–56.

Vonasch, A. J., Reynolds, T., Winegard, B., & Baumeister, R. F. (2018). Death before dishonor: Incurring costs to protect moral reputation. *Social Psychological and Personality Science, 9*(5), 604–613.

Vonasch, A. J., & Sjåstad, H. (2020). Future-orientation (as trait and state) promotes reputation-protective choice in moral dilemmas. *Social Psychological and Personality Science, 12*(3), 194855061989925.

Vonasch, A. J., Vohs, K. D., Ghosh, A. P., & Baumeister, R. F. (2017). Ego depletion induces mental passivity: Behavioral effects beyond impulse control. *Motivation Science, 3,* 321–336.

Weatherford, J. (1997). *The history of money.* New York: Three Rivers Press.

Webb, T., & Sheeran, P. (2003). Can implementation intentions help to overcome ego-depletion? *Journal of Experimental Social Psychology, 39,* 279–286.

Weinberger, D. A., Schwartz, G. E., & Davidson, R. J. (1979). Low-anxious, high-anxious, and repressive coping styles: Psychometric patterns and behavioral and physiological responses to stress. *Journal of Abnormal Psychology, 88,* 369–380.

Weinstein, N. D. (1980). Unrealistic optimism about future life events. *Journal of Personality and Social Psychology, 39,* 806–820.

Weintraub, K. J. (1978). *The value of the individual: Self and circumstance in autobiography.* Chicago: University of Chicago Press.

Weiskrantz, L., Elliott, J., & Darlington, C. (1971). Preliminary observations on tickling oneself. *Nature, 230,* 598–599.

Weiss, J. M. (1971a). Effects of coping behavior in different warning signal conditions on stress pathology in rats. *Journal of Comparative and Physiological Psychology, 77,* 1–13.

Weiss, J. M. (1971b). Effects of coping behavior with and without a feedback signal on stress pathology in rats. *Journal of Comparative and Physiological Psychology, 77,* 22–30.

Weiss, J. M. (1971c). Effects of punishing the coping response (conflict) on stress pathology in rats. *Journal of Comparative and Physiological Psychology, 77,* 14–21.

Wenzlaff, R. M., Wegner, D. M., & Roper, D. W. (1988). Depression and mental control: The resurgence of unwanted negative thoughts. *Journal of Personality and Social Psychology, 55,* 882–892.

Wesnes, K. A., Pincock, C., Richardson, D., Helm, O., & Hails, S. (2003). Breakfast reduces declines in attention and memory over the morning in schoolchildren. *Appetite, 41,* 329–331.

West, A. (1999). The flute factory: An empirical measurement of the effect of division of labor on productivity and production. *American Economist, 43,* 82–87.

Whitman, W. (2013). *Leaves of grass.* New York: Penguin Random House. (Original work published 1855)

Wicklund, R., & Duval, S. (1971). Opinion change and performance facilitation as a result of objective self-awareness. *Journal of Experimental Social Psychology, 7,* 319–342.

Wicklund, R. A. (1975). Objective self-awareness. In L. Berkowitz (Ed.), *Advances in experimental social psychology* (Vol. 8, pp. 233–275). New York: Academic Press.

Wicklund, R. A., & Gollwitzer, P. M. (1982). *Symbolic self-completion*. Hillsdale, NJ: Erlbaum.

Wiese, C., Tay, L., Duckworth, A., D'Mello, S., Kuykendall, L., Hofmann, W., . . . Vohs, K. (2018). Too much of a good thing?: Exploring the inverted-U relationship between self-control and happiness. *Journal of Personality, 86*(3), 380–396.

Wildschut, T., Pinter, B., Vevea, J. L., Insko, C. A., & Schopler, J. (2003). Beyond the group mind: A quantitative review of the interindividual-intergroup discontinuity effect. *Psychological Bulletin, 129,* 698–722.

Wilson, P. N., & Kennedy, A. M. (1995). Trustworthiness as an economic asset. *International Food and Agribusiness Management Review, 2,* 179–193.

Wilson, T. D. (2002). *Strangers to ourselves: Discovering the adaptive unconscious*. Cambridge, MA: Harvard University Press.

Winegar, K. (1990, November 27). Self-esteem is healthy for society. *Star Tribune,* Minneapolis, MN, pp. 1E–2E.

Wood, W., & Neal, D. (2007). A new look at habits and the habit-goal interface. *Psychological Review, 114,* 843–863.

Woolfolk, R. L., Parrish, M. W., & Murphy, S. M. (1985). The effects of positive and negative imagery on motor skill performance. *Cognitive Therapy and Research, 9,* 335–341.

Zimbardo, P. G. (1977). *Shyness: What it is, what to do about it*. New York: Jove.

Zuckerman, M. (1979). Attribution of success and failure revisited or: The motivational bias is alive and well in attribution theory. *Journal of Personality, 47,* 245–287.

Zullow, H. M., Oettingen, G., Peterson, C., & Seligman, M. E. P. (1988). Pessimistic explanatory style in the historical record: CAVing LBJ, presidential candidates, and East versus West Berlin. *American Psychologist, 43,* 673–682.

Index

Abduction by aliens, 331, 332
Academic achievement
    effects of self-affirmation and, 163
    identity crisis and, 323–324
    self-control and, 85, 93
    self-esteem and, 178–180
    See also School performance
Acceptance
    self-deception and, 204–206
    self-esteem and, 191
    social integration function of self and, 17–18,
        21
Accountability, 97–99
Accuracy
    in information sharing, 227
    as motivation, 156–157, 164
    in self-beliefs, 192–193, 196–213
Actions
    activities of the self and, 222–230
    effects of self-affirmation and, 162–164
    following orders, 223
    motivation and, 219–220
    overview, 217–218
    self-knowledge and, 140–142, 144–146,
        150–151, 172–173, 174
    task performer activity, 222–223
    See also Behavior
Active agent, 267–268
Active responding, 246–247, 250
Addiction
    as a self-defeating behavior, 350, 355, 357
    self-regulation and, 343
    unity of self and, 119–121
    as a way to escape self-awareness, 329–330,
        334
    See also Substance use

Adequacy, 163–164
Adolescence
    beginnings of self and, 92–93
    evolution of the western self and, 29–30
    identity crisis and, 323, 325
    narrative self and, 149
    self-beliefs and, 192–193
    self-esteem and, 177, 181–182
    See also Developmental processes
Adulthood
    beginnings of self and, 92–93
    narrative self and, 149
    self-beliefs and, 193
    self-esteem and, 181–182
    See also Developmental processes
Affirmation, 162–164. See also Self-affirmation
Agency, 89–90, 219–220
Aggression
    displacement and, 212
    mirrors and, 131
    self-control and, 233–234
    self-esteem and, 182–185
    self-presentation and, 293, 300
    threatened egotism and, 184–185
Alcohol use
    self-awareness and, 133, 236
    as a self-defeating behavior, 352, 355, 357
    as a way to escape self-awareness, 329–330,
        334
    See also Substance use
Alien abduction, 331, 332
Altruism, 108
Alzheimer's disease, 112
Animals other than humans
    aggression and, 185
    autonomy and, 263

407

Animals other than humans *(cont.)*
  brain development and, 75
  choice and, 253–255, 257
  continuity of self and, 121, 122–123
  cooperation and morality and, 106–107
  deception and, 200–201
  experience of unity and, 67–68
  exploring the existence of self in, 15–17
  groups and, 98–99, 284
  interpersonal self and, 87
  moral reputation and, 110
  ownership and, 69–70
  reputation management and, 296–297
  self across time and, 76
  self-awareness and, 130
  shame and, 77–78
  unity of self and, 115
Anonymity, 98
Anxiety and anxiety disorders, 207, 339, 343.
    See also Social anxiety disorder
Approval from others, 77. *See also* Praise
Arab self-beliefs, 38. *See also* Culture
Arguments, 313–314
Asian self, 36–41, 43, 44. *See also* Culture
Aspects of self, 6–7, 76–89, 93, 110, 129. *See
    also* Executive self; Interpersonal self;
    Self-awareness; Self-beliefs
Attention, 207–208
Attention-deficit/hyperactivity disorder
    (ADHD), 207, 343
Attitudes, 155–156, 166
Attributes
  narrative knowledge and, 147
  self-knowledge and, 143, 144–146, 149,
    150–151, 161–162
Attributions, 207
Authenticity, 52–58
Autism spectrum disorder, 340–341
Automatic mental processes, 154–155,
    166–167
Autonomy
  continuity of self and, 121–122
  depression and, 338
  free will and, 263–264
  functional autonomy, 41, 83, 93, 161–162
  morality and, 83, 93
  overview, 268
  responsible autonomy, 20, 21, 117–118,
    121–122, 266–268
  self as active agent and, 267–268
  self-knowledge and, 161–162
  True Self and, 54–55
  unity project and, 116–118, 264–265
Avoidance, 207–208, 354

Babies. *See* Developmental processes; Infancy
Backfires of self-defeating behaviors, 355–356,
    359. *See also* Self-defeating behavior
Barnum effect, 173–174

Beginnings of self
  acting as a unity, 67–68
  from adolescence into adulthood, 92–93
  aspects of self and, 76–89
  boundary of "me" and "not me" and,
    65–67
  culture and, 72–73
  executive self and, 80–86
  groups and, 68–69
  interpersonal self and, 86–89
  learning how to play roles and, 90–92
  narrative self and, 89–90
  overview, 65, 73, 93
  ownership and, 69–72
  self-beliefs and, 78–80
  self-control and, 84–86
  social origins of self, 69–72
  See also Developmental processes
Behavior
  choice and, 253–254
  conscious and unconscious processes and,
    134–138
  effects of self-affirmation and, 164
  ego depletion and, 238
  mirrors and, 131
  moral self and, 81
  multiple-self theories and, 49
  quitting addiction and, 119–121
  relationships and, 313–314
  self-awareness and, 132–133, 138
  self-control and, 85
  self-knowledge and, 140–142, 144–146,
    150–151, 172–173, 174
  self-presentation and, 290–291, 299–301
  True Self and, 54–55
  See also Actions; Self-defeating behavior
Belonging, 271–272, 274–275, 279, 370–371
Bias
  ego depletion and decision fatigue and,
    260–261
  introspection and, 167
  selective criticism and, 209–210
  self-beliefs and, 192–193, 196, 305
  self-deception and, 207, 209–210
  self-knowledge and, 152
Big Five dimensions of personality, 170–171.
    See also Personality
Binges
  as a self-defeating behavior, 355, 357, 358
  self-regulation and, 343
  as a way to escape self-awareness, 330, 332,
    334
Biological processes, 7–8
Bipolar disorder, 336–337
Blame, 332–333, 334
Bliss, 333
Body, 4–6, 74–76, 221–222
Body dysmorphic disorder, 339
Borderline personality disorder, 340

Boundary of "me" and "not me," 65–67
Bragging, 300
Brain
  communication and, 371
  development of boundary between body and, 74–76
  energy and, 372–373
  glucose levels and, 243
  role of in the self, 5–6, 13–15
  unity of self and, 116–117, 118
Brain fog, 96
Buddhist philosophy, 43–45
Bullying, 88, 183

Career achievement, 85, 93, 323–324
Categories, 280–284
Central nervous system, 116–117
Ceremonies, 279
Change, 221–222, 230, 235, 250
Cheating, 195
Childhood
  autonomy and, 267
  beginnings of self and, 93
  choice and, 255
  evolution of the western self and, 29–30
  interpersonal self and, 86–89
  learning how to play roles and, 90–92
  morality and, 80–84, 110
  narrative self and, 89–90, 148–149
  self-control and, 84–86, 231–234
  self-esteem and, 181
  self-reference effect and, 168
  See also Developmental processes
Choices
  adolescence and, 92–93
  behavior and, 18–19, 253–254
  complex choices, 255–256
  difficulty of choosing, 254
  ego depletion and decision fatigue and, 246–247, 259–261
  emotion and, 258–259
  energy and, 372–373
  free will and, 265–267
  memory and, 168–169
  morality and, 108
  narrative self and, 89
  overview, 251–253, 268
  process of, 256–257
  self-expression and, 261–262
  self-knowledge and, 257–258
  self-reference effect and, 168–169
  simple choices, 254–255
  social integration function of self and, 18–19, 21
  willpower and, 246
  See also Decision making
Choosing how to act, 21
Cigarette smoking, 350, 355, 357. See also Substance use

Cognitive processes
  choice and, 252–253, 268
  cognitive dissonance, 155–156, 172–173, 291–292, 293
  overview, 45
  self-deception and, 206–213
  self-defeating behavior and, 357
  self-regulation and, 248–249
Cognitive-affective crossfire, 154
Cognitive–experiential self-theory (CEST), 153
Coherence, 227, 264–265
Collective brain fog, 96
Collective identity
  in the early Middle Ages, 23–25, 34
  groups and, 101
  overview, 280
  social identity theory and, 280–284
  See also Groups
Communication
  choice and, 262
  information agent and, 226
  overview, 18, 21, 371
  unity of self and, 373
Comparison
  downward comparison, 210
  looking-glass self and, 169–172
  self-awareness and, 132–134
  self-esteem and, 160–161
  self-improvement motive and, 160
  self-knowledge and, 210
Compartmentalization, 340, 363–365, 366–367
Competence
  autonomy and, 263
  beginnings of self and, 79–80
  effects of self-affirmation and, 163
  morality and, 112
  overview, 18, 21
  self-esteem and, 185–186
Competition, 92, 101, 106
Complex self-concepts, 16, 29–30. See also Self-concept
Compromise, 253, 260
Concealing aspects of self, 125
Concept of self. See Self-concept
Confidence
  beginnings of self and, 79
  illusion in self-beliefs and, 195–196
  overestimating control illusion and, 199–200
  self-esteem and, 185–186, 188
Conflict, 313–314
Conformity, 56, 227, 292–293
Connections across time, 16. See also Self across time
Consciousness
  introspection and, 166–167
  overview, 134–138
  unity of self and, 116–117, 118
Consensus, 227

Consequences of one's choices
  escape from self and, 332
  responsible autonomy and, 20, 21
  unity of self and, 123, 124–125, 126
Consistency
  mirrors and, 131
  self-knowledge and, 154–157, 164, 173–174
  self-presentation and, 292
  society and, 124–125
  unity of self and, 115–116, 124–125, 126
  See also Self-verification
Contact hypothesis, 273–275
Continuity of self, 71, 121–123, 375. *See also*
    Self across time; Unity project
Control, 199–200, 220–222, 230, 309. *See also*
    Self-control
Controlled mental processes, 154–155
Cooperation
  activities of the self and, 223
  morality and, 104–107, 113, 230
  overview, 18, 21, 106, 371–372
  reputation and, 108–110
Creativity, 96
Credibility, 300
Crime, 233–234
Criticism, 209–210
Culture
  autonomy and, 263
  brain development and, 75
  evolution and, 7–8, 72–73
  face and dignity cultures, 40–41
  functions of self and, 20
  groups and, 99, 100–101
  interdependent and independent selves and,
    36–40
  interpersonal self and, 86–89
  overview, 7, 9, 11–13, 36, 41, 369–370, 375
  ownership and, 69–70
  reality of selfhood and, 43–44
  role of in the self, 5–6, 20–21
  self as a central value and, 319–321
  self as active agent and, 267–268
  self-knowledge and, 27–28
  social integration function of self and, 17–20
  stress of self and, 333–334
  unity of self and, 121–123
  See also Western self
Curiosity, 226

Death, 66–67, 189–190
Decision making
  ego depletion and decision fatigue and, 246,
    259–261
  overview, 251–252
  process of, 256–257
  self-knowledge and, 268
  unity of self and, 373–374
  willpower and, 246–247, 250
  See also Choices

Defense mechanisms, 163, 164, 207–208,
    211–213
Dementia, 112, 338–339
Denial, 211–213
Dependency, 338
Depersonalization, 337
Depression
  organization of self-beliefs and, 361
  overestimating control illusion and, 199
  overview, 338
  self-serving bias and, 207
Desire
  agency and, 219–220
  choice and, 254, 268
  effects of self-affirmation and, 162–164
  executive agent and, 218, 230
  quitting addiction and, 119–121
Destiny, 59
Developmental processes
  from adolescence into adulthood, 92–93
  aspects of self and, 76–89
  boundary between brain and body, 74–76
  interpersonal self and, 86–89
  learning how to play roles and, 90–92
  morality and, 80–84, 110
  narrative self and, 89–90, 148–149
  overview, 93
  self across time and, 76
  self-control and, 84–86
  See also Adolescence; Adulthood; Beginnings
    of self; Childhood; Infancy
Differentiation, 365–366
Dignity culture, 40–41. *See also* Culture
Disorganized self, 336–342. *See also*
    Organization of self-beliefs
Displacement, 212
Dissociation, 337, 340
Divided self, 125, 336–342
Division of labor, 97
Double life, 125
Downward comparison, 210. *See also*
    Comparison
Doxa
  information agent and, 102–103
  interpersonal self and, 86, 88
  overview, 7, 228
Drug use. *See* Substance use
Dynamic self-concepts, 16. *See also* Self-concept

Early experiences, 168
Eating disorders, 330, 332, 334, 343, 344
Economic systems
  activities of the self in regards to, 223–225
  morality and, 112
  ownership and, 70–71
  suicide and, 329
Effort
  division of labor and, 97
  groups and, 102

mirrors and, 131
social loafing and, 96
Ego and egotism, 43–44, 306–307, 356, 357–358. *See also* Ego depletion; Threatened egotism
Ego depletion
choice and, 259–261
controversies regarding the theory of, 243–245
effects of, 238–243
overview, 236–245, 250
planning and, 249
willpower and, 246–247
See also Ego and egotism
Elastic criteria, 210–211
Emotion
choice and, 258–259, 268
mirrors and, 131
self-defeating behavior and, 357–358, 359
See also Feelings
Encouragement, 312–313
Endowment effect, 169
Energy, 218, 237–238, 242–243, 245, 250, 372–373. *See also* Ego depletion
Environment, 221–222
Error-monitoring system, 341
Escapes from self
overview, 334
reasons for, 332–333
themes and patterns among, 328, 331–332
ways of escaping self-awareness, 328–331
See also Stress of self
Evaluation, 256–257, 292–293. *See also* Judgment; Self-evaluation
Evolution
aggression and, 185
beginnings of self and, 65–67
culture and, 7–8, 11–12, 72–73
executive agent and, 220
groups and, 98, 101
morality and, 107
overview, 369–370
self-control and ego depletion and, 242–243
self-knowledge and, 139–140
Exaggeration in self-beliefs, 193–196. *See also* Illusion in self-beliefs; Self-beliefs
Executive function, 6, 313–314, 357, 359
Executive self
activities of the self and, 222–230
beginnings of self and, 76, 80–86
control and harmony and, 220–222
moral reputation and, 110
motivation and, 219–220
overview, 218, 219, 230, 374
relationships and, 313–314
self-regulation and, 248–249
See also Actions; Agency
Expectations, 155
Extended-time self, 372

Face culture, 40–41. *See also* Culture
Failure of the self, 348–349. *See also* Self-defeating behavior
Fairness, 82–83. *See also* Morality
False beliefs
escape from self and, 331, 332, 334
self-beliefs and, 142–150, 161–162
self-enhancement motive and, 153–154
See also Illusion in self-beliefs; Self-beliefs; Self-deception
False selves, 55, 56–58, 299–300
Family factors
identity crisis and, 323
interdependent and independent selves and, 39
narcissism and, 309
self-beliefs and, 304–306
self-control and, 234
See also Parenting relationships
Feelings
escape from self and, 333, 334
introspection and, 166–167
self-deception and, 201–202
self-esteem and, 186, 191
self-knowledge and, 140–142
self-regulation and, 248
See also Emotion
Following instructions, 223
Forgiveness, 122–123
Free will
autonomy and, 263–264
moral self and, 81
overview, 254–255, 265–266, 268
quitting addiction and, 119–121
as responsible autonomy, 266–267
self as active agent and, 267–268
Fulfillment, 59–60
Fun, 333, 334
Functional autonomy
morality and, 83, 93
overview, 41
self-knowledge and, 161–162
See also Autonomy
Functions of self, 17–20. *See also* Purpose of self
Future
autonomy and, 267
continuity of self and, 121–122
illusion in self-beliefs and, 195–196
morality and, 111
narrative self and, 148–149
optimism and, 206
self across time and, 76
self-defeating behavior and, 350
self-improvement motive and, 160
self-regulation and, 248–249, 343
unity of self and, 115–116, 117–119, 123–125
See also Goals; Planning; Time

Gambling, 355, 358
Games, 90–92

Gender
  culture and, 38
  processes that undermine a sense of self and,
    317–318, 325
  self-esteem and, 177, 185
  stress of self and, 326–328
Global self-esteem, 161–164. *See also* Self-esteem
Glucose levels, 240–243, 250
Goals
  effects of self-affirmation and, 162–164
  goal contagion, 341–342
  information agent and, 227
  mental illness and, 343
  self-regulation and, 235–236
  task performer activity and, 222–223
Gratitude, 83
Groups
  activities of the self in regards to, 222–230
  bad sides of, 95–96
  beginnings of self and, 68–69
  contact hypothesis and, 273–275
  different selves in, 99–103
  good sides of, 96–99
  group boundaries, 284–285
  individuality and, 286
  interpersonal self and, 276–277
  learning how to play roles and, 90–92
  mixing groups, 284–285
  morality and, 82–83, 108–110, 113, 278
  overview, 94–95, 103, 280, 287–288, 370–371
  perception of the group and, 287
  self-presentation and, 301
  social identity theory and, 280–284
  tokenism and, 285–286
  See also Collective identity; Interpersonal
    self; Social context of self
Groupthink, 95
Guilt, 259, 348–349

Habits
  choice and, 259–260
  ego depletion and, 239–241, 250
  multiple-self theories and, 51–52
Harmony, 220–222, 230
Health outcomes
  self-control and, 85, 232
  self-esteem and, 187
  self-presentation and, 290–291
  See also Outcomes
Hidden aspects of self. *See* Unconscious self
Hierometer theory, 190
Hoarding, 339, 343
Honesty
  deceiving others and, 204–206
  economic systems and, 255
  illusion in self-beliefs and, 195–196
  self-deception and, 204–206
  self-presentation and, 299–300
Humility, 307, 314

Ideal self, 295, 297–298. *See also* Self-
  presentation
Identity
  brain development and, 75–76
  compared to the self, 3–4
  compartmentalization and, 363–365
  concealing aspects of self and, 125
  escape from self and, 332, 334
  evolution of the western self and, 29–30
  groups and, 99–103
  identity conflict, 322, 323
  identity crisis, 30, 321–325
  identity deficit, 322, 323
  interpersonal self and, 271
  learning how to play roles and, 90–92
  other people's concepts of yourself, 275–277
  overview, 7
  relation of individual to society and, 31–34
  social identity theory and, 100, 280–284
  unity of self and, 115, 125
  See also Social identity
Illusion in self-beliefs
  illusion of selfhood, 42–48
  limited exaggeration and, 193–196
  overview, 192–193, 213
  positive illusions, 197–200
  See also False beliefs; Self-beliefs; Self-
    deception
Illusory control, 222. *See also* Control
Imitation, 87
Implicit Attitudes Test (IAT), 118
Imposter phenomenon, 351
Impression management
  interpersonal self and, 275–277, 279
  overview, 295, 296–297
  self-awareness and, 133–134
  See also Self-presentation
Impulse
  choice and, 252–253, 255–256
  conscious and unconscious processes and,
    136
  ego depletion and decision fatigue and,
    246–247, 261
  overview, 13–14
  True Self and, 54–55
  unity of self and, 116–118, 124–125
Inauthenticity, 57
Inconsistency, 115–116
Independent selves, 36–40, 41
Individuality, 99–103, 286
Infancy
  aspects of self and, 76–89
  boundary between brain and body, 74–76
  overview, 74, 93
  self across time and, 76
  True Self and, 54
  See also Childhood; Developmental processes
Inflation of self, 193–196. *See also* Illusion in
  self-beliefs

Information agent, 88–89, 102–103, 225–228
Information loss, 96
Information processing, 169, 174, 236–237
Instructions, following, 223
Integration, 17–21, 54–55, 118–119, 123–125.
   See also Unity project
Intelligence testing, 238–239
Intention, 341
Interdependent selves, 36–40, 41
Interests, 143, 146, 149–151, 258
Intergroup situations, 282–283, 288. *See also*
   Groups
Interpersonal factors
   autonomy and, 263
   effects of self-affirmation and, 163
   self-deception and, 204–206
   self-enhancement motive and, 159
   See also Interpersonal self
Interpersonal self
   beginnings of self and, 76, 86–89
   contact hypothesis and, 273–275
   first self question, 272–273
   mental illness and, 347
   morality and, 110, 277–279
   need to belong and, 271–272
   other people's concepts of yourself, 275–277
   overview, 6, 271, 279, 374
   as a self-defeating behavior, 354
   See also Groups; Interpersonal factors;
     Relationships; Social context of self
Introspection, 16, 165–167, 174
Irrational bias, 261
Irrational optimism illusion, 200
Isolation defense, 211–213

Japanese self-beliefs, 37. *See also* Culture
Joint attention, 88–89
Judgment
   choice and, 256–257, 261–262
   information sharing and, 227
   morality and, 229–230

Know thyself, 139–140. *See also* Self-knowledge
Knowledge, self. *See* Self-knowledge

Labor, division of, 97
Language
   communication and, 371
   reputation and, 371
   role of in the self, 5–6
   unity of self and, 373
Leadership, 281
Learned helplessness, 356
Learning
   interpersonal self and, 86–89
   learning how to play roles and, 90–92
   self-knowledge and, 173–174
   unity of self and, 373
Legal problems, 85, 121

Life, 66–67
Limited exaggeration, 193–196. *See also*
   Illusion in self-beliefs
Logical reasoning, 238–239
Loneliness, 102
Looking-glass self, 169–172, 196. *See also*
   Mirrors
Love, 308–311

Marriage
   idealizing one's partner and, 307–308
   identity crisis and, 323–324
   improvement of each partner within, 311–314
   interdependent and independent selves and,
     39
   processes that undermine a sense of self and,
     318, 325
   self-actualization and, 60–61
   self-beliefs and, 305–306
   self-love and other-love and, 308–311
   See also Relationships
Mastery, 77, 79, 93
Materialism, 331, 334
Medical treatment adherence, 354, 357, 358
Meditation, 43–44, 330, 334
Memory
   morality and, 111–112
   organization of self-beliefs and, 360–361,
     367
   selective memory, 208–209
   self-deception and, 208–209
   self-knowledge and, 174
   self-reference effect and, 167–169
   unity of self and, 117
Mental illness
   interpersonal self and, 347
   overview, 335–336, 347
   poorly organized self and, 336–342
   self-awareness and, 345–347
   self-control and, 342–345
   self-serving bias and, 207
Mental processes
   automatic mental processes, 154–155,
     166–167
   choice and, 252–253, 254, 268
   mental shifting as an escape from self, 333,
     334
   self-deception and, 202–203
Michelangelo phenomenon, 312–313, 314
Middle Ages, 23–25, 34
Midlife crisis. *See* Identity
Mirrors, 129–130, 131, 133–134. *See also*
   Looking-glass self
Misregulation, 247–248, 344–345, 359. *See*
   also Self-regulation
Mob violence, 95
Modern period, 25–27, 31–35
Modesty, 301, 303, 306–307, 314
Monitoring, 235–236, 250

Moral licensing patterns, 262
Morality
  activities of the self in regards to, 229–230
  choice and, 262
  continuity of self and, 121
  cooperation and, 104–107
  costs of to the self, 108–110
  evolution of the western self and, 27
  importance of to the self, 111–112
  interpersonal self and, 277–279
  mirrors and, 131
  moral reasoning, 81
  moral responsibility and, 16, 102
  moral self and, 80–84, 93, 148, 229–230
  motivations other than, 112–113
  overview, 7, 18, 21, 104, 113, 374–375
  reputation and, 289, 296–297
  self-deception and, 207
  time and, 111
  unity of self and, 125
Mother–infant/child relationships, 304–305.
    See also Family factors; Relationships
Motivation
  accuracy as, 156
  agency and, 219–220
  consistency as, 154–156
  culture and, 37–38
  executive agent and, 218, 230
  morality and, 112–113
  motivational conflict, 254, 255–256
  ownership and, 71
  self-defeating behavior and, 356
  self-destructive tendencies and, 348
  self-improvement motive, 159–160
  self-knowledge and, 152–153, 156–157, 164
  True Self and, 54
Multiple selves, 48–52, 61, 298–299

Narcissism
  aggression and, 184
  narcissistic entitlement, 301, 303
  in relationships, 314
  self as a central value and, 320
  self-love and other-love and, 308–311
Narrative knowledge, 142, 147–149, 150–151
Narrative self, 89–90, 148–149
Nature versus nurture, 11–13. *See also* Culture
Negative beliefs, 188–189
Neuroscience, 45
Nonaggression, 131
Norm violations, 88
"Not me," 65–67
Nurture. *See* Culture
Nutrition, 240–243, 250

Objections to selfhood, 42–45. *See also* Reality
    of selfhood
Obsessive–compulsive disorder (OCD),
    337–338, 343

Ongoing self, 255–256
Online self-presentation, 301–303, 334. *See
    also* Self-presentation
Optimal margin of illusion, 193–196. *See also*
    Illusion in self-beliefs
Optimism
  illusion in self-beliefs and, 200
  overview, 195
  self-deception and, 202–203, 206
Orders, following, 223
Organization of self-beliefs
  compartmentalization and, 363–365
  memory and, 360–361
  overview, 366–367
  self-complexity and, 361–363
  self-concept differentiation, 365–366
  See also Self-beliefs
Other-love, 308–311
Outcomes
  effects of self-affirmation and, 162–164
  ego depletion and, 238–243
  escape from self and, 332
  identity crisis and, 323–324
  self-control and, 85, 93, 231–234
  self-deception and, 203
  self-esteem and, 176–178, 191
Overestimating control illusion, 199–200
Overimitation, 87
Ownership
  activities of the self in regards to, 224
  continuity of self and, 121
  endowment effect and, 169
  self-knowledge and, 169
  social origins of self and, 69–72, 73

P. T. Barnum effect, 173–174
Pain, 326–327
Paranoid thinking, 345–346
Parenting relationships, 304–305, 309, 323. *See
    also* Family factors; Relationships
Passive responding, 246–247, 250
Patterns
  ego depletion and decision fatigue and,
    260–261
  escape from self and, 328, 331–332, 334
  other people's concepts of yourself,
    275–277
  self-defeating behaviors and, 352–354,
    358–359
  self-knowledge and, 144–145
Perceptions, 44, 144–146, 151
Perceptual defense, 207–208
Perfection, 53, 338, 343
Performances
  groups and, 103
  overview, 4–5, 9, 217–218
  self-defeating behavior and, 356
  task performer activity, 222–223
Perseverance, 356

Personality
  evolution of the western self and, 26–27
  hidden aspects of self and, 319
  looking-glass self and, 170–171
  multiple-self theories and, 49
  narrative knowledge and, 147
  other people's concepts of yourself, 275–277
  self-destructive tendencies and, 348
  self-knowledge and, 144–146, 150–151
  See also Traits
Perspectives of others
  adolescence and, 93
  choice and, 261–262
  groups and, 287
  limited exaggeration and, 194
  looking-glass self and, 169–172
  overview, 275–277
  self-deception and, 207–208
  self-knowledge and, 144–146, 151, 169–172, 174
Philosophical objections to the reality of selfhood, 42–45. *See also* Objections to selfhood; Reality of selfhood
Physical outcomes, 85. *See also* Outcomes
Planning, 246–247, 248–249, 250. *See also* Future
Play, 90–92
Political factors, 320, 327–328
Poorly organized self, 336–342. *See also* Organization of self-beliefs
Positive beliefs
  beginnings of self and, 78–80, 93
  effects of self-affirmation and, 162–164
  overestimating control illusion and, 199–200
  self-deception and, 202–203
  See also Self-beliefs
Posttraumatic stress disorder (PTSD), 337, 343
Potential, 52–61, 62
Power, 326–328
Praise
  beginnings of self and, 77, 93
  effects of self-affirmation and, 164
  illusion in self-beliefs and, 197–198
  self-deception and, 207–208
Predictions, 155, 195–196
Preference, 154–156
Prejudice
  conscious and unconscious processes and, 136–138
  contact hypothesis and, 273
  reputation and, 289
  selective criticism and, 209–210
  self-deception and, 211
  unity of self and, 118
Premenstrual syndrome (PMS), 243
Present time, 76, 111, 115, 116–117. *See also* Time
Presentation of self. *See* Self-presentation
Pressure, choking under, 356, 359

Primary control, 221–222, 230. *See also* Control
Privacy, 31–32, 227–228
Processes
  choice and, 252–253, 256–257, 268
  ego depletion and decision fatigue and, 260–261
  escape from self and, 332–334
  overview, 4–5, 9
  self-regulation and, 248–249
  that undermine a sense of self, 317–318, 325
Procrastination, 352–354, 357, 359
Production, 97
Progress, 76, 77
Projection, 211–213
Pronouns, 69–72
Propositional knowledge, 142, 143, 144–146, 149, 150–151
Prospection, 249. *See also* Planning
Public image of self, 275–277
Public self-consciousness, 106
Punishment, 348–349
Purpose of self, 17–20. *See also* Functions of self
Pygmalion phenomenon, 312–313

Rational thought, 249
Reactions, 163, 164, 211–213
Reality of selfhood, 42–48, 61
Reasoning, 81, 238–239
Reassurance seeking, 311
Regressors, 360–361
Regret, 259, 372
Rejection, 309–310, 354, 357
Relapse, 247–248
Relationships
  idealizing one's partner and, 307–308
  improvement of each partner within, 311–314
  interdependent and independent selves and, 39
  limited exaggeration and, 194
  modesty in, 306–307
  morality and, 278
  overview, 304, 314
  self-beliefs and, 304–306
  self-concept differentiation, 365–366
  self-deception and, 204–206
  self-enhancement motive and, 159
  self-esteem and, 187
  self-love and, 308–311
  See also Interpersonal self; Marriage
Religion
  compartmentalization and, 364
  identity crisis and, 323
  morality and, 105
  processes that undermine a sense of self and, 318, 325
  self as a central value and, 320
  self-awareness and, 132

Religious objections to the reality of selfhood, 42–45. *See also* Objections to selfhood; Reality of selfhood
Reproduction function of self, 17
Reputation
  choice and, 261–262
  groups and, 283
  ideal self and, 297–298
  morality and, 107, 108–110, 113
  more than one reputation and, 298–299
  overview, 301, 303, 371–372
  self-destructive behavior and, 349
  self-esteem and, 184–185
  self-knowledge and, 151, 156–157, 164
  unity of self and, 125
  See also Reputation management; Self-enhancement; Self-presentation
Reputation management
  moral self and, 81–82
  overview, 16, 19, 21, 289, 295, 296–297, 303
  self theories and, 60–61, 62
  See also Reputation; Self-presentation
Respect, 18, 21, 284–285, 309
Responsibility, 97–99, 121–122, 207
Responsible autonomy
  continuity of self and, 121–122
  free will and, 266–267
  overview, 20, 21, 268
  self as active agent and, 267–268
  unity of self and, 117–118
  See also Autonomy
Revenge, 354–355, 357
Right-now unity
  choice and, 254–256
  overview, 115, 116–117, 126, 373–374
  ownership and, 224
  planning and, 249
  See also Unity project
Roles
  continuity of self and, 121
  groups and, 103
  multiple-self theories and, 49, 51–52
  overview, 370–371
  self-concept differentiation and, 365–366
  self-deception and, 196–197
  unity of self and, 126
Rouge test, 130. *See also* Mirrors

Sadness, 259
Satiation, 162, 163
Schemas, 143
Schizophrenia, 341–342
School performance, 176–180. *See also* Academic achievement
Secondary control, 221, 222, 230. *See also* Control
Selective criticism, 209–210
Selective memory, 208–209. *See also* Memory

Self across time, 16, 76. *See also* Continuity of self; Time
Self in general
  animals and, 15–17
  aspects of self, 6–7, 76–89
  communication and, 371
  cooperation and, 371–372
  energy and, 372–373
  evolution and culture and, 7–8, 369–370
  functions of, 17–20
  groups and, 370–371
  morality and, 374–375
  origin of the self, 13–15
  overview, 3–4, 5–6, 9, 375
  self as a system, a process, or a performance, 4–5
  unity of self and, 373–375
Self over time, 22–23. *See also* Time
Self theories
  multiple selves, 48–52
  overview, 42, 61–62
  reality of selfhood, 42–48
  self-actualization, 58–61
  self-knowledge and, 152–153
  True Self and, 52–58
Self-acceptance, 176
Self-actualization, 58–61, 62
Self-affirmation
  choice and, 262
  effects of, 162–164
  self-deception and, 202–203
  self-knowledge and, 164
  See also Affirmation
Self-appraisal
  beginnings of self and, 79–80
  limited exaggeration and, 193–196
  self-enhancement motive and, 159
  self-esteem and, 181–182, 184
Self-awareness
  beginnings of self and, 93
  conscious and unconscious processes and, 134–138
  ego depletion and, 236–245
  escape from self and, 333, 334
  groups and, 287–288
  introspection and, 165–167
  mental illness and, 345–347
  mirrors in the study of, 131
  overview, 5–6, 129–131, 138, 235–236
  self-evaluation and, 132–134
  self-regulation and, 235–236
  social identity theory and, 282
  ways of escaping, 328–331
  See also Self-knowledge
Self-beliefs
  accuracy of, 192–193, 196–213
  beginnings of self and, 76, 78–80
  culture and, 37–38
  organization of, 360–367

organization of self-beliefs and, 366–367
overview, 192–193, 213
relationships and, 304–306, 308
self-knowledge and, 142–150
Self-blame, 332–333, 334
Self-complexity, 361–363
Self-concept
  adolescence and, 92–93
  compared to self-knowledge, 142–143
  compared to the self, 3–4, 6
  complex and dynamic self-concepts, 16
  conscious and unconscious processes and,
    135–136
  consistency and, 155
  evolution of the western self and, 29–30
  groups and, 101
  self as a system, a process, or a performance,
    4–5
  self-concept differentiation, 365–366
Self-consciousness, 77–78, 93, 106
Self-control
  beginnings of self and, 84–86, 93
  benefits of, 231–234
  choice and, 256–257
  executive agent and, 218, 230
  mental illness and, 342–345, 347
  moral self and, 81
  overview, 231, 250, 374
  relationships and, 314
  self-defeating behaviors and, 359
  unity project and, 248–249
  See also Control; Self-regulation
Self-deception
  backfires and, 355–356
  cognitive strategies for, 206–213
  deceiving others and, 204–206
  hidden aspects of self and, 319
  overview, 196–213
  positive illusions, 197–200
  reasons for, 200–206
  self-esteem and, 190–191
  See also False beliefs; Illusion in self-beliefs
Self-defeating behavior
  backfires and, 355–356
  emotion and, 357–358
  how and why it happens, 349–354
  overview, 348–349, 358–359
  See also Behavior; Systemic failure of the self
Self-destructive behavior, 349–354. *See also*
  Self-defeating behavior
Self-determination theory, 263
Self-distancing, 134, 138
Self-doubt, 185–186
Self-enhancement
  compared to self-improvement motive, 160
  culture and, 37
  healthiness of, 158–159
  illusion in self-beliefs and, 197–198
  overview, 153–154, 192–193

self-deception and, 205–206
self-knowledge and, 145–146, 156–157,
  158–159, 164
See also Motivation; Reputation
Self-esteem
  aggression and, 182–185
  beginnings of self and, 78–80
  compartmentalization and, 364
  conscious and unconscious processes and,
    135–136
  effects of self-affirmation and, 162–164
  efforts to raise, 178–180
  flaws in the research evidence regarding,
    180–182
  high self-esteem, 175–176, 185–187
  illusion in self-beliefs, 197–198
  low self-esteem, 176–178, 188–189
  mental illness and, 347
  overview, 175, 189–191
  relationships and, 310–311
  selective criticism and, 209–210
  self-deception and, 203, 210–211
  self-defeating behavior and, 356
  self-enhancement motive and, 154, 158–159
  self-knowledge and, 160–162, 164
  social identity theory and, 283
Self-evaluation
  overview, 132–134, 138
  reality of selfhood and, 43–44
  self-deception and, 201–202, 210–211
  self-knowledge and, 161–162, 164
Self-expression, 61, 261–262
Self-government. *See* Autonomy
Self-handicapping, 351–352, 359
Self-harm, 188
Self-improvement motive, 159–160, 164, 201.
  See also Motivation
Self-indulgence, 261
Self-injurious behavior, 349
Self-interest, 82–83, 277–279, 372
Selfish practices, 95–96, 278, 320–321
Self-knowledge
  accuracy as motive and, 156
  aspects of self and, 76–89
  behavior and, 172–173
  choice and, 257–258, 268
  compartmentalization and, 363–366
  consistency as motive and, 154–156
  depression and, 338
  effects of self-affirmation and, 162–164
  evolution of the western self and, 27–28, 35
  hidden aspects of self and, 319, 325
  as interests and values, 149–150
  introspection and, 165–167
  as a list of personality traits, 144–146
  looking-glass self and, 169–172
  moral reputation and, 110
  motives for, 152–153, 156–157, 164
  multiple kinds of, 150–151

Self-knowledge *(cont.)*
	narrative self and, 89–90, 147–149
	organization of, 360–367
	overview, 6, 139–140, 151, 164, 165, 174, 374
	self as a central value, 319–321
	self-beliefs and, 142–150
	self-deception and, 197
	self-enhancement motive and, 153–154,
		158–159
	self-esteem and, 160–162
	self-improvement motive and, 159–160
	self-reference effect, 167–169
	thinking and, 173–174
	thoughts and feelings versus actions and,
		140–142
	See also Self-awareness
Self-love, 308–311
Self-presentation
	goals of, 293–294
	ideal self and, 297–298
	morality and, 296–297
	more than one reputation and, 298–299
	narcissism and, 309
	overview, 289–291, 299–301, 303, 371–372
	in relationships, 306–307
	research studies regarding, 291–293,
		294–296
	social media and, 301–303
	See also Reputation; Reputation management
Self-protection orientation, 188
Self-reference effect, 167–169, 174, 340–341
Self-regulation
	compared to self-improvement motive, 160
	ego depletion and, 236–245
	energy and, 372–373
	interpersonal self and, 278
	misregulation and, 247–248
	overview, 231, 250, 251
	self-defeating behaviors and, 358–359
	standards and, 235–236
	unity project and, 248–249
	willpower and, 246–247
	See also Self-control
Self-schemas, 143
Self-serving bias, 207. *See also* Bias
Self-verification, 154–156, 173–174, 308
Sexual masochism, 326–328, 333, 334
Shame, 77–78
Shared knowledge and assumptions, 113,
	276–277, 370. *See also* Doxa
Shared reality. *See* Doxa
Shyness, 354, 357, 359
Side effects, 332
Sincerity, 26, 52–58
Situational factors, 49
Skepticism, 226
Social anxiety disorder
	overview, 339
	self-defeating behavior and, 354, 357, 359

	self-regulation and, 343
	See also Anxiety and anxiety disorders
Social class, 23–24
Social context of self
	activities of the self in regards to, 222–230
	autonomy and, 263
	beginnings of self and, 69–72, 73, 93
	brain development and, 74–76
	contact hypothesis and, 273–275
	culture and, 11–13
	deception and, 200–201
	interpersonal self and, 86–89
	learning how to play roles and, 90–92
	limited exaggeration and, 194
	need to belong and, 271–272
	overview, 10–11, 370–371, 375
	ownership and, 69–72
	self-awareness and, 130–131, 138
	self-deception and, 201, 204–206
	self-esteem and, 191
	social integration function of self and, 17–21
	unity of self and, 121–123, 126
	See also Groups; Interpersonal self; Social
		identity; Society
Social environment, 39–40
Social identity
	compared to the self, 3–4
	evolution of the western self and, 23–25
	groups and, 100
	overview, 9
	social identity theory, 100, 280–284,
		287–288
	unity of self and, 115
	See also Identity; Social context of self
Social loafing, 96
Social media
	identity crisis and, 324
	self-presentation and, 301–303
	stress of self and, 334
Social mobility
	evolution of the western self and, 27, 29–30
	group boundaries and, 284–285, 288
	relation of individual to society and, 31–32
	social identity theory and, 283
	See also Social rank and class; Status
Social promotion in schools, 179
Social rank and class, 23–24, 318, 325. *See also*
	Social mobility; Status
Society
	activities of the self in regards to, 222–230
	autonomy and, 263
	choice and, 256
	consistency and, 124–125
	cooperation and, 104
	evolution of the western self and, 23–25, 35
	groups and, 99, 101, 103
	morality and, 105, 107, 108–110, 112–113
	motivations other than morality and,
		112–113

overview, 7, 9, 99, 369–370, 375
reality of selfhood and, 43
relation of individual to society and, 31–34
responsible autonomy and, 268
role of in the self, 5–6, 13–15
self as a central value and, 319–321
self as active agent and, 267–268
self-esteem movement and, 176–178
selves in conflict with, 32–34
unity of self and, 121–123, 124–125
See also Social context of self
Sociometer theory, 189–190
Specialized performance, 103. *See also*
        Performances
Specific self-esteem, 161–162. *See also* Self-
        esteem
Spiritual practices, 42–45
Standards
    escape from self and, 332, 334
    self-awareness and, 132–133, 138, 235–236
    self-regulation and, 235, 250
Status
    groups and, 283, 284–285
    morality and, 108
    processes that undermine a sense of self and,
        318, 325
    suicide and, 329
    See also Social mobility; Social rank and class
Status quo bias, 260, 283
Stereotypes, 101, 118, 136–138
Stigma, 125
Stimulus, 253–254, 264
Stress
    compartmentalization and, 364
    escape from self and, 333, 334
    self-esteem and, 186
    self-regulation and, 247–248
Stress of self, 326–328, 333–334. *See also*
        Escapes from self
Sublimation, 212
Subselves, 49. *See also* Multiple selves
Substance use
    self-awareness and, 133, 236
    self-control and, 85
    as a self-defeating behavior, 350, 352, 355,
        357
    self-presentation and, 290
    self-regulation and, 247–248
    as a way to escape self-awareness, 329–330,
        334
    See also Addiction
Substitution, 163
Suicide, 329, 332, 334, 349
Superiority, 163–164
Suppressing negative thoughts, 211–213
Survival function of self, 17
Systemic failure of the self, 348–349. *See also*
        Self-defeating behavior
Systems, 4–6, 9

Task initiation, 246–247
Task performer activity, 222–223
Teasing, 87–88
Terror management theory, 190
Theories, self. *See* Self theories
Thoughts
    effects of self-affirmation and, 162–164
    introspection and, 166–167
    self-knowledge and, 140–142, 173–174
Threatened egotism, 184–185, 357–358, 359.
        See also Ego and egotism
Time
    cooperation and, 372
    dementia and, 338–339
    morality and, 111
    reputation management and, 296–297
    unity of self and, 373–374, 375
    See also Continuity of self; Future; Present
        time; Self across time; Unity project
Tokenism, 285–286, 287, 288
Trade, 223–225
Tradeoffs of self-defeating behaviors, 349–354,
        359. *See also* Self-defeating behavior
Traits
    choice and, 257
    effects of self-affirmation and, 163
    hidden aspects of self and, 319
    looking-glass self and, 170–171
    narrative knowledge and, 147
    other people's concepts of yourself, 275–277
    self-deception and, 201
    self-knowledge and, 143, 144–146, 149, 150–151
    See also Personality
Trauma, 168, 337
Trichotillomania, 339–340
True Self, 52–58, 61, 261–262
Trust, 233, 255
Twenty Statements Test, 37

Uncertainty, 254, 268
Unconscious self
    effects of self-affirmation and, 164
    introspection and, 166–167
    overview, 134–138, 319
    See also Consciousness
Underachievement, 352
Underregulation, 247, 343, 344, 359. *See also*
        Self-regulation
Undoing, 212
Unity project
    autonomy and, 264–265
    beginnings of self and, 67–68
    boundary between brain and body, 75
    interpersonal self and, 86–89
    multiple-self theories and, 50–51
    organization of self-beliefs and, 362–363,
        364–365
    overview, 6–7, 114, 115–116, 117–119,
        123–125, 126, 373–375

Unity project *(cont.)*
  quitting addiction and, 119–121
  self-knowledge and, 142–143, 148
  self-reference effect and, 168
  self-regulation and, 235, 248–249
  society and, 121–123
  types of, 114–119
  See also Continuity of self; Time

Values
  effects of self-affirmation and, 162–164
  endowment effect and, 169
  identity crisis and, 322–323
  self as a central value, 319–321
  self-knowledge and, 149–151
Violence, 95, 182–185, 354–355, 357
Virtue, 131, 193, 374–375

Wanting, 219–220, 230. *See also* Desire
Western self
  conflict between individual and society and, 32–34
  early Middle Ages and, 23–25

early modern period and, 25–27
face and dignity cultures, 40–41
interdependent and independent selves and, 36–40
modern identity and, 29–30
overview, 22–23, 34–35
relation of individual to society and, 31–34
self-knowledge and, 27–28
See also Culture
Willpower
  choice and, 259–261
  ego depletion and, 236–245
  mental illness and, 344–345
  overview, 250
  unity project and, 248–249
  See also Self-regulation
Withdrawal, 311
Withholding information, 227–228
Within-group similarity, 283, 287–288. *See also* Groups

Yoga, 43–44